Taking Stock of Environmental Assessment

Environmental assessment is a process for predicting the likely effects of a proposed project, plan, or policy on the environment prior to a decision being made about whether these should proceed. Through the regulation of this process, law is now commonly engaged in dilemmas about the appropriate balance between conservation and development, as well as the place for participation and popular protest. The main aim of this edited collection is to analyse this engagement.

This collection of work from experts working on environmental assessment in the United States and Europe provides a detailed treatment of key issues in environmental assessment, in order to encourage an appreciation of where environmental assessment has come from and, perhaps most importantly, how it could develop in the future. This collection is a full 'stocktaking' exercise, encompassing a broad range of concerns, timescales and legal and policy contexts. It is both reflective and up to date, providing a current assessment of the state of the growing discipline of environmental assessment scholarship and practice, whilst also pointing towards future developments. Although the emphasis is firmly on law, the book also provides a good sense of the political, scientific and technological settings in which environmental assessment has developed.

Individual chapters discuss the development of EIA in the United States and Europe, the interrelation of environmental assessment with other regulatory regimes (water protection, environmental justice initiatives, the European spatial strategy), and the prospects for the digitalisation of the environmental assessment process. Its jurisdictional reach means that it provokes comparative analysis on the roots and current state of environmental assessment in the United States and Europe.

Dr Jane Holder Reader in Environmental Law, Faculty of Laws, University College London, is a member of the Centre for Law and the Environment, UCL and co-editor of *Current Legal Problems*.

Donald McGillivray Senior Lecturer, Kent Law School, University of Kent, lectures in environmental law and is case analysis editor for the *Journal of Environmental Law*.

Taking Stock of Environmental Assessment

Law, policy and practice

Edited by
Jane Holder and
Donald McGillivray

Routledge·Cavendish
Taylor & Francis Group

First published 2007
by Routledge-Cavendish
2 Park Square, Milton Park, Abingdon, Oxon OX14 4RN

Simultaneously published in the USA and Canada
by Routledge-Cavendish
270 Madison Ave, New York, NY 10016

Routledge-Cavendish is an imprint of the Taylor & Francis Group, an informa business

© 2007 Jane Holder and Donald McGillivray

Typeset in Times New Roman by
Newgen Imaging Systems (P) Ltd, Chennai, India
Printed and bound in Great Britain by
Cromwell Press Ltd, Trowbridge, Wiltshire

British Library Cataloguing in Publication Data
A catalogue record for this book is available from the British Library

Library of Congress Cataloging in Publication Data
A catalog record for this book has been requested

ISBN 10: 1-84472-101-9 (hbk)
ISBN 10: 1-84472-100-0 (pbk)
ISBN 10: 0-203-94494-1 (ebk)

ISBN 13: 978-1-84472-101-6 (hbk)
ISBN 13: 978-1-84472-100-9 (pbk)
ISBN 13: 978-0-203-94494-3 (ebk)

Contents

List of contributors and biographical details

Daniel A Farber is the Sho Sato Professor of Law and Director of the Environmental Law Program at the School of Law, University of California, Berkeley. He received a BA in Philosophy with high honours in 1971 and an MA in Sociology in 1972, both from the University of Illinois. In 1975 he earned his JD from the University of Illinois. After graduating Daniel clerked in the Court of Appeals and the Supreme Court and practised law before joining the University of Illinois Law School. In 1981 he became a member of the University of Minnesota Law School Faculty. During his years there he became the first Henry J. Fletcher Professor of Law in 1987, serving as a visiting professor at Stanford Law School, Harvard Law School and the University of Chicago Law School. His books include *Environmental Law: Cases and Materials* (7th edn, 2005, with Carlson and Freeman), *Eco-Pragmatism: Making Sensible Environmental Decisions in an Uncertain World* (1999) and *Disasters and the Law: Katrina and Beyond* (2006, with Chen).

Jane Holder is Reader in Environmental Law at the Faculty of Laws, UCL. She obtained a PhD from Warwick University on the subject of environmental assessment and has taught environmental law and policy at UCL since 1992. Her research interests focus upon environmental assessment, commons and environmental protection and landscape issues. She has recently published *Environmental Assessment: The Regulation of Decision Making* (Oxford University Press, 2004) and *Environmental Protection, Law and Policy* (Cambridge University Press, 2007, with Maria Lee). Jane is a member of the Centre for Law and the Environment and the Centre for European Law and Governance, both at the Faculty of Laws, UCL.

William Howarth is Professor of Environmental Law at Kent Law School, University of Kent. His research interests focus upon environmental and ecological law, with particular emphasis upon the legal protection of the aquatic environment and the ecosystems that it supports. His major works include *Water Pollution and Water Quality Law* (Shaw and Sons, 2001, with Donald McGillivray) and *Flood Defence Law* (Shaw and Sons, 2002). William Howarth is the General Editor of the journal *Water Law*.

Stephen Jay is a Senior Lecturer in Urban and Regional Studies at Sheffield Hallam University. He has research interests in the role of environmental assessment in development planning, and has recently focused on the application of strategic environmental assessment in the private sector, as exemplified by the privatised electricity industry. He is also engaged in research into the current development of offshore windfarms and the emergence of marine spatial planning.

Carys Jones is a Senior Lecturer in Environmental Planning in the School of Environment and Development, University of Manchester, and Director of the EIA Centre. She has a PhD from the University of Wales, Aberystwyth. Her work on environmental assessment has included studies for the European Commission, UK government departments and research councils. Recent studies include archaeology and EIA in North West Europe, scoping practice in England, and offshore oil and gas EIA practice. She is the author of a number of EIA and SEA related publications, most recently the co-edited book *SEA and Land-Use Planning* published by Earthscan. Since 2001 she has been a Co-editor of *Impact Assessment and Project Appraisal* the Journal of the International Association for Impact Assessment.

Bradley C Karkkainen, Henry J. Fletcher Chair in Law, Law School, University of Minnesota, conducts research and teaches in the fields of environmental and natural resources law. His research centres on innovative strategies for environmental regulation and natural resource management with an emphasis on mechanisms that promote continuous adaptive learning, flexibility, transparency and policy integration. He has published widely on each of these areas, including in relation to environmental assessment.

Ludwig Krämer is a Visiting Professor at both the Centre for Law and the Environment, University College London and Bremen University. He was until recently the Head of Environmental Governance of DG Environment in the European Commission, from which position he campaigned for the effectiveness of environmental legislation at the EU level. Ludwig Krämer has published numerous works on EU environmental law. His retirement from the Commission was marked by the publication of a major work, *Reflections on Thirty Years of EU Environmental Law: A High Level of Protection?* (Europa, 2005).

Donald McGillivray, Senior Lecturer in Law at the Kent Law School, University of Kent, has conducted research upon water law, the land torts and the environment, and compensation in nature conservation. He is the co-author of *Water Pollution and Water Quality Law* (Shaw and Sons, 2001, with William Howarth) and *Environmental Law* (Oxford University Press, 6th edn, 2005, with Stuart Bell).

Áine Ryall, Senior Lecturer, Faculty of Law, University College Cork, Ireland, holds a PhD in European environmental law from the European University Institute, Florence. She is also a barrister and was called to the Irish Bar in 1995. She specialises in European Community environmental law. Áine has published widely on environmental law, most recently *Effective Judicial Protection and the EIA Directive in Ireland* (Hart, 2007).

Paul Slinn is Environmental Projects Team Leader with the Merseyside Environmental Advisory Service, providing technical support to local government on Environmental Assessment and the environmental management of major development projects. He was previously a Research Associate at the EIA Centre, University of Manchester. He holds a BSc in Archaeology and an MA in Environmental Impact Assessment and Management. His key interest lies in the relationship between environmental assessment and environmental management, and he has recently completed a research project examining current practice in trading estate developments in England and Wales.

Jonathan B Wiener is the William R. and Thomas L. Perkins Professor of Law, and Professor of Environmental Policy and Public Policy Studies, at Duke University. He is also a University Fellow of Resources for the Future and the President-elect of the Society for Risk Analysis. In 2003 he received the Chauncey Starr Young Risk Analyst Award from the Society of Risk Analysis for exceptional contributions to the field of risk analysis by a scholar aged 40 or under. He has written widely on the United States and international environmental law and risk regulation including *Reconstructing Climate Policy* (AEI Press, 2003, with Richard Stewart) and *Risk vs Risk* (Harvard, 1995, with John Graham). He worked on these topics at the White House Council of Economic Advisors, at the White House Office of Science and Technology Policy, and at the United States Department of Justice, serving in both the first Bush and Clinton administrations. He received his undergraduate and law degrees from Harvard University, and served as a law clerk to US federal judges Jack Weinstein and Stephen Breyer.

Christopher Wood, OBE, Emeritus Professor of Environmental Planning, University of Manchester was Co-director of the EIA Centre, University of Manchester, and Co-editor of the journal *Impact Assessment and Project Appraisal*. He was awarded the International Association for Impact Assessment's Rose-Hulman award in 2003 'for a lifetime of excellence in promoting environmental assessment'. He has written extensively about environmental planning generally and about EIA and strategic environmental assessment in particular. He has published *Environmental Impact Assessment: A Comparative Review* (Prentice Hall, 2nd edn, 2002) and co-edited *Strategic Environmental Assessment and Land Use Planning: An International Perspective* (Earthscan, 2005).

Preface

This collection is rooted in a seminar on 'The Current State of Environmental Impact Assessment in Law and Custom' held at University College London under the auspices of the Centre for Law and Environment, at the Faculty of Laws in December 2003. The seminar brought together leading scholars in environmental assessment, many of whom understood and presented environmental assessment from both academic and legal practice perspectives.[1] A real sense of the dynamism and theoretically intriguing nature of environmental assessment was successfully portrayed by those who presented papers. This seminar provided an important starting point.

The project has since expanded considerably to encompass US scholarship in the area (where environmental assessment has been a long-standing and controversial feature of the law and has stimulated much academic debate) and a very detailed treatment of key issues at the European level, in order to more fully appreciate where environmental assessment has come from and, perhaps most importantly, how it could develop in the future. In short, this collection became a full stocktaking exercise, encompassing a broad range of concerns, timescales, and contexts. We are particularly grateful to that elite group of environmental assessment scholars from the United States who allowed us to considerably broaden the focus of the collection and to provoke comparisons. Closer to home, we are delighted that so many of our top environmental assessment and law specialists were willing to engage with the subject in an attempt to work out the current reach, and potential influence, of environmental assessment. The end result is a collection which is both reflective and also up to date, providing a current assessment of the state of the growing discipline of environmental assessment scholarship and practice whilst also pointing towards future

1 We would like to thank Professors Richard Macrory, Philippe Sands and Ludwig Krämer, all at the Centre for Law and the Environment, UCL, Professor Chris Wood, University of Manchester, William Sheate, Imperial College, Wiek Schrage, United Nations, Geneva, Professor Laurence Boisson de Chazournes, University of Geneva, Professor Jan Jans, University of Amsterdam, Professor Malcolm Grant, Provost, UCL, Judge Konrad Schiemann, Stephen Hockman QC, Jeffrey Jowell, QC and William Upton for their involvement in the seminar and their support of this project.

developments. Whilst the emphasis is firmly on law, it also provides a good sense of the political, scientific and technological settings in which environmental assessment has developed. In sum, through this collection we have been involved in a very fruitful process of exchange and one which will hopefully sustain future academic relations and research projects on environmental assessment and beyond.

Our thanks are due to Briar Towers at UCL Press and Fiona Kinnear and Madeleine Langford at Routledge-Cavendish for their patience and efficiency and to Christopher Campbell-Holt for his assistance with the editorial process.

Jane Holder
Donald McGillivray
December 2006

Chapter 1

Taking stock

Donald McGillivray and Jane Holder

Introduction

Whether one inclines to the view that environmental assessment (EA) is a potent, perhaps even radical, regulatory mechanism, or a deceit of no substance (and perhaps even of some mischief), there can be little doubting the extent to which EA is an increasingly pervasive part not just of modern environmental law but of regulatory law in general.

Environmental impact assessment laws emerged, as keystones of modern environmental regulatory law, from the early 1970s onwards, the first major development being the US federal National Environmental Policy Act 1969 (NEPA). As Bradley Karkkainen, one of the three US-based legal scholars to contribute to this collection, recounts, in some ways EA was an 'afterthought' for the drafters of NEPA, unaware of the importance of the apparently minor amendment tabled during the later stages of the Bill's passage to the effect that, prior to undertaking any action 'significantly affecting the quality of the human environment', the 'responsible official' must produce a 'detailed statement' on the environmental consequences of, and alternatives to, the proposed action.

As Carys Jones and her colleagues recount, despite its low-key origins, national environmental impact assessment laws of various kinds soon followed suit, using the passage of NEPA's action-forcing obligation as inspiration, including in a number of European states, before – as Ludwig Krämer notes – lengthy and at times unprincipled bargaining led to a European Community Directive on EIA finally being adopted in 1985. At European level, as elsewhere (and as NEPA has always done in principle, though as Karkkainen notes, not greatly in practice), legislation has extended beyond project-level assessment, and now encompasses the strategic assessment of plans and programmes. And as we discuss further below, impact assessment as a regulatory technique has spread into new fields beyond environmental protection, with regulatory impact assessment now an increasingly ubiquitous feature of modern public administrative life.

A useful way of capturing these developments is by reference to three periods or 'waves' of EA scholarship and concern. These time-frames are not intended as devices for a perfect mapping of all developments across all jurisdictions, but are rather aimed at providing a framework around which developments can be fitted and conceptualised.

The first wave

The principal feature of the first wave of scholarship is a concern for the implementation of the first generation of EA laws (mainly project-level EIA laws). One might think of this as the period when the soul of EIA was searched for. One way in which this was done was administrative – as Jones *et al* note, by issuing guidance, building capacity, training and so on, sometimes being linked to the provision of development assistance. But the generality and ambiguity of some of the legislative provisions – and the compound problem that this can give rise to when this legislation requires further implementation, as in the EC – meant that this was a task that also fell in great measure to the courts (though, as Aine Ryall notes, for partly institutional reasons the Irish courts have played comparatively little part in the evolution of EA law). In the US, the high-water mark was reached in the judgment of Judge Skelley Wright in *Calvert Cliffs* in 1973 which, although it turned its face to merits review, suggested that EIA required an assessment (by which Judge Skelly Wright said he meant, as noted in the chapter by Jonathan Wiener, a cost benefit assessment) of federal projects, so as to take into account their previously neglected environmental costs. The more substantive reading of *Calvert Cliffs*, however, failed to stick – although the US courts did require fairly stringent consideration of alternatives – and it soon became clear that the courts regarded the impact assessment provisions of NEPA as purely procedural in nature.[1]

In Europe, as Krämer notes, it also 'fell on the courts to try to make Directive 85/337 operational'. By contrast to US experience, in the EC the procedural nature of the EIA Directive has never seriously been challenged, and the focus of judicial scrutiny in the early years of the Directive tended to be on challenges to incomplete implementation at Member State level, with the European Court of Justice trimming the exercise of Member States' discretion in areas such as which Annex II projects, where EIA was not necessarily required, would require assessment (although, as Krämer notes, this did not curb the scope for 'sometimes quite remarkable' divergences between Member States on the applicable national thresholds for particular project categories). An important article from 1993 by John Alder, for example, explored the minimalist and often grudging approach to the Directive's implementation in the UK.[2] In particular, Alder criticised the way in which the courts took a narrow approach to interpretation of the legislation which, it was argued, was fuelled both by an unwillingness for a system which traditionally gave a wide degree of administrative law discretion to take procedural rights seriously and by a lack of sympathy to environmental values. Even if Alder may have made too much of the substantive dimension to the US 'hard look'

---

1 *Strycker's Bay Neighborhood Council Inc. v Karlen*, 444 U.S. 223 (1980); *Robertson v Methow Valley Citizens Council*, 490 U.S. 332 (1989).

2 John Alder, 'Environmental Impact Assessment – the Inadequacies of English Law' (1993) *Journal of Environmental Law* 203.

approach, his work nevertheless provided an important pause for thought about the tensions between EA and traditional, liberal legal values.

The first age of EA scholarship, therefore, ends with an acceptance of the courts' unwillingness to give EIA a directly substantive edge at project level. It can also be characterised by a mixture of informed scepticism and uncertainty about whether, and if so to what extent, EIA could really influence decision-makers in ways that gave added voice to environmental interests. Such scepticism found particular expression in works which highlighted the power of environmental impact assessment 'to seduce',[3] and in the putting together of 'pseudo-EIAs' (mainly in the context of infrastructure projects in developing countries).[4]

The second wave

Partly in response to the acknowledged limitations of environmental assessment and the sceptical views described above, attention then turned in two directions; first, to securing a better legislative and judicial appreciation of (in the main, individual) participatory rights and, second, to expanding the scope of EA outwards and upwards to the level of the wider planning processes within which project decisions are nested. The former sees in enhanced public participation the route to the carriage of environmental values into the decision-making process; the latter, on the other hand, sees better decision-making as about the level decisions are taken at. Both of these are reflective of a turn in emphasis in EA to its role as a component of wider regulatory governance structures.

Taking the former first, we can see certain tensions between EA's participatory and substantive objectives. In the EC regime, for example, the courts have recently been called upon to strike the balance between these objectives when considering the extent to which pre-decision mitigation by developers obviates the requirement for EIA. Since the environmental statement must describe any remedial and mitigation measures, a strict approach would suggest that developers cannot duck the need for EIA in this way since mitigating measures could only be a secondary issue. On the other hand, the main aim of EIA should be to prevent environmental harm and if this can be designed out before the project is submitted for approval then EIA can be said to have done its job. In the leading case from the English courts, *Bellway Urban Renewal Southern v Gillespie*,[5] the Court of Appeal held that mitigation measures are not in principle to be ignored for the purposes of screening since that would distort the reality of the project proposal. Notably, then, a purposive construction of the Directive does not always require

---

3 Francoise Ost, 'A Game without Rules? The Ecological Self-Organisation of Firms', in Gunther Teubner, Lindsay Farmer and Declan Murphy (eds) *Environmental Law and Ecological Responsibility: the Concept and Practice of Ecological Self-Organisation* (Chichester: Wiley, 1994), p 351.

4 Prasad Modak and Asit Biswas (eds) *Environmental Impact Assessment for Developing Countries* (London: Heinemann, 1999), pp 240–241.

5 [2003] Env LR 30.

its provisions to be construed strictly so that EIA is more likely to be required.[6] On the other hand, the mere fact that conditions can take the effects of the development below the threshold of significance are not enough in themselves to rule out the need for EIA. A matrix of factors needs to be considered, including the nature of the remedial measures, their complexity and the degree of detail stipulated and, in particular, the prospects that they will be successfully implemented. But how can this ensure that the *best* advice about mitigating environmental impact emerges (which would be in line with the preventive and participatory nature of the Directive), not simply advice that is standard or sufficient? Or that mitigation measures are successful (which, if secured at all, probably falls to other regulatory regimes).[7]

The US has taken a broadly similar approach to this tension. In the US, resort to 'mitigated FONSIs' – findings that projects are not of significant impact because of the mitigation measures proposed – indicate that impact assessment under NEPA has a substantive edge to some degree, if only insofar as agencies appear to mitigate the environmental impact of projects to bring them beneath the threshold for preparing a full environmental impact statement. The background to mitigated FONSI's is provided in Bradley Karkkainen's chapter, and it is notable that their development was actively encouraged by the courts. As Daniel Farber notes, through use of the mitigated FONSI, agencies are 'presumably achieving these environmentally beneficial results at a lower cost and in less time than would be required if they went through the full-blown EIS process. That is a positive outcome, not a negative one. It is evidence that NEPA works'. Karkkainen agrees – mitigated FONSI's allow substantive standards in and indirectly achieve NEPA's original purposes by an 'unanticipated backdoor route' – and the expense for agencies of otherwise conducting a full-blown EIA acts as an important driver to mitigate environmental harms.

Nevertheless, the judicial interpretation of EIA on both sides of the Atlantic has ensured, albeit in limited and instrumental ways, that the public have a right to be involved, even if this may in practice be constrained by lack of resources. In the United Kingdom, the courts' (relatively late) protection of the public's right to participate in environmental assessment may be thought to have democratized development consent procedures, at least at the local level.[8] In summary, the courts have played their part in securing for EA a central role in relation to this important aspect of wider environmental governance.[9] As to the latter, SEA has

---

6   *World Wildlife Fund v Autonome Provinz Bozen* [1999] ECR I-5613 para. 37 ('actual characteristics').

7   See Stuart Bell and Donald McGillivray, *Environmental Law* (Oxford: OUP, 6th edn 2005), pp 531–532.

8   Most notably in *Berkeley v Secretary of State for the Environment and Fulham Football Club* ('Berkeley No. 1') [2001] AC 603.

9   See further Joanne Scott and Jane Holder, 'Law and New Environmental Governance in the European Union', in Grainne de Burca and Joanne Scott (eds) *Law and New Governance in the EU and US* (Oxford: Hart, 2006).

the capacity to be more transformative of environmental decision-making and, as Jones *et al* document, SEA laws are now found in more than 30 jurisdictions, though with its evolution 'probably lagging 15 years behind that of EIA'. In the EU, it is too soon after the coming into force of the SEA Directive to draw any firm conclusions about its effectiveness, but it is clear that assessment can no longer be restricted to projects, and in other areas, such as with the assessment obligations under the 1992 EC Habitats Directive, the Court of Justice has recently had cause to rule on this.[10]

In summary, in this era of EA development the informed scepticism and uncertainties about the potential of the instrument to contribute to 'better' decision-making – to make not just bureaucracies, but also governments and firms, 'think'[11] – gave way to greater optimism about the place of environmental assessment in new governance experiments, particularly as a means to secure participation, encourage information exchange, foster partnerships and joint responsibility, and perhaps most importantly, encourage the operation and fulfilment of each of these vital components of governance at multiple, but related, levels. In terms of the form of regulation exercised by environmental assessment, though originally out of synch with the European Union's command and control approach, the EA procedure has been seen as typical of the Union's favoured approach of 'new governance', and has been embraced as providing rich material on its working in practice.[12] Some strains of scepticism remained, particularly as a result of empirical findings that developers continued to manipulate the search for alternatives and use the form of environmental assessment to favourably, rather than objectively, present their development proposals.[13] Interestingly, having initially bolstered the claims of new governance by providing evidence of the apparent workability of its key elements, such critiques of environmental assessment have contributed to a broader and more thorough review of new governance methods, and especially proceduralism.

---

10 Case C-6/04 *Commission v UK* [2006] Env LR 27.
11 We borrow this concept from the classic work by Serge Taylor, *Making Bureaucracies Think: The Environmental Impact Statement Strategy of Administrative Reform* (Stanford: Stanford University Press, 1984).
12 For example, by Hubert Heinelt, Tanja Malek, Randall Smith and Annette E. Toller (eds) *European Union Environment Policy and New Forms of Governance: A Study of the Implementation of the Environmental Impact Assessment Directive and the Eco-management and Audit Scheme Regulation in Three Member States* (Aldershot: Ashgate, 2001). Though, see also Katharine Holzinger, Christopher Knill and Ansgar Shafer, 'Rhetoric or Reality? "New Governance" in EU Environmental Policy' (2006) 12(3) *European Law Journal* 403 on why context-oriented regulation has failed to emerge in practice in the EU; the data – at least up until 2000 – demonstrates that regardless of the innovations in governance ideas, interventionist instruments still play a dominant role.
13 For example, Jane Holder, *Environmental Assessment: The Regulation of Decision Making* (Oxford: OUP, 2004).

The third wave

Here, we pick out two developments that our contributors spend much time discussing, being areas where EA is, and ought to be, expanding into. The first of these is to *ex post* assessment, the going beyond of formal *ex ante* predictions. Did EA predict the environmental impact of development, and perhaps more importantly did it correctly predict whether our assumptions about how likely impacts were to be mitigated were right? Everything we know about forecasting generally suggests that this is unlikely, but we use the tools that we have at our disposal and, hopefully, make the best use of them. But the best use of the tool is to constantly inquire whether it is working properly, to evaluate its use and adapt it for the future. Many of the contributors see this area as one of EA's major weak spots, and various corrective suggestions are made, both for EIA and for regulatory impact assessment (discussed below) including making EAs accessible to the public so they can judge whether mitigation has been successful.

Second, looking beyond the environmental arena, as a general mechanism impact assessment can now be found in a huge array of settings. These include – mostly at the project level – health, social and ecological impact assessments. But beyond this, and at a more strategic level, we find trade impact assessments and regulatory impact assessments. Indeed, as Jones *et al* note: 'It is perhaps a compliment to the perceived success of EIA in incorporating environmental considerations into decision-making procedures that, over a lengthy period, as it has spread geographically around the world and been applied at different levels of environmental decision-making, it has been imitated and applied to specific impact types not necessarily related to the environment.'

Yet as Jones *et al* note in the context of regulatory impact assessment, there is concern that a regulatory model with its roots in the environmental field may lose its connections to environmental problems when applied to general government regulation, as with the more economically driven regulatory impact assessment process. This point is echoed by Krämer, who suggests that the environment is losing out the more that EIA evolves into IA more generally, though for Wiener, who defends the use of IA as an environmental protection tool, there is no necessary reason why this should be the case.

The collection in outline

As is clear from the above, the collection brings together policy, regulatory and legal scholarship, and divergent views on EA, from both sides of the Atlantic.

The opening chapter, by Carys Jones and her colleagues, provides a comprehensive overview of developments in EA policy over the last 35 years, charting the rise first of EIA, then SEA and now the emergence of sustainability assessments and appraisals. A particular feature of the paper is its marshalling of the literature on whether, across a large sample of jurisdictions, the different forms of EA 'work'. They suggest that there is little strong evidence supporting the conclusion that EA works directly in the sense of altering decision-making processes, though in contributing to wider environmental awareness raising it may be responsible for more indirect yet transformative benefits in terms of institutional environmental learning. In particular, they note a divergence between the role performed by EIA at project level, which tends to conform to rationalist models of decision-making dominant at the time when EIA laws were first being adopted, with that performed by SEA, where more radically effective dimensions are hoped for: 'It is clear that a considerable shift is taking place within EA thinking, specifically in relation to SEA, and that a greater alertness and responsiveness to the realities of strategic planning is developing.'

Of particular note from a legal point of view is their brief consideration of ways in which EA might be given a substantive edge. These include EA being made more central to implementing sustainable development policies, especially if – as in the UK – these are formulated in terms of environmental limits. Echoing the influential Royal Commission on Environmental Pollution's 2002 report on *Environmental Planning*, this might be done through a statutory principle of 'ensuring that the quality of the environment is safeguarded and wherever appropriate enhanced'.[14] Another option considered is that there should be no net environmental deterioration from assessment decisions. This taps into the growing movement trying to make certain decisions at worst environmentally neutral – for example, carbon neutrality, zero waste, policy objectives of no net loss of biodiversity – and is an objective that is expressed, in varying degrees, in recent English planning guidance on mitigating and compensating for adverse nature conservation effects of development.[15] This would significantly enhance the mitigation obligations currently found in most EA laws. If a no net loss baseline could not be met, then as a way of emphasising the weight to be given to environmental interests at the expense of claims in favour of development, the precautionary principle could be made central to assessment decisions. In the nature of their general overview, none of these are worked up in any detail, but each provide avenues worthy of being explored further (indeed, Jonathan Wiener explores the role that the proportionality principle and the precautionary principle could both play in regulatory impact assessment).

By contrast to Jones *et al*'s broad overview, Bradley Karkkainen's chapter locates the passage into law of NEPA and its EIA provisions in the context of various factors at play in the United States in the 1960s, including Rachel Carson's *Silent Spring*; the seminal *Scenic Hudson* case (a case of some importance in the rise of environmental law generally in the US);[16] and the work of Joseph Sax

---

14 Royal Commission on Environmental Pollution, Twenty-third report, *Environmental Planning* Cm 5459 (HMSO, 2002), para. 8.33.

15 ODPM Circular 06/05 (DEFRA Circular 01/05) *Biodiversity and Geological Conservation – Statutory Obligations and their Impact Within the Planning System.*

16 See, e.g., Richard Lazarus, *The Making of Environmental Law* (Chicago: University of Chicago Press, 2004) p 81 ('*Scenic Hudson* established a pattern for environmental litigation in general that persisted throughout the 1970s').

in advocating giving legal voice to environmental interests by promoting the public trust doctrine and environmental citizen suits. Ironically, NEPA did not contain any citizen suit provision: 'Nonetheless, in the spirit of the times and with environmental litigation of all kinds swirling around them, courts in the 1970s had little trouble discerning, or simply assuming *sub silentio*, an implied private cause of action to enforce NEPA's procedural duties against reluctant federal officials. . . . From the outset, the post-enactment development of NEPA would be driven mainly by citizen-initiated litigation.' The courts are focal points in his account of the development of EA law in the US, with NEPA being both valued and loathed for its part in delaying projects to the point of cancellation, or forcing modifications, through drawn out litigation (a feature of NEPA that came as something of an unwelcome surprise to its main legislative sponsor).[17] Karkkainen provides a number of helpful lenses through which debates about the value of NEPA's impact assessment provisions can be looked at, and concludes his chapter with an assessment of proposed deregulatory reforms to streamline NEPA, both on cost grounds and to counteract its use as a delaying tactic. These general reform proposals have been attacked by the environmental lobby and have as yet failed to command legislative support.[18] But Karkkainen does not see NEPA as immune from further efforts at deregulation, and concludes with a plea for those who value NEPA to seize the high ground in the debate about how best EA should operate in an age when the production and consumption of environmental information has spiralled, and where the demands on those who are tasked with managing the environment in a climate of increased scientific and regulatory complexity have also increased sharply.

The chapter by Ludwig Krämer gives an evolutionary account of EA law and practice in the EU, from before the first EIA Directive up to the contemporary use of regulatory impact assessment (RIA) within the European Commission. Reflecting his experience of the negotiation and enforcement of EC environmental law, the chapter gives a unique insight into the reception of EA ideas within the EC over the last 30 years. Krämer argues that, as initially adopted, the EIA Directive gave too much implementing discretion to the Member States, was silent on studying alternatives and weak on mitigation measures, and even left unclear whether a formal written impact assessment document was required. Some of these criticisms persist, although they have been ameliorated to a degree by the adoption of Directive 2001/42 requiring the strategic assessment of plans and programmes at Member State level which is somewhat more prescriptive in its

---

17 See A Dan Tarlock, 'The Story of Calvert Cliffs: A Court Construes the National Environmental Policy Act to Create a Powerful Cause of Action', in Richard J Lazarus and Oliver A Houck (eds) *Environmental Law Stories* (New York: Foundation Press, 2005), p 83.

18 The Administration of George W. Bush has made an inroad into NEPA in relation to forest management; see the Healthy Forests Restoration Act of 2003, Pub. L. 108–148, 117 Stat. 1887, which expedites NEPA reviews and limits the consideration of alternatives, see Tarlock, ibid, p 106.

requirements on decision-makers to show how environmental impacts have been taken into account.

Krämer then turns to considering EA within the European Community's own decision-making processes. He notes how the assessment of the EC's own plans and programmes has been resisted from within – in implementing the Aarhus Convention to apply to its own institutions, recent legislation gives public participation rights but does not directly require that EC plans and programmes are subject to EA.[19] He is also critical of the way in which, when it comes to assessing legislative proposals by the European Commission, the absence of agreed rules can lead to a proliferation of impact studies on behalf of a range of interested parties (noting how the proposal for a directive on chemicals regulation – the REACH proposal – was the subject of 50 different impact studies by different EC institutions, Member States and private organisations, which necessarily calls into question the added value of impact assessment here.

Finally, Krämer concludes his chapter with a coruscating critique of wider regulatory impact assessment in Europe which, he argues, simply serves the deregulatory agenda at the expense of environmental protection. Even where the environment is mentioned – which is not in every case, and often only marginally – there is no 'identification, description and evaluation' of the direct and indirect effects of the planned measures on the environment, as the SEA Directive requires. Rather, 'the statements are either short or general and limit themselves to the declaration that the measure is favourable to sustainable development or to the environment. Or the "assessment" is reduced, as far as the environmental impact is concerned, to the question of how much the measure would cost. It is clear that such a question can hardly ever be answered'. As Krämer concludes, 'the "impact assessment" approach by the Commission cannot . . . be considered a serious contribution to assess the environmental effects of proposed legislation and policy orientation'. Indeed, he argues, the effect of internal impact assessment may in fact have environmentally harmful consequences, resulting in no significant amendments to proposals with adverse environment consequences, while frustrating environmental legislation.

In contrast to Krämer, Jonathan Wiener's chapter on 'Better Regulation' takes a more optimistic approach to RIA, albeit one that recognises that current practices need to be changed. In the context of looking back and forth across the Atlantic at better regulation initiatives, and IA as a component of these, he argues that 'the current borrowing of better regulation tools has not been much constrained by abstract ideological or rhetorical commitments, nor by supposed national styles or mentalities of law'. For Wiener, IA is a key tool for better regulation

---

19 See Regulation (EC) No 1367/2006 of the European Parliament and of the Council of 6 September 2006 on the application of the provisions of the Aarhus Convention on Access to Information, Public Participation in Decision-making and Access to Justice in Environmental Matters to Community institutions and bodies, Art 9, OJ L264/13.

in the EU – there is a case for substantive decision-making, centrally through cost–benefit analysis, or as the EU guidance puts it, assessing 'positive and negative impacts', both quantitative and qualitative, where regulation is 'better' where it is expected to produce net benefits. Wiener argues for what he terms a 'warm' approach to IA, taking environmental and other less easily quantifiable costs and benefits fully into account and without any instinct towards deregulation. The impediment to this, he argues, is institutional, not analytic – what is needed, and what the EU can learn from the US experience, are the best mechanisms to give voice to the various interests at play, determine their importance, and weigh them in the decision-making process. But, like EA in its procedural guise, IA and cost–benefit analysis are 'tools, not rules', with ultimate decisions resting with public officials exercising judgement. For Wiener, 'the criticisms of IA (especially using [cost benefit analysis]) seem to me to be worth taking seriously, but not fatal to a sensible application for weighing pros and cons of important decisions. There is no better alternative way of making policy.' Contra the examples given by Krämer, Wiener cites evidence that the *ex ante* estimate of *both* benefits and costs tend to be overstated in RIA, and that cost-benefit analysis can also be used to 'prompt' desirable new regulations to protect the environment.

For Wiener, the heart of effective impact assessment is not the quantification of costs and benefits of individual decisions – though these are important – but rather the consideration of the full pros and cons of a range of alternatives in a transparent and reasoned way (extending, for example, to serious consideration of multiple risks). His 'warm' version of IA tries to steer a path between taking decisions based either from acting out of 'hot' moral outrage or, at the other end of the spectrum, from pure 'cold' desk-top number crunching. ' "Warm analysis" would occupy the centre of this spectrum, embodying serious analysis of the full variety of impacts and tradeoffs, some quantitative and some qualitative, with compassion for both those who incur risks and those who incur abatement costs.'

None of this, of course, takes away from political judgment in the sharpening of the tools being used. For example, Wiener notes that the EU value for a statistical life appears to be lower than that taken in the US, while discount rates – so central to assessing the future costs of current plans – also vary across time and space according to preference, and were lowered in the second Bush administration.[20] Wiener further advocates using cost–benefit analysis across more of the board, for example, to spur good new regulatory proposals rather than just to block existing weak ones and equally to appraise deregulatory and administrative simplification initiatives. Wiener further considers the review of impact assessment, noting the weaknesses of relying on the courts to do this through judicial review, and offering suggestions for independent institutional review procedures.

---

20 For a critique of discounting generally, see also Frank Ackerman and Lisa Heinzerling, *Priceless* (New York: New Press, 2004), ch. 8; Richard Revesz, 'Environmental Regulation, Cost–Benefit Analysis, and the Discounting of Human Lives' (1999) 98 *Columbia Law Review* 941.

Finally, he considers the case for *ex post* review of RIA – as is now being undertaken in the US, and is being facilitated, for future review, in the EU – as an essential part of a wider outcome-based approach in this area.

As befits the subject-matter of his chapter, Wiener's is a thorough analysis – not just of RIA but of the current state of the debate about regulation more generally – and provides much food for thought about how in particular environmental impacts are best determined and weighed by legislators and other decision-makers. At the very least, it must be hoped – as Wiener does – that IA in effect gives environmental interests a substantive presence in the decision-making process rather than, as Jones *et al* recount of EA generally, being a factor that must be taken into account by decision-makers who, ultimately, are more heavily swayed by other factors.

The difference between the EC's 2001 SEA Directive and its 2000 Water Framework Directive is the subject of the chapter by William Howarth. The obvious point of contrast is that while the SEA Directive is a procedural tool for gathering together and considering environmental information at the level of plans and programmes, the WFD's requirements for reviews of the impacts of human activity on water bodies, which precedes the adoption of plans and programmes under the Directive, is based upon explicit and reasonably precise environmental objectives and standards against which assessments are to be made. As Howarth argues, in setting the benchmark in both the EIA and SEA Directives as the requirement of assessment where there are likely to be significant environment effects, but then not defining what is 'significant' means that, 'put bluntly, the exercise is "aimless" '. Whatever position one takes on the spectrum between convert and sceptic, EA can only be guaranteed to have any real-world cutting edge if it has express substantive content. The WFD, he argues, shows one way in which such substantivisation could be achieved, for example, by reference to baseline, non-deterioration standards (see also Jones *et al* above) and environmental quality standards laid down in the WFD and other legislation.

Taking this argument further, Howarth suggests that compliance with existing Community legislation be the 'threshold for acceptability' for any EIA or SEA. This is a variant of the debate as to whether planning or pollution control decision-makers have the whip hand, a debate that has rumbled through the UK courts over the last decade or so and which the courts have attempted to resolve by giving planning authorities some room for discretion to deny planning permission, on locational grounds, even where compliance with regulatory permissions will be likely, whilst rejecting challenges based on possible regulatory ineffectiveness.[21] The immediate attraction of Howarth's proposal is clear; however, what is not discussed is how much added value his proposals contain. Arguably, the strength of EA lies in its requirement – seen more strongly in the EC in SEA than in EIA – that

---

21   The leading case is *Gateshead MBC v Secretary of State for the Environment* [1995] Env LR 37; see more recently *Hopkins Development Ltd v First Secretary of State* [2006] EWHC 2823 (Admin).

alternatives be transparently considered and mitigated for; for all their weaknesses, these aim to reduce impacts rather than merely require existing norms to be complied with at the preferred location or through the relevant planning process. A sceptical view might be that the aim of EA is merely being used as a supplement, *ex ante*, to force compliance with environmental quality norms that ought to be complied with in any case. But for Howarth, the introduction of environmental standards into EA may be seen, positively, both in the immediate context of reinforcing environmental standards and in the longer term of 'substantivizing' EA.

Áine Ryall's chapter also provides an in-depth analysis of EA law in the EC, in this case scrutinising the links between the EIA Directive and the Aarhus Convention. The Aarhus Convention on access to environmental information, public participation and access to justice is widely heralded as an important breakthrough, at a global level, in terms of articulating the public interest in environmental decision-making. In terms of access to justice, the Convention has given rise to provisions amending the EIA Directive which require access to a review procedure for 'the public concerned', allowing a qualified challenge to the 'substantive or procedural legality' of decisions subject to the participation requirements established in the Directive. While it is clear that the amendments to the Directive are aimed at granting standing to bodies like NGOs, as Ryall notes the law on standing in Ireland has relatively recently been amended if anything to *restrict* the scope for public interest challenges by requiring a 'substantial interest' rather than a 'sufficient interest' to be shown. She makes the case that, in areas where Community law rights are concerned, national courts ought to take a generous approach to the substantial interest requirement, and suggests that there may also be a need for a concomitant approach to courts orders to ensure that Community rights are able to be vindicated.

Ryall also queries what standard of judicial review is to be required. Although any challenge must be to the 'legality' of decisions rather than its merits, Ryall comments on the highly deferential standard of review taken by the Irish courts in planning cases because of the complex balancing of factors involved. In an echo of Alder's earlier article in relation to the UK courts, however, she queries whether this is an appropriate legal standard to adopt; many issues within EIA law involve matters of mixed fact and law or, as the English courts have now accepted, some matters which were formally deemed to be matters of fact and degree must now, following European Court of Justice case law, be seen as matters of law for which an objective approach is needed.[22] There are echoes here of the changing emphases taken by the English courts to the issue of substantial compliance, with the House of Lords in *Berkeley No. 1*[23] stressing that a process which appeared to gather together all the information required under the Directive was not sufficient

---

22 *R(Goodman) v London Borough of Lewisham ('Big Yellow')* [2003] Env LR 28.
23 *Berkeley v Secretary of State for the Environment (Berkeley No.1)* [2000] AC 603.

because the rights of the public to participate meaningfully in the decision-making process could be frustrated if it was not clear *to the public concerned* where to locate this information. As Ryall notes, these issues have yet to come before the Irish Supreme Court, though it may not be long before they do.

Providing information to decision-makers is of course at the very heart of any type of EA. But what happens to this information once the decision on the project or plan etc has been made? This is the question that informs the chapter by Daniel Farber, who in 'Bringing Environmental Assessment into the Digital Age' considers it a 'no brainer' that this information – laboriously (and expensively) collated for the purposes of individual EAs – should not effectively be lost thereafter to other researchers, participants and decision-makers, not least because the information that we have publicly available about the environment is so riddled with gaps. Given that EA is a procedural rather than substantive mechanism, aimed at forcing the disclosure of information, Farber wonders what the point of a disclosure statute is 'that does not in fact make information available in usable form to the public'.

Forcing this information out would also allow EA to play an accountability role, with access to environmental assessments allowing the public the chance to see what kinds of mitigating measures have been proposed in relation to other, similar, developments, and therefore to give some added weight to calls for their consideration in the development under question. This *ex ante* function might also be coupled, *ex post*, by using access to environmental assessments to see how development is measuring up to the claims made for it when it was being proposed, especially in terms of mitigation measures. The importance of this is underscored by the fact that, although mitigated FONSIs are widely used, 'there is at best haphazard monitoring of the success of mitigation measures, and even if there were compulsory monitoring, the difficulty of obtaining the EAs themselves would prevent any systematic comparison of predictions with outcomes'. All of this would feed in to a more adaptive orientation for EA generally, as well as for specific projects.

Farber sees a 'virtual global ecosystem' through a geographic information system (GIS) which included EA data as the ultimate ambition, but suggests that much more modest steps might go a long way, for example, simply making environmental assessments online. (Writing from a US perspectives, his remarks are not immediately translatable into a EU context, because there is not necessarily a written environmental assessment – the closest equivalent would be the proponent's environmental statement or environmental report, but this gives an initial appraisal, from the proponent's point of view, of likely impacts, and as things stand could not be taken as the final *assessment* of impacts.) He asks of the current system some straightforward questions about accessing EA information: Are they accessible? Are they searchable? Is information about specific sites integrated to build up a picture of a region? Is there post-project follow-up information? Answering these, he concludes that 'the current system flunks in all four of these dimensions'. All of these areas could be improved through digital EA.

But this era is a long way off. Indeed, as he poignantly remarks: 'Sadly, current environmental assessment is largely a creature of the nineteenth century. Hard copies of documents languish in obscure file cabinets, just as they might have done in the days of Dickens' "circumlocution bureau".'

Finally, Jane Holder's chapter on 'The Prospects for Ecological Impact Assessment' provides a 'back to the future' analysis of environmental assessment by paring it back to its roots in ecological science, but in so doing, also offers a new direction for its future development. This paper is a response and a reaction to the steady broadening of environmental assessment to encompass sustainability criteria of social and economic impacts, of the sort now commonplace in the European Union, as 'sustainability analysis'. This process of broadening the remit of environmental assessment appears to have permeated beyond policy-making at the European Union level, so that, for example, a strategic environmental assessment of offshore renewable energy projects also includes analysis of the prospects of this type of development for increasing employment opportunities and contributing to the British renewables industry. Even at the EIA level, statements assessing the environmental impact of projects habitually include similar references to local economic conditions. Holder argues that whereas there is a place for such considerations to be taken into account in broader decision-making processes, there is a risk that environmental assessment is being used as a means to prejudge, or package, such choices. Holder, perhaps idealistically, looks to a form of environmental assessment which is more sensitive to ecological requirements and realities in three ways: first, the lengthening of timeframes for both *ex ante* and *ex post* assessment to better reflect the ecological condition of sites, migration patterns and colonisation of an area over time, rather than according to standard administrative frameworks (for example for licensing purposes); second, the setting of boundaries for a study based on the ecological condition of the land, which might extend well beyond the boundaries of ownership as legally defined, or land which forms the subject of an application for development consent; and, finally, an ecologically sensitive treatment of issues of compensation and mitigation. The apparent oversight of ecology in environmental assessment procedures is illustrated by the case of the proposed wind farm on the Isle of Lewis, on the west coast of Scotland. This case serves also to underline that predictions made in the course of environmental assessment procedures are open to contrary interpretations and that environmental assessment itself provides a site for contest and dispute, about both fact and values.

Closing remarks

In summary, each of the contributions to the stocktaking exercise that we have engaged upon is unashamedly empirical in the sense that their overriding concern is with how environmental assessment works, typically and most obviously in law, but also in policy and practice. The contributors share a (possibly unfashionable) belief in the rationality and 'workabilty' of environmental assessment – in its ability to produce 'better decisions' – which is broadly representative of the current state of the environmental assessment discipline. As a legal mechanism, environmental assessment is therefore thought to be well worth the considerable time, trouble, and resources involved in 'getting it right', which has in the past included numerous preparatory drafts of forms of environmental assessment, extensive and repeated reporting and information exchange exercises, the promulgation of amending legislation and (with SEA) the introduction of more far-reaching and, arguably, more complex instruments. However, the contributors to this book do not make light of the inherent problems with environmental assessment. They also recognise that environmental assessment is a complex and mediated social and legal experience in which decision-making is shaped by the changes in, for example, the physical environment of an area, political priorities, regulations or policies, societal views and scientific knowledge as well as by negotiations, persuasion and bargaining.[24] Looking further beyond the rationality of decision-making, informed and shaped by environmental assessment, it is perhaps time to include within the frames of reference in this area the significance of the 'irrational', the 'subjective', or 'unmeasurable' in environmental assessment – how it acts as an avenue for protest (or at least for delay as a variant of this), a power of expression and communication, and as a critical meeting point between (legal) text, culture and nature.[25] Legal engagement with these qualities of environmental assessment might, in time, produce a 'fourth wave' of scholarship. Pointers in this direction may be found in this collection. We offer the faint hope that, as Wiener argues of IA, here the academic is also the policy entrepreneur. But, if this is our ultimate aspiration, in this collection our minimum objective is 'just' to highlight vital aspects of law, policy and practice relating to environmental assessment, and, most importantly, to give a sense of the impacts, influences and dynamic inter-relationships between these.

24 Such complexities are captured well by Angus Morrison-Saunders and Jos Arts (eds) *Assessing Impact: Handbook of EIA and SEA Follow-up* (London: Earthscan, 2004), p 30.
25 We note here Lord Hoffmann's (somewhat disparaging, but possibly accurate) remarks in *Berkeley No. 1* about the use of environmental assessment as a conduit for public expression and participation: 'the directly enforceable right of the citizen which is accorded by the [EC EIA Directive] ...requites the inclusive and democratic procedure prescribed by the Directive, in which the public however misguided or wrong headed its views may be, is given an opportunity to express its opinion on the environmental issues'.

Chapter 2

Environmental assessment: dominant or dormant?

*Carys Jones, Stephen Jay, Paul Slinn and Christopher Wood**

Introduction

Environmental assessment (EA) is used in this chapter as a portmanteau term for environmental impact assessment (EIA) and strategic environmental assessment (SEA). EIA is the evaluation of the effects likely to arise from a major project significantly affecting the natural and man-made environment. Consultation and participation are integral to this evaluation. EIA is a systematic and integrative process for considering possible impacts prior to a decision being taken on whether or not a proposal should be given approval to proceed. EIA requires, *inter alia*, the publication of an EIA report describing in detail the environmental impacts likely to arise from an action. SEA is an equivalent process undertaken at the policy, plan and/or programme (PPP) level.

The EA process should supply decision makers with an indication of the likely environmental consequences of their actions. EA is thus an anticipatory, participatory, environmental management tool, of which the EA report is only one part. It can contribute towards achieving sustainable development (SD) by a number of mechanisms, including design changes.[1]

The EA takes place in a wider decision-making political context so it is inevitable that economic, social, or political factors will outweigh environmental factors in many instances. Although EA can lead to the abandonment of environmentally unacceptable actions, it was never intended to prevent actions with significant environmental impacts from being implemented. Rather, the intention was that actions be authorised in the full knowledge of their environmental consequences. This is why the mitigation of environmental impacts is so central to EIA. Decisions on projects in which the environmental effects have palpably been ameliorated are much easier to make and justify than those in which mitigation has not been achieved.

After over 35 years of practice and development, project level EIA has become an accepted environmental management tool in a wide range of jurisdictions around the world. Its intentions are widely agreed and, legally and procedurally, it is now

---

* The authors gratefully acknowledge the late Dr Norman Lee's stimulating comments on a draft of this chapter.
1 C M Wood, *Environmental Impact Assessment: A Comparative Review*, 2nd edn (Harlow: Prentice Hall, 2003).

embedded in the broader project planning culture. The EIA has evolved over time and in accordance with local contexts and circumstances. More recently, SEA practice has begun to burgeon. However, while there is considerable evidence that EA has influenced decisions affecting the environment, it is generally accepted that this influence is less than its originators anticipated.[2] The purpose and practice of EA are therefore ripe for reconsideration.

This chapter will attempt to establish whether EA is as dominant as its current context allows or whether it is lying dormant. The chapter will briefly describe the origins and diffusion of EA and then discuss emerging forms of assessment, EA and SD, the performance of EA, the effect of EA on decision-making, EA and decision-making models, and increasing the effectiveness of EA. Finally, conclusions are drawn.

Origins and diffusion

EA first appeared in the United States as a result of the National Environmental Policy Act of 1969 (NEPA). NEPA was enacted at a time when environmental damage had become a substantive issue of major public concern thrust upon often reluctant governments ill-organised to provide the necessary cross-departmental interdisciplinary response: national environment departments did not then exist. As Lynton Caldwell, its principal architect, stated, NEPA 'became law because of an undeniable groundswell of public demand in the late 1960s for government "to do something about the environment"'.[3] As he averred, 'the United States appears to have been the first nation to respond comprehensively to an insistent (though inchoate) public demand for action to protect the quality of the environment'.[4]

One of the purposes of NEPA is 'to promote efforts which will prevent or eliminate damage to the environment and biosphere'.[5] This environmental policy goal is coupled with a prescient SD aspiration:

> The Congress, recognizing the profound impact of man's activity on the... natural environment...and...the critical importance of restoring and maintaining environmental quality...declares that it is the continuing policy

2   B Sadler, *Environmental Assessment in a Changing World: Evaluating Practice to Improve Performance*, Final Report of the International Study of the Effectiveness of Environmental Assessment (Ottawa: Ministry of Supply and Services, Canadian Environmental Assessment Agency and International Association for Impact Assessment, 1996); Wood, *Environmental Impact Assessment*, ibid; M Cashmore, R Gwilliam, R Morgan, D Cobb, and A Bond, 'The Interminable Issue of Effectiveness: Substantive Purposes, Outcomes and Research Challenges in the Advancement of Environmental Impact Assessment Theory' (2004) 22 *Impact Assessment and Project Appraisal* 295.

3   L K Caldwell and K Shrader-Frechette, *Policy for Land: Land and Ethics* (Lanham, MD, USA: Rowman Littlefield, 1993), 146.

4   L K Caldwell, *The National Environmental Policy Act: An Agenda for the Future* (Bloomington, IN, USA: Indiana University Press, 1998), 4.

5   NEPA, s 2; Caldwell, ibid.

of the Federal Government ... to use all practicable means and measures ... to create and maintain conditions under which man and nature can exist in productive harmony, and fulfil the social, economic, and other requirements of present and future generations of Americans.[6]

This policy was intended, *inter alia*, to 'fulfil the responsibilities of each generation as trustee of the environment for succeeding generations'.[7] However, it was recognised that the policy alone was insufficient: 'it was necessary in realizing national environmental policy objectives to lay unequivocal mandatory requirements on the Federal bureaucracies whose inbred attitudes were resistant to the new environmental objectives'.[8] Accordingly, NEPA requires that '[a]ll agencies of the Federal Government shall ... include in every recommendation for major Federal actions significantly affecting the quality of the human environment, a detailed statement on ... the environmental impact of the proposed action'.[9] This was the origin of the environmental impact statement (EIS) and the phrase 'environmental impact assessment' evolved to describe the process leading up to, and on from, the EIS. The preparation of an EIS was an 'action-forcing' measure imposed upon federal agencies to require them to consider the environmental consequences of their decisions.

California was the first of the American states to introduce an effective 'little NEPA', in 1970.[10] The majority have chosen not to do so. The ramifications of NEPA were beginning to be accepted internationally as a result of several celebrated legal cases which clarified its significance at a time when the unprecedented surge of environmental concern culminated in the United Nations conference on the environment in Stockholm in 1972. The problems of burgeoning development, pollution and destruction of the natural environment that NEPA was intended to address were perceived as universal. The rigorous project-by-project evaluation of significant impacts inherent in EIA was seized upon as a powerful weapon in the fight to resolve these environmental problems by many other jurisdictions which adopted elements of the US EIA process. Most were, however, very cautious about importing NEPA-style litigation with EIA and made strenuous efforts to avoid doing so.

The methods of adoption varied, including cabinet resolutions, advisory procedures, regulations, and laws were all employed. Probably the first overseas jurisdiction to adopt an environmental impact policy was the Australian state of New South Wales in January 1972. Canada approved a federal cabinet directive on EIA in 1973 and the Commonwealth of Australia announced an EIA policy in

6 NEPA, s 101(a).
7 Ibid, s 101(b).
8 Caldwell, *The National Environmental Policy Act*, n. 4 above, 6.
9 NEPA, s 102(2)(c); Caldwell, ibid.
10 The majority have chosen not to do so. See R E Bass, A I Herson, and K M Bogdan, *CEQA Deskbook: A Step-by-Step Guide on How to Comply with the California Environmental Quality Act* 2nd ed. (Point Arena CA, USA: Solano Press, 1999).

1972 and passed an act in 1974. New Zealand instituted EIA procedures by cabinet minute in 1974. Columbia and Thailand established EIA systems through specific legislation in 1974 and 1975 respectively, followed by France in 1976. Ireland passed legislation that permitted, but did not require, EIA in 1976 and the cabinet of the West German government approved an EIA procedure by minute in the same year. The Netherlands governmental standpoint on EIA followed in 1979. There was also considerable EIA activity in numerous developing countries.[11]

Several international agencies involved themselves with EIA. In 1974 the Organisation for Economic Cooperation and Development recommended that member governments adopt EIA procedures and methods and that they use EIA in the process of granting aid to developing countries. In addition, in 1985 the Council of the European Communities adopted the EIA Directive that required member states to implement formal EIA procedures by 1988. These procedures were subsequently strengthened in 1997 by an amended version of the EIA Directive 1985, which came into effect in 1999.[12]

In 1989 the World Bank ruled that EIA for major projects should normally be undertaken by the borrower country under the Bank's supervision. The United Nations Environment Programme also made recommendations to member states regarding the establishment of EIA procedures, established goals and principles for EIA and issued guidance on EIA in developing countries. The 1992 Earth Summit provided additional momentum to these initiatives. EIA is now practised in more than one hundred countries.[13]

The earliest legislation requiring the use of SEA was NEPA. The term 'major Federal actions' was subsequently defined to include projects and programmes, rules, regulations, plans, policies, procedures, and legislative proposals advanced by federal agencies.[14] SEA procedures are not distinguished from project EIA procedures in the United States where EISs for PPPs are often called programmatic EISs.

Although the preparation of programmatic EISs for federal programmes that might involve numerous actions was recommended as early as 1972, to ensure that cumulative impacts were addressed, it was not until the late 1980s that the opportunities afforded by NEPA began to be realised. California's SEA system, however, dates from the mid-1970s and several hundred SEAs have been undertaken to date, mostly of land-use plans.[15]

SEA practice has received considerable impetus from a number of international organisations. The need to integrate environmental considerations with

---

11 N Lee and C George (eds) *Environmental Assessment in Developing and Transitional Countries* (Chichester: Wiley & Sons, 2000).

12 See Council Directive 97/11/EC of 3 March 1997, which amended Council Directive 85/337/EC of 27 June 1985 on the assessment of the effects of certain public and private projects on the environment.

13 Wood, *Environmental Impact Assessment*, n. 1 above.

14 NEPA, s 102(2)(c); Caldwell, *The National Environmental Policy Act*, n. 4 above.

15 Bass, *CEQA Deskbook*, n. 10 above.

development became an accepted part of World Bank policy in 1987. The same philosophy was echoed in the Brundtland Report.[16] Two of the outputs of the 1992 Earth Summit, Agenda 21 and the Rio Declaration,[17] provided further impetus for national governments to incorporate environmental considerations into all levels of decision-making. Similarly, the United Nations Economic Commission for Europe (UNECE) has championed the extension of EIA principles to PPPs, most recently by promoting the SEA protocol.[18] A European directive on the assessment of plans and programmes – commonly referred to as the Strategic Environment Assessment (SEA) Directive, even though the term SEA is not actually used in the Directive – came into effect in 2004.[19] In some ways this is surprisingly stronger than the amended European EIA Directive on which it was based.

The implementation of the European SEA Directive in all twenty-five member states and of SEA procedures in other developed and, to a lesser extent, developing countries has resulted in more than thirty jurisdictions making formal provision for SEA.[20] Notwithstanding this, the evolution of SEA probably lags 15 years behind that of EIA.

Emerging forms of assessment

Petts has concluded that no single tool can provide for all environmental management contexts but her evaluation of various decision aiding tools indicated that both EIA and SEA provide examples of optimality in that they address uncertainty, cover a range of impacts and include participatory mechanisms.[21] It is perhaps a compliment to the perceived success of EIA in incorporating environmental considerations into decision-making procedures that, over a lengthy period, as it has spread geographically around the world and been applied at different levels of environmental decision-making, it has been imitated and applied to specific impact types not necessarily related to the environment.[22]

This proliferation of other forms of impact assessment reflects the recognised value of a structured and consistent approach to evaluating environmental, and

---

16 Brundtland Report, also known as *Our Common Future: World Commission on Environment and Development* (Oxford: Oxford University Press, 1987).

17 See United Nations Environment and Development Agenda 21, also known as 'Agenda 21'; and see United Nations Conference on Environment and Development (UNCED), Rio de Janeiro, 3–14 June 1992, also known as 'the Rio Earth Summit'.

18 See United Nations Economic Commission For Europe Protocol On Strategic Environmental Assessment to the Convention on Environmental Impact Assessment in a Transboundary Context.

19 See Council Directive 2001/42/EC on the assessment of the effects of plans and programmes on the environment.

20 B Dalal-Clayton and B Sadler, *Strategic Environmental Assessment: A Sourcebook and Reference Guide to International Experience* (London: Earthscan, 2005).

21 J Petts, 'Environmental Impact Assessment Versus Other Environmental Management Decision Tools' in J Petts (ed.) *Handbook of Environmental Impact Assessment* Volume 1, (Oxford: Blackwell, 1999).

22 A Porter and J Fittipaldi (eds) *Environmental Methods Review: Retooling Impact Assessment for the New Century* (Fargo, ND, USA: Press Club, 1998).

other, aspects when taking decisions. Thus, Sadler regarded EA as largely being successful as a policy instrument because it had developed to include new areas and impacts.[23] However, Benson considered that EA was too limited in application to answer fully the broad questions involved in considering the full effects of human activities in sustainability terms.[24] Sadler saw the future of EA as being part of a framework, linking it in an integrated way to other instruments such as lifecycle analysis, environmental auditing and environment accounting, and sustainability approaches such as the principles espoused in Agenda 21.[25]

Over the years, a growing body of increasingly diffuse impact assessment practice and experience, together with a wide appreciation of the need to strengthen impact assessment systems, has emerged. Even without the inexorable rise of SD up the political agenda, it was perhaps inevitable that there would be pressure to reintegrate these types of impact assessment with their progenitor, EA.

A list of more specialised forms of assessment of, principally project, impacts is potentially lengthy but examples include:

- social impact assessment;
- ecological impact assessment; and
- health impact assessment.

Social impact assessment (SIA) has evolved as a discipline with theoretical underpinning, a methodology and a growing body of experience.[26] Although precise definitions vary, SIA possesses many similarities to EIA in terms of process but its focus is explicitly on 'people'. Nevertheless, its routine practice generally remains confined to North America, Australasia, and the development banks.

Treweek emphasised that the main role of ecological impact assessment is to support EIA and SEA, but also to contribute to wider issues of implementing the principles of sustainability, the 'wise use' of land, and natural resource planning more generally, including integrated pollution control.[27] Thus, the development of a specific type of impact assessment focussing on a particular topic does not necessarily result in a narrow and exclusive assessment of that topic.

The assessment of health impacts has often been an underlying factor in impact assessment rather than an explicit requirement.[28] The amended European directive on EIA indicates the intention of assessing the effects of

23 B Sadler, 'On Evaluating the Success of EIA and SEA' in A Morrison-Saunders and J Arts (eds) *Assessing Impact: Handbook of EIA and SEA Follow-up* (London: Earthscan, 2004).

24 J Benson, 'What's The Alternative? Impact Assessment Tools and Sustainable Planning' (2003) 21 *Impact Assessment and Project Appraisal* 261.

25 See Agenda 21, n. 17 above; Sadler, *Environmental Assessment in a Changing World*, n. 2 above.

26 F Vanclay, 'Social Impact Assessment' in Petts, *Handbook*, n. 20 above.

27 J Treweek, *Ecological Impact Assessment* (Oxford: Blackwell, 1999), xi.

28 British Medical Association, *Health and Environmental Impact Assessment: An Integrated Approach* (London: Earthscan, 1998).

development projects is, *inter alia*, 'to take account of concerns to protect human health'.[29] Human health is included as an impact area to be included in environmental reports undertaken under the SEA Directive.[30] Links between health impact assessment and SIA are also evident[31] although in practice integration is uncommon.[32]

Despite initial enthusiasm for, and promotion of, these impact assessment types their impetus has not always been sustained and their general acceptance into mainstream practice, either as a separate entity or in an integrated form, is not universal. This is mainly due to lack both of specific regulatory requirements and of clarity regarding their inclusion within the coverage of current EIA or SEA procedures.

In addition, other forms of, principally PPP, assessment have developed rather more independently of EA. These assess impacts of potential significance for broader planning and decision-making which tend to fall outside the usual scope of EA. They include:

- trade impact assessment; and
- regulatory impact assessment.

Trade impact assessment involves the assessment of the likely positive or negative direct and indirect environmental, economic, and social consequences of trade liberalisation measures.[33] Regulatory impact assessment (RIA) relates to the assessment of the impacts of proposed legislative and regulatory measures. The consideration of environmental impacts in RIA tends to be limited since economic impacts are often a key aspect. Although there has been recognition that other forms of quantitative and qualitative analyses are also relevant, there are few links between RIA and EA.[34]

The development of various forms of assessment raises several concerns about their effective implementation, including the resources required, the potential for inconsistencies in approach, the lack of linkages between assessments, and whether the impacts covered are appropriate for broader planning and decision-making purposes. The integration of assessment tools and approaches

29 EIA Directive, Preamble, n. 12 above.
30 See SEA Directive, n. 18 above.
31 M Birley, 'Health Impact Assessment, Integration and Critical Appraisal' (2003) 21 *Impact Assessment and Project Appraisal* 313.
32 B Ahmad, 'Integrating Health Into Impact Assessment: Challenges and Opportunities' (2004) 22 *Impact Assessment and Project Appraisal* 2.
33 N Lee and C Kirkpatrick, 'Methodologies for Sustainability Impact Assessments of Proposals for New Trade Agreements' (2001) 3 *Journal of Environmental Assessment Policy and Management* 395.
34 Organisation for Economic Cooperation and Development, Reforming Environmental Regulation in OECD Countries (Paris, OECD, 1997).

has therefore attracted attention[35] although integration can be interpreted in different ways:

1   integrated definition of the environment incorporating social and economic factors;
2   integrated approaches to decision-making which place projects in the context of relevant policies and strategies;
3   integrated use of assessments in decision-making;
4   integrated use of combinations of assessment and other environmental management tools to counteract inherent deficiencies and limitations; and
5   integrated use of EIA and environmental management systems.

It has long been recognised that the reconciliation of these different understandings is necessary to progress towards a truly integrated approach that will allow decisions to be undertaken in the full knowledge of the consequences for the environment, including social and economic impacts. This has led to emerging interest in integrated forms of, principally PPP, assessment that incorporate EA, with particular focus on:

•   extended impact assessment; and
•   sustainability assessment/appraisal.

Extended impact assessment was intended to cover environmental, economic, and social impacts and to replace several separate forms of impact assessment previously applied to European Commission policy proposals.[36] These included business impact assessment, gender assessment, environmental assessment, small and medium enterprises assessment, trade impact assessment, and regulatory assessment.

There has also been increasing interest in, and development of, approaches to the integration of EA with sustainability approaches, particularly at the strategic level.[37] Sustainability (impact) assessment, or appraisal, includes social and economic impacts alongside environmental impacts. Inevitably, the assessment of the very different and often conflicting impacts of an action can presage tensions during decision-making.

EA and sustainable development

The pressure to move from a focus on the assessment of environmental impacts, whether EIA at the project level or SEA at PPP levels, to the assessment of

---

35 See Sadler, *Environmental Assessment in a Changing World*, n. 2 above; Lee and Kirkpatrick, *Methodologies for Sustainability Impact Assessments*, n. 33 above.
36 N Lee, 'Bridging the Gap Between Theory and Practice in Integrated Assessment' (2006) 26 *Environmental Impact Assessment Review* 57.
37 Ibid.

a wider range of human concerns is perhaps inevitable given the current trend of using SD as an aspirational target. Sustainability assessment (or sustainability appraisal), or some means of assessing environmental, social, and economic impacts, especially of PPPs, in an integrated manner, seems likely to be a popular assessment tool in the future.

The increasing focus on achieving SD provides a fresh challenge for the role of EA in informing decision-making.[38] The oft-quoted 'Brundtland' definition of SD is that which 'meets the needs of the present without compromising the ability of future generations to meet their own needs'.[39] This definition is essentially anthropocentric with a focus on promoting the human element. Other interpretations advocate a more eco-centric approach with the integrity of the biosphere underpinning social and economic development.[40]

The recognition that environmental, social, and economic issues need to be addressed is not a new concept in EA. The originators of EA always acknowledged that, in the end, decision-making should take into account a full and balanced range of issues. Although the use of the term 'sustainability' effectively dates from the Brundtland Report,[41] NEPA, made environmental quality the necessary precondition for SD. In recognising NEPA's legacy is both environmental impact assessment and strategic environmental assessment, it follows there may be dangers in widening the approach to assessment.

The emergence of the concept of SD, and of sustainability assessment, has posed a particular challenge in relation to the environment as it has allowed decision makers to make trade-offs between its economic, social, and environmental strands. This has led to a perception that the environment may not generally enjoy equal status with social and especially economic factors in the mainstreaming of SD decisions. The Royal Commission on Environmental Pollution (RCEP)[42] highlighted the concern that environmental and social issues may well be marginalized by the dominant economic assessments undertaken in current sustainability appraisals. The RCEP castigated both the appraisal and the justification of an initiative with economic drivers using economic criteria as meaningless. It stated the purpose of EA was to 'integrate environmental concerns into primarily non-environmental areas of decision-making. We believe that the environmental component of sustainability appraisal must be strengthened, as a condition for its retention'.[43]

Just as the environmental revolution in the late 1960s encountered the sectoral division of environmental responsibilities, the concept of SD often proved to be too

---

38 E.g. see the EC 'SEA Directive', Art 1, n. 18 above.
39 Brundtland Report, n. 16 above, 43.
40 T O'Riordan and H Voisey, 'The Political Economy of Sustainable Development' (1997) 6 *Environmental Politics* 1.
41 Brundtland Report, n. 16 above.
42 See Royal Commission on Environmental Pollution, 23rd Report, *Environmental Planning* (2002).
43 RCEP, ibid, para. 7.47.

diffuse for narrowly based government departments to advance policies supported equally by all its pillars.[44] The inevitable consequence has been that 'in practice, different agencies focused on those one or two most relevant to them'.[45] The UK initially formulated four equally weighted SD objectives: social; environmental; natural resource; and economic. In 2005, however, these were replaced by five principles in which the twin goals were 'living within environmental limits' and a 'strong, healthy and just society', and a sustainable economy, good governance, and sound science were the means to achieve these.[46] Living within environmental limits was defined as: '[r]especting the limits of the planet's environment, resources and biodiversity – to improve our environment and ensure that the natural resources needed for life are unimpaired and remain so for future generations'.[47]

This environmental emphasis amongst the five sustainable development principles may in time lead to a strengthening of the environmental component of sustainability assessment.

Performance of EA

While the difficulties of reaching an objective overall judgement about the performance of any EIA or SEA system are numerous,[48] there is a need for evaluative frameworks to compare the formal legal EA procedures, the arrangements for their application, and practice in their implementation. A distinction must be made between quality and effectiveness in evaluating EA practice.[49] The former refers to determinants of quality that can be split into legal, institutional, and other arrangements, EA procedures and methods. The latter relates to outputs, both direct and indirect, for example the achievement of identified goals such as the influence on decisions. Judgements about the quality and effectiveness of the EA process involve the use of different types of criteria.

Wood evaluated seven EIA systems employing a set of fourteen criteria focussed upon the requirements and operation of the EIA process, that is, mainly procedural inputs, although they also encompassed effectiveness, efficiency, and equity considerations.[50] Table 2.1 summarises the overall performance of these

---

44 S C Young, 'The United Kingdom: From Political Containment to Integrated Thinking' in W M Lafferty and J Meadowcroft (eds) *Implementing Sustainable Development: Strategies and Initiatives in High Consumption Societies* (Oxford: Oxford University Press, 2000).

45 Her Majesty's Government, Scottish Executive, Welsh Assembly Government and Northern Ireland Office, *One Future – Different Paths: The UK's Shared Framework for Sustainable Development* (DEFRA, 2005), 15.

46 Ibid, 17.

47 Ibid, 16.

48 Sadler, *Environmental Assessment in a Changing World*, n. 2 above; Cashmore, 'The Interminable Issue of Effectiveness', n. 2 above.

49 W Thissen, 'Criteria for Evaluation of SEA' in M Partidario and E Clark (eds) *Perspectives On Strategic Environmental Assessment* (Boca Raton, FL, USA: Lewis, 2000).

50 Wood, *Environmental Impact Assessment*, n. 1 above.

Table 2.1 Performance of EIA systems

Evaluation criterion	United States	United Kingdom	Netherlands	Canada	Australia	New Zealand	South Africa
Legal basis	■	■	■	■	■	■	■
Coverage	◪	■	■	□	◪	■	■
Alternatives	■	◪	■	■	■	◪	■
Screening	■	■	■	■	■	■	■
Scoping	■	◪	■	■	■	◪	■
EIA report preparation	■	□	■	□	■	□	□
EIA report review	■	◪	■	□	■	□	□
Decision-making	◪	◪	◪	□	□	□	□
Impact monitoring	□	◪	□	□	◪	◪	◪
Mitigation	■	■	■	■	■	■	■
Consultation and participation	■	◪	■	■	■	□	□
System monitoring	◪	□	■	■	■	□	◪
Benefits and costs	■	■	■	■	■	■	■
Strategic EA	■	□	■	□	□	□	□

■ Yes   ◪ Partially   □ No

Source: C M Wood, *Environmental Impact Assessment: A Comparative Review*, 2nd edn (Harlow: Prentice Hall, 2003), 358.

Table 2.2 Performance of land use plan SEA systems

Evaluation criterion	Canada	Denmark	Germany	Hong Kong	Hungary	Ireland	Netherlands	New Zealand	Portugal	South Africa	Sweden	United Kingdom	United States	World Bank
SYSTEM CRITERIA														
Legal basis	□	■	■	□	■	■	■	□	□	□	■	■	■	□
Integration	■	■	■	■	□	■	□	■	■	□	□	□	□	□
Guidance	■	□	□	■	□	□	□	□	■	□	■	■	□	□
Coverage	□	■	■	□	■	■	■	□	■	□	■	■	■	■
Tiering	□	■	□	■	□	■	□	■	?	□	□	□	□	□
Sustainable development	■	■	□	■	□	□	□	□	?	■	■	□	□	■
PROCESS CRITERIA														
Alternatives	□	■	■	■	■	■	□	■	□	■	□	■	□	□
Screening	■	■	■	■	■	■	■	□	□	□	□	■	■	■
Scoping	□	■	■	■	■	■	?	□	□	■	□	□	■	□
Prediction/ evaluation	□	■	■	■	■	■	■	□	□	■	□	□	□	□
Additional impacts	□	■	□	□	□	□	■	□	□	□	□	■	□	□

OUTCOME CRITERIA

Report preparation
Review
Monitoring
Mitigation
Consultation and public

Decision making
Costs and benefits
Environmental quality
System monitoring

■ Yes   □ Partially   □ No   ? Don't know

Source: C Jones, M Baker, J Carter, S Jay, M Short, and C Wood (eds) *Strategic Environmental Assessment and Land Use Planning: An International Evaluation* (London: Earthscan, 2005), 279.

Note
Country performance comparisons should be made with great caution as they involve different authors' uncalibrated judgements.

EIA systems against the fourteen criteria. Many of the EIA systems performed strongly, reflecting the progress made as a result of many years' experience. Over time, legal requirements have been strengthened, guidance has been improved, expertise has been developed and expectations have been raised. The Netherlands EIA system, in particular, met most of the evaluation criteria.

A similar set of twenty criteria was employed to evaluate the quality and effectiveness of the SEA process in fourteen jurisdictions.[51] These were split into three broad categories: system, process, and outcome criteria. It is clear from Table 2.2 that the frequently embryonic SEA systems evaluated left much to be desired in comparison with the more mature EIA systems. Denmark and Hong Kong were adjudged to perform best against the evaluation criteria.

The performance of the EIA systems in Table 2.1 and SEA systems in Table 2.2 against decision-making criteria demonstrates why the analysis of decision-making mechanisms has become an important focus for debate about how, 35 years after its establishment, EA can achieve better environmental outcomes.

Effect of EA on decision-making

Recently, the focus of EIA evaluation has been less on procedural implementation and more on increasing effectiveness and efficiency and achieving better environmental outcomes.[52] Assessing the substantive output, the effectiveness of EIA in delivering its desired outcome, the enhancement of environmental protection, is a different, and ultimately more difficult, task. However, Sadler believed the 'litmus test' of EIA effectiveness was the influence the process had on decision-making.[53]

Put simply, the aim of evaluating the effectiveness of EA can be expressed as: 'how much difference is EA making?' Ideally, this question should be addressed with reference to EA's ultimate aim of 'restoring and maintaining environmental quality'.[54] There are obvious problems, however, in comparing the environmental conditions that might prevail without EA with those with EA. Not only is this a very hypothetical comparison to make, but it is difficult to define in a measurable way the various aspects of environmental quality. Even more elusive are the concepts of SD and sustainability, which are increasingly being adopted as the fundamental goals of EA. These concepts might be valuable statements of the ultimate purpose of EA but are too indeterminate to allow a meaningful answer to be given about the difference that EA might be making.

More helpful in trying to appraise the performance of EA is its specific regulatory aim of ensuring that environmental considerations are properly

---

51 C Jones, M Baker, J Carter, S Jay, M Short, and C Wood (eds) *Strategic Environmental Assessment and Land Use Planning: An International Evaluation* (London: Earthscan, 2005).

52 Cashmore, 'The Interminable Issue of Effectiveness', n. 2 above.

53 Sadler, *Environmental Assessment in a Changing World*, n. 2 above.

54 NEPA, s 101(a). See Caldwell, *The National Environmental Policy Act*, n. 4 above.

taken into account in individual cases. This is frequently stated to be the immediate aim of EA in legislation, guidance and the academic literature.[55] When a development project or a strategic initiative is proposed, EA requires the possibility of harmful environmental consequences to be considered and if these are likely a thorough study to be carried out of the potential environmental effects. The findings of this study should then be incorporated into the decisions made about the proposal. It is in the realm of decision-making about mooted projects and strategic actions that the influence of EA can best be tested. This can be explored by considering whether or not EA is leading to better decisions from an environmental point of view and whether projects and strategic actions are being significantly changed, or even halted, because of EA.

These issues were addressed in research into the effectiveness of EIA in UK planning decisions in the mid-1990s.[56] This involved a study of 40 cases in which environmental statements (ESs) were submitted with planning applications for consideration by local planning authorities. It was found that within this sample EIA decided the outcome of the application in only one case, and here the EIA indicated the development should be permitted rather than refused. Nonetheless, planning officers involved in the cases generally felt the ESs helped them to make their recommendations about the applications. EIA was not determinative but gave planners added confidence that their consideration of the proposals was sufficiently well informed. However, at the committee stage, when final decisions were made, the environmental statements played a significant role only in a minority of cases. Overall, other planning considerations were more important at this stage in decision-making, such as the responses from consultation and public participation that took place as part of the normal planning process.

It seems the actors involved in these 40 cases were operating primarily within the parameters of the planning procedures to which they were accustomed, and EIA was commonly seen as external to those procedures. The findings of EIA were often regarded as a useful contributory factor but EIA was not as fully integrated into the institutional patterns of decision-making as its originators hoped. The only area of decision-making where EIA played a consistent role was in the setting of conditions on planning permissions. Here the mitigation measures recommended in ESs were frequently referred to and used as the basis for some of the conditions set. EIA was resulting in some modification of projects,

---

55 E.g. see Sadler, *Environmental Assessment in a Changing World*, n. 2 above; Lee and George, *Environmental Assessment*, n. 11 above; B Noble, 'Strategic Environmental Assessment: What Is It? And What Makes It Strategic?' (2000) 2 *Journal of Environmental Assessment Policy and Management* 203.

56 C M Wood and C Jones, 'The Effect of Environmental Assessment on UK Local Planning Authority Decisions' (1997) 34 *Urban Studies* 1237.

although not usually of a major kind. The overall purposes, scales, and types of development were not affected.[57]

While these results are limited in their geographical and institutional scope, they are in line with other studies of EIA performance, both UK based[58] and international.[59] In his comparative review, Wood employed the criterion: 'must the findings of the EIA report and the review be a central determinant of the decision on the action?'[60] Table 2.1 illustrates that none of the seven EIA systems fully met this criterion. In order to do so, an EIA system needs to demonstrate not only that decisions should be influenced by EIA, as all seven did, but that the EIA report actually influences each decision. Although all seven jurisdictions employed differing mechanisms for ensuring the EIA was considered, in practice it was still not unusual, as a result of regulatory weaknesses, for 'decision makers to circumvent...EIA mechanisms where this is convenient'.[61] Wood concluded that EIA does exert some influence on development decisions, but it is common for the findings of EIA to be marginalised in favour of other considerations.

While modifications to the project design were made prior to the formal application and/or during the formal EIA process in nearly every case reported, these were mostly minor and designed to mitigate the worst effects of development, the need for which was seldom questioned on environmental grounds. None of the systems examined was judged to have made adequate use of EIA findings during the decision-making process. This suggests that more could be done to improve the quality of the information that EIA produces but also perhaps that decision makers do not consistently give appropriate weight to environmental issues when balancing the advantages and disadvantages of a proposal.

These findings raise the question of whether the immediate objective of EIA, to provide environmental information, is an adequate expression of its ultimate aim as expressed in NEPA. The insistence that EIA, and EA more generally, is a decision aiding, rather than decision-making, tool may be unduly limiting and may be placing too great a level of trust on decision makers to act in accordance with the environmental information provided to them. In its own restrictive terms,

---

57 Wood and Jones, 'The Effect of Environmental Assessment on UK Local Planning Authority Decisions' (1997) 34 *Urban Studies* 1237.

58 J Weston, 'EIA and Public Inquiries' in J Weston (ed.) *Planning and Environmental Impact Assessment in Practice* (Harlow: Longman, 1997).

59 N Lee, 'Environmental Assessment In The European Union: A Tenth Anniversary' (1995) 10 *Project Appraisal* 77; Sadler, *Environmental Assessment in a Changing World*, n. 2 above; E ten Heuvelhof and C Nauta, 'The Effects Of Environmental Impact Assessment In The Netherlands' (1997) 12 *Project Appraisal* 25; A Barker and C M Wood, 'An Evaluation Of EIA System Performance In Eight EU Countries' (1999) 19 *Environmental Impact Assessment Review* 387; J Glasson, 'Environmental Impact Assessment: Impact on Decisions' in Petts, *Handbook*, n. 20 above; E Leknes, 'The Roles Of EIA In The Decision-Making Process' (2001) 21 *Environmental Impact Assessment Review* 309; P Christensen, L Kørnøv, and E H Nielsen, 'EIA As Regulation: Does It Work?' (2005) 48 *Journal of Environmental Planning and Management* 393.

60 Wood, *Environmental Impact Assessment*, n. 1 above.

61 Ibid, 239.

it could be said that EIA is performing well: it is providing the information, and decision makers are 'taking account' of it. It is just that they are frequently being swayed by other perspectives!

The actual decisions taken are likely to be based more upon the norms and values of elected decision makers and their advisers, acting within a political arena, than upon an impartial consideration of the environmental information. In this regard, it has been argued that EIA is inevitably constrained by being merely a procedural tool that does not require decision makers to adopt any particular environmental standards.[62] There is not even an obligation on decision makers to give any specified weight to the environmental information. On the other hand, it could be argued that the 'information-providing' function of EIA is as much as is currently politically acceptable and that the spread of statutory EIA systems around the world in a few decades should in itself be taken as a measure of its success.

There has been less empirical research into the effectiveness of SEA in shaping decision-making. This is partly because SEA is much less established than EIA, both in legislative and practice terms, and consequently has a less well-defined and 'measurable' place in decision-making processes. In addition, SEA relates to an extremely diverse range of strategic proposals, making it difficult to draw generalised conclusions about its influence. Although there is a growing body of literature documenting the development of SEA in different contexts around the world, much of the ensuing discussion is normative in nature, suggesting how SEA should be carried out rather than evaluating its actual performance.[63]

In the UK, however, there has been a relatively long history of a simplified form of SEA, the environmental/sustainability appraisal of land-use plans. Appraisal has been studied since soon after its inception in the early 1990s and some checking of its effectiveness has been undertaken. In a large-scale survey of local authority appraisals, Therivel found that the appraisal led to changes in plan content in a small majority (55 per cent) of cases.[64] Similarly, Therivel and Minas compared plans before and after appraisal was carried out and found some environmental/sustainability appraisal related changes in many cases.[65] So there is some evidence that 'direct benefits'[66] are resulting even from this rudimentary form of SEA. However, these studies do not indicate the relative extent or importance of changes to plans resulting from appraisal. In another study, when planning officers were asked about the influence of appraisals on their plans,

---

62 Benson, 'What's The Alternative?', n. 24 above.
63 Partidario and Clark, *Perspectives*, n. 49 above; M Schmidt, E Joao, and E Albrecht (eds) (2005) *Implementing Strategic Environmental Assessment* (Berlin: Springer, 2005).
64 R Therivel, 'Strategic Environmental Assessment of Development Plans in Great Britain' (1998) 18 *Environmental Impact Assessment Review* 39.
65 R Therivel and P Minas, 'Ensuring Effective Sustainability Appraisal' (2002) 20 *Impact Assessment and Project Appraisal* 81.
66 Thissen, 'Criteria for Evaluation', n. 49 above.

87 per cent responded that appraisal had brought benefits but approximately two-thirds stated that it had had little or no influence on plan objectives and policies, and believed that their plan would have developed in the same manner without any appraisal having been undertaken.[67] Benson and Jordan confirmed that sustainability appraisal had little effect on plans, explaining this as being due to a lack of integration into the plan preparation process.[68]

Other work has also suggested that SEA is making only a limited difference to strategic actions. For instance, Fischer, in a study of the SEA of transport-related plans in three north European regions, painted a mixed picture of its strengths and weaknesses and found no consistent achievement of the intended benefits of SEA.[69] Recently documented practice from around the world suggests some 'success stories'.[70] For instance in the Czech Republic, where SEA legislation has been in place since 1992, significant modifications or even rejection of plans and policies have sometimes resulted from SEA practice.[71] But there are also examples of SEA having limited influence, such as in New Zealand, where a form of SEA was enshrined in legislation in 1991 but has struggled to find acceptance in strategic planning practice.[72]

The decision-making criterion applied in the international evaluation of the SEA of land-use plans was: 'do SEAs have any discernible influence on the content of land-use plans or the treatment of environmental issues during decision-making?'[73] It can be seen from Table 2.2 that using this criterion SEA was thought to influence land-use planning decisions beneficially in some of the countries studied. Thus, SEA was considered to have a discernible influence during the decision-making process in Denmark, Hong Kong, and Germany. In New Zealand, the UK, and the US, SEA was adjudged to have a partial influence on the outcome of land-use planning decisions, whilst in two cases the criterion was not believed to be met. In nearly half the countries the influence of SEA on decision-making was unknown because the SEA systems were not sufficiently advanced.

However, if EA's record of demonstrably changing the decisions made about projects and strategic actions is not strong, it is possible that influence is being

---

67 M Short, C Jones, J Carter, M Baker, and C Wood, 'Current Practice in the Strategic Environmental Assessment of Development Plans in England' (2004) 38 *Regional Studies* 177.

68 D Benson and A Jordan, 'Sustainability Appraisal in Local Land Use Planning: Patterns of Current Performance' (2004) 47 *Journal of Environmental Planning and Management* 269.

69 T Fischer, 'Benefits Arising From SEA Application: A Comparative Review of North West England, Noord-Holland, and Brandenburg-Berlin' (1999) 19 *Environmental Impact Assessment Review* 143.

70 Schmidt, *Implementing Strategic*, n. 63 above; Dalal-Clayton and Sadler, *A Sourcebook*, n. 20 above.

71 L Vaclavikova and H Jendrike, 'National Strategy for the Implementation of SEA in the Czech Republic' in Schmidt, ibid.

72 A Memon, 'SEA of Plan Objectives and Policies to Promote Sustainability in New Zealand' in Schmidt, ibid.

73 Jones *et al*, *Strategic Environmental Assessment*, n. 51 above.

exerted on decision-making in more subtle and possibly long-term ways. For instance, an international survey of EA practitioners in the mid-1990s suggested that quite apart from its immediate influence on proposals, EA conferred other benefits such as increasing environmental awareness and learning amongst participants.[74] This should contribute to greater consideration of environmental concerns in the future, both by proponents whose plans may become more environmentally acceptable from the outset, and by decision makers who may come to demand higher standards of environmental protection. It was also anticipated that wider public and stakeholder understanding of the environmental issues associated with development and strategic planning would result from the consultation and public participation carried out as part of EA. The actual extent to which EA is achieving these 'indirect outcomes' is difficult to ascertain,[75] but a number of studies suggest that gains of this kind have been made.[76] Moreover, this knock-on effect of environmental learning should assist the fundamental purposes of EA, improving environmental quality and contributing to the achievement of SD.

EA and decision-making models

In parallel with the increased focus on the influence of EA on decisions, the nature of EA is being examined more fundamentally and its place within the decision-making process is being considered more conceptually. EA was developed at a time when rationalist thinking prevailed in decision-making circles.[77] According to this paradigm, decision makers would give objective consideration to an issue, taking into account all possible alternatives, each of which would be assessed on the basis of the technical information available, and would come to a decision that was in the best interests of society as a whole. The 'environmental information' provided by EA fits this rational planning model perfectly. The rational model of decision-making has, however, been largely discredited not least because of its claim to value free objectivity.[78] Within the realm of development planning, as in others, decisions involve a wide range of pressures, not least social and political. Other theories of how decisions are reached in reality, and even of how they should be reached, have long since taken centre stage.[79]

---

74 Sadler, *Environmental Assessment in a Changing World*, n. 2 above.
75 Thissen, 'Criteria for Evaluation', n. 49 above.
76 C Jones, C Wood, and B Dipper, 'Environmental Assessment in the UK Planning Process' (1998) 69 *Town Planning Review* 315; Therivel, 'Strategic Environmental Assessment Of Development Plans', n. 64 above; Short, 'Current Practice', n. 67 above.
77 J Weston, 'EIA, Decision-making Theory and Screening and Scoping in UK Practice' (2000) 43 *Journal of Environmental Planning and Management* 185.
78 J Dryzek, *Discursive Democracy: Politics, Policy, and Political Science* (Cambridge: Cambridge University Press, 1990).
79 M Hill, *Studying the Policy Process* (Harlow: Prentice Hall, 1997).

If EIA remains wedded to rationalism, it is perhaps unsurprising that its record in influencing decisions is poor. However, EIA does not completely fail to engage with other understandings of decision-making. As both Bartlett and Kurian, and Lawrence, have demonstrated, various aspects of EIA can be shown to relate to different models of how planning decisions are made.[80] For instance, from an institutionalist perspective, EIA could be seen as a means of bringing about change in the values, rules, and priorities that govern the institutions responsible for planning decisions. Rather than being a key factor in individual planning decisions, EIA may be having a gradual transformative effect on decision-making authorities through their experience of dealing with applications for EIA development, from which environmental learning ensues. Whether intended or not, EA is not just operating within the confines of its narrow rationalist beginnings but has a more complex role within decision-making processes, in which environmental perspectives are being brought to bear in a variety of ways. Moreover, it is itself subject to some of the dynamics currently being observed within land-use planning, such as more 'communicative' approaches, by which emphasis is placed upon participation and consensus building, rather than expert-led technical solutions.[81]

Interest in understanding the relationship between EA and decision-making has been particularly strong in relation to SEA. This arises partly from the manner in which strategic actions are drawn up and 'decided upon', which is quite different to that of projects subject to EIA. In the case of projects, a proponent generally presents well-defined proposals for approval by a separate decision-making authority. EIA plays an important role at this point as a result of the environmental information it provides, the crucial decision-making question being 'how much weight will be given to this information?' In contrast, strategic actions tend to gain approval gradually as they take shape, often being prepared by the decision-making authority itself. Final approval is likely to be the culmination of an incremental process of plan or policy-making. Even at this point, there will not usually be the option of totally rejecting a strategic proposal, only that of further revision. For SEA to have any meaningful role in this evolution of strategic actions it must engage closely with the entire process. Hence, the constant refrain from commentators that SEA should begin early during plan or policy-making, and should be fully integrated into the process that is being assessed.[82] This has meant that SEA methodologies are being

80 R V Bartlett and P A Kurian, 'The Theory of Environmental Impact Assessment: Implicit Models of Policy-Making' (1999) 27 *Policy and Politics* 415; and see D Lawrence, 'Planning Theories and Environmental Impact Assessment' (2000) 20 *Environmental Impact Assessment Review* 607.

81 T Richardson, 'Environmental Assessment and Planning Theory: Four Short Stories About Power, Multiple Rationality, and Ethics' (2005) 25 *Environmental Impact Assessment Review* 341.

82 T Fischer, 'Practice of Environmental Assessment for Transport and Land-use Policies, Plans and Programmes' (2001) 19 *Impact Assessment and Project Appraisal* 41; R Therivel, *Strategic Environmental Assessment in Action* (London: Earthscan, 2004).

developed with the detailed elements of the strategic planning process, including decision-making, in mind. It has also led to a rethinking about how EIA works.[83]

In addition, strategic actions are extremely diverse in their form and context, ranging from local, sector-specific programmes to wide-ranging, national, and even international, strategies. This diversity adds to the difficulty of establishing common approaches to SEA, and provides further incentives for the development of SEA processes that are closely adapted to the strategic proposals being assessed.[84] It also forces attention on to the process of plan or policy-making itself and raises questions about how best to influence final outcomes. For example, Caratti recommended that the starting point for SEA should be to analyse the decision-making process itself and that SEA activity should be directed towards any 'decision windows' where there is the greatest opportunity for bringing environmental considerations into play.[85]

It is clear that a considerable shift is taking place within EA thinking, specifically in relation to SEA, and that a greater alertness and responsiveness to the realities of strategic planning is developing. Partidario sets this flexible and decision oriented approach against the 'technocratic characteristics of project EIA.[86] This growing concern to understand the processes that SEA is seeking to influence is starting to translate into more theoretical debate about the place of SEA within decision-making.[87] However, much of this discussion is still aspirational, the hope being that making SEA more context specific will enhance its effectiveness.[88] It is perhaps too soon to assess whether or not this more adaptive approach is paying dividends in terms of shaping strategic outcomes.

Increasing the effectiveness of EA

The limited influence that EA is perceived to be having on decisions that affect the environment has inevitably stimulated discussion about the best means of

---

83 S Owens, T Rayner, and O Bina, 'New Agendas for Appraisal: Reflections on Theory, Practice, and Research' (2004) 36 *Environment and Planning A*, 1943.

84 M Partidario, 'Strategic Environmental Assessment: Principles and Potential' in Petts, *Handbook*, n. 21 above; M Partidario, 'Elements of an SEA Framework: Improving the Added-Value of SEA' (2000) 20 *Environmental Impact Assessment Review* 647; T Nitz and A Brown, 'SEA Must Learn How Policy-Making Works' (2001) 3 *Journal of Environmental Assessment Policy and Management* 329.

85 P Caratti, H Dalkmann, and R Jiliberto (eds) *Analysing Strategic Environmental Assessment: Towards Better Decision-Making* (Cheltenham: Edward Elgar, 2004).

86 Partidario, 'Strategic Environmental Assessment', n. 84 above, 72.

87 L Kørnøv and W Thissen, 'Rationality in Decision and Policy Making: Implications For Strategic Environmental Assessment' (2000) 18 *Impact Assessment and Project Appraisal* 191; M Nilsson and H Dalkmann, 'Decision-Making and Strategic Environmental Assessment' (2001) 3 *Journal of Environmental Assessment Policy and Management* 305.

88 R Verheem and J Tonk, 'Strategic Environmental Assessment: One Concept, Multiple Forms' (2000) 18 *Impact Assessment and Project Appraisal* 177.

enhancing its effectiveness. Traditionally, the emphasis has been on doing this by diffusing and strengthening EA processes such as capacity building, guidance, and training. However, more recently there has been a focus on the more fundamental issues surrounding the purpose of EA. This suggests that effectiveness could be improved by linking it to a 'statutory purpose', fundamental goals and/or clear environmental standards.

Diffusing and strengthening EA processes

Institutional and professional EA capacity increases have taken place in both developing and developed countries as part of the continuing diffusion and strengthening of EA for many years.[89] These developments in EA capacity have been supported and 'locked in' by research, guidance, and training activities. In the developing world, EA has often been introduced as a condition of development assistance programmes into countries that lack the broad framework of environmental and social protection present in the developed world and where institutional capacity is often limited.[90] In this context EIA often has a significant role in environmental protection, hence the World Bank's 'environmental and social impact assessment' policy, and there may be particular political, cultural, and resource constraints that apply when the increases in EA capacity are being considered.[91]

Strengthening SEA is occurring as a result of burgeoning activity, not least because of the need to implement the SEA Directive.[92] EIA can provide an impetus to the development and strengthening of SEA by contributing methods and approaches, but also by indicating key areas where SEA can deliver particular value, for example, in addressing cumulative impacts. SEA has benefited from some aspects of the experience of EIA over many years but now faces many unique challenges of its own, including the implementation of the various measures necessary to assimilate it successfully within sustainability assessment.[93]

The traditional approach to increasing EA effectiveness and efficiency has included demands that EA be applied more rigorously on the assumption that if it is given greater legislative weight and conducted more thoroughly it would fulfil its aims more successfully. For instance, Glasson suggested a number of areas where EIA could be improved, including the mandatory consideration of alternatives and better prediction of cumulative impacts.[94] Lee and George found

---

89 See Figure 2.1.
90 Lee and George, *Environmental Assessment*, n. 11 above; Dalal-Clayton and Sadler, *A Sourcebook*, n. 20 above.
91 H Abaza, 'Strengthening Future EA Practice: An International Perspective' in Lee and George, ibid.
92 Jones, *Strategic Environmental Assessment*, n. 51 above.
93 Lee, 'Bridging the Gap', n. 36 above.
94 J Glasson, R Therivel and A Chadwick, *Introduction to Environmental Impact Assessment* (London: UCL Press, 2005).

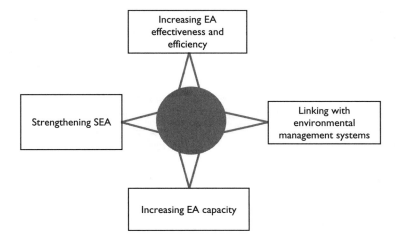

Figure 2.1 Trends in environmental assessment.

Source: C M Wood, *Environmental Impact Assessment: A Comparative Review*, 2nd edn (Harlow: Prentice Hall, 2003), 369.

similar procedural weaknesses in EIA in developing countries.[95] The limited degree of leverage being exerted by EA has also provoked concerns for better 'follow-up' of actions after they have been approved, to ensure that they remain within acceptable environmental limits.[96]

There have been ongoing incremental improvements in technical impact assessment methodology and legal procedures for EIA. Local context is very important in determining how improvements in EA effectiveness can be achieved.[97] For instance, for historical reasons the legal and institutional frameworks in the transitional countries of central and eastern Europe have their own specific characteristics that cannot be ignored if any attempt to achieve improved effectiveness, however well resourced, is to have the desired effect.[98]

The existence of published guidance on EA systems is clearly useful to those responsible for preparing EA reports, to those making decisions, to those consulted, and to the public. General guidance of this type can be accompanied by the provision of more detailed guidance on the different stages of the EA process.[99] The provision of EA training for EA project managers, for technical

95 Lee and George, *Environmental Assessment*, n. 11 above.
96 Morrison-Saunders and Arts, *Assessing Impact*, n. 23 above.
97 Lee, 'Bridging the Gap', n. 36 above.
98 J Dusik and B Sadler, 'Reforming Strategic Environmental Assessment Systems: Lessons From Central and Eastern Europe' (2004) 22 *Impact Assessment and Project Appraisal* 89.
99 Wood, *Environmental Impact Assessment*, n. 1 above.

specialists and for others involved in the EA process, is an effective method of increasing the standard of practice even in mature EA systems. A variety of different training methods is appropriate in most EA systems.[100]

There is a continuing need for research on various aspects of EIA and SEA, both general and specific. EA research has largely been process and procedure led and only fairly recently has a substantive body of literature begun to develop focussing on its theoretical aspects. While research on forecasting and other methodological aspects of EA is necessary, it is research on the integration of EA into decision-making, including the assimilation of EA into sustainability assessment, that is the most crucial. Owens recommended that well-designed longitudinal work, incorporating research on EA as it happens, be undertaken.[101] It has also been argued that the research agenda needs to broaden further to encompass an examination of the causal relationships between EA and particular outcomes, particularly in terms of decision-making, despite the conceptual difficulties involved.[102]

Influencing ongoing project management through links with environmental management systems following project authorisation is also occurring and has scope for development. These developments include better translation of commitments made in EISs into conditions applied to development consents and subsequently improving their integration into environmental management systems.

New approaches to EA and decision-making

The emphasis in all these suggestions for making EA more effective is still on adapting, improving and extending the procedures for assessment. The essential orthodoxy of the EA process is not questioned and there is relatively little consideration given to the fundamental character of EA and whether it has the ability to bring real influence to bear on decision-making. Attention therefore needs to turn to the policy framework in which EA is being implemented. If the political decisions that EA is intended to inform are the crucial factor in environmental protection,[103] then EA systems need to be developed to ensure that they are given appropriate weight by decision makers. In other words, recommendations for improving the effectiveness of EA need to reflect the studies of the role of EA in decision-making summarized above.

One of the great strengths of EA, and particularly of EIA, is that it enjoys widespread statutory status and acceptance and it should be possible to build upon this strength by progressively incorporating improvements. There are several

---

100 Wood, *Environmental Impact Assessment*, n. 1 above.
101 Owens, 'New Agendas for Appraisal', n. 83 above.
102 Cashmore, 'The Interminable Issue of Effectiveness', n. 2 above.
103 Wood, *Environmental Impact Assessment*, n. 1 above.

avenues through which EA might be given a more central and determinative place in decisions with environmentally significant implications:

- Assessment for environmentally sustainable development;
- No net environmental deterioration in assessment decisions; and
- Precautionary principle in assessment decisions.

Assessment for environmentally sustainable development

The connection of EA to the increasingly accepted concept of SD provides an opportunity to increase the influence of EA in decision-making, especially now that 'living within environmental limits' has been elevated to one of the twin goals of SD in the UK.[104] SD strategies already make explicit reference to the importance of EA and open the way to the fuller integration of EA into decision-making processes through both regulatory instruments and institutional practice. Enhancing the emphasis given to environmental resources and capacities in EIA to enable the effects of individual projects or PPPs on cumulative impacts, climate change, and biodiversity losses to be estimated and tracked would be one way forward.[105] Another would be increasing the weight given to EA to enable it to play its full role in balanced development decision-making. Both would support progress towards a new policy framework for environmentally sustainable development, which would set limits for development according to the resilience or regenerative ability of an environment expected to be affected by proposed development.[106]

To implement environmentally SD would require the incorporation of principles, criteria, thresholds, and limits concerning aspects of SD into EA practice. This would necessitate the inclusion of a 'statutory principle' which might include 'ensuring that the quality of the environment is safeguarded and wherever appropriate enhanced' within the legislative framework for EA.[107] This would give EA greater substantive content, building on the environmental idealism which has always been implicit.[108]

No net environmental deterioration from assessment decisions

Adopting a principle of no net environmental deterioration from assessment related decisions would take EA beyond its traditional role of identifying and mitigating significant impacts, towards being the vehicle for proposing environmental enhancement(s) to offset any negative impacts remaining after mitigation.

---

104 HM Government *et al*, n. 45 above, 16.
105 Wood, *Environmental Impact Assessment*, n. 1 above.
106 Sadler, *Environmental Assessment in a Changing World*, n. 2 above.
107 RCEP, *Environmental Planning*, n. 42 above, 108.
108 Lawrence, 'Planning Theories', n. 80 above.

In 1976, the German Impact Mitigation Regulation introduced this principle by formalising the concept of 'compensation pools',[109] consisting of approved locations where developers could conduct approved environmental enhancement to compensate for negative impacts elsewhere.[110] The idea has gained currency over the years and has been introduced into the German Building Code and the Nature Conservation Act. The use of air pollution emission offsets has been required in non-attainment areas in the United States for many years.[111] Similar approaches, including measures to achieve net environmental gain, have begun to appear in other countries such as the Netherlands and Sweden and have been suggested in the UK.[112] For example, EA could result in the use of planning obligations which 'might be used, when appropriate, to offset through substitution, replacement or regeneration the loss of, or damage to, a feature or resource present or nearby, for example, a landscape feature of biodiversity value, open space or right of way'.[113]

Precautionary principle in assessment decisions

Similarly, the widely accepted notion of the precautionary principle could be incorporated into assessment decisions. This would have the effect of forcing decision makers to take a much more sceptical line on development proposals in the absence of convincing environmental analysis. The precautionary principle is gaining currency in environmental protection and is included as part of the EC Integrated Pollution Prevention and Control (IPPC) Directive.[114] One of the main recommendations of the RCEP is that the IPPC licensing procedure and the precautionary principle should be integrated with EIA and the land-use planning regime, with the use of a single procedure for the implementation of European EIA and IPPC requirements leading to a common environmental statement.[115]

Conclusions

The last 35 years have shown huge advances in EIA. EIA systems in many developed countries have been strengthened and much is being achieved in improving EIA capacity in developing countries.[116] As EIA has developed there

---

109 Also known as 'mitigation banks'.
110 W Wende, A Herberg, and A Herzberg, 'An Innovative Approach to Procedures' (2005) 23 *Impact Assessment and Project Appraisal* 101.
111 C M Wood, *Planning Pollution Prevention: A Comparative Study of Siting Controls Over Air Pollution Sources in the UK and the USA* (Oxford: Heinemann Newnes, 1989).
112 Countryside Agency, English Heritage, English Nature and Environment Agency (2005) *Environmental Quality in Spatial Planning* (Cheltenham: Countryside Agency, 2005), 9.
113 Office of the Deputy Prime Minister, *Planning Obligations*, Circular 05/2005 (2005), para. B16.
114 Directive 96/61/EC concerning integrated pollution prevention and control.
115 RCEP, *Environmental Planning*, n. 42 above, 92.
116 Lee and George, *Environmental Assessment*, n. 11 above.

has been an increasing emphasis on its relationship with the broader decision-making and environmental management context and recognition of its subjective and political nature.

There is no doubt that, in the more mature EIA systems, the way decisions are made has changed because the behaviour of proponents, consultants, consultees, the public, and the decision-making authorities has been modified. EIA has made a contribution to the achievement of SD through design changes, through corporate, institutional, and scientific changes, and through stakeholder empowerment.[117] The quality of decisions involving EIA has improved as a result of the increased use of modification or mitigation, the use of more stringent conditions upon permissions and the non-implementation of some potentially environmentally damaging proposals which might previously have been approved. However, overall EIA's contribution to the achievement of SD has fallen short of its full potential. EIA is an invaluable tool but it needs to be developed further to place it more firmly in the context of other policy and environmental instruments to provide more adaptive environmental management.[118]

The strengthening of SEA to make it more effective is gathering pace but requires further effort. It appears that while the potential of SEA to reduce the negative and enhance the positive environmental impacts associated with PPP implementation remains, many of the opportunities presented by SEA have not yet been achieved. Perhaps the most obvious future development in SEA is the clarification and strengthening of its institutional and legal basis. Hopefully, the inevitable improvements to SEA practice in the future will be accompanied by the realization of many of these opportunities.[119]

Certain general shortcomings in the current state of EIA practice can be observed, of which weakness in integrating EIA into decision-making is the most significant. A number of specific measures can be used to strengthen different EIA systems by introducing or bolstering appropriate procedural requirements. Additional initiatives are needed in relation to guidance, training, and research. Linkages with environmental management systems and capacity building for EIA are also essential.

However, the crucial factor in environmental protection remains the political decision that EA informs.[120] The influence of EA on decision-making is by far its most important characteristic. It is necessary not only to improve EA procedures but also to ensure that they receive the public and political endorsement necessary for them more fully to deliver their aims. EA was introduced as part of an environmental awakening responding to widespread popular concern about the

---

117 Cashmore, 'The Interminable Issue of Effectiveness', n. 2 above; Christensen, 'EIA As Regulation', n. 61 above.
118 Sadler, *Environmental Assessment in a Changing World*, n. 2 above; Wood, *Environmental Impact Assessment*, n. 1 above.
119 Jones, *Strategic Environmental Assessment*, n. 51 above.
120 Bartlett and Kurian, 'The Theory of Environmental Impact Assessment', n. 80 above.

despoliation of the natural environment. As Caldwell has complained, in the US '[t]he courts have treated [NEPA] as essentially procedural – enforcing its means (the impact statement) but generally declining to consider its ends'.[121] In the US, as elsewhere, the unfulfilled nature of EA probably accurately reflects public and political ambivalence to adopting the means to make it more effective.

There remains widespread concern that despite the establishment and refinement of EA systems, the achievement of SD goals remains elusive. While the linkage between EA and SD is widely accepted, principles, criteria, thresholds and limits concerning aspects of SD have not been incorporated into EA practice sufficiently. This has resulted in continuing incremental environmental deterioration.

It is probably time to reconsider the nature of Caldwell's 'unequivocal mandatory requirement' and give EA a statutory purpose.[122] Much could be achieved by increasing the weight given to environmental resources and capacities in existing EA systems. The same end could be achieved by ensuring that EA was linked to clear 'environmentally sustainable development' objectives. The effectiveness of EA would be bolstered if it incorporated a clearly articulated 'no net environmental deterioration' principle and, if this could not be met, if it required the application of the precautionary principle in decision-making.

Overall, the conclusion must be that EIA is now a mature adult, if less dominant than its originators hoped. While SEA is developing, it is still an immature younger sibling competing for dominance with other environmental management tools. Neither process is dormant. However, there is no doubt that, if the public and politicians truly will the ends, EA can provide truly effective means of beneficially amending decisions to achieve more sustainable development. It must be hoped that the awakening that is needed to realise the undoubted potential of EA will occur without having to be triggered by untold environmental harm.

121 Caldwell and Shrader-Frechette, *Policy for Land*, n. 3 above, 257.
122 Caldwell, *The National Environmental Policy Act*, n. 4 above.

Chapter 3

NEPA and the curious evolution of environmental impact assessment in the United States

Bradley C Karkkainen[1]

The first major statutory enactment of America's 'environmental decade' of the 1970s, the National Environmental Policy Act (NEPA)[2] launched the most widely emulated environmental policy innovation of the twentieth century: environmental impact assessment (EIA).[3] From inauspicious beginnings as an obscure procedural device appended as afterthought to a broader environmental policy statute, EIA has grown to become a ubiquitous tool of environmental policy at the international, national, and sub-national levels.[4]

NEPA's global impact was largely a fortuitous accident, for initially the statute was not intended as an EIA measure at all. Its central purpose, as its name implies, was to establish a comprehensive national environmental policy, articulating broad substantive goals that federal agencies would be expected to integrate into all their programs, policies, and operations.[5] NEPA proclaims national goals to 'encourage productive and enjoyable harmony between man and his environment, to promote efforts which will prevent or eliminate damage to the

1 The author thanks Dan Farber and Alex Klass for helpful comments on earlier drafts, and Mary Mullen for invaluable research assistance.
2 See also National Environmental Policy Act of 1969, Pub. L. 91–190, as amended, (1 January 1970), codified at 42 U.S.C. ss 4321–4347.
3 See L K Caldwell, *The National Environmental Policy Act: An Agenda for the Future* (Bloomington: Indiana University Press, 1998), stating that due to widespread adoption of EIA requirements, NEPA is 'probably the most imitated US law in history' (internal citation omitted).
4 Ibid, 71, noting that EIA has been embraced in the Espoo Convention on transboundary environmental impact assessment, Agenda 21, EU directives to member states, and elsewhere; and ibid, 164, stating that twenty-two US states have their own 'little NEPA' EIA statutes; Council on Environmental Quality, *The National Environmental Policy Act: A Study of Its Effectiveness After Twenty-Five Years* (Washington DC: Council on Environmental Quality, 1997), 3, stating that EIA requirements have been adopted by at least 80 countries and such global institutions as the World Bank.
5 See L K Caldwell, 'Implementing NEPA: A Non-Technical Political Task' (hereafter 'Implementing NEPA'), in R Clark and L W Canter (eds), *Environmental Policy and NEPA: Past, Present, and Future* (hereafter '*Environmental Policy*') (Boca Raton: Fla., St. Lucie Press, 1997), 25, 35–37, stating that NEPA's framers conceived it as establishing a broad national environmental policy applicable to all federal agencies.

environment and biosphere and stimulate the health and welfare of man; [and] to enrich the understanding of the ecological systems and natural resources important to the Nation'.[6] To achieve these lofty ambitions, the statute announces 'the continuing policy of the Federal Government' that federal agencies should 'use all practicable means, consistent with other essential considerations of national policy, to improve and coordinate Federal plans, functions, programs, and resources' to achieve such key environmental objectives as intergenerational trusteeship, provision safe and healthful surroundings, beneficial use of the environment, preservation of cultural and natural heritage, and protection of renewable resources.[7]

Early drafts of NEPA made no mention of environmental impact assessment.[8] That requirement was added relatively late in the legislative process, after political scientist Lynton K Caldwell, a longtime champion of a national declaration of environmental policy[9] and advisor to the bill's chief Senate sponsor, Senator Henry M 'Scoop' Jackson,[10] urged inclusion of an 'action-forcing' procedural mechanism to bring NEPA's substantive goals to the attention of agency officials at key points in their decision-making processes.[11] Senator Jackson thereupon inserted language during committee mark-up of the bill requiring that prior to undertaking any action 'significantly affecting the quality of the human environment', the 'responsible official' must produce a 'detailed statement' on the environmental consequences of, and alternatives to, the

6 NEPA s 2, 42 U.S.C. s 4321.
7 NEPA s 101, 42 U.S.C. s 4331(a)–(b). The six key policy objectives are: (1) to fulfill the responsibilities of intergenerational trusteeship; (2) to assure 'safe, healthful, productive, and esthetically and culturally pleasing surroundings'; (3) to 'enjoy the widest range of beneficial uses of the environment without degradation, risk to health or safety, or other undesirable or unintended consequences'; (4) to preserve 'historic, cultural, and natural aspects of our national heritage' and maintain an 'environment which supports diversity and a variety of environmental choice'; (5) 'achieve a balance between population and resource use' affording 'high standards of living and a wide sharing of life's amenities'; and (6) 'enhance the quality of renewable resources and approach the maximum attainable recycling of depletable resources'. ibid, s 4331(b).
8 See Caldwell, n. 3 above, 64: 'The impact statement requirement did not appear in the early versions of the legislation because the primary concern at that time was to formulate a national environmental policy and a council . . . to oversee its implementation'.
9 See L K Caldwell, 'Environment – A New Focus for Public Policy', (1963) 23 *Public Administration Review* 1329.
10 Democrat, Washington.
11 See Caldwell, n. 3 above, 49, stating that the EIS provision was intended to 'bring agency policy into conformity' with NEPA's substantive provisions by 'forc[ing] the Federal agencies to consider the environmental consequences' of proposed actions; Caldwell, n. 4 above, 40–41, stating the 'action-forcing' EIS requirement was added at a Senate committee hearing when committee staff argued that 'without a justiciable provision the act might be no more than a pious resolve that the federal bureaucracy could ignore with impunity'; D Bear, 'The National Environmental Policy Act: Its Origins and Evolution' (hereafter 'NEPA: Origins') (1995) 10 *Journal of Natural Resources & the Environment* 3, attributing the recommendation for an 'action–forcing' device to Caldwell.

proposed action.[12] Jackson's seemingly modest little 'action-forcing' amendment would transform NEPA into the world's first EIA statute, but it drew little notice at the time, provoking neither debate, nor opposition, nor affirmative endorsement.[13] Congress passed NEPA as thus amended, and President Richard Nixon signed the measure into law on New Year's Day, 1 January 1970, accompanied by a statement proclaiming the 1970s the 'decade of the environment'.[14]

In the months and years that followed, it would be NEPA's broadly framed substantive provisions, the statute's original *raison d'etre*, that would fall by the wayside. Courts deemed these requirements too vague and indefinite to provide a judicially enforceable standard,[15] and the political branches, Congress and the White House, declined to intervene when agencies went about their business as usual, largely ignoring the substantive policy goals set out in the Act.[16]

Procedural requirements were another matter, however. NEPA section 102(2)(C), the 'action-forcing' Environmental Impact Statement provision, was framed in specific and unmistakably mandatory language. It stated that:

> *all* agencies of the Federal Government *shall*...include in *every* recommendation or report on proposals for legislation and other major Federal actions significantly affecting the quality of the human environment, a *detailed statement* by the responsible official on...the environmental impact...[and] alternatives to the proposed action...[17]

---

12 NEPA s 102(2)(c), 42 U.S.C. s 4332(2)(c).

13 Caldwell, n. 3 above, 64: 'In retrospect, it appears curious that the EIS provision occasioned no debate and almost no external opposition or endorsement'.

14 Ibid, 17.

15 See *Calvert Cliffs Coordinating Comm. v Atomic Energy Commission*, 449 F.2d 1109, 1112 (D.C. Cir. 1971): 'the general substantive policy of the Act is a flexible one [that] may not require particular substantive results in particular problematic circumstances'; ibid, 1115: 'reviewing courts probably cannot reverse a substantive decision on its merits'; *Vermont Yankee Nuclear Power Corporation v Natural Resources Defense Council*, 435 U.S. 519, 558 (1978): 'NEPA does set forth significant substantive goals for the Nation, but its mandate to agencies is essentially procedural'; *Strycker's Bay Neighborhood Council v Karlen*, 444 U.S. 223, 227–28 (1980): 'once an agency has made a decision subject to NEPA's procedural requirements, the only role for a court is to insure that the agency has considered the environmental consequences; it cannot interject itself within the area of discretion of the executive as to the choice of action to be taken' (internal quotation and citations omitted); *Robertson v Methow Valley Citizen's Council*, 490 U.S. 332, 350 (1989): 'NEPA itself does not mandate particular results, but simply prescribes the necessary process'.

16 See Caldwell, n. 3 above, 26, stating that full implementation of NEPA's substantive policies 'requires a degree of political will that has not yet been evident in either Congress or the White House'; ibid, 89, stating that the 'general indifference of Congress' and 'inattention of successive presidents' have allowed agencies to ignore NEPA's substantive policies.

17 NEPA s 102(2)(C), 42 U.S.C. s 4332(2)(C) (emphasis added).

Mandatory procedures were something courts could and would enforce, especially under the command of unambiguous statutory terms like 'all', 'shall', 'every', and 'detailed statement'.[18] The threat of judicial enforcement, in turn, prompted agencies to be attentive to procedural detail, lest important agency actions be held up by litigation and injunction.[19] Procedure soon overtook substance, transforming NEPA into what has become, in practice, almost purely a procedural statute.[20] It was this NEPA-as-it-devolved, rather than NEPA as originally envisioned, that would inspire EIA procedures worldwide.

Antecedents: *Silent Spring*, Storm King, Santa Barbara, and Sax

The 1960s were a time of turmoil in American society and politics, the decade of the Civil Rights movement, urban riots, Vietnam War protests, campus radicalism, flower children, the rebirth of modern feminism, and the assassinations of John and Robert Kennedy, Martin Luther King, and Malcolm X. The 1960s were also the decade that ushered in modern environmentalism. American environmentalists like to claim as intellectual forebears the early nineteenth century transcendentalist writer Henry David Thoreau, the late nineteenth century preservationist John Muir, the progressive era conservationists Gifford Pinchot and Teddy Roosevelt, and the game biologist-turned-ecologist Aldo Leopold.[21] But the seminal events that molded the modern environmental sensibility occurred against the rough-and-tumble tableau of the 1960s.

The early years of that decade had already witnessed an uptick in pollution control regulation at the state and municipal levels,[22] together with increased federal funding for wastewater treatment[23] and heightened attention to conservation

---

18 See *Calvert Cliffs*, n. 15 above, 1115: 'Section 102 of NEPA mandates a particular sort of careful and informed decision-making process and creates judicially enforceable duties', and if agencies fail to observe these procedures 'it is the responsibility of the courts to reverse'.

19 See Caldwell, n. 3 above, 68, stating that the threat of judicial enforcement led agencies to focus their attention almost exclusively on NEPA's action-forcing procedural requirements.

20 See Bear, 'NEPA: Origins', n. 11 above, 5, stating that in practice NEPA's substantive policy provisions have been less important and its judicially enforced procedural requirements more important than the framers of the legislation anticipated.

21 See R B Smythe, 'The Historical Roots of NEPA' in R Clark and L W Canter, *Environmental Policy*, 3, 4–10, tracing the intellectual roots of American environmentalism to such figures as Thoreau and Emerson, Muir, Pinchot, and Leopold; R F Nash, *The Right of Nature: A History of Environmental Ethics* (Madsion, Wisconsin: University of Wisconsin Press, 1989), 34, stating that popular environmentalism developed in the US in the 1960s and 'Thoreau did not become an environmental hero until well into the twentieth century'.

22 See R N L Andrews, *Managing the Environment, Managing Ourselves: A History of American Environmental Policy* (Yale University Press, 1999), 207, 209, stating that 14 states had enacted air pollution control laws by 1963, prompting key industries to begin to demand moderate and uniform federal regulation.

23 See ibid, 205, stating that federal funding for municipal wastewater treatment grew from $50 million per year in 1960 to $3.5 billion over five years beginning in 1966.

of the nation's public lands.[24] Conservation causes in the American West, especially, had helped to revitalize nature preservation groups like the Sierra Club and the Wilderness Society.[25] But it was the publication of a book, Rachel Carson's *Silent Spring*,[26] a searing indictment of the indiscriminate use of toxic pesticides that galvanized public opinion and launched the mass environmental movement that eventually would win enactment of the major federal environmental laws of the 1970s.[27]

Trained as a marine biologist, Carson had worked mainly as a science writer and editor for the federal government's principal wildlife management agency, the Fish and Wildlife Service, before retiring from government service to write popular books and articles. *Silent Spring* reflects Carson's profoundly ecological perspective.[28] Humans are interdependent with nature, Carson wrote, and our actions, like the spraying of DDT and other pesticides, can have powerful, lasting, and unintended consequences for non-target species like birds and beneficial insects, and perhaps ultimately for ourselves as these poisons return to us through environmental exposures and food chains.[29] Carson emphasized that she did not oppose the use of pesticides, only their 'indiscriminate use' at a time when their environmental consequences were not fully understood.[30]

The publication of *Silent Spring* created an instant political demand for government action to address these very scary threats, helping to launch the modern environmental movement and eventually ushering in the enactment of NEPA, the Clean Air Act, the Clean Water Act, the Endangered Species Act, and a dozen other major federal environmental statutes, as politicians of both major parties competed to appeal to the new environmental constituency.[31] *Silent Spring*

24 See ibid, 194–96, stating that growing public opposition to intensive logging on public lands led to enactment of the Wilderness Act in 1964, providing for strict preservation of the most pristine areas; ibid, 222, stating that President Kennedy appointed a Western environmentalist, Stewart Udall, as his Secretary of Interior and convened a White House Council on Conservation in 1961, policies that continued into the Johnson Administration.

25 See Smythe, 'Historical Roots', n. 20 above, 9, stating that the Sierra Club and the Wilderness Society were reinvigorated by successful campaigns in the 1960s to defeat Western dam projects and to enact national wilderness protection legislation.

26 R Carson, *Silent Spring* (Boston: Houghton Mifflin, 1962).

27 R J Lazarus, *The Making of Environmental Law* (Chicago: University of Chicago Press, 2004), 58: 'the publication of *Silent Spring* was an epochal event in the history of environmentalism'.

28 See L Lear, *Rachel Carson: Witness for Nature* (New York: Owl Books, 1997), 429, stating that *Silent Spring*: 'forced a public debate over the heretofore academic idea that living things and their environment were interrelated'.

29 Carson, *Silent Spring*, n. 26 above, 5–6.

30 Ibid, 12: 'It is not my contention that chemical insecticides must never be used. I do contend that we have put poisonous and biologically potent chemicals indiscriminately into the hands of persons largely or wholly ignorant of their potential for harm.'; ibid, 13: 'I contend, furthermore, that we have allowed these chemicals to be used with little or no investigation of their effect on soil, water, wildlife, and man himself'.

31 Lazarus, n. 27 above, 53–54.

has been called 'the book that launched a movement' and 'one of the two most influential books in American history' alongside Harriet Beecher Stowe's *Uncle Tom's Cabin*.[32] These are very strong claims, but they are not hyperbole. Whatever one thinks of the work on its merits, and it has had plenty of detractors over the years,[33] there can be no doubt as to its influence.

Beyond its contribution to the formation of modern environmentalism, *Silent Spring* influenced the enactment of NEPA in more specific ways. Carson's most compelling theme was that we were introducing chemical pollutants wantonly, without taking the time to consider possible adverse side effects. Carson wrote '[t]he public must decide whether to continue on the present road, and it can do so only when in full possession of the facts. In the words of Jean Rostand, "The obligation to endure gives us the right to know".'[34]

Echoing Carson's clarion call for a public 'right to know', the Senate committee report on NEPA, the closest thing we have to an official explanation of congressional intent, states the rationale for the statute thusly: 'The survival of man, in a world in which decency and dignity are possible, is the basic reason for bringing man's impact on his environment under informed and responsible control.'[35]

This 'right to know' theme inspired NEPA's proponents to frame the measure not only as a technical aid to better-informed governmental decision-making, but also as a means to inform the public about the environmental impacts of proposed government actions, enhancing transparency, accountability, and public participation in governmental decision-making.[36] As former Interior Secretary

---

32 See e.g. F Moreno, *Rachel Carson and the Book that Launched a Movement*, New York Academy of Sciences Update (November/December 2005), naming *Silent Spring* 'one of the two most influential books in American history' alongside *Uncle Tom's Cabin*; A Gore, 'Introduction', in Carson, *Silent Spring*, xviii–xvix, stating the publication of *Silent Spring* 'can properly be seen as the beginning of the modern environmental movement' and stating the book's impact was comparable to that of *Uncle Tom's Cabin*. Stowe's *Uncle Tom's Cabin* stoked Northern abolitionist sentiments in the mid-nineteenth century and is widely seen as a proximate cause of the US Civil War.

33 See Lear, *Witness for Nature*, n. 28 above, 428–439, describing attacks on *Silent Spring* from reviewers, news organizations, food and pesticide industry groups, government agencies, and scientists; ibid, 451–452 stating that a report by the President's Science Advisory Committee largely vindicated Carson's principal claims.

34 Carson, *Silent Spring*, n. 26 above, 13.

35 Senate Committee on Interior and Insular Affairs, S. Rep. No. 196 to accompany S. 1075, at 4 (9 July 1969).

36 See M Herz, 'Parallel Universes: NEPA Lessons for the New Property' (1993) 93 *Columbia Law Review* 1668, 1708–1709, stating that NEPA's legislative history 'underlines the centrality of public participation' and that public disclosure of the EIS 'is a step toward openness, inclusion, and participation' by the public in environmental decisions; S A Shapiro, 'Administrative Law after the Counter-Reformation: Restoring Faith in Pragmatic Government' (2000) 48 *University of Kansas Law Review* 689, 696, stating that NEPA's public disclosure requirements 'made it easier for environmentalists and other public interest groups to monitor agencies, like the Department of Agriculture, that were perceived by them to be excessively friendly to corporate and business interests'. For example, Senator Jackson argued the 'basic principle' of NEPA is

Stewart Udall has written, 'it is undeniable that Rachel Carson's concepts inspired...the enactment of the National Environmental Policy Act'.[37]

A number of other dramatic events contributed to the cauldron in which NEPA's EIA requirements were brewed. One was the Federal Power Commission's decision to permit an electric utility to build a massive pump-storage hydroelectric plant atop Storm King Mountain in the scenic Hudson River Valley north of New York City. Environmentalists and local preservationists joined forces under the banner of the Scenic Hudson Preservation Conference in an effort to block the development on aesthetic and environmental grounds. Scenic Hudson's first major legal victory was a landmark 1965 Second Circuit Court of Appeals ruling that the Federal Power Commission was under an 'affirmative duty to inquire into and consider all relevant facts' to support the statutorily mandated finding that issuance of the permit was 'in the public interest'. Specifically, the court held that the agency was obligated to study a full range of alternatives to the proposed project in light of its aesthetic and environmental impacts, including effects on the spawning grounds of a commercially and recreationally valuable fish species, the striped bass.[38] The court's order in the *Scenic Hudson* case presaged, and served as the prototype for, NEPA's subsequent environmental impact assessment requirement.[39]

Another dramatic precipitating event was the 1969 Santa Barbara oil spill in which a blowout at an offshore oil rig spilled more than 70,000 barrels of crude oil into southern California's scenic Santa Barbara channel, harming wildlife and waterfowl and disrupting aesthetic and recreational uses along 30 miles of California coastline, with devastating consequences to the state's valuable tourism industry. The Santa Barbara oil spill fueled public demands that such potentially catastrophic environmental impacts be considered as part of the approval process for offshore oil and gas leasing, an approach that a few months later would win statutory codification in NEPA.[40]

that 'we must strive in all that we do, to achieve a standard of excellence in man's relationships to his physical surroundings', and that any departures from that standard 'will have to be justified in the light of public scrutiny as required by section 102'. See (1969) 115 *Congressional Record* 40, 416.

37 S L Udall, *The Quiet Crisis and the Next Generation* (Salt Lake City: Peregrine Smith Books, 1988), 202–203.

38 *Scenic Hudson Preservation Conference v Federal Power Commission*, 354 F.2d 608, 621 (2d Cir. 1965).

39 See N A Robinson, 'Enforcing Environmental Norms: Diplomatic and Judicial Approaches' (2003) 26 *Hastings International and Comparative Law Review* 387, 404, stating that 'the logic of "look before you leap" was sufficiently compelling that the Federal Power Act model, as interpreted by the courts, became a precedent for the EIA procedures...of NEPA'; O Houck, 'Unfinished Stories' (2002) 73 *University Colorado Law Review* 867, 878, stating that the original *Scenic Hudson* decision 'opened the way' for 'the principles of review of environmental impacts and alternatives that are at the heart of NEPA'.

40 K Harb, 'The Legal and Policy Dilemma of Offshore Oil and Gas Development' (2004) 19 *Natural Resources and Environment* 23, stating that the Santa Barbara spill led to a moratorium on offshore oil leasing in the Pacific and contributed to enactment of NEPA and the Coastal Zone Management Act.

Finally, any history of NEPA would not be complete without mention of the pioneering work of a leading legal academic, Joseph L. Sax, one of the 'founding fathers' of modern American environmental law. In a seminal 1970 article, Sax argued that a common law of environmental protection might be fashioned by updating and expanding the public trust doctrine, an ancient common law doctrine holding that the sovereign holds title to the submerged lands beneath tidal waters in trust for the benefit of the public generally, for use in navigation, commerce, and fishing.[41] This doctrine, Sax argued, both empowered the sovereign to manage certain common resources for the public's benefit, and yet constrained the exercise of sovereign authority over those resources by placing the sovereign itself under a quasi-fiduciary duty to the public.[42] In some circumstances, the public trust doctrine gave citizens a cause of action against private parties who interfered with the public's rights in trust resources, or against the sovereign itself for breach of its duties as trustee.

Now suppose, Sax argued, that the public trust doctrine were expanded along two dimensions: first, by expanding the public trust *corpus* to include other natural resources providing diffuse public benefits, such as wildlife, air quality, and water quality; and secondly, by extending judicially cognizable public trust *purposes* to include recreational, aesthetic, and ecological values.[43] Such an expanded public trust doctrine would place the sovereign under an obligation to manage these common pool resources for the benefit of the public, and grant members of the public a right of action to enjoin any private interference with or damage to such resources, or to compel the sovereign itself to manage the resources for the public's benefit.

Sax's article set off a flurry of subsequent scholarship and led eventually to partial adoption of his environmental public trust theory in a number of leading American jurisdictions, notably California.[44] Perhaps Sax's most important contribution, however, was to crystallize the idea of the environmental citizen suit. The idea that citizens should be entitled to sue to protect environmental quality

---

41 J L Sax, 'The Public Trust Doctrine in Natural Resources Law: Effective Judicial Intervention' (1970) 68 *Michigan Law Review* 471, 474: 'only the public trust doctrine seems to have the breadth and substantive content which might make it useful as a tool of general application for citizens seeking to develop a comprehensive legal approach to resource management problems'.

42 Ibid, 476–477, noting the public trust doctrine has a dual aspect, both authorizing the sovereign to act to protect public trust resources and restraining the sovereign's discretion with respect to those resources.

43 Ibid, 556–557, noting the 'historical scope of public trust law is quite narrow' but arguing that the same underlying logic of diffuse public interests in uniquely valuable resources in implicated 'controversies involving air pollution, the dissemination of pesticides, the location of rights of way for utilities, and strip mining or wetland filling on private lands'.

44 See e.g. *National Audubon Society v Superior Court of Alpine County* (Mono Lake), 658 P.2d 709 (CA 1983), holding that public trust extends to non-navigable freshwater tributaries of a navigable saltwater lake, and judicially cognizable public trust purposes include protection of aesthetic, recreational, and ecological values.

was not entirely new, of course.[45] The *Storm King* litigation stands out as a successful early example, predating Sax's public trust scholarship. In most other contexts, however, would-be environmental plaintiffs had been frustrated by the difficulty of finding statutory or common law causes of action that would allow them to maintain successful lawsuits to resolve environmental problems.[46] Of particular note, many of the new environmental organizations that emerged in the 1960s had tried to litigate to end the abuses of DDT and other pesticides that Rachel Carson had documented in *Silent Spring*,[47] but faced with ongoing scientific controversy, data gaps, inherently probabilistic causation models, and the difficulty of finding plaintiffs whose injuries were sufficiently concrete and clearly traceable to pesticide applications, their litigation strategy had largely ended in failure.

One of these new environmental groups, the West Michigan Environmental Action Council, enlisted Sax, then on the law faculty at the University of Michigan, to help them develop a new statutory cause of action for environmental harms.[48] Sax obliged by drafting the landmark Michigan Environmental Protection Act (MEPA),[49] which codified the expanded public trust principles he was then exploring in his academic writings. MEPA authorizes 'any citizen' to seek injunctive or declaratory relief against 'any person' for 'the protection of the air, water, and other natural resources and the public trust in these resources from pollution, impairment, or destruction'.[50] Impelled by the newly emergent environmental movement and aided by health-and-safety activists from the

45 See B H Thompson, Junior, 'The Continuing Innovation of Citizen Enforcement' (2000) *University of Illinois Law Review* 185, 195–196, tracing the idea of public enforcement of environmental laws to an English statute of 1388, noting that private lawsuits play a major role in enforcing federal securities, antitrust, and civil rights laws, and describing efforts in the 1960s to use *qui tam* actions to enforce the 1899 Refuse Act against polluters. Prominent administrative law scholars like Louis Jaffe and Kenneth Culp Davis had long advocated expanded 'public' rights of action in other legal contexts. See e.g. L L Jaffe, *Standing to Secure Judicial Review: Public Actions*, (1961) 74 *Harvard Law Review* 1265; K C Davis, 'Standing: Taxpayers and Others' (1968) 35 *University of Chicago Law Review* 601.

46 See Thompson, ibid, acknowledging that environmental litigation predicated upon *qui tam* actions ultimately proved unsuccessful; Sax, 'The Public Trust Doctrine', n. 40 above, 473–474, noting the diversity of legal theories advanced, usually unsuccessfully, by environmental plaintiffs in the 1960s; J L Sax, *Defending the Environment* (New York: Knopf, 1971), 125–148, documenting the 'uncertain state of development' of environmental litigation in the late 1960s in the absence of clear statutory causes of action.

47 One of America's most prominent environmental organizations, Environmental Defense, originally Environmental Defense Fund, was organized to press the legal battle against DDT and other pesticides. See C J Bosso, *Pesticides and Politics* (University of Pittsburgh Press, 1987), 135–137, describing formation of EDF and its role in early pesticide litigation. The organization still bills its successful campaign to ban DDT as one of its signal accomplishments.

48 D Dempsey, *Ruin and Recovery: Michigan's Rise as a Conservation Leader* (Ann Arbor, University of Michigan Press, 2001), 171.

49 See Michigan Environmental Protection Act, codified at Mich. Comp. L. ss. 324.1701ff.

50 Mich. Comp. L. s 324.1701(1).

United Auto Workers Union, MEPA passed the Michigan legislature and was signed into law by an environmentally minded Republican Governor in 1970.[51]

Thus was born the idea of the statutory environmental citizen suit, one of the principal driving forces behind the subsequent development of US environmental law. From MEPA, a stand-alone all-purpose environmental citizen suit provision, it was a short step for Sax to argue for inclusion of a statutory citizen suit provision in the Clean Air Act, then being debated in Congress, and in subsequent federal environmental statutes.[52] Since the 1970s, literally thousands of environmental citizen suits have been filed, usually against private defendants for failure to observe regulatory standards, but frequently against federal officials for failure to exercise mandatory duties under the relevant statutes. These suits have profoundly shaped the development of environmental law in the United States, resulting in its vigorous enforcement even when government enforcement efforts have been lax, and forcing government officials to adhere strictly to their statutory duties under the nation's environmental laws.[53]

Ironically, NEPA, unlike most of the nation's major environmental statutes, does not contain an express citizen suit provision.[54] Nonetheless, in the spirit of the times and with environmental litigation of all kinds swirling around them, courts in the 1970s had little trouble discerning, or simply assuming *sub silentio*, an implied private cause of action to enforce NEPA's procedural duties against reluctant federal officials.[55] More recently courts have held that NEPA can be enforced through the federal Administrative Procedure Act[56] which allows any

---

51 See Dempsey, *Ruin and Recovery*, n. 48 above, 170–176, describing the events leading to MEPA's enactment.

52 Sax was in close communication with the principal sponsor of the Clean Air Act, Senator Edmund Muskie (Democrat, Maine) and his staff. Senators Hart (Democrat, Michigan) and McGovern (Democrat-South Dakota) also introduced a federal version of Sax's MEPA legislation at the time the Clean Air Act was under consideration. See R E Schiller, 'Enlarging the Administrative Polity: Administrative Law and the Changing Definition of Pluralism, 1944–1970', (2000) 53 *Vanderbilt Law Review* 1389, 1448–1449.

53 See Thompson, 'Citizen Enforcement', n. 45 above, 189–193, 198–199.

54 See M C Stephenson, 'Public Regulation of Private Enforcement: The Case for Expanding the Role of Administrative Agencies' (2005) 91 *Vanderbilt Law Review* 93, stating that NEPA and the Federal Insecticide, Fungicide and Rodenticide Act (FIFRA) are the only major federal environmental statutes without citizen suit provisions.

55 See e.g. *Aberdeen & Rockfish R. Co. v Students Challenging Regulatory Agency Procedures*, 422 U.S. 289 (1975), holding that NEPA creates 'a discrete procedural obligation on government agencies' and 'a right of action in adversely affected parties to enforce that obligation'; *Atchison, Topeka & Santa Fe. Ry. Co. v Callaway*, 431 F. Supp. 722, 728 (D.D.C. 1977), holding that NEPA's EIS requirement is enforceable by implied private right of action; *Calvert Cliffs coordinating Committee v Atomic Energy Commission*, 449 F.2d 1109 (D.C. Cir. 1971), holding that s 102 of NEPA 'creates judicially enforceable duties', without discussing who has a right to maintain an action to enforce these duties.

56 See e.g. *Public Citizen v Office of U.S. Trade Representative*, 970 F.2d 916, 919 (1992): 'NEPA does not include a private right of action, so plaintiffs rest their claim for judicial review on the Administrative Procedure Act'.

'aggrieved person' to seek judicial review of a 'final agency action' that is 'arbitrary and capricious' or otherwise contrary to law,[57] although the APA 'final agency action' requirement narrows the occasions on which judicial review may be available.[58]

From the outset, the post-enactment development of NEPA would be driven mainly by citizen-initiated litigation, a development that likely would not have occurred but for the pioneering contributions of Joe Sax.

Reshaping NEPA: the role of the courts

NEPA's enactment unleashed a flood of litigation. By April 1970, a federal court had relied on NEPA to enjoin construction of the trans-Alaska oil pipeline pending completion of an environmental impact statement.[59] Within months, environmental plaintiffs won injunctions halting several highways,[60] a barge canal,[61] and a dam project.[62] The message to federal agencies was unmistakable: ignore NEPA at your peril.

The defining case of the era was *Calvert Cliffs Coordinating Committee v Atomic Energy Commission*.[63] In that case, environmental plaintiffs challenged the NEPA compliance rules the Commission had devised for itself, which all but guaranteed that information contained in an EIS would not reach the eyes of the commissioners making the key decisions. Declaring its own duty to 'see that important legislative purposes, heralded in the halls of Congress, are not lost or misdirected in the vast hallways of the federal bureaucracy',[64] the Court of Appeals for the D.C. Circuit first held that NEPA's substantive provisions established a 'flexible' standard that affords agencies considerable discretion and 'may not require particular substantive results in particular problematic circumstances'.[65]

---

57 5 U.S.C. ss 701–706.

58 In *Public Citizen v USTR*, n. 56 above, for example, Public Citizen attempted to force production of an EIS on the proposed North American Free Trade Agreement, negotiated by the US Trade Representative on behalf of the President. The D.C. Circuit held, however, that Public Citizen had no cause of action against the Trade Representative who only made non-binding recommendations to the President; because these recommendations were not 'final agency action', APA review was not available. Nor could Public Citizen sue the President who was not considered an 'agency' for purposes of the APA.

59 See *Wilderness Society v Hickel*, 325 F. Supp. 422 (D.D.C. 1970), holding Secretary of the Interior had not complied with NEPA requirements before issuing construction permits.

60 See e.g. *Named Individual Members of the San Antonio Conservation Society v Texas Highway Department*, 446 F.2d 1013 (5th Cir. 1971); *Harrisburg Coalition Against Ruining the Environment v Volpe*, 330 F.Supp. 918 (M.D. Pa. 1971).

61 See *Environmental Defense Fund v Army Corps of Engineers*, 324 F. Supp. 878 (D.D.C. 1971).

62 See *Environmental Defense Fund v Army Corps of Engineers*, 325 F. Supp. 749 (D. Ark. 1971), enjoining dam construction until NEPA compliance is achieved.

63 449 F.2d, 1109 (D.C. Cir. 1971).

64 Ibid, 1111.

65 Ibid, 1112.

In stark contrast, however, the court held that NEPA's procedural duties 'establish a strict standard of compliance'[66] mandating 'a particular sort of informed and careful decision-making process and...judicially enforceable duties'.[67] Applying that strict standard, the court concluded that the Commission's NEPA compliance procedures 'make a mockery of the Act' by insulating key decision-makers from meaningful consideration of the information contained in the Environmental Impact Statement. On that ground, the court reversed and remanded the agency's decision.

Bifurcating substance from procedure and emphasizing strict compliance with the latter while rendering the former all but non-justiciable, *Calvert Cliffs* set the tone for subsequent judicial interpretations of NEPA, with profound consequences for the future direction of agency compliance efforts. A short time later the Supreme Court would affirm in *Kleppe v Sierra Club* that the 'only role for a court is to insure that the agency has taken a "hard look" at environmental consequences; it cannot interject itself within the area of discretion of the executive as to the course of action to be taken'.[68] By 1980, the Supreme Court would flatly hold NEPA's substantive requirements non-justiciable.[69]

A second influential D.C. Circuit case was *NRDC v Morton*.[70] In that case, a national environmental organization contended that the Secretary of the Interior had not adequately considered alternatives to a proposed program of offshore oil and gas leases in the Gulf of Mexico. Specifically, plaintiffs said, the Secretary should have considered whether the nation's energy needs could be met by lifting restrictions on oil imports. The Secretary defended on grounds that such an action would require congressional action and involved 'complex factors... including national security' which were beyond the scope of NEPA review. The court held for the plaintiffs, stating the agency must consider 'reasonable' alternatives, even if they require action by parties other than the agency itself, because the purpose of the EIS is not only to inform the agency conducting the analysis but more broadly to inform the governmental decision-making process. Since *NRDC v Morton*, analysis of alternatives has been central to the NEPA compliance process.

The Second Circuit got into the act with a third profoundly influential early case, *Hanly v Kleindienst*.[71] In that case, residents and neighboring businesses challenged a federal agency's decision not to produce a full-scale environmental impact statement in conjunction with its decision to build a federal detention

---

66 449 F.2d, 1112.
67 Ibid, 1115.
68 *Kleppe v Sierra Club*, 427 U.S. 390, 411 (1976) (internal citation and quotation omitted).
69 *Strycker's Bay Neighborhood Council v Karlen*, 444 U.S. 223, 227–228 (1980); see also *Robertson v Methow Valley Citizens Council*, 490 U.S. 332, 350 (1989): 'it is now well settled that NEPA itself does not mandate particular results, but simply prescribes the necessary process'.
70 *NRDC v Morton*, 458 F.2d 827 (D.C. Cir. 1972).
71 471 F.2d 823 (2d Cir. 1972).

facility in lower Manhattan. The Second Circuit Court of Appeals held that by the terms the statute, a full EIS was required only if environmental impacts rose to the level of 'significant', and since the statute itself did not define the term 'significant', the implementing agency had some discretion in making that threshold determination. The court ruled, however, that such a threshold determination must be based on a 'reviewable environmental record' compiled after giving the public notice and an opportunity to be heard.[72] This ruling set in motion the establishment of a formalized Environmental Assessment (EA) process, a kind of truncated mini-EIA leading to a Finding of No Significant Impact (FONSI) justifying the agency's decision not to conduct a full-scale EIS. This procedure, nowhere mentioned in the NEPA statutory text, was codified and elaborated in subsequent NEPA implementing regulations, and is now a standard feature, indeed the central mechanism, of federal agencies' NEPA compliance practice. Each year approximately 50,000 EAs are conducted, the vast majority of them leading to FONSIs. In contrast, fewer than 500 full-scale EISs are completed each year.

A fourth crucial step in NEPA's procedural evolution was the development of the so-called 'mitigated FONSI', again with the courts' blessing. Once it became apparent to federal agencies that an EA leading to a FONSI was generally a cheaper and faster route to NEPA compliance than a full-scale EIS, the question arose whether proposed projects might be re-jigged to include mitigation measures calculated to keep environmental impacts below the EIS-triggering threshold of 'significant', thus justifying the agency in proceeding on the EA fast track. This sidestepping approach, dubbed the 'mitigated FONSI', has generally been approved by the courts, with the D.C. Circuit again leading the way. In a 1973 case, *Maryland-National Park & Planning Commission v U.S. Postal Service*,[73] the D.C. Circuit first suggested in dicta that an agency might be able to avoid NEPA's EIS production requirement if mitigation measures added to the project kept expected environmental impacts below the threshold of 'significant', stating that this approach 'is to be encouraged'.[74] In 1982 this suggestion ripened into a D.C. Circuit holding in *Cabinet Mountains Wilderness v Peterson* that if 'the proposal is modified prior to implementation by adding specific mitigation measures' which reduce adverse impacts, 'the statutory threshold of significant environmental effects is not crossed and an EIS is not required'.[75] Other courts have generally concurred.[76]

Although exact figures are not available, it is believed that a large fraction of all federal projects approved under the fast-track EA procedure now include mitigation

---

72 Ibid, 836.
73 487 F.2d 1029 (D.C. Cir. 1973).
74 Ibid, 1040 & fn. 11.
75 685 F.2d 678, 682 (D.C. Cir. 1982).
76 See e.g. *Friends of Endangered Species v Jantzen*, 760 F.2d 976, 987 (9th Cir. 1985); *Louisiana v Lee*, 758 F.2d 1081, 1083 (5th Cir. 1985); *C.A.R.E. Now v F.A.A.* 844 F.2d 1569, 1575 (11th Cir. 1988).

measures designed to reduce environmental impacts below the statutory threshold of 'significant'. Some commentators have opined that this approach subverts NEPA's central analytical requirements. It is precisely in circumstances where environmental impacts could rise to the level of 'significant' that the statute instructs the agency to undertake a full-scale EIS to identify all impacts and a reasonable range of alternatives before selecting its course of action. The mitigated FONSI short-circuits that inquiry: so long as the agency can identify and incorporate any mitigation measures that reduce expected impacts below the EIS-triggering threshold of 'significant', it can avoid the more detailed EIS analysis.

On another view, however, the mitigated FONSI appears to have salutary consequences. By inducing agencies to identify and implement mitigation measures that reduce expected environmental impacts below the EIS-triggering threshold of 'significant', the mitigated FONSI effectively reincorporates a judicially enforceable substantive standard into NEPA, and almost certainly leads agencies to include environmentally beneficial mitigation measures in their projects, thus indirectly achieving NEPA's original purposes by an unanticipated backdoor route. Ironically, the NEPA-mandated EIS, intended to operate as the analytical vehicle by which agencies inform themselves about the environmental consequences of their actions and identify environmentally beneficial alternatives prior to deciding upon a course of action, instead comes to operate as a costly procedural penalty that agencies must pay in cases where environmental harms cannot be avoided or adequately mitigated.

Filling in the details: from guidelines to regulations

From the outset, federal agencies required assistance in interpreting NEPA and determining how they might comply. Shortly after the statute's enactment, President Nixon directed his Council on Environmental Quality to produce non-binding 'guidelines' to help steer federal agencies through the interpretive thicket.[77] These guidelines underwent several revisions in subsequent years in response to major court rulings and agency implementation experience.

In 1977, President Carter issued an executive order authorizing CEQ to issue mandatory NEPA implementation 'regulations' and directing federal agencies to comply.[78] This measure, undertaken pursuant to the President's inherent executive authority over federal agencies, places the CEQ regulations under a different legal status than most agency regulations. In the usual case, Congress expressly delegates subsidiary rulemaking authority to the agency, and under the *Chevron* doctrine in US administrative law, reviewing courts must defer to the agency's regulatory interpretation of the requirements of its governing statute so long as

---

77 Executive Order No. 11,514, 35 Fed. Reg. 4247 (5 March 1970).
78 Executive Order No. 11,911, 42 Fed. Reg. 26967 (24 May 1977).

that interpretation is 'reasonable'. However, CEQ's NEPA implementation rules are not promulgated pursuant to a congressional delegation of authority and they are not entitled to *Chevron* deference. Courts have sometimes been reluctant to enforce CEQ regulations strictly on the theory that the President has sufficient means at his disposal to enforce his own orders against federal agencies without aid or interference from the courts.[79] Nonetheless, courts have held that CEQ regulations are entitled to 'substantial' deference as a guide to the meaning of the NEPA statute itself.[80]

In 1978, CEQ issued comprehensive regulations filling in the details of NEPA compliance.[81] These procedural rules have been remarkably stable over the course of nearly three decades, undergoing only minor revisions during that time.[82] The CEQ rules spell out, with far greater precision than the statute itself, whether,[83] when,[84] how,[85] and by whom[86] an Environmental Impact Statement or Environmental Assessment shall be prepared, together with its required contents.[87] CEQ rules also set out additional procedural steps agencies may or in some cases must take,[88] many of them aimed at ensuring adequate public notice and opportunity to be heard.[89] In addition, CEQ rules require each federal agency, in consultation with CEQ and consistent with the generally applicable CEQ regulations, to develop and publish its own supplemental NEPA implementation procedures and criteria for determining when an EIS is required, together with explanatory guidance.[90]

Thus each agency is bound by three tiers of NEPA law: the sparse procedural requirements of the statute itself, vigorously enforced by the courts; detailed CEQ regulations made mandatory by Presidential executive order, given substantial

---

79 See e.g. *Taxpayers of Michigan Against Casinos*, 433 F.3d 852, 861 (D.C. Cir. 2006): 'the binding effect of CEQ regulations is far from clear' because CEQ 'has no express regulatory authority' under the statute, but CEQ's interpretations of NEPA are nonetheless 'entitled to substantial deference'.

80 See *Andrus v Sierra Club*, 442 U.S. 347, 358 (1979).

81 43 Fed. Reg. 55990 (28 November 1978), codified as amended at 40 C.F.R. Part 1500.

82 See W H Rodgers, Junior, *Environmental Law* (Thomson and West, 1994), 816–817.

83 40 C.F.R. ss 1501.4, 1502.4, 1509.2.

84 Ibid, ss 1501.2, 1501.3.

85 Ibid, ss 1502.7 (page limits), 1502.8 (writing), 1502.10 (format).

86 Ibid, ss 1505.5 (lead agency), 1501.6 (cooperating agencies).

87 Ibid, ss 1502.14 (alternatives), 1502.15 (affected environment), 1502.16 (environmental impacts).

88 See e.g. 40 C.F.R. 1508.4 (establishing procedure for 'categorical exclusions', minor or routine actions not requiring environmental assessment or environmental impact statement); 1508.22 (use of environmental assessment to reach FONSI and avoid EIS requirement).

89 See e.g. 40 C.F.R. ss 1508.22 (publication of notice of intent to prepare EIS), 1501.4 ('finding of no significant impact' made available to public); 1501.7 (public participation in 'scoping' process to determine key elements of environmental impact analysis); 1506.6 (public notice of NEPA hearings and full public disclosure of EIS, comments received, and underlying documents used in analysis), 1506.10 (publication of draft EIS at least 45 days before decision on agency action).

90 40 C.F.R. s 1507.3.

deference but not rigidly enforced by the courts; and the agency's own NEPA implementation rules and procedures. Deviation from any of these might provide grounds for a court to hold the agency's action 'arbitrary and capricious' and to enjoin the agency from undertaking the proposed project until NEPA procedures are properly satisfied.

NEPA in action: five contrasting views

NEPA has come in for wide-ranging praise and criticism over its first three-and-a-half decades. Many defend it ardently as a cornerstone of US environmental policy that has forced agencies to be more attentive to the environmental consequences of their actions, while simultaneously opening up governmental decision-making to public scrutiny and an unprecedented measure of public participation.[91] Indeed, some argue that NEPA's core environmental impact assessment requirement has assumed quasi-constitutional status as one of the foundational operating principles of the modern administrative state.[92]

This view, call it 'NEPA optimism', can be contrasted with a somewhat more cynical view held by others in the environmentalist camp who might be described as the 'NEPA monkey wrenchers'. This group is more skeptical of the claim that NEPA's procedural formalities actually induce better-informed decision-making or genuine opportunities for public participation. Nonetheless, the 'monkey wrenchers' find NEPA an invaluable tool because it gives them leverage to resist environmentally harmful government projects by means of costly and dilatory environmental reviews or drawn-out litigation. In many cases, the added political and financial costs of NEPA compliance, especially when coupled with litigation, can force cancellation or modification of the proposed project.[93]

A contrasting but closely related view is that held by the 'NEPA skeptics', including many agency managers and proponents of private projects requiring government approvals. For much the same reason 'monkey wrenchers' love

---

91 See e.g. *Council on Environmental Quality, NEPA: A Study* (hereafter '*CEQ Study*'), (Washington DC: Council on Environmental Quality, 1997), iii, concluding that NEPA is 'a success' because it 'has made agencies take a hard look at the potential environmental consequences of the actions, and it has brought the public into the agency decision making process like no other statute'.

92 See T W Merrill, *Capture Theory and the Courts, 1967–1983* (1997) 72 *Chicago-Kent Law Review* 1039–1040, describing NEPA and the Administrative Procedure Act as foundational 'framework statutes' of modern administrative law and comparing their role to that of the US Constitution.

93 See P J Culhane, 'NEPA's Impacts on Federal Agencies, Anticipated and Unanticipated' (1990) 20 *Environmental Law* 681, 700, stating that 'decisional gridlock' due to 'interminable delay' and 'protracted NEPA litigation' is an 'acceptable outcome' to opponents of agency projects; J Dao, 'Environmental Groups to File Suit over Missile Defense', *New York Times*, 28 August 2001, A10, quoting an environmental activist as stating 'the hope is that delay [occasioned by NEPA litigation] will lead to cancellation . . . That's what we always hope for in these suits'.

NEPA, the skeptics fear and despise it, seeing it as a tool of obstructionism and a source of needless and unproductive cost, delay, and procedural red tape.[94]

A fourth view, predominant among legal academics, is that of the 'legalist critics'. The general thrust of this view is that by exalting procedure over substance, NEPA has gone seriously astray. Some have held this view from the very beginning. For example, Joe Sax famously wrote in 1973 that NEPA's 'emphasis on the redemptive quality of procedural reform is about nine parts myth and one part coconut oil.'[95] For others, the fault lies primarily with the courts for their role in eviscerating NEPA of its substantive content.[96]

A fifth view is that of the 'progressive reformers'. The reformers are generally sympathetic with NEPA's aims and accomplishments to date but also acutely sensitive to its limitations. Their reform proposals are many and varied. Some argue for increased emphasis on strategic environmental assessment at higher levels of decision-making, rather than the project-specific approach to impact assessment typically taken by agencies.[97] Some call for stronger centralized data collection and supervisory review over the highly decentralized and possibly non-uniform NEPA compliance practices of federal agencies.[98] Others call for more effective use of digital information management technologies, arguing this can streamline data collection and presentation while also improving the quality and usefulness of NEPA analyses.[99] Still others emphasize the need for post-implementation monitoring and adaptive management, or 'adaptive mitigation', recognizing that in a complex world our *ex ante*

94 See F B Cross, 'The Judiciary and Public Choice' (1999) 50 *Hastings Law Journal* 355, 375, stating that NEPA is 'notorious for special interest abuse' because it 'can be used by anyone interested in frustrating or delaying a major government action'.

95 J L Sax, 'The (Unhappy) Truth About NEPA' (1973) 26 *Oklahoma Law Review* 239, 239. Sax later modified his views, calling NEPA 'one of the very few means by which the obligation to gather adequate information and then to subject it to careful and detailed consideration can be enforced'. See J L Sax, 'The Search for Environmental Rights' (1990) 6 *Journal of Land Use & Environmental Law* 93, 98.

96 See e.g. N C Yost, *NEPA's Promise–Partially Fulfilled* (1990) 20 *Environmental Law* 533, 540, arguing that the courts' narrow view 'truncate[d] NEPA's substantive development and deprive[d] the nation of the full reach of Congress' purpose in enacting the statute'.

97 See *CEQ Study*, n. 91 above, 11–12, stating that 'agencies tend to examine identified project-level environmental effects in microscopic detail' but devote less attention to considering the environmental consequences of broader policies and programmes.

98 See e.g. J F C DiMento and H Ingram, 'Science and Environmental Decision Making: The Potential Role of Environmental Impact Assessment in the Pursuit of Appropriate Information' (2005) 45 *Natural Resources Journal* 283, 300–303, recommending collection of EIA and other environmental data in centralized clearinghouses to provide better baseline information and cross-check for compatibilities and inconsistencies in environmental assessments; W L Andreen, 'In Pursuit of NEPA's Promise: The Role of Executive Oversight in the Implementation of Environmental Policy' (1989) 64 *Indiana Law Journal* 205, 253–260, calling for strengthened CEQ and EPA oversight of NEPA compliance by federal agencies.

99 See e.g. D A Farber in this collection.

predictions as to likely environmental impacts may often turn out to be inaccurate or just plain wrong.[100]

Whither NEPA?

Notwithstanding its many critics, NEPA has proven remarkably stable since its enactment. Repeated efforts to revise it have foundered under opposition from environmentalists to any changes they perceive as undermining or weakening the statute, and amidst cross-cutting pressures for widely divergent, and possibly incompatible, visions of NEPA reform.

Efforts to amend NEPA appeared to gain some traction with the September 2003 release of a report by an *ad hoc* NEPA Reform Task Force commissioned by the president's Council on Environmental Quality. That report, entitled 'Modernizing NEPA Implementation',[101] called for several broad categories of changes, including:

- improved use of information technology;
- heightened attention to information security in situations where information divulged through the NEPA process might implicate national security concerns;
- improved collaboration among federal agencies and between federal and non-federal parties;
- greater emphasis on programmatic, as opposed to project-specific, analyses;
- incorporation of adaptive management techniques into the NEPA compliance process;
- expanded use of 'categorical exclusions', that is, categories of minor actions exempted from NEPA review by regulation; and
- 'streamlining' the EA process through standardized reporting, page limitations, expanded use of checklists and forms, and simplification of analytical requirements.

A short time later, the House Resources Committee appointed a House Task Force on Improving the National Environmental Policy Act, which issued its

---

100 An early proponent of this view was C S 'Buzz' Holling, generally credited with coining the concept of adaptive management. Holling's early work in this area, which he called 'adaptive environmental assessment and management', grew out of his experience, and frustrations, as an ecologist called on to participate in the production of EISs in complex situations requiring integration across multiple scientific disciplines, and highly speculative predictions based on incomplete data, underlying scientific uncertainties, and incomplete and untested predictive models. A sounder approach, Holling argued, would be to construct policy interventions as testable hypotheses, generating post-implementation monitoring data that could help reduce scientific uncertainties and improve predictive models over time. See C S Holling, *Adaptive Environmental Assessment and Management* (New York: Wiley, 1978).

101 NEPA 'Task Force Report to the Council on Environmental Quality, Modernizing NEPA Implementation', September 2003.

own report in December 2005, after holding seven months of hearings around the country.[102] The House Task Force report emphasized the need to limit NEPA litigation and other causes of 'cost and delay' in the NEPA process. It recommended, *inter alia*, mandatory timelines for completion of NEPA reviews, increased use of categorical exclusions, limitations on the 'alternatives' required to be studied in an EIS, and additional limitations on citizen access to the courts.

The general thrust of these proposals is to limit information production and citizen-initiated litigation, and they have been subjected to withering criticism by environmentalists.[103] They appear not to have gained majority support in either house of Congress. Consequently, notwithstanding the recent flurry of administrative and legislative proposals, legislation to amend NEPA has not advanced in the current Congress.

Yet the current state of the debate over NEPA's future must be judged a stalemate rather than a clear-cut victory for any side. Efforts to 'reform' NEPA from a variety of perspectives can be expected to continue. Much is at stake in these ongoing debates. NEPA has done much to improve government's environmental performance by compelling the production and disclosure of information on expected environmental outcomes, but it remains a relatively crude and unsophisticated instrument with which to address the environmental challenges of the twenty-first century. Ours is an age of explosive growth in sheer information and the technological means to manage and distribute it. NEPA has kept pace neither with contemporary information management capabilities, nor with contemporary scientific understandings of the complexity of the environmental management task. We therefore face both a need and an opportunity to make NEPA an even more effective environmental management tool than it has been over the first three-and-a-half decades of its existence. But if we botch that opportunity, we risk setting environmental management back a generation or more.

102 United States House of Representatives Committee on Resources, 'Task Force on Improving the National Environmental Policy Act, Initial Findings and Draft Recommendations', December 1995.

103 See e.g. R G Dreher, 'NEPA Under Siege: The Political Assault on the National Environmental Policy Act' (2005) *Georgetown Environmental Law & Policy Institute* 8–11, characterizing the House Task Force report as 'proposals to weaken NEPA [by] exempting broad categories of federal agency action, [imposing] restrictions on the substance of environmental reviews, [and] restrict[ing] public participation and judicial review'; Natural Resources Defense Council, Statement on Release of the NEPA Task Force Report (press release), 21 December 2005, stating that the House Task Force report 'suggests no less than 13 recommendations to weaken the National Environmental Policy Act in profound and fundamental ways'.

Chapter 4

Better Regulation in Europe

Jonathan B Wiener[1]

Introduction

"Better Regulation" is sweeping Europe. Based on a White Paper on Governance[2] and an expert group report,[3] both issued in 2001, the European Commission under President Prodi adopted a suite of regulatory reform measures in 2002, including guidelines on impact assessment.[4] Following a Communication from the new Barroso Commission in March 2005,[5] these guidelines were revised in 2005[6] and updated again in 2006.[7] Impact Assessment (IA) is now required for all regulatory proposals on the Commission's Work Programme. In addition, the Commission is pressing for simplification of existing laws (through consolidation,

1 A previous version of this chapter was published in *Current Legal Problems* 59, 447–518 (Oxford: Oxford University Press, 2006). For support of this research, the author thanks the Eugene T. Bost, Jr Research Professorship of the Charles A. Cannon Charitable Trust No 3 at Duke University. For helpful comments and discussion, the author thanks Joanne Caddy, Luigi Carbone, Cary Coglianese, Heidi Dawidoff, Marie-Anne Frison-Roche, John Graham, Olivier Godard, Robert Hahn, James Hammitt, Jane Holder, Stephane Jacobzone, Josef Konvitz, Gert-Jan Koopmans, Andreas Kraemer, Ragnar Lofstedt, Giandomenico Majone, Richard Macrory, Nikolai Malyshev, Patrick Messerlin, Lars Mitek Pederson, Charles-Henri Montin, Shainila Pradhan, Ray Purdy, Cornelia Quennet-Thielen, Manuel Santiago, Robert Scharrenbourg, Michel Setbon, Bernard Sinclair-Désgagné, Richard Stewart, Cass Sunstein, Tim Swanson, Nicolas Treich, Matti Vainio, and participants in meetings held at University College London, the OECD, the US–EU High-Level Regulatory Cooperation Forum, and the French Ministry of Finance Economy & Industry.
2 European Commission, "European Governance: A White Paper," COM(2001) 428.
3 Mandelkern Group on Better Regulation, Final Report, November 2001.
4 European Commission, Communication from the Commission on Impact Assessment, COM(2002) 276, June 5, 2002 (hereafter "IA Guidelines 2002").
5 European Commission, Communication from the Commission to the Council and the European Parliament, "Better Regulation for Growth and Jobs in the European Union," COM(2005) 97, SEC(2005) 175, March 16, 2005.
6 European Commission, Impact Assessment Guidelines, SEC(2005) 791, June 15 2005 (hereafter "IA Guidelines 2005").
7 European Commission, Impact Assessment Guidelines, SEC(2005) 791, June 15, 2005, with March 15, 2006 update (hereafter "IA Guidelines 2006").

codification, and repeal), reduction of administrative costs ("cutting red tape"), and consultation with those affected by regulatory policies.

The member states of the European Union (EU) are likewise adopting programs of Better Regulation, some predating and spurring the Commission's efforts, and others in turn spurred by the Commission.[8] In 2004, a coalition of four of the rotating six-month Presidencies of the European Union (Ireland, Netherlands, Luxembourg, and Britain) issued a joint statement of their intention to pursue Better Regulation efforts during their upcoming Presidencies; this letter played an important role in spurring the European Commission to update and strengthen its IA Guidelines.[9] To note one prominent example of action by a member state, the UK has launched a Better Regulation Executive[10] and an external advisory Better Regulation Commission. In May 2005, UK Prime Minister Tony Blair delivered a speech on "Risk and the State," emphasizing that risk regulation is absolutely necessary, but criticizing over regulation of small risks in the futile effort to reduce risks to zero (often as an overreaction to a recent crisis), thus impeding innovation and inducing perverse effects that "do more damage than was done by the problem itself." As a remedy, he advocated the program of "Better Regulation" based on a "rigorous risk-based approach" that will employ impact assessments and "regulate only after reflection."[11]

Will Better Regulation make a difference? Will it make things better? This study begins by examining the Better Regulation initiative as an exercise of legal borrowing, and by framing the question whether Better Regulation will really yield better results. After several transatlantic conflicts over regulatory topics such as the precautionary principle, genetically modified foods, and climate change, Europe and America now appear to be converging on the analytic basis for regulation. In a process of hybridization, European institutions are borrowing "Better Regulation" reforms from both the US approach to regulatory review using benefit-cost analysis and from European member states" initiatives on administrative costs and simplification; in turn the European Commission is helping to spread these reforms among the member states.

In the following sections, this study addresses in more detail the main components of Better Regulation – impact assessments and administrative simplification – and advocates the adoption of several institutional improvements. (Other aspects of regulatory reform in Europe, such as transparency, consultation,

---

8 The Communication of March 16, 2005, COM(2005) 97, above, included a colourful chart of relative progress on Better Regulation among the member states. Highest marks went to Denmark, the UK, and Poland; lowest marks went to France, Portugal, and Cyprus. See below in the section on European Experience at n. 88.

9 See Joint Initiative on Regulatory Reform, a Letter from the EU Presidencies of Ireland, Netherlands, Luxembourg, and the UK, January 26, 2004, at http://www.finance.gov.ie/documents/ pressreleases/2004/janmcc12462. pdf.

10 See http://www.betterregulation.gov.uk/ and http://www.cabinetoffice.gov.uk/ regulation/.

11 Prime Minister Tony Blair, "Speech on Risk and the State," May 26, 2005, available at http://www.number-10.gov.uk/output/Page7562.asp.

and subsidiarity, are mentioned here but are not the focus.) In many respects, the Better Regulation initiative promises salutary reforms, such as wider use of regulatory impact assessments and a reduction in unnecessary bureaucracy. In other respects, the European initiative speaks more of Procrustean deregulation than of better regulation. Meanwhile the European Commission still needs to establish the institutional infrastructure needed to succeed. I argue that the European program of Better Regulation is well-founded but could be even better if it adopted several strategies: enlarging the scope of impact assessment and benefit-cost analysis toward a broader, "warmer," and more evenhanded application of these tools, with greater attention to multiple risks; moving beyond a narrow focus on cutting administrative costs or simplification for their own sake, toward criteria that address benefits as well as costs; centralizing expert oversight so that impact assessments actually influence decisions, both to say "no" to bad ideas and "yes" to good ideas; and undertaking *ex post* evaluation of policies for adaptive policy revision and for improvement of *ex ante* assessment methods. These reforms would help Better Regulation achieve its true objective: better, not just less or more. In turn, the US could study these European innovations and borrow from them where they prove successful.

Legal borrowing

The Better Regulation initiative is a conscious exercise of legal borrowing. This borrowing has been both horizontal and vertical. Horizontal legal borrowing occurs when one co-equal legal system borrows from another, such as Europe borrowing from the US, or one European member state from another EU member state.[12] Vertical legal borrowing occurs when a supra-governmental regime borrows from its own constituent members, such as the EU-level institutions borrowing from EU member states.[13]

The Better Regulation initiative in Europe borrows along both of these dimensions. It is an outgrowth of ideas percolating up from (vertically) and spreading across (horizontally) the EU member states; of the integration of EU institutions and the current EU platform of competitiveness, good governance, and sustainable development;[14] and also of deliberate (horizontal) borrowing from

---

12 The literature on horizontal legal borrowing (across states) is extensive; the classic is Alan Watson, *Legal Transplants: An Approach to Comparative Law* (2nd edn) (Athens, Ga: University of Georgia Press, 1993).

13 A framework of legal borrowing that adds the vertical dimension (between states and federal and international bodies) is developed in Jonathan B Wiener, "Something Borrowed for Something Blue: Legal Transplants in the Evolution of Global Environmental Law" (2001) 27 *Ecology Law Quaterly* 1295.

14 A useful history of the connections of Better Regulation to these three elements of the EU platform is provided in Ragnar Lofstedt, "The Swing of the Regulatory Pendulum in Europe: From Precautionary Principle to (Regulatory) Impact Analysis" (2004) 28 *Journal of Risk and Uncertainty* 237–260.

American law. It is thus a perfect example of legal "hybridization," an evolutionary process involving the exchange and recombination of traits (here, legal ideas) from different species (here, legal systems) into new hybrid versions in response to changing needs.[15] As in biological evolution, legal hybrids do not always succeed. Mixing together legal concepts can be ineffective or incoherent.[16] As in biology, legal hybrids succeed when they possess novel combinations of traits that enable them to occupy new niches opened up by changing external demands. Better Regulation in Europe is a hybrid package of reforms attempting to respond to changing needs for regulatory management.

In its Impact Assessment Guidelines, the Commission tellingly quotes US President Woodrow Wilson: "I not only use all the brains that I have, but all that I can borrow."[17] The Commission's immediate point here is to espouse borrowing ideas from public input and interservice consultation to improve regulation, but the quotation simultaneously invokes the larger project of legal borrowing involved in the European initiative on Better Regulation, which emulates key concepts and tools of regulatory reform developed in the American administrative state over the past four decades.[18]

What is now emerging is a global movement toward regulatory reform and Better Regulation, drawing significantly on American administrative law and oversight mechanisms.[19] The American sources of European Better Regulation are

---

15 For further discussion on "hybridization" of legal ideas and the counterpart concepts in evolutionary biology, see Jonathan B Wiener, "Whose Precaution After All? A Comment on the Comparison and Evolution of Risk Regulatory Systems" (2003) 13 *Duke Journal of Comparative and International Law* 207, 254–261. An overview of evolutionary biology concepts applied to legal evolution is Simon Deakin, "Evolution for Our Time: A Theory of Legal Memetics" (2002) 55 Current Legal Problems 1–42. See also sources cited in nn 29–31 below on legal borrowing and diffusion.

16 See Wiener, n. 15 above (noting failure of hybrids until new niches open); Willam Reppy, "Eclecticism in Choice of Law: Hybrid Method or Mishmash?" (1983) 34 Mercer L Rev 645 (criticizing eclecticism as unpredictable and standardless, while endorsing careful construction and transparent selection of new hybrid methods). Moreover, diffusion itself can sometimes undermine incentives to innovate or can invite fads. See David Lazer, "Regulatory Capitalism as a Networked Order," (March 2005) Annals of the American Academy 52–66.

17 Quoted in IA Guidelines 2006, at 9.

18 On the US history, see Richard Pildes and Cass R Sunstein, "Reinventing the Regulatory State" (1995) 32 University of Chicago Law Review 1; Elena Kagan, "Presidential Administration" (2001) 114 Harvard Law Review 2246.

19 See Benedict Kingsbury, Nico Krisch, and Richard B Stewart, "The Emergence of Global Administrative Law," (summer/autumn 2005) 68 *Law and Contemporary Problems* 15; Richard B Stewart, "Accountability and the Discontents of Globalization: US and EU Models for Regulatory Governance" (draft 2006); Robert W Hahn and Robert E Litan, "Counting Regulatory Benefits and Costs: Lessons for the US and Europe" (2005) 8 *Journal of International Economic Law* 473–508; Robert W Hahn, *Reviving Regulatory Reform: A Global Perspective* (Washington, DC: AEI Press, 2001).

well recognized. For example, the head of Irish government recently observed:

Better Regulation and EU – US perspectives are foremost in my mind these days. Better Regulation is a core theme of our EU Presidency and featured prominently at the recent Spring Economic Council.... There is a long tradition in American Public Administration of focussing on the quality and impact of regulation. Many of the policies, institutions and tools that support Better Regulation have their origins in the USA. For example, a lot of very significant anti-trust and consumer protection measures were put in place in the USA in the first decades of the 20th century. There is much that we have learned from the United States in relation to regulatory management and, through occasions like this, much that we can continue to learn.... We hope too that there will be shared learning. While we in the European Union are newer to the game, I hope that we have moved beyond our rookie season! The Union is making up ground quickly in respect of Better Regulation. This is as it should be. There is a deeper understanding within the European Institutions and Member States of the need for regulatory reform.[20]

This process is not one-way: American legal ideas are not the only ones being adopted in other countries. At the same time that the Better Regulation initiative is bringing the methods of impact assessment and regulatory review from the US to Europe, other legal concepts are also spreading from Europe and elsewhere to the US and beyond.[21] The precautionary principle is perhaps the best example of a European regulatory law export (adopted, for example, in US statutes and judicial decisions in the 1970s and by the city of San Francisco in 2003); environmental contracts or covenants are another. The larger picture of globalization is one of shared hybridization across legal systems, that is, the mutual borrowing of many legal ideas across many countries and the creation of new hybrid legal concepts.[22] The Better Regulation initiative is itself a hybrid, combining the American tool of regulatory impact assessment (RIA) with European strands such as simplification and a standardized approach to measuring administrative costs.

Moreover, Better Regulation is not just an American idea. Considered as a form of structured reasoning to inform sound public policy and bureaucratic

20 Speech by the Taoiseach (Head of Government of Ireland), Mr Bertie Ahern, TD, at the IBEC Conference on EU – US Perspectives on Regulation, Dublin, April 19, 2004, available at http://www.betterregulation.ie/index.asp?docID=57.

21 This mixed and multi-directional pattern stands in contrast to the claim that the globalization of law is a one-way process of imperious Americanization, e.g. Ugo Mattei, "A Theory of Imperial Law: A Study on US Hegemony and the Latin Resistance" (2003) 10 Indiana J Global Legal Studies 383. Contrary to Mattei, European legal ideas are also being borrowed, including by America. And (as Mattei also recognizes) America is frequently a borrower of other countries' immigrants and ideas, so even the export of nominally "American" legal ideas is often the reception, recombination, and re-export of others' ideas.

22 On the spread of the precautionary principle and hybridization across legal systems, see Wiener, n. 15 above.

governance, as I describe below (recalling Benjamin Franklin's "prudential algebra,") it is also a European idea: one need only think of Bentham, Hume, Smith, and Mill, and of Montaigne, Descartes, Rousseau, Voltaire, and Max Weber, to name a few. America did not invent the ideas of forecasting future risks, reasoned decision-making, and rigorously assessing public policy options, even if the US government has by now constructed a highly developed system for implementing these concepts. In recent years, British, Australian, and Italian scholars have made important contributions to Better Regulation.[23] And French scholars, across the political spectrum, have championed evidence-based reasoning for government policy; they include figures as diverse as Bertrand de Jouvenel[24] and Pierre Bourdieu.[25] It is worth noting that US Supreme Court Justice Stephen Breyer, in his book on what is now called Better Regulation, held up the French *Conseil d'Etat* as a model to transplant to the US.[26] And it was a French expert, Dieudonné Mandelkern, who led the multinational group whose report proposed the EU Better Regulation initiative in 2001.[27]

23 E.g. N Gunningham and P Grabosky, *Smarter Regulation: Designing Environmental Policy* (Oxford: Oxford University Press, 1998); Christopher Hood, Henry Rothstein, and Robert Baldwin, *The Government of Risk: Understanding Risk Regulation Regimes* (Oxford: Oxford University Press, 2001); Richard Macrory, "Regulatory Justice: Sanctioning in a Post-Hampton World" (The Macrory Review of Penalties) (consultation document, March 2006); Claudio Radaelli, *What Does Regulatory Impact Assessment Mean in Europe?* AEI-Brookings Joint Center for Regulatory Studies, Related Publication 05–02, January 2005; Andrea Renda, *Impact Assessment in the EU* (Brussels: CEPS, 2006); Giandomenico Majone, *Regulating Europe* (London: Routledge, 1996).

24 Bertrand de Jouvenel, *L'Art de la Conjecture* (Monaco: Editions du Rocher, 1964). This call for rigorous thinking about the future influenced Herman Kahn and Anthony J Wiener, *The Year 2000: A Framework for Speculation* (New York: Macmillan, 1967), which helped bring scenario-based forecasting and decision-making to the US government.

25 Bourdieu is cited by Joseph Stiglitz, *Globalization and its Discontents* (London: Penguin, 2002), p x for the point that politicians need to engage in scientific debate based on facts and evidence before adopting public policies. Bourdieu was a leading French sociologist, 1930–2002, at L' Ecole des Hautes Etudes en sciences sociales (EHESS) and then at the Collège de France, a theorist of social fields and social capital, a leftist activist, and an opponent of liberal markets and globalization; he was the author of *Acts of Resistance: Against the Tyranny of the Market* (New York: New Press, 1999) and "Utopia of Endless Exploitation: The Essence of Neoliberalism" *Le Monde Diplomatique*, December 1998, at http://mondediplo.com/1998/12/08bourdieu (denouncing market liberalism promoted by economists, and favoring public interest based on collective institutions and empirical verification of theory); he was also the subject of the documentary film *La Sociologie est un Sportde Combat* (2003). Said Bourdieu: "Observation of reality puts us on our guard against the temptation to construct over-simple models" (from Bourdieu's work on the peasantry in Béarn; quoted in Douglas Johnson, "Obituary: Pierre Bourdieu" the *Guardian* January 28, 2002, at http://www.guardian.co.uk/obituaries/story/0,,640396,00.html).

26 Stephen G Breyer, *Breaking the Vicious Circle: Toward Effective Risk Regulation* (Cambridge, Mass: Harvard University Press, 1993), part III.

27 Mandelkern Group Report, n. 3 above.

Legal borrowing of the concepts and nomenclature of "better regulation" and "regulatory impact assessment" does not necessarily mean convergence in the content of policies and procedures adopted to implement those ideas. As Claudio Radaelli has emphasized, the "diffusion of a common RIA 'bottle'" does not necessarily produce the same "wine."[28]

Nonetheless, it is striking that European regulatory policy is now expressly borrowing ideas from American law, even when transatlantic relations are relatively strained. It is even more striking that chief among these borrowed ideas is impact assessment as a check on regulation, or more precisely as a way to shape regulation. The contrast to the debate over the precautionary principle in the 1990s is stark: there Europe sought to export its aggressive platform over the objections of a reluctant US government, and to position Europe (at least rhetorically) as a distinct pro-environment alternative to American pro-market regulatory policy in the post-Cold War era.[29]

What explains this rapprochement? First, it illustrates the view that legal borrowing is ubiquitous, occurring all the time in multiple directions.[30] Legal

---

28 Claudio M Radaelli, "Diffusion without Convergence: How Political Context Shapes the Adoption of Regulatory Impact Assessment," (October 2005) 12 *Journal of European Public Policy* 924–943.

29 See Wiener, n. 15 above (reporting the evolution of precaution in EU and US legal systems, and the claim that the EU had become more precautionary than the US by the 1990s). Studies in the 1980s typically found that the US used scientific and economic analysis more than did Europe, although the ultimate standards set were similar. E.g. Sheila Jasanoff, *Risk Management and Political Culture* (New York: Russell Sage, 1986); David Vogel, *National Styles of Regulatin: Environmental Policy in Great Britain and the United States* (Ithaca, NY: Cornell University Press, 1986). Whether Europe *actually* adopted a more precautionary regulatory system than the US in the 1990s is, however, open to question. Several cases support that claim, including greater European precaution on hormones in beef, genetically modified foods, climate change, and toxic chemicals. On the other hand, several cases point the other way, including greater US precaution on mad cow disease (BSE) and vCJD in blood, particulate matter emissions from power plants and diesel vehicles, youth violence, and terrorism, see Wiener, n. 15 above. But these cases are not a representative sample from which reliable generalizations can be drawn about trends in all risk regulation. We therefore studied a data set of all of the 2878 risks identified in the US and Europe over 1970–2004; we found no significant trend toward greater European precaution over the period. James K Hammitt, Jonathan B Wiener, Brendon Swedlow, Denise Hall, and Zheng Zhou, "Precautionary Regulation in Europe and the United States: A Quantitative Comparison" (October 2005) 25 *Risk Analysis* 1215–1228.

30 See Watson, n. 12 above, 22; cf Jack L Walker. "The Diffusion of Innovation Among the American States" (1969) 63 *Amercian Political Science Review* 880–9 (within the US); Anne-Marie Slaughter, *A New World Order* (Princeton: Princeton University Press, 2004) (across international networks). There are parallel literatures on the diffusion of business and technological innovations, see Everett M Rogers, *Diffusion of Innovations* (5th edn) (New York: Free Press, 2003) (first pub 1963); on the diffusion of social innovations, see e.g. Torsten Hägerstrand, "The Diffusion of Innovations" (1968) 4 *International Encyclopedia of Social Sciences* 194; A J Toynbee, (1961) 12 "A Study of History: Reconsiderations" 343 (describing as "mimesis" the process of cross-cultural diffusion); and on the diffusion of political systems, see e.g. Kurt Weyland, "Theories of Policy Diffusion," (2005) 57 *World Politics* 262–295;

borrowing has played a strong role in the evolution and diffusion of environmental regulation in the past.[31] Borrowing has helped spread such legal concepts as environmental impact assessment, pollution discharge information disclosure registries, economic incentive instruments including emissions trading, and precaution. Scholars often write about these patterns of diffusion after they have occurred. Sometimes scholars also play a role in the process of transplantation as it occurs;[32] Better Regulation is one of those cases, as experts share ideas across the Atlantic through papers, conferences, and sabbaticals. A central point here is that the current borrowing of Better Regulation tools has not been much constrained by abstract ideological or rhetorical commitments, nor by supposed national styles or mentalities of law.[33] Contrasts between allegedly US and European approaches to law and regulation are overstated,[34] as intergroup contrasts often are.[35] Instead, the ongoing Better Regulation experience suggests

Zachary Elkins and Beth Simmons, "On Waves, Clusters and Diffusion: A Conceptual Framework" (2004) *Annals of the American Academy* (AAPSS); Beth Simmons, Frank Dobbin, and Geoffrey Garrett, "The International Diffusion of Liberalism," (Fall 2006) *International Organization*.

31 See Peter H, Sand, *Transnational Environmental Law: Lessons in Global Change* (The Hague and Boston: Kluwer Law International, 1999) 241; Wiener, n. 13 above; Per-olof Busch and Helge Jörgens, "The International Sources of Policy Convergence: Explaining the Spread of Environmental Policy Innovations" (October 2005) 12 *Journal of European Public Policy* 860–884.

32 Watson argues that much borrowing is carried out by elite jurists who borrow what they happen to know or come across in their travels, communications, and research (n. 15 above, at 112–113). In a similar way, Peter Galison writes about the exchange of ideas across scientific disciplines occurring when experts participate in a "trading zone" such as by collaborating on a common research tool. Peter Galison, *Image & Logic: A Material Culture of Microphysics* (Chicago: The University of Chicago Press, 1997).

33 For the view that national styles or mentalities of law are highly influential, see Vogel, n. 29 above; K Zweigert and H Kotz, *An Introduction to Comparative Law* (3rd edn, T Weir trans) (Oxford: Oxford University Press, 1998) (styles of legal systems are seen in their history, their "predominant and characteristic mode of thought," their institutions, and their ideology, ibid 68); Pierre Legrand, "European Legal Systems are Not Converging" (1996) 45 ICLQ 52 (emphasizing distinctive national legal mentalities); Robert A Kagan, *Adversarial Legalism: The American Way of Law* (Cambridge, Mass: Harvard University Press, 2001). But see John Bell, *French Legal Cultures* (London: Cambridge University Press/Butterworths, 2001) (finding different legal cultures in the different institutions within France).

34 Some have argued that Europe now follows the Precautionary Principle whereas the US does not, e.g. David Vogel, "The Hare and the Tortoise Revisited: The New Politics of Consumer and Environmental Regulation in Europe," (2003) 33 *British Journal of Political Science* 557–580, but our research finds little evidence of such a divergence. See Wiener, n. 15 above (reviewing the debate); Hammitt *et al*, n. 29 above (surveying a large array of risks and finding little or no trend toward greater European precaution).

35 Cf Henri Tajfel, "Experiments in Intergroup Discrimination" (1970) 223 *Scientific American* 96–102 (showing that people tend to exaggerate intergroup differences); Amartya Sen, *Identity and Violence: The Illusion of Destiny* (New York: WW Norton, 2006) (showing that group characterizations are misleading because they ignore enormous variation among individuals).

that legal borrowing can readily occur across ostensibly different legal systems, as change agents of legal evolution (such as scholars or policy entrepreneurs within government) import legal concepts and as those legal concepts offer net benefits to the receiving society or its institutions.[36]

Second, economic and political globalization are increasing the opportunities for exchange of legal ideas. Trade, transnational and transgovernmental networks, epistemic communities of experts, and telecommunications (especially the internet) have made it more likely, even in just the last 15 years, that legal concepts used in one country can be researched and cross-fertilized in another country. Even if national legal styles or mentalities governed in the past, increasing exchange across legal systems is leading those old ways to evolve toward more open, cosmopolitan attitudes, and a process of "hybridization" in which mixtures of legal ideas create new hybrid modes that populate both sources.[37]

Third, "it's the economy." A major objective of Better Regulation is economic competitiveness.[38] The US adopted regulatory reform efforts in the 1970s and 1980s in part to combat inflation and recession. Europe turned to Better Regulation in the last five years to remedy its sluggish economy, which has been growing at about 2 percent per year of late, in contrast to roughly 3 to 4 percent per year in the US and nearly 10 percent per year in China. The Lisbon Strategy adopted in 2000 aims to make Europe the most productive economy in the world by 2010, while maintaining the European social model and fostering environmentally sustainable growth. The Better Regulation initiative is explicitly tied to the Lisbon Strategy. The Prodi Commission stressed good governance; the Barroso Commission stresses competitiveness.[39] Slow economic growth and high unemployment in Europe prompted the Lisbon Strategy to boost growth and jobs; the World Bank's "Doing Business" reports added pressure on

---

36 For a model of legal borrowing supplied by change agents and potentially subject to benefit-cost analyses in the receiving jurisdiction (depending on the voting rules for adoption of law in the receiving institutions), see Wiener, n. 13 above, at 1344–1362.

37 On hybridization of regulatory law, see Wiener, n. 15 above, at 254–261.

38 Better Regulation builds on the continuing program of regulatory reform of *economic* regulation – reform or deregulation of price controls, subsidies, and limits on market access in regulated industries such as aviation, trucking, and banking. Despite the predictions of public choice theory that reform of economic regulation was unlikely to occur (because such regulation benefits concentrated industry interests who would lobby to maintain it), much reform and deregulation have in fact occurred. On the US experience focusing on telecommunications, see Robert Horwitz, *The Irony of Regulatory Reform* (Oxford: Oxford University Press, 1991); on the experience in the UK and Japan, see Steven Kent Vogel, *Freer Markets, More Rules: Regulatory Reform in Advanced Industrial Countries* (Ithaca, NY: Cornell University Press, 1998).

39 In the Communication of March 16, 2005, COM(2005) 97, SEC(2005) 175, "Better Regulation for Growth and Jobs in the European Union," the first objective identified is "competitiveness," ibid 3.

European governments to attract business through legal reform.[40] The four Presidencies' letter of January 2004 began with this opening paragraph:

> The European Commission's recent review of the European economy pointed out that regulatory reform is a key element in seeking to achieve the goals of the Lisbon strategy. The IMF has made it clear that improvements in the EU regulatory framework could deliver as much as a 7 per cent increase in GDP and a 3 per cent increase in productivity in the longer term.[41]

It almost goes without saying that one key purpose of regulatory reform is to reduce costs.[42] In the 1980s the US had a Task Force on Regulatory Relief, later called the Competitiveness Council; the EU now has a Competitiveness Council of Commissioners. The UK Better Regulation Executive was earlier called the Regulatory Impact Unit, and before that the Deregulation Unit in the 1990s. Reducing the costs of regulation is driven by both internal and external pressures. Because regulation imposes costs on the domestic economy, there is internal pressure for reform. Because some regulation favors domestic producers over foreign producers, yielding international trade disputes, there is external pressure for reform. (Meanwhile, of course, regulations also may have benefits, such as health and environmental protection, which could be lost if regulations were rescinded or diluted.)

Corroborating this point is the remarkable fact that Europe has also borrowed the regulatory tool of emissions trading from the US in order to implement the Kyoto Protocol. During the 1990s, European negotiators resisted and criticized US proposals for greenhouse gas emissions trading. Now, even while criticizing the US for its reluctance to join the Kyoto Protocol, Europe has adopted the very policy proposal that the US had been urging as the flagship instrument to achieve greenhouse gas emissions reductions.[43] The basic reason is no mystery: cost-effectiveness. When Europe ratified Kyoto and finally got down to implementing its targets, it became clear that emissions trading would be

---

40 See n. 177 below.

41 See Joint Initiative on Regulatory Reform, n. 9 above, at 1, citing European Commission, "The EU Economy: 2003 Review," COM(2003) 729, and IMF, "When Leaner isn't Meaner: Measuring Benefits and Spillovers of Greater Competition in Europe" (2003).

42 Much of the debate addresses its efficacy in reducing costs. See Robert Baldwin, "Is Better Regulation Better for Business?" (2004), at http://www.lse.ac.uk/collections/pressAnd InformationOffice/newsAndEvents/archives/2004/Is_BetterRegulation_betterForBusiness.htm (criticizing inadequate regulatory relief meant to help industry); Corporate Environment Observer, "Better Regulation: For Whom?" (2004), at http://www.corporateeurope.org/observer9/ regulation.html (criticizing regulatory relief undertaken at industry's behest).

43 See Wiener, n. 13 above; Joseph Kruger and William Pizer, "Greenhouse Gas Trading in Europe" (October 2004) *Environment* magazine, 8–23.

a cost-saving, highly effective method of reducing emissions.[44] Cost drove legal borrowing of emissions trading, despite a previously strong rhetorical opposition to this very legal tool and to its source – a rhetoric that one no longer hears in Europe.

Fourth, a related but somewhat different motivation for regulatory reform is to enable the Executive (the President, Prime Minister, or other head of government) to respond to the growth of the regulatory state. The Executive is held accountable by the public for both the costs of regulation (hence pressure to reduce regulation or its costliness), and for the harms of risks not prevented (hence pressure to regulate effectively). In the US, the Administrative Procedure Act of 1946 followed the New Deal expansion of administrative regulation, and Presidential Executive Orders on regulatory review in the 1970s, 1980s, and 1990s followed the Great Society adoption of major health and environmental legislation. The President was compelled to deal with Congressional enactment of regulatory statutes (often delegating substantial power and discretion to regulatory agencies, and foisting on agencies the hard choices of reconciling competing objectives such as health versus cost); and to respond to judicial review of agency action (which is non-expert and not politically accountable, and may distort or ossify regulatory policy). Likewise in Europe, the Better Regulation initiative follows the increasing integration of EU institutions and the greater competency of the EU to regulate health and the environment after the Single European Act and the Maastricht, Amsterdam, and Nice treaties. Better Regulation is in part a move to find a common basis for regulation among the EU institutions (in particular the Commission, the Parliament, and the Council) and the member states, facilitating trade in the Single European Market and ensuring political accountability of government policy.[45] And Better Regulation responds

---

44 One current concern is that states may distort the operation of the CO_2 allowance market, partly by allocating excess allowances to shield their industries, arguably leading to price volatility in the EU Emissions Trading System (ETS) in the spring of 2006 when this allocation pattern became apparent (and the market price dropped from 30 to 9 euros in one week). On the general problem, see Jonathan B Wiener, "Global Environmental Regulation: Instrument Choice in Legal Context" (1999) 108 *Yale Law Journal* 677–800, at Part V (warning that nation-states may interfere or "meddle" with the operation of international allowance trading markets). Carol Rose observed that such "meddling" is not always "frivolous," because states may be protecting against local hotspots, see Carol Rose, "Expanding The Choices for the Global Commons: Comparing Newfangled Tradable Allowance Schemes to Old-Fashioned Common Property Regimes," 10 *Duke Environmental Law and Policy Forum* 45, 61 and n. 69 (2000). But in CO_2 markets there are no serious hotspot concerns to justify state interference.

45 This is true even though the EU does not have the same type of executive branch as the US, headed by a President popularly elected for a term of four years. The EU has a college of Commissioners, appointed as a slate for a term of five years; the President of the Commission is its leader but is also a somewhat equal colleague and is not popularly elected. And the EU as a whole has a Presidency held in rotation by each member state for six months at a time. In these respects, the EU Executive function is weaker or more decentralized than the US Presidency. At the same time, the European Commission has a monopoly on the initiation of legislation, a power that the US President lacks.

to the need to re-establish the credibility and legitimacy of effective regulation in Europe after a series of public health crises such as mad cow disease (BSE), foot and mouth disease, and scares over dioxin in animal feed, benzene in Perrier, and genetically modified foods. In short, Better Regulation recognizes the need for sound management of the regulatory state, on both sides of the Atlantic.

Is better regulation better?

Given that the EU is borrowing regulatory reform from the US, a normative evaluation of this exercise is in order. It would perhaps be typical for an American legal expert to espouse this flattering imitation, saying, yes, do as we have done, copy our system. But here I write to say: do as we have learned, not simply as we have done. Europe should not simply borrow directly from the US. Europe should innovate, not imitate. Moreover, regulatory reform in Europe must be adapted to suit European institutions. Through this process, Europe should experiment with institutional innovations that can make Better Regulation even better. Europe has an opportunity to do a better job at Better Regulation than the US has done, or, at least, to try out new approaches that can be compared to the US system. If Europe demonstrates improvements in regulatory policy, those advances can and should be borrowed back by the US. Further, the adoption of Better Regulation in Europe can itself create a common language and platform for greater transatlantic communication and collaboration about regulatory policy.[46]

A key theme of this article is that where there are problems in regulatory reform and Better Regulation, such as the debate over benefit-cost analysis (BCA), there are valuable institutional remedies. Where there are controversies regarding the limitations or biases in analytic methods, the underlying sources of these problems are often institutional, not analytic, and can often be ameliorated by institutional reorientations. Thus Europe, and in turn the US, can make Better Regulation even better by investing in intelligent institutional structures and approaches.

"Better regulation" clearly expresses a more sympathetic view of regulation than does "deregulation," or cost-cutting for greater competitiveness, or even than "regulatory reform." "Reform" could imply improvement, but also pruning and paring, whereas "better" casts a brighter light on creative approaches.[47] Critics of

---

46 One example is the series of US – High-Level Regulatory Cooperation Forum meetings now being held (the latest in January and May 2006).

47 The Irish government defines "Regulatory reform" as "changes that improve regulatory quality i.e. enhance the performance, cost-effectiveness or legal quality of regulations and related government formalities' [quoting OECD, *Regulatory Reform in Ireland* (2001), at 17]. ... Examples of changes to the process of regulation include: impact analysis/assessment techniques; the use of alternatives to traditional regulation such as market mechanisms and economic incentives and "sunsetting" arrangements whereby regulations are formally reviewed at a future date to establish whether or not they are still valid or if they could be improved, reduced or even revoked." By contrast, "Regulatory management, Better Regulation and Smarter Regulation" are the

regulatory reform fear that it really means less regulation, that is, less protection, not better. Of course, cost reduction is desirable, as long as benefits are not reduced even more. European legal systems may need cost reduction and increased flexibility, for example in labor law. But "better" regulation puts the focus on better results, outcomes, performance – not just on less regulation per *se* (nor more). The European initiative on Better Regulation has not gone into detail about what it means by "better" results, apart from emphasizing accountability and competitiveness. At a first approximation, better results should mean improving societal well-being, that is, increasing societal net benefits, through less cost or more protection or, ideally, both.[48] "Better" could in some cases imply "less," but that depends on the calculus of better outcomes, not on a pre-analytic commitment to less regulation for its own sake. And sometimes "less is more,"[49] in the sense that better results can be achieved by more streamlined and lower-cost approaches, but again this is "less" as a route to "better" rather than less for its own sake. (Meanwhile, one can also question whether a much-touted program of Better Regulation is really making a difference, or whether it is just rhetoric and symbolic politics. Answering this question requires assessing the quality of impact assessments, the staff and resources being brought to bear, the structures and rules being adopted, and the actual influence on regulatory decisions. I discuss these issues further in the sections on Impact Assessment and Oversight below.)

The Better Regulation initiative could indeed yield better results. The use of impact assessment has the potential to improve regulatory policies and outcomes, increasing net benefits. Administrative cost reduction and simplification can reduce regulatory burdens and untangle needless bureaucratic rigidity. And the Better Regulation initiative, especially the use of IA, is moderating the earlier fervor for the precautionary principle;[50] indeed the European Commission has

---

terms which are increasingly being used to convey the concept of an ongoing commitment to improving the processes of policy formulation, legislative drafting and enhancing the overall effectiveness and coherence of regulation. The idea of "Better Regulation" also helps to draw an important distinction between the wide reform agenda and deregulation. It is accepted that in some cases consumer, investor and the broader public interest may be better served by introducing new regulation and that in other cases it may be better served by removing regulation. No initial assumption is being made about either the existing quality or quantity of regulation or the need to deregulate. Instead, it is suggested that the goal of Better Regulation will not be achieved by simply seeking to minimise the volume of regulation but rather by using as simple and straightforward measures as possible to achieve policy objectives." See http://www.betterregulation.ie/index.asp?locID=20&docID=-1.

48 This is plainly a first approximation. There is no space here to compare alternative conceptions of welfare, efficiency, Bentham, Kaldor-Hicks, Pareto, fairness, and other formulations. Suffice to say here that competitiveness is only one element of the overall social well-being that "better" should entail; and that the European stewards of Better Regulation should develop a more thorough explanation of what they mean by "better." See below on "warm analysis."

49 See UK Better Regulation Task Force report, *Regulation: Less is More* (March 2005).

50 See Wiener, n. 15 above, at 220–225; Lofstedt, n. 14 above.

redefined the precautionary principle as requiring benefit–cost analysis.[51] Precaution can be worth-while to prevent uncertain and potentially irreversible risks, but it can also be excessive, incurring the costs of false positives, innovation foregone, and new countervailing risks (themselves uncertain and potentially irreversible).[52] Yet if the Better Regulation initiative focuses exclusively on competitiveness, that is, on reducing costs to industry, without considering social and environmental benefits, it risks yielding less regulation instead of better results. Moreover, increasing net benefits expands the social surplus that can be distributed to engage allies. To succeed and endure, the Better Regulation initiative needs to increase the net benefits of regulation.

In my experience, both in government and in academia, there is a huge swath of interests who favor less regulation regardless of its benefits, and a huge swath who favor more regulation regardless of its costs. In both cases, the alternative to analysis is sanctimony-supposing one knows the right answer without analyzing the consequences. In between these two potent and vocal campaigns is a narrow slice of those who genuinely want to compare the consequences (benefits and costs) of regulatory choices. It is very difficult for governments to maintain a steady commitment to comparing benefits and costs when great political pressure is brought to bear from one swath or the other.

In that light, I assess the Better Regulation initiative in terms of the major reform strategies it invokes, and their counterparts in US law. I address Impact Assessment (including both benefit-cost analysis (BCA) and risk assessment as an input to BCA), the problem of addressing multiple risks in concert, administrative costs, simplification, oversight, and *ex post* evaluation. For each of these issues, I offer suggestions on how to make Better Regulation even better, focusing on institutional innovations.

Impact assessment

US experience

In the United States, every President since the 1970s has formally required some form of regulatory impact assessment. President Nixon ordered a Quality of Life review, and President Ford ordered an inflationary impact review. President Carter issued Executive Order (EO) 12044 (March 23, 1978), requiring economic analysis of regulations, and creating the Regulatory Analysis Review Group to

---

51 See European Commission, Communication from the Commission on the Precautionary Principle, COM(2000) 1, Brussels, February 2, 2000 (available at http://europa.eu.int/comm/dgs/health_consumer/library/pub/pub07_en.pdf) (providing that precautionary regulation must satisfy proportionality and must be based on an analysis of benefits and costs).

52 See Jonathan B Wiener, "Precaution in a Multirisk World" in Dennis J Paustenbach (ed), *Human and Ecological Risk Assessment: Theory and Practice* (New York: John Wiley, 2002) 1509–1531.

provide interagency oversight. In 1980, through the Paperwork Reduction Act,[53] the US Congress created the Office of Information and Regulatory Affairs within the Office of Management and Budget (OMB/OIRA). On February 17, 1981, less than a month after taking office, President Reagan signed EO 12291,[54] requiring regulations to yield benefits that "outweigh" their costs, with a goal of maximizing net benefits, and directed OMB/OIRA to serve as the White House office with the authority to oversee regulatory impact analyses (RIAs).

On September 30, 1993, President Clinton issued EO 12866,[55] which confirmed the bipartisan commitment to RIA using benefit-cost analysis (BCA). EO 12866 replaced the word "outweigh" with "justify" (a less quantitative term, embracing a broader public judgment about the policy's merits). Section 1 of EO 12866 maintained the requirement to "maximize net benefits," and in section 6 it expressly required full analysis of the range of types of costs and benefits, including economic, social, and environmental. EO 12866 also added emphasis on qualitative and distributional impacts, added an instruction to evaluate the countervailing health and environmental risks induced by regulation of a target risk (risk-risk tradeoffs), and added new procedures for transparency (including reporting by OIRA of outside contacts, inclusion of agency representatives at OIRA meetings held to discuss the agency's policies, and oversight of OIRA by a committee chaired by the Vice President).

Since the year 2001, the administration of current President Bush has retained the Clinton EO, reconfirming the bipartisan character of regulatory review. The Bush administration OIRA has issued more "return" letters (saying "no" to deficient regulations) than did the Clinton administration OIRA, but at the same time the Bush OIRA has also innovated the new device of "prompt letters" (using BCA to say "yes" to desirable regulations and urging agencies to adopt them; examples include requiring trans-fat content labels on food to reduce heart disease, and installing automatic electronic defibrillators in the workplace). OIRA has also issued new RIA Guidelines in Circular A-4,[56] calling for more use of cost-effectiveness analysis (C–EA), lower discount rates (3 percent as well as 7 percent, and potentially even lower than 3 percent for long–term intergenerational effects), risk-risk tradeoff analysis, and probabilistic scenarios of impacts exceeding $1 billion. Further, OIRA has issued guidelines as required by the

---

53 Codified at 44 USC 3501 ff. Despite the name of this law, the US approach (mandated by the series of Presidential EOs) focuses on BCA – full assessment of both benefits and costs – rather than on trying to reduce paperwork costs (administrative costs) alone.

54 46 Fed Reg 13193 (published February 19, 1981).

55 Executive Order 12866, "Regulatory Planning and Review," 58 Fed Reg 51735 (October 4, 1993), available at http://www.whitehouse.gov/omb/inforeg/eo12866.pdf. As a senior staff person in the President's Council of Economic Advisers (CEA) at the time, I assisted in the drafting of EO 12866.

56 OMB/OIRA, Circular A–4, "Regulatory Analysis," September 17, 2003, available at http://www.whitehouse.gov/omb/circulars/a004/a-4.pdf.

Information Quality Act, a bulletin on peer review, and a proposed Bulletin on Risk Assessment. President Bush transferred oversight of OIRA from the office of the Vice President to the office of the White House Chief of Staff.[57] And OIRA now posts all significant documents on its website, http://www. whitehouse.gov/omb/inforeg/regpol.html.

In short, there is a bipartisan consensus among US Presidents of both political parties over the last four decades to require agencies to produce RIAs and to use BCA for risk management. One prominent author has heralded the era of the "cost-benefit state."[58] Another says that monetized BCA has become "the norm for government policy."[59] It should also be noted that BCA in the US addresses all types of costs and benefits – including economic, social, and environmental – and thus is comparable to the "Integrated Impact Assessment" conducted in the EU.[60]

But BCA is still not applied to all regulatory policies in the US Federal agencies in the US appear to quantify some benefits or costs of regulatory proposals most of the time, but to quantify and monetize both benefits and costs only about half the time.[61] One reason for this incomplete use of BCA may be that federal statutes vary in whether they require, permit, or prohibit reliance on BCA in agency regulatory decision-making. Congress often requires agencies to use BCA, as in the Consumer Product Safety Act (CPSA 1972) (consumer products), Federal Insecticide, Fungicide and Rodenticide Act (FIFRA, 1975) (pesticides), Toxics Substances Control Act (TSCA, section 6 (1977) (toxic substances), and Unfunded Mandates Reform Act (UMRA, 1995) ("unfunded mandates" on states, businesses). Sometimes Congress permits BCA without requiring its use in decision-making, for example, in the Occupational Safety and Health Act (OSH Act 3(8), 1972) (as to workplace hazards other than toxics), Clean Water Act (CWA, section 304, 1972) (water pollution technology standards), and Safe Drinking Water Act (SDWA, 1996 amendments) (drinking water contaminants). But some Congressional statutes prohibit agencies' use of BCA in regulation, such as the Clean Air Act (CAA, section 109, 1970) (national

---

57   EO 13258 (2002), at http://www.whitehouse.gov/omb/inforeg/eo13258.pdf. This shift in roles was apparently requested by Vice President Cheney, who preferred to focus on other issues. In some administrations, there can be a difference of perspectives and even competition between the President and Vice President, so the transfer of oversight from the Vice President to the White House Chief of Staff may bring regulatory review more closely in line with the President's policy agenda. This would continue a trend toward Presidential direction of regulatory matters that was already under way in the earlier Carter, Reagan, Bush, and Clinton administrations, see Elena Kagan, "Presidential Administration," (2001) 114 *Harvard Law Review* 2246.

58   Cass R Sunstein, *The Cost-Benefit State: The Future of Regulatory Protection* (Chicago: American Bar Association, 2002).

59   W Kip Viscusi, "Monetizing the Benefits of Risk and Environmental Regulation" (2006) 33 *Fordham Urban Law Journal* 1033–1044.

60   IA Guidelines 2006, Annex 13, make clear that BCA in the EU also includes economic, environmental, and social impacts.

61   Hahn and Muething, (2003) 55 *Administrative Law Review* 608–642.

ambient air quality standards), OSH Act section 6(b)(5) (1972) (workplace toxics), Endangered Species Act (ESA, section 7, 1973) (endangered species), Resource Conservation and Recovery Act (RCRA, section 3004m, 1984) (hazardous waste treatment standards), and Comprehensive Environmental Response, Compensation and Liability Act (CERCLA, section 121, 1986) (hazardous waste cleanup standards). The Presidential EOs requiring BCA do not countermand a Congressional prohibition on using BCA to set standards, but they can require the agency to conduct a BCA as an informative analytic matter even if the agency is prohibited by the statute from relying on the BCA in setting a standard. Thus, the incomplete application of BCA suggests that OMB/OIRA has limited resources to supervise agency conduct, that some impacts are difficult to quantify or monetize, and that spreading the culture of impact assessment across the agencies is still a work in progress.

Moreover, BCA is not required for several other aspects of US regulation. It is not required for Congressional legislation, although the Unfunded Mandates Reform Act (UMRA, 1995) encourages it. Nor is it required for international treaties involving regulatory commitments.[62] Nor is BCA adequately employed in evaluating federal spending decisions, including both new spending and cutbacks,[63] nor in evaluating public works such as water resource projects (despite the history of BCA being developed to evaluate dams since the 1930s),[64] nor in evaluating national forest logging (despite section 6(k) of the 1976 National Forest Management Act (NFMA), requiring economic suitability for

---

62 Agency regulations adopted pursuant to an international treaty would presumably be subject to EO 12866, but by the time such a regulation reaches OIRA the international treaty has already been negotiated and ratified and the regulation is therefore difficult to revise. To address this problem, the US State Department has recently proposed requiring agencies to consult with OMB/OIRA earlier, on the regulatory impacts of pending new international agreements. 71 Fed Reg 28831 (May 18, 2006). The State Department already requires agencies to consult with OMB before making new budgetary commitments in international agreements. See 22 CFR s 181.4(e).

63 See Robert W Hahn, "The Cost-Benefit of Budget Cutting," AEI-Brookings Policy Matters 06–12 (May 2006).

64 The federal Reclamation Act of 1902 required economic analysis of projects, and the federal Flood Control Act of 1936 required projects to demonstrate that "the benefits to whomsoever they may accrue are in excess of the estimated costs," 33 USC s 701a. Although federal water agencies such as the Bureau of Reclamation, US Department of the Interior, evaluate some project benefits and costs, they typically have not conducted a full BCA including environmental impacts. See Alan V Kneese, "Whatever Happened to Benefit-Cost Analysis?" (2000) 116 Water Resources Updates 58–61, at http://www.ucowr.siu.edu/updates/116/index.html. Economists have long argued for correcting this omission and thereby protecting the environment by making *greater* use of BCA, including environmental impacts. See Maynard M Hufschmidt, "Benefit-Cost Analysis: 1933–1985" (2000) 116 Water Resources Update 42–49, at http://www.ucowr.siu.edu/updates/116/index.html (noting studies in 1950, 1958, and 1962 espousing this view, and changes proposed by the Carter administration to expand BCA to ensure environmental protection in water projects). Economist and BCA advocate Kip Viscusi wrote an early paper for the proenvironment Ralph Nader group making this point: federal

timber cutting). Nor is BCA required for major federal actions (such as projects or policy decisions) under the environmental impact statement (EIS) provision of the National Environmental Policy Act (NEPA), despite an early effort to incorporate BCA into the EIS as a way to strengthen environmental protection.[65] Nor is BCA adequately employed in evaluating trade measures, despite the requirement in Section 201 of the Trade Act of 1974 that trade safeguards must "provide greater economic and social benefits than costs."[66] Nor is BCA yet employed to evaluate counter terrorism operations (despite the early history of BCA and systems analysis being brought to the US military by Defense Secretary Robert McNamara's "Whiz Kids" in the 1960s), and it is only beginning to be applied (with difficulty) to the new wave of homeland security regulations.[67]

water agencies" BCA was unduly narrow and should be expanded to account for environmental impacts. See Richard L Berkman and W Kip Viscusi, *Damming The West: Ralph Nader's Study Group Report on the Bureau of Reclamation* (New York: Grossman Publishers, 1973). Viscusi continues to advocate BCA for both public works projects and regulations, see W Kip Viscusi, "Monetizing the Benefits of Risk and Environmental Regulation," AEI-Brookings Joint Center Working Paper 06–09 (April 2006).

65 See Judge Skelley Wright's opinion in *Calvert Cliffs Coordinating Committee v AEC*, 449 F 2d 1109 (DC Cir 1971) (finding that the EIS provision in NEPA section 102(2)(C) requires BCA of federal projects, in order to take into account their previously neglected environmental costs), *cert denied*, 404 US 942 (1972). The US Supreme Court subsequently held that NEPA requires only a "purely procedural" exercise of informed decision-making – a so-called "stop and think" exercise – with no substantive criteria for such decisions. See *Stryker's Bay Neighborhood Council Inc v Karlen*, 444 US 223 (1980). NEPA has been held by the courts not to apply to international trade agreements like NAFTA, see *Public Citizen v United States Trade Representative*, 5 F 3d 549 (DC Cir 1993), nor to federal spending laws, *Andrus v Sierra Club*, 442 US 347 (1979). In addition, various exemptions to NEPA have been adopted, including statutory exemptions for EPA actions under the Clean Air Act, 15 USC s 793(c)(1), and many actions under the Clean Water Act, 33 USC s 1371(c)(1); and judicial exemptions for EPA actions under environmental laws deemed to require the "functional equivalent" of the EIS process. See Jonathan M Cosco, "NEPA for the Gander: NEPA's Application to Critical Habitat Designations and Other "Benevolent" Federal Action" (1998) 8 *Duke Environmental Law and Policy Forum* 345.

66 19 USC 2251 (a).

67 See Jessica Stern and Jonathan B Wiener, "Precaution Against Terrorism" (2006) 9 *Journal of Risk Research* 393–447 and also in Paul Bracken, Ian Bremmer, and David Gordon (eds), *Managing Strategic Surprise* (Cambridge: Cambridge University Press, forthcoming 2007). Analysis of counter terrorism policies (both domestic homeland security and external intelligence and military operations) is particularly urgent, because effective counter-terrorism is essential, but counterproductive policies can do serious damage to national security as well as to human life. See ibid (arguing that little serious *ex ante* analysis was done of the Iraq invasion, with the result that serious countervailing risks were neglected, including collateral civilian deaths, blowback, bog-down, distraction, and theft; and advocating subjecting counter terrorism policies to a joint OIRA-NSC oversight process using analytic tools of BCA and risk-risk tradeoff analysis); Linda Bilmes and Joseph E Stiglitz, "The Economic Costs of the Iraq War" (2006) National Bureau of Economic Research (NBER) Working Paper 12054, available at www.z.gsb.columbia.edu/faculty/jstiglitz/newworks.cfm (arguing that the costs of the Iraq War were greatly underestimated *ex ante*, and calling for BCA of future such interventions).

European experience

In the European Union, Impact Assessment of new regulations is now required in almost all countries and at the EU level, and BCA is increasingly employed. There is a long history of the use of environmental impact assessment used to inform decision-makers (as under NEPA in the US), with some versions requiring actual financial compensation for the environmental harms of projects,[68] and thus a kind of BCA imposed on projects through tort law or the law of expropriation (takings) of neighbors' property.

BCA applied to modern regulatory decisions is also increasingly required in Europe. Most generally, the Proportionality Principle, a general principle of European law,[69] has been held to imply some version of BCA. In the *Pfizer* case, the court observed (paras 410–411):

> The Court considers that a cost/benefit analysis is a particular expression of the principle of proportionality in cases involving risk management...the principle of proportionality, which is one of the general principles of Community law, requires that measures adopted by Community institutions should not exceed the limits of what is appropriate and necessary in order to attain the legitimate objectives pursued by the legislation in question, and where there is a choice between several appropriate measures, recourse must be had to the least onerous, and the disadvantages caused must not be disproportionate to the aims pursued...[70]

The Communication on the Precautionary Principle of February 2000 requires precautionary regulations to be *proportional* to the chosen level of protection, *non-discriminatory* in their application, *consistent* with similar measures already taken, *based on an examination of the potential benefits and costs* of

---

See generally Barbara Tuchman, *The March of Folly* (New York: Knopf, 1984) (on the counterproductive results of military campaigns undertaken without adequate analysis of likely outcomes). Yet these policies are difficult to analyze because information may be classified, because terrorists are strategic agents who respond to preventive measures hence requiring dynamic game theory models, and because some consequences may be hard to quantify (e.g. loss of privacy and freedom).

68 See Jane Holder, *Environmental Assessment: The Regulation of Decision Making* (Oxford: Oxford University Press, 2005) (focusing on the history in the UK), including her discussion of the compensation requirement under the writ *ad quod damnum* in the thirteenth century.

69 Nicholas Emiliou, *The Principle of Proportionality in European Law: A Comparative Study* (London: Kluwer Law International, 1996).

70 Case T-13/99, *Pfizer Animal Health SA v Council*, 2002 WL 31337 (European Court of First Instance, September 11, 2002). But the court remarked in para 456: "The Court observes that the importance of the objective pursued by the contested regulation, i.e. the protection of human health, may justify adverse consequences, and even substantial adverse consequences, for certain traders...The protection of public health, which the contested regulation is intended to guarantee, must take precedence over economic considerations."

action or lack of action (including, where appropriate and feasible, an economic cost/benefit analysis), *subject to review* in the light of new scientific data, and *capable of assigning responsibility for producing the scientific evidence* necessary for a more comprehensive risk assessment. In effect, the Communication reclaims the PP as part of decision analysis.[71]

Adopted late in 2000, the Nice Treaty of the EU (building on the Amsterdam and Maastricht treaties) provides in Art 174(3) that European environmental policy must be based on an assessment of "the potential benefits and costs of action or lack of action." Unlike in the US, it does not appear that any European Union laws prohibit the use of BCA, although such prohibitions may exist in member states' laws.

The new EU "Better Regulation" initiative has launched Impact Assessment Guidelines (2002, revised 2005, updated 2006) requiring a form of BCA.[72] The IA Guidelines require identification of the problem, consideration of alternative policy options (including no action), and assessment of the "positive and negative" economic, social, and environmental impacts (including direct and indirect impacts) of each policy option.[73] The Guidelines use the terminology of "positive and negative impacts" to include both a fully quantified and monetized BCA, and a partially quantified/partially qualitative "multi-criteria analysis," as well as a cost-effectiveness analysis where relevant.[74] This is similar to the provisions of US EO 12866 and of OMB Circular A-4, calling for an RIA including both quantitative and qualitative evaluation of all benefits and costs and giving guidance on BCA and C-EA. (The US uses the term BCA to refer to both the

---

71 Several scholars have developed approaches to melding the PP with consequentialist decision analysis. See e.g. Ralph L Keeney and Detlof von Winterfeldt, "Appraising the Precautionary Principle–A Decision Analysis Perspective" (2001) 4 *Journal of Risk Research* 191; John D Graham, "Decision-Analytic Refinements of the Precautionary Principle" (2001) 4 *Journal of Risk Research* 127; Olivier Godard, Claude Henry, Patrick Lagadec, and Erwann Michel-Kerian, *Traitédes Nouveaux Risques* (Paris: Gallimard, 2002); Richard B Stewart, "Environmental Regulatory Decisionmaking under Uncertainty" (2002) 20 *Research in Law and Economics* 71–152; Michael Dekay, Mitchell Small, Paul Fischbeck, Scott Farrow, Alison Cullen, J B Kadane, Lester Lave, Granger Morgan, and K Takemura, "Risk-Based Decision Analysis in Support of Precautionary Policies" (2002) 5 *Journal of Risk Research* 391; Scott Farrow, "Using Risk-Assessment, Benefit-Cost Analysis, and Real Options to Implement a Precautionary Principle" (2004) 24 *Risk Analysis* 727; Christian Gollier and Nicolas Treich, "Decision Making under Uncertainty: The Economics of the Precautionary Principle" (2003) 27 *Journal of Risk and Uncertainty* 77; Pauline Barrieu and Bernard Sinclair-Dégagné, "On Precautionary Policies" (forthcoming 2006) Management Science.
72 See IA Guidelines 2005 and 2006, nn. 6–7 above. For discussion, see Andrea Renda, *Impact Assessment in the EU* (Brussels: Center for European Policy Studies, 2006); Lucas Bergkamp, *European Community Law for the New Economy* (Antwerp: Intersentia, 2004), 169. By "a form of BCA," I mean some analysis of benefits and costs, i.e. of positive and negative impacts, and not a particular version that e.g. requires or eschews quantified monetized values.
73 IA Guidelines 2006, Part III, at 16–46.
74 See IA Guidelines 2006 at 13 and at 39 and n. 45, and Annex 13, "Methods on Comparing Impacts."

fully quantified and monetized BCA, and the partially quantified/partially qualitative analysis of benefits and costs, described in the EU Guidelines.) Further, like EO 12866, the EU Guidelines provide that "A measure is considered justified where net benefits can be expected from the intervention."[75]

Of the 70 Extended IAs conducted by the European Commission so far (2003–2005), fewer than 40 percent quantify and monetize either benefits or costs, and only 17 percent compared net benefits.[76] These figures are lower than the comparable statistics for the US (cited above), but the EU system has been in operation for a much shorter period of time. Also, in principle, the EU RIA system applies to all legislation, at least to directives and regulations initiated by the European Commission, and to amendments adopted by the European Parliament. The Commission's monopoly on initiating legislation means that requiring IA of European Commission proposals is in a sense more akin to requiring IA of Congressional bills in the US – a power that US Presidents and OMB/OIRA do not have.

Several EU member states have adopted strong Better Regulation programs with RIA procedures.[77] For example:

- The UK has conducted several reviews of its risk regulation system,[78] created the Better Regulation Executive[79] in the Cabinet Office, and the external advisory Better Regulation Commission. The government announced a Better Regulation Action Plan,[80] and developed comprehensive guidelines on risk management which instruct government bodies to seek transparency and proportionality through the use of risk assessment, analysis of market failures, valuation (of monetary and non-monetary impacts, including attention to public concerns), impact assessment including benefit-cost analysis of alternative policy options, and monitoring of policy implementation.[81]

---

75 See IA Guidelines 2006, Annex 13.1.

76 Andrea Renda, *Impact Assessment in the EU*, n. 72 above, at 63.

77 For more on RIAs in a variety of countries, see OECD, *RIA Inventory* (Paris: OECD, 2003).

78 These include the Hampton review on Reducing Administrative Burdens (2005) at http://www. hm-treasury.gov.uk/budget/budget_05/press_notices/bud_bud05_presshampton.cfm, the Macrory review on Regulatory Penalties (interim consultation document, May 2006) at http://www. cabinetoffice.gov.uk/regulation/reviewing_regulation/penalties/index.asp, and the Davidson review on implementation of EU legislation (forthcoming 2006), as well as the Better Regulation Task Force (now Commission) report on *Regulation – Less is More* (March 2005) at http://www. brc.gov.uk/publications/lessismoreentry.asp. For further details and links to each document see http://www.cabinetoffice.gov.uk/regulation/.

79 See http://www.cabinetoffice.gov.uk/regulation/.

80 See http://www.hm-treasury.gov.uk./newsroom_and_speeches/press/2005/press_ 50_05.cfm.

81 See HM Treasury, *The Green Book* (2003); HM Treasury, "*Managing Risks to the Public: Appraisal Guidance*" (June 2005). For an overview of these efforts, see UK House of Lords, Economic Affairs Committee, *Government Policy on the Management of Risk* (June 2006), at http://www.publications.parliament.uk/pa/ld200506/ldselect/ldeconaf/183/183i.pdf.

- Ireland has created a regulatory reform office in the Department of the Taoiseach, and a Statutory Law Revision and Consolidation Unit in the Office of the Attorney General.[82] Ireland began these efforts through a Coordinating Group of Secretaries in 1995, which issued a report on Delivering Better Government in 1996.[83] These efforts were organized under the Strategic Management Initiative and its Working Group on Regulatory Reform. The government issued a report on Reducing Red Tape in 1999,[84] and a report on Regulating Better in 2004,[85] committing to rigorous use of Regulatory Impact Analysis. In June 2005 it decided to require RIA across all departments, and in October 2005 the government issued RIA Guidelines.[86]
- The Netherlands has adopted a strong program of Administrative Cost reduction, including pioneering the Standard Cost Model which is now being borrowed by many other countries,[87] and setting a goal of 25 percent reduction of administrative burden.[88] But it remains to be seen whether the Netherlands will undertake a broader program of Better Regulation using Impact Assessment and BCA.
- France, although it did not begin to adopt Better Regulation measures until more recently, has now created a Better Regulation office at the Ministry of Finance, Economy and Industry (transferring functions there from the *Réforme de l'Etat* previously in the Prime Minister's office, in order to combine regulatory oversight with budgetary oversight). France has also launched a Better Regulation program in the *Conseil d'Etat*. And France has proposed a new law requiring impact assessment of all new legislation.
- Germany, under its new coalition government headed by Chancellor Angela Merkel, has made better regulation a high priority. Under the rubric "Scaling Back Bureaucracy," the Merkel government has appointed a minister to lead the program, adopted the Standard Cost Model as well as RIA Guidelines, and begun an assessment of administrative burdens with a view to adopting a political goal to reduce such burdens in the near future.

---

82 See http://www.betterregulation.ie/.

83 Available at http://www.betterregulation.ie/attached_files/upload/static/1151.pdf.

84 Available at http://www.betterregulation.ie/index.asp?docID=37.

85 Department of the Taoiseach, *Regulating Better: A Government White Paper Setting out Six Principles of Better Regulation* (January 2004), available at http://www.betterregulation.ie/upload/Regulating_Better_hrml/index.html.

86 See RIA Guidelines: "How to Conduct a Regulatory Impact Analysis," and "Regulatory Impact Analysis: Lessons from the Pilot Exercise," both available at http://www.betterregulation.ie/eng/index.asp?docID=80.

87 The Standard Cost Model Network, a consortium of countries using this approach, is at www.administrative-burdens.com.

88 See Bert Doorn and Christiaan Prins, "A Dutch Treat: The Netherlands Presidency and Regulatory Reform," *Challenge Europe*, Issue 13 – What Future for Europe's Economic and Social Model? (January 30, 2005), at http://www.theepc.be/en/ce.asp?TYP=CE&LV=177&see=y&t=42&PG=CE/EN/detail&l=2&AI=417.

In its March 16, 2005 Communication on Better Regulation, the European Commission attached a chart summarizing progress on Better Regulation and Impact Assessment (See below, p 89).[89] Events are moving quickly in this field, so this chart may already be out of date. Still, the chart is noteworthy for its very clear effort to shame laggard countries into adopting Impact Assessment procedures. Denmark, Poland, and the UK scored the highest (10 points out of a possible 11); France, Portugal, and Cyprus scored zero. But as noted above, already France has taken important actions since this chart was published.

Of course, even where countries have adopted IA systems, they may be implementing such reviews in different ways. For example, Radaelli finds that IA is aimed at improving substantive policy consequences in the US, at managing the bureaucracy in the UK, at transparency in the Netherlands, and at formal adherence to rules in countries like France and Germany.[90] But IA arguably serves all of these objectives in each of these countries; certainly it does in the US. And IA is also an evolving program, so that the substantive consequentialism of US regulatory review and the transparency of Dutch administrative cost measurement may well be adopted in other countries over time.

A brief evaluation

It is by now fairly clear that the choice to use IA and BCA is not a partisan matter. IA is a tool for better decision-making employed on both the center-left and the center-right, and it is a mechanism of interbranch relations – to enable Presidential management of the regulatory state (both in the US and in the European Union). It has become the mainstream consensus approach, albeit with critics on each flank. In the United States, IA using economic analysis such as BCA has been espoused by a wide array of actors across the political spectrum, including not only Republican Presidents Nixon, Ford, Reagan, and both Bushes, but also Democratic Presidents Carter and Clinton, Judge Skelley Wright (in the *Calvert Cliffs* case cited above), US Supreme Court Justice Stephen Breyer[91] (appointed to the Court by President Clinton), and law professors Cass Sunstein[92]

---

89 Adapted from European Commission, Communication from the Commission to the Council and the European Parliament, "Better Regulation for Growth and Jobs in the European Union," COM(2005) 97, SEC(2005) 175, March 16, 2005, n. 4 above, at 17 (footnote omitted). The footnote in the table (omitted here) references the chart to "Commission Staff Working Paper: Report on the Implementation of the European Charter for Small Enterprises in the Member States of the European Union – SEC(2005) 167, 8.2.2005, p 36," but the chart addresses Impact Assessment procedures in general and only the last two columns address impacts on small businesses.

90 See Radaelli, n. 28 above.

91 Breyer, n. 26 above.

92 Cass R Sunstein, *Risk and Reason* (New York: Cambridge University Press, 2002); Sunstein, n. 58 above. Sunstein is also the author of *Radicals in Robes: Why Extreme Right-Wing Courts are Wrong for America* (New York: Basic Books, 2005).

and Buzz Thompson,[93] among many others, as well as many economists of diverse political persuasions,[94] including Alan Blinder[95] and Joseph Stiglitz.[96] In Europe, Better Regulation through IA is espoused by a chorus of political leaders across the political spectrum, including Tony Blair, Gordon Brown, Bertie Ahern, Romano Prodi, Jose Manuel Barroso, Gunther Verheugen, and others; and it has been adopted by both the European Commission and the EU member states.

At the same time, IA of regulations, especially IA using BCA, has been criticized as anti-environmental, chiefly on the grounds that it tends to delay regulations and to overstate costs and understate health and environmental benefits (such as human life, ecological vitality, and aesthetics) which are difficult to measure.[97] Similarly, environmental IA under NEPA has been criticized – notably by industry and the military – for delaying new projects. (As I point out below, another distinct problem with BCA occurs when it focuses narrowly on a target risk and on industry compliance costs, to the neglect of countervailing risks and ancillary benefits.)

Advocates of BCA answer that if BCA is done well, it will measure all important impacts. They are optimistic about the ability of economic methods to

---

93 Barton Thompson, Jr, "People or Prairie Chickens: The Uncertain Search for Optimal Biodiversity," (1999) 51 *Stanford Law Review* 1127.

94 E.g. Kenneth Arrow, Maureen Cropper, George Eads, Robert Hahn, Lester Lave, Roger Noll, Paul Portney, Milt Russell, Richard Schmalensee, Kerry Smith, and Robert Stavins, "Is There a Role for Benefit-Cost Analysis in Environmental, Health, and Safety Regulation?," (1996) 272 *Science* 221–222 (advocating the use of BCA as a tool to help inform regulatory policy decisions).

95 See Alan Blinder, *Hard Heads, Soft Hearts: Tough-Minded Economics for a Just Society* (Reading, Mass: Addison-Wesley, 1988). Prof Blinder was a member of the Council of Economic Advisers (CEA) appointed by President Clinton.

96 Joseph Stiglitz was first a member and later Chair of CEA under President Clinton, and winner of the Nobel Prize. While a critic of *laissez-faire* globalization (see Stiglitz, n. 25 above), Prof Stiglitz has espoused BCA with improvements to reflect advances in economic understanding, as reflected in his support and role in the drafting of President Clinton's EO 12866, and in his scholarship such as Joseph E Stiglitz, *Economics of the Public Sector* (3rd edn) (New York: WW Norton, 2000); Joseph E Stiglitz, "The Rate of Discount for Cost-Benefit Analysis and the Theory of the Second Best," in R Lind (ed), *Discounting for Time and Risk in Energy Policy* (Washington, DC: RFF Press, 1982) 151–204. And he has recently written: "The most important things in life – like life itself – are priceless. But that does not mean that issues involving the preservation of life (or a way of life), like defense, should not be subjected to cool, hard economic analysis." Joseph E Stiglitz, "Analysis on True Cost-Benefit of Iraq "Project" Virtually Absent," Daily Yomiuri Online, March 4, 2006, at http://www.yomiuri.co.jp/dy/columns/syndicate/20060313dy02.htm. See also Bilmes and Stiglitz, n. 66 above (advocating BCA).

97 See David Driesen, "Is Cost-Benefit Analysis Neutral?" (2006) 77 *University of Colorado Law Review* 335; Frank Ackerman, Lisa Heinzerling, and Rachel Massey, "Applying Cost-Benefit to Past Decisions: Was Environmental Protection ever a Good Idea?" (2005) 57 *Administrative Law Review* 155. Other critiques attack the ethics of monetizing health and environmental benefits, see Frank Ackerman and Lisa Heinzerling, *Priceless: Knowing the Price of Everything and the Value of Nothing* (New York: The New Press 2004). Rebuttals to these critiques include Viscusi, n. 59 above; and Robert W Hahn, In *Defense of the Economic Analysis of Regulation* (Washington, DC: American Enterprise Institute Press, 2005).

Table 4.1 Overview of measures in the area of Better Regulation and impact assessment*

	Better regulation programme policy	Specific RIA policy	Obligatory RIA	Alternative instruments considered	Guidelines on RIA	Coordinating body for RIA	Consultation part of RIA	Formal consultation procedures	Direct stakeholder consultation	Tests of impact on small enterprises	Exemptions for SMEs	Total Y + (Y)
Belgium	(Y)	N.A.	(Y)	N.A.	(Y)	(Y)	N	(Y)	(Y)	(Y)	N	7
Czech Republic	Y	N.A.	N	Y	N.A.	N.A.	N.A.	N.A.	N.A.	(Y)	N	3
Denmark	Y	Y	Y	Y	Y	Y	Y	Y	Y	Y	N	10
Germany	Y	N.A.	N.A.	N.A.	Y	Y	N.A.	Y	N.A.	N.A.	N.A.	5
Estonia	N	N	Y	Y	Y	N.A.	N.A.	N	N	N	Y	4
Greece	(Y)	(Y)	N	N	(Y)	(Y)	Y	N	N	N	N.A.	3
Spain	Y	(Y)	Y	N.A.	N.A.	N	N.A.	N	N	N	N.A.	6
France	N.A.	N.A.	N	N.A.	N.A.	N	N.A.	N.A.	N	N.A.	N	0
Ireland	Y	N	N	(Y)	(Y)	(Y)	(Y)	(Y)	N	(Y)	N	5
Italy	(Y)	Y	N	(Y)	Y	Y	(Y)	N	Y	N	N	8
Cyprus	N	N	N	N	N	N	N	N	N	Y	N	0
Latvia	Y	Y	Y	Y	Y	Y	Y	Y	N	N.A.	N.A.	9
Lithuania	N.A.	N.A.	Y	N	N.A.	N.A.	N.A.	N.A.	N	N	N.A.	4
Luxembourg	Y	(Y)	Y	N	N	Y	(Y)	(Y)	N	N	Y	7
Hungary	Y	N.A.	N.A.	N	N.A.	(Y)	N	N	N	N	Y	6
Malta	Y	N.A.	N.A.	N	N.A.	Y	(Y)	N	Y	N	Y	4
Netherlands	Y	Y	Y	Y	Y	N	N	N	Y	(Y)	Y	8
Austria	Y	Y	Y	Y	Y	N	Y	Y	Y	N.A.	N	8
Poland	Y	N	N	Y	N	Y	Y	Y	(Y)	N	Y	10
Portugal	N	N	N.A.	N.A.	N	N.A.	N.A.	N.A.	N.A.	N.A.	N	0
Slovenia	Y	N.A.	N.A.	N.A.	N.A.	N.A.	N.A.	N.A.	N.A.	N.A.	N.A.	1
Slovakia	N.A.	N.A.	N.A.	N.A.	N.A.	N.A.	N.A.	N.A.	N.A.	N.A.	N	1
Finland	Y	Y	Y	Y	Y	(Y)	Y	Y	(Y)	N.A.	N.A.	9
Sweden	Y	Y	Y	Y	Y	Y	Y	Y	Y	N	N	9
United Kingdom	Y	Y	Y	Y	Y	Y	Y	Y	Y	Y	N	10
Total Y + (Y)	19	13	12	15	15	14	12	12	11	7	5	

Legend:

Y Measures exist; (Y) Measures planned/Available partially; N No measures exist; N.A. Information not available.

Note

* See above p. 87, n. 89.

develop quantified and monetized measures even of amenities not traded in markets.[98] And they point to the transparency gains of forcing decisions to be based on a rigorous analysis made available to the public.

An additional point is that, if costs to industry will inevitably be pressed by industry lobbyists (with or without BCA), then failing to quantify health and environmental benefits (by eschewing BCA) will actually lead to under protection of those social values. If interest group politics favors concentrated industry groups over diffuse environmental beneficiaries, then BCA is more important to clarify the benefits than the costs. If risk reduction or other benefits are not quantified and compared through BCA, those benefits will be neglected in a political calculus that inevitably focuses on cost. To be sure, much costly environmental legislation has been enacted without quantification of benefits (or costs), but those laws may represent interest group deals more than a maximization of public net benefits.

And, fundamentally, advocates respond: if government does not use some version of comparing benefits and costs, then on what alternative basis will it make decisions? Critics of BCA often fail to explain an alternative method for making decisions.[99] Not comparing benefits and costs may simply lead to decisions which are less transparent, less subject to debate and correction, and more arbitrary and biased than is BCA, that is, to decisions which are driven by overreaction to crisis events,[100] under reaction to routine, systemic, or unseen concerns,[101] and raw political power (especially of concentrated industry groups)

---

98 E.g. Viscusi says: "any regulatory benefit from a risk regulation or environmental regulation that should be legitimately recognized in the policy analysis process potentially can be quantified in monetary terms." Viscusi, n. 59 above.

99 Some advocate setting standards "as low as feasible," but a feasibility test would be insensitive to benefits, would regulate more profitable industries more tightly than less profitable industries (sending perverse signals and potentially conflicting with environmental justice concerns by protecting poorer communities less than richer communities), and would be less protective than BCA where BCA would warrant shutting down a noxious industry but the "feasible" constraint would keep the industry in business.

100 See Robert V Percival, "Environmental Legislation and the Problem of Collective Action," (1998) 9 *Duke Environmental Law and Policy Forum*; Thomas Birkland, *After Disaster: Agenda Setting, Public Policy, and Focusing Events* (Washington, DC: Georgetown University Press, 1997); Thomas Birkland, *Lessons of Disaster: Policy Change after Catastrophic Events* (Washington, DC: Georgetown University Press, 2006).

101 See Cass R Sunstein, "Cognition and Cost-Benefit Analysis" (2000) 29 *Journal of Legal Studies*, reprinted in Mathew Adler and Eric Posner (eds), *Cost-Benefit Analysis* (Chicago: University of Chicago Press, 2001); Richard Posner, *Catastrophe: Risk and Response* (New York: Oxford University Press, 2004) (arguing that the public and government give inadequate attention to low-probability high-consequence risks of extreme events, but that on BCA criteria such risks should be addressed more aggressively); Jonathan B Wiener, Book review of Richard Posner, *Catastrophe: Risk and Response* (2004) and Jared Diamond, *Collapse: How Societies Choose to Fail or Succeed* (2005), in (2005) 24 *Journal of Policy Analysis & Management* 885–889; Cass R Sunstein, "On the Divergent American Reactions to Terrorism and Climate Change," AEI-Brookings Joint Center for Regulatory Studies, Working Paper 06–13 (May 2006).

rather than analysis. The alternative to analysis may often be sanctimony – acting without analyzing, on the supposition that we "know" the right answer – hastily choosing regulation or deregulation, green technologies or counterterror tactics, depending on who is in power.

In advising the European Commission on these questions, the Mandelkern Group Report rejected claims of bias:

> Some see RIAs as an excuse to impose a business-focused, deregulatory agenda on policy makers. For a RIA done well, this is absolutely not the case. Rather, as stated elsewhere, the RIA simply sets out the information in a clear and concise way to inform – not control – the political decision. This point needs to be stressed as appropriate and real efforts need to be made to ensure that both benefits and costs are included in the assessment.
>
> Another possible problem is the political pressure to do something – anything – now, irrespective of a proper assessment (sometimes known in its most extreme form as a "knee-jerk reaction") . . . development of a good RIA system is likely to reduce the incidence of this reaction as the need for good assessment becomes commonly understood and supported. . . .
>
> A further situation can be where the main political decision has already been taken (perhaps in a government programme or party manifesto). In these cases there can be a reluctance to undertake assessment of the implementation options available. However, almost always details remain to be resolved where an assessment can play an important role in informing, in a very explicit manner, those taking the decisions on the details about the trade-offs that they are making. Finally, there is often the perception that doing RIA takes too much time and delays the policy development process to an unacceptable degree. However, when RIA is an integrated part of the process, any delays in the earlier stages are minimised and often outweighed by time and cost savings later in the process where the greater defensibility of the policy solutions and the increased buy-in by stakeholders are important.[102]

There is not the space here to sort out this entire debate. After briefly assessing the pros and cons of IA in this subsection, I suggest in the next subsection that Europe, committed as it already is to using IA in Better Regulation, should experiment with a set of institutional innovations which will test whether the criticisms can be overcome and whether IA can thus be made to perform even better than it has so far.

The criticisms of IA (especially using BCA) seem to me to be worth taking seriously, but not fatal to a sensible application of weighing the pros and cons of important decisions. There is no better alternative way of making policy, and it has become the mainstream consensus approach. The criticisms should therefore

---

102 Mandelkern Group Report (2001), n. 3 above, at 25.

motivate better policy analysis, not its rejection. The concerns about omission of important impacts, including countervailing risks and ancillary benefits, are crucial; as I suggest below, they warrant a broader more embracing form of BCA. The concern about delay is quite important, but delay is amenable to a weighing of its own pros and cons. The benefit of delay is that additional analysis can improve decisions (and defer policy burdens); the cost is that delay can forfeit the value of earlier policy adoption (e.g. earlier protection of victims, or earlier authorization of a useful invention). Weighing these conflicting effects is the task of Value of Information/Cost of Information (VOI/COI) techniques, one component of BCA. This idea is reflected in the European IA Guidelines' doctrine of "proportionate analysis," and roughly in the difference between initial IA and Extended IA in Europe, as well as initial Environmental Assessments versus full Environmental Impact Statements under US NEPA law, and insignificant versus significant regulatory actions under OMB review. Note that the cost of delay cuts both ways: who bears its costs depends on the default rule in force while the analysis is pending. Regulatory impact assessment (RIA) may delay regulation of private actors, while environmental impact assessment (EIA) may delay projects sought by private actors. The delays posed by RIA themselves can cut both ways, depending on who bears the cost of the delay: if the law requires IA before adopting a regulation that would restrict a risky product or facility (as for many pollution controls), then delay favors industry and the cost is borne by victims; but if the law requires IA before licensing of a new product or site (as for new drugs or pesticides or energy facilities), then delay favors victims and the cost is borne by industry and consumers. The question is institutional rather than analytic. Moreover, as the Mandelkern group points out, a careful IA can resolve and avoid problems that would yield delay later on, so it can achieve less delay overall. In short, delay turns out to be a problem that calls for better BCA, not avoiding BCA.

Meanwhile, retrospective analyses of a variety of policies do not bear out the concern that BCA is biased toward overstating costs and understating benefits. *Ex post* evaluations of a growing set of cases (though not yet a representative sample) have found that *both* benefits and costs appear to have been overstated in *ex ante* RIAs.[103] Certainly specific cases can be cited of BCA recommending less stringent regulation, but perhaps those recommendations were warranted. In several other key cases, RIA and BCA have been used to identify and promulgate some of the most important advances in more stringent environmental and health protection. These include the phase out of CFCs, the phase down of lead (Pb) in gasoline (petrol), and the restrictions on particulate matter emissions from power

---

103 See OMB, *Validating Regulatory Analysis: 2005 Report to Congress on the Costs and Benefits of Federal Regulations and Unfunded Mandates on State, Local, and Tribal Entities* (Washington, DC: US Office of Management and Budget, 2005), ch III, 41–49; Winston Harrington, Richard D Morgenstern, and Peter Nelson, "On the Accuracy of Regulatory Cost Estimates" (2000) 19 *Journal of Policy Analysis and Management* 297–332.

plants and diesel engines.[104] Indeed these are three policies on which the US, using BCA, adopted policies that were substantially more precautionary (earlier and more stringent) than Europe.[105] Critics contend that in the past BCA has more often been used to reduce than to increase the stringency of new regulations.[106] As I argue below, even if this is true, it is as much or more a result of the institutional posture of BCA as of the analytic methodology of BCA, and both of these can be ameliorated in the European program of Better Regulation.

Why might costs and benefits be over- or understated in *ex ante* BCA? Costs may be overstated *ex ante* if industry opposes regulation citing high cost estimates, and then once a rule is imposed, industry finds less costly means of complying than it thought or said it could (though at some expense of managerial time); and if the extent of implementation of the policy is predicted *ex ante* to be greater than it actually turns out to be. On the other hand, costs could be understated *ex ante* if they focus on a subset of costs such as industry compliance costs and neglect wider or longer-term effects such as foregone innovation.

Benefits may be understated *ex ante* if risk assessments focus on one risk at a time and omit multiple simultaneous exposures; if they neglect low-probability extreme events; if they neglect sensitive subpopulations; or if they omit ancillary benefits from unintended reductions in other risks. And benefits may be understated *ex ante* if monetized BCA omits or underestimates impacts that are difficult to measure in monetary terms. On the other hand, benefits may be overstated *ex ante* if the implementation of the policy is predicted to be greater than actually turns out to occur; if countervailing risks created by the policy are omitted; if the methods of valuation used to monetize environmental benefits (such as contingent valuation surveys regarding non-market assets such as ecosystems) tend to overstate benefits or if the risk assessments which underlie the calculation of policy benefits use conservative default assumptions and

---

104 Ackerman *et al*, n. 97 above, review the Lead Phasedown and argue that it does not show the success of BCA in supporting a more stringent policy on lead (Pb) in gasoline because the BCA came late in the story (in the 1980s), after several decades of the use of lead in gasoline (since the 1920s) and after a prior regulation to reduce lead in gasoline had been adopted in the 1970s without reliance on BCA. By contrast, Driesen, n. 97 above, at 364, states that "this case does seem to offer reasonably good evidence of CBA motivating an increase in stringency." In addition, the conclusion to be drawn from the Ackerman *et al* critique is not that BCA did not support a more aggressive phaseout of lead in gasoline (it did), but that BCA should have been undertaken decades earlier. Ackerman *et al* say that BCA could not have been conducted earlier because the data on health effects of lead were lacking, yet they cite evidence of the longstanding scientific appreciation of the adverse health effects of lead exposure; and they neglect the endogenous character of benefits data: if BCA had been required or undertaken, evidence to quantify the benefits would have been sought and collected. The reduction in lead emissions due to the first regulation in the 1970s was not the only way to generate exposure and dose-response data, as Ackerman *et al* assert; variations across locations, and changes in exposure over prior decades, could also have been studied.
105 See Wiener, n. 15 above.
106 See Driesen, n. 97 above.

methods that tend to overstate risks and hence benefits (due to such factors as overstated linear no-threshold dose-response extrapolations, use of most sensitive test species, identifying any observed effect as adverse, making animal-to-human extrapolations without accounting for mechanistic differences ("modes of action") using "maximum exposed individual" exposure assumptions, and using large safety factors for extrapolation to human subpopulations).

The result is that risk assessment exhibits simultaneous excessive attention to some (small) risks, and inattention to other (larger) risks. To address many of these problems, US EPA has adopted new cancer risk assessment guidelines,[107] which require greater use of evidence before resorting to conservative default assumptions, greater attention to modes of action, and more attention to children and other susceptible sub-groups. And US OMB/OIRA has issued a proposed Bulletin on Risk Assessment in January 2006,[108] seeking to ensure greater transparency and realism, use of central estimates, and consistent criteria for identifying adverse effects. In addition, although few statutes specify the criteria for scientific risk assessment,[109] courts have begun to apply general statutory edicts to use the "best available science" to require agencies to conduct high-quality risk assessments.[110]

To make Better Regulation effective, European institutions need to address these questions of risk assessment as well. So far, the approach of European institutions to risk assessment has been ad hoc or ill-defined. In the EU, the move toward quantitative risk assessment has been more recent than in the US (where it accelerated in the 1980s following the US Supreme Court's *Benzene* decision[111] and the 1983 publication of the National Academy of Sciences "Redbook"[112]). EU use of risk assessment has been driven in part by WTO decisions under the Agreement on Sanitary and Phytosanitary Standards (SPS), which requires

---

107 US Environmental Protection Agency (2005), Guidelines for Carcinogen Risk Assessment, EP/630/P-03/0001F www.epa.gov/cancerguidelines.

108 US OMB, Proposed Bulletin on Risk Assessment, January 9, 2006, available at www.whitehouse.gov/omb/inforeg/infopoltech.htm#iq. This initiative is endorsed in concept by Nicholas Bagley and Richard L Revesz, "Centralized Oversight of the Regulatory State," AEI-Brookings Joint Center for Regulatory Studies, Related publication 06–12 (April 2006), at 44–53 (forthcoming in (2006) 106 *Columbia Law Review*, Section IV.A).

109 See Kelsey Stansell, Mark Marvelli, and Jonathan B Wiener, " 'Adverse Effects' And Similar Terms In U.S. Law," Report for the Dose Response Specialty Group of the Society for Risk Analysis (SRA) (July 2005), available at www.sra.org/drsg/docs/Adverse_ Effects_Report.pdf.

110 E.g. *Chlorine Chemistry Council v EPA*, 206 F 3d 1286 (DC Cir 2000) (vacating goal for maximum level of chloroform because agency set goal based on linear low-dose extrapolation when it had just found that a threshold model was superior). See also Leather Industries *v* EPA, 40 F 3d 392 (DC Cir 1994) (remanding standard for selenium content in sewage sludge because the exposure assumption–children eating sludge on highway median strips–was not credible).

111 *Industrial Union Dept, AFL-CIO v American Petroleum Institute*, 448 US 607 (1980).

112 NAS/NRC, *Risk Assessment in the Federal Government: Managing the Process* (Washington, DC: National Academies Press, 1983).

a scientific risk assessment to support international trade restrictions.[113] The European Commission has espoused scientific risk assessment as a predicate to any invocation of the precautionary principle,[114] and the European Court of Justice held, in a case on mad cow disease (BSE) quite reminiscent *of Benzene*, that member state governments may not invoke precaution to regulate risks that the Commission has deemed insignificant.[115] Still, major risk regulations within the EU sometimes proceed without risk assessments, as in the recent *Pfizer* and *Alpharma* cases regarding antibiotics in animal feed,[116] in which the Court of First Instance held that a ban could be adopted without a risk assessment and even when the relevant scientific advisory committee had recommended against a ban or had not been consulted at all (despite a requirement for such consultation). The court ruled in the *Pfizer* case, paras 139 and 142–144:

> ...a risk assessment cannot be required to provide the Community institutions with conclusive scientific evidence of the reality of the risk and the seriousness of the potential adverse effects were that risk to become a reality.... [But] a preventive measure cannot properly be based on a purely hypothetical approach to the risk, founded on mere conjecture which has not been scientifically verified...a preventive measure may be taken only if the risk, although the reality and extent thereof have not been "fully demonstrated by conclusive scientific evidence," appears nevertheless to be adequately backed up by the scientific data available at the time when the measure was taken.

This statement is confusing. The court appears to misunderstand the purpose of a risk assessment, which is never to provide "conclusive scientific evidence" (which does not exist) but rather to provide a forecast of (inevitably uncertain) future risks. The court holds that a "purely hypothetical" risk or "mere conjecture" is inadequate, but that a risk assessment is not required, and it remains unclear what the court means by its alternative of "adequately backed up by the scientific data" – an invitation to further litigation. The Better Regulation initiative should resolve these confusions by requiring risk assessment (as called for in the European Commission's February 2000 Communication on the Precautionary Principle),

113 See Steve Charnovitz, "The Supervision of Health and Biosafety Regulation by World Trade Rules" (2000) 13 *Tulane Environmental Law Journal* 271.

114 Commission of the European Communities, Communication from the Commission on the Precautionary Principle, COM(2000) 1, Brussels, February 2, 2000, available at http://europa.eu.int/comm/dgs/health_consumer/library/pub/pub07_en.pdf.

115 Case C-1/00, *Commission of the European Communities v French Republic* (Failure of a Member State to fulfill its obligations – Refusal to end the ban on British beef and veal), [2001] ECR I-09989 (European Court of Justice, 2001).

116 Case T-13/99, *Pfizer Animal Health SA v Council*, 2002 WL 31337 (European Court of First Instance, September 11, 2002); *Case* T-70/99, *Alpharma Inc v Council*, 2002 WL 31338 (European Court of First Instance, September 11, 2002).

setting criteria for risk assessments, and explaining that risk assessment is a method to forecast uncertain future scenarios.

Nor is incomplete information a reason to reject BCA. Information about future events is never complete or certain. Given uncertainty, some form of BCA seems superior to the alternative methods of decision-making. A raw political (non-analytic) choice of goals would be arbitrary or distorted by rent-seeking politics; even if well-intentioned, it may simply neglect important costs and benefits (especially to those who lack effective political voice) and thereby yield policy errors.[117] The Mandelkern Group advised that it is certainly sometimes the case that there is a

> paucity of good quality data on benefits and costs, including the difficulty of estimating the value of non-marketed goods (e.g. environmental degradation or damage to human health). Whilst this will indeed affect the overall quality of the assessment – which can only be as good as the inputted data – it is not a sufficient argument for not carrying out any assessment at all. Use of error estimation and ranges (rather than single figures) for benefits and costs can help, as can the input from consultation with stakeholders and intelligent use of available data, consultants and academic expertise. Seeking input from a wide range of stakeholders can help avoid the kind of bias otherwise possible from vested interests.[118]

Likewise, the US Council on Environmental Quality (CEQ) guidelines for environmental IA under NEPA address uncertainty by requiring the agency to obtain additional information at reasonable cost, to describe the remaining uncertainties, and to make an express judgment about the importance of such questions for the impacts being assessed.[119] As noted above, in its IA Guidelines

---

117 See John D Graham and Jonathan B Wiener, *Risk vs. Risk: Tradeoffs in Protecting Health and the Environment* (Cambridge, MA: Harvard University Press, 1995) (arguing that failure to analyze full impacts of policy choices often results in selective neglect of impacts on constituencies lacking effective political voice; thus, good impact assessment can advance both efficiency and equity).

118 Mandelkern Group Report (2001), n. 3 above, at 24.

119 40 CFR 1502.22 (promulgated at 51 Fed Reg 15625, April 25, 1986) ("(a) If the incomplete information relevant to reasonably foreseeable significant adverse impacts is essential to a reasoned choice among alternatives and the overall costs of obtaining it are not exorbitant, the agency shall include the information in the environmental impact statement. (b) If the information relevant to reasonably foreseeable significant adverse impacts cannot be obtained because the overall costs of obtaining it are exorbitant or the means to obtain it are not known, the agency shall include within the environmental impact statement: (1) A statement that such information is incomplete or unavailable; (2) a statement of the relevance of the incomplete or unavailable information to evaluating reasonably foreseeable significant adverse impacts on the human environment; (3) a summary of existing credible scientific evidence which is relevant to evaluating the reasonably foreseeable significant adverse impacts on the human environment, and (4) the agency's evaluation of such impacts based upon theoretical approaches or research

in 2005, the European Commission addressed this issue through the doctrine of "proportionate analysis," requiring services of the Commission to invest in additional information where the benefits of doing so (in improved decisions) justify the costs.[120]

Institutional innovations

Given its commitment to IA as the key tool for Better Regulation, Europe now faces the debate over the pros and cons of BCA, and, at the same time, an opportunity to make progress through institutional innovations. Many of the real problems with IA and BCA are institutional, not analytic. Economics is not fundamentally opposed to ecology: both words derive from the Greek *oikos* for household, and they should be able to cohabit graciously. The concern that the tools of IA and BCA are biased against environmental protection arises largely because of the institutional postures in which the tools are applied: too coldly, to "just say no," and too narrowly. Making progress on these institutional biases by using BCA more "warmly," using it to say "yes" as well as no, and using it more widely, would make Better Regulation even better.

IA and BCA are tools, not rules. They are mechanisms to inform decision-making, not the decision itself. The decision itself is and must be an exercise of judgment by a public official. Policy must be based on and express that judgment, rather than be dictated by a cold numerical calculus. At the same time, that public policy judgment will often be better made when it is informed by a careful structured comparison of consequences, whether that is termed an analysis of "benefits and costs" or "positive and negative impacts." Simply choosing policy goals on unstated or raw political criteria would be arbitrary, invite partisan volatility, and lack transparency. At least some version of BCA offers a transparent opportunity to evaluate and debate the reasons given. The key should be this function of considering alternatives and consequences and giving reasons for decisions, rather than quantification *per se*.

Here I suggest several institutional innovations that Europe could pursue to make Better Regulation even better.

Warm Analysis

Given its determination to use IA and BCA, Europe should employ what I will call "Warm Analysis." Along a spectrum from "hot" to "cold," one can locate policy based on moral outrage at the hot end (imagine the crowd or the politician who

methods generally accepted in the scientific community. For the purposes of this section, "reasonably foreseeable" includes impacts which have catastrophic consequences, even if their probability of occurrence is low, provided that the analysis of the impacts is supported by credible scientific evidence, is not based on pure conjecture, and is within the rule of reason.").

120 IA Guidelines 2006, Part II, s 5, at 8.

reacts intensely, often to a recent crisis or scandal, expressing moralistic norms of sin, blame, and punishment, and giving little or no attention to, or even opposing, analysis of wider consequences), and one can locate policy based on strict monetized BCA at the end of cool or cold analysis (imagine the accountant wearing a green eye shade who counts statistics, manages only what is measured, and maximizes wealth dispassionately).[121] "Warm analysis" would occupy the center of this spectrum, embodying serious analysis of the full variety of impacts and tradeoffs, some quantitative and some qualitative, with compassion for both those who incur risks and those who incur abatement costs. As I will argue here, warm analysis can be understood as the application of BCA to BCA – or optimal optimization – recognizing that information and analysis are themselves costly (chiefly in delay) and that omitting important effects is itself a costly error of analysis. Sensible application of BCA requires applying it not only to regulatory policies but also to the analytic review process itself. Hot moral outrage neglects important impacts and tradeoffs, and is vulnerable to heuristic errors; cold analysis applies monetized BCA to policies but neglects the costs of delay and of omitting important but unquantified impacts. Warm analysis is thus more embracing than either hot or cold approaches, while remaining truer to the core principle of BCA.

The crucial task for good public policy is to think through decisions. It is therefore to engage in a structured consideration of the major alternatives and consequences, in order to inform sound judgment through reason. The crucial task is not just an accounting exercise, nor strict economic optimization, though economic tools can be helpful. That is the key reason that in EO 12866 we chose to use the term "justify" in place of "outweigh," and to expressly allow consideration of non-quantified impacts (while encouraging quantification). "Warm analysis" compares pros and cons in a structured decision framework but without limiting the comparison to strictly quantified and monetized impacts.

This approach is the "prudential algebra" recommended by Benjamin Franklin in 1772:

> In the Affair of so much Importance to you, wherein you ask my Advice, I cannot for want of sufficient Premises, advise you *what* to determine, but if

---

121 See Christopher H Schroeder, "Cool Analysis Versus Moral Outrage in the Development of Federal Environmental Criminal Law," (1993) 35 *William and Mary Law Review* 251, 253–258. Schroeder limits "cool analysis" to self-interested utility maximization in which risks are calculated as the "thin" expected value of probability and harm. Two aspects that Schroeder puts under the heading of "moral outrage" – the inclusion in an individual's utility function of effects on others and on society as a whole, and the recognition of "thick" qualitative attributes of risk–do not seem to me to fit the notion of moral outrage, and would fit better under what I am calling "warm analysis." By contrast, moral outrage at the hot end of the spectrum is characterized by an intense and moralist or absolutist response focused on sin, blame, and prohibition, lacking (or even opposed to) analysis of consequences, tradeoffs, and proportionality. Schroeder describes the moral outrage felt by environmentalists who see pollution as a sin and compliance as an obligation; consider also the moral outrage felt after a terrorist attack and the call for a "crusade" of "shock and awe" to strike back. See Stern and Wiener, n. 67 above.

you please I will tell you *how*. When those difficult Cases occur, they are difficult, chiefly because while we have them under Consideration, all the Reasons *pro* and *con* are not present to the Mind at the same time; but sometimes one Set present themselves, and at other times another, the first being out of Sight.... To get over this, my Way is, to divide half a Sheet of Paper by a Line into two Columns; writing over the one Pro, and over the other Con. Then during three or four Days Consideration, I put down under the different heads short Hints of the different Motives, that at different Times occur to me, *for* or *against* the Measure. When I have thus got them all together in one View, I endeavour to estimate their respective Weights... and thus proceeding I find at length where the Ballance lies... And, tho' the Weight of Reasons cannot be taken with the Precision of Algebraic Quantities, yet, when each is thus considered, separately and comparatively, and the whole lies before me, I think I can judge better, and am less liable to make a rash Step; and in fact I have found great Advantage from this kind of Equation, in what may be called *Moral or Prudential Algebra*.[122]

Franklin describes a careful structured approach to ensuring that all the important consequences are "on screen,"[123] quantifying their weights as much as possible but not insisting on algebraic precision, and coming to a considered judgment about the best course of action. He emphasizes that errors – "rash Steps" – are principally due to omitting important reasons and not to quantifying each reason too little or too much. Similarly, John Maynard Keynes remarked that "it is better to be roughly right than precisely wrong."[124] Cass Sunstein has advocated BCA as a cognitive approach to informed decision-making rather than as a strictly numerical calculus of optimization,[125] and Amartya Sen has advocated broadening the types of impacts and valuations incorporated into BCA.[126] As quoted above, the Mandelkern Group urged the use of ranges rather than point estimates, to account for uncertainties in the forecasts of benefits and costs – an insight borne out in the *ex post* studies of BCAs.

Warm Analysis is not a rejection of BCA using quantified, monetized values. Indeed, BCA itself justifies the Warm Analysis approach. With limited resources to analyze decisions, there is some tradeoff between accuracy (getting the

---

122 Benjamin Franklin, "Letter to Joseph Priestley," London, September 19, 1772, in *Benjamin Franklin: Representative Selections, with Introduction, Bibliography and Notes*, Frank Luther Mott and Chester E Jorgenson (eds), (New York: American Book Company, 1936), 348–349.

123 See Howard Margolis, *Dealing with Risk* (Chicago: University of Chicago, Press 1996).

124 Quoted in Alan Greenspan, Chairman of the Federal Reserve Board, "Bias in the Consumer Price Index," Testimony before the Committee on the Budget, US House of Representatives, March 4, 1997, at http://www.federalreserve.gov/Boarddocs/testimony/1997/19970304.htm.

125 See Sunstein, n. 101 above.

126 See Amartya Sen, "The Discipline of Cost-Benefit Analysis," (2000) 29 *Journal of Legal Studies* 931–952 (favoring BCA if it uses a broader set of values instead of only market valuations).

decision right) and precision (calculating exact numbers), which suggests that on standard BCA criteria, it would often do more to improve policy decisions to get the full set of consequences before the decision-maker (so that "the whole lies before me," in Franklin's words) than it would to invest in precisely quantifying only a few of those consequences while neglecting others or unduly delaying the decision. This is akin to the question of how much analysis is optimal: more analysis yields fewer policy errors, but also incurs costs in money and time (delay), so one must compare the Value of Information (VOI) versus the Cost of Information (COI). Such a BCA of BCA, or meta-BCA, shows that it is better to assess the full consequences than to quantify precisely just a few. A Cold Analysis that quantifies some impacts but omits other recognized important impacts (or takes too long) is in effect assigning a weight of zero to those omitted impacts, which is a greater error than including them in a qualitative or partly quantified way.[127] If the cost (including delay) of precisely quantifying all the impacts is lower than its benefits, then full quantification is warranted. And this meta-BCA suggests that, over time, as we find ways to quantify and monetize more impacts – to reduce the COI or increase the VOI – more exacting analysis would be warranted. Our methods of quantification and valuation are endogenous and should respond to the use of BCA, as qualified by meta-BCA, to become "Warm Analysis" by improving our ability to make diverse impacts more understandable.[128]

127 Thus either inadequate comparison of benefits and costs (as espoused by critics of BCA) or excessive quantification of a few benefits and costs (as undertaken in some BCAs) would threaten what Franklin called a "rash step." In a similar vein, the late Allen Kneese – an economist and advocate of using BCA in environmental policy – worried that overly precise BCAs may "let method outrun content." Kneese, n. 64 above, at 60. Likewise, the joint statement by eleven noted economists advocating BCA was careful to say that BCA has an important role to play in helping inform regulatory decision-making, although it should not be the sole basis for such decision-making, that agencies "should not be bound by strict benefit-cost tests," and that agencies should take into account uncertainties, ranges of estimates, unquantified impacts, and distributional impacts. See Arrow *et al*, n. 94 above.

128 I do not propose to leave everything "blurry," as one critic of BCA has urged, see Lisa Heinzerling, "Regulatory Costs of Mythic Proportions," (1999) 107 *Yale Law Journal* 1981, 2069. My point is that a comprehensive Warm Analysis offers greater clarity than either a Cold Analysis that omits important factors, or a non-BCA approach that omits important factors. Nor do I agree that a careful structured analysis of pros and cons lacking full quantification would be "vacuous" (see Sunstein, n. 101 above) or "vapid" (see Driesen, n. 97 above). The key point is to get the decision-maker to consider the full portfolio of important choices and consequences, see Margolis, n. 123 above, Graham and Wiener, n. 117 above. This approach avoids the "false promise of determinacy" that critics fear in strictly quantified BCA, see Amy Sinden, "Cass Sunstein's Cost-Benefit Lite: Economics for Liberals," (2004) 29 *Columbia Journal Environmental Law* 191, 194. At the same time, I am optimistic about the ability to improve methods of analysis over time to quantify more kinds of impacts (especially through investment in research and staff capacity, through greater demand for such analysis through initiatives such as Better Regulation, and through *ex post* evaluations to improve *ex ante* methods, as discussed below). For another effort to find a "middle way between all or nothing analytically" that bears similarities to my version of "warm analysis" – yet authored by a critic

While the academic debate over BCA often pits advocates of Cool Analysis against sharp critics who reject statistics and monetization without clearly identifying a preferred alternative decision-making method (implying a preference for populist moral outrage), the practical reality is that the approach to Warm Analysis that I am describing is already available, even required, under the major legal requirements for BCA. In the US, EO 12866 expressly requires analysis of both qualitative and quantitative factors, and calls on agencies to show that benefits "justify" (not "outweigh") the costs. OMB/OIRA Circular A-4 requires attention to unquantified as well as quantified impacts. CEQ guidelines on environmental IA require assessment of impacts despite incomplete information. In the EU, the IA Guidelines require analysis of "all positive and negative impacts," with the possibility of using formal BCA or C-EA where warranted.[129] (They do not, however, set a goal of "maximizing net benefits," as the US orders do; the EU should consider adding this objective in its next updated IA Guidelines.) And the EU IA Guidelines call for "Proportionate Analysis," to choose the degree of analysis warranted by the problem.[130]

A particular question, to which little space can be devoted here, is – given a decision to monetize valuations of impacts – what monetary estimates should be used for the values of health, life, and environmental impacts? Willingness-to-pay (or to accept) is a useful but imperfect proxy for utility, limited by ability to pay and variations in marginal utility of income, by market imperfections in mobility and information, and by heuristic misperceptions of risk.[131] There is

---

of quantitative analysis – see Richard Parker, "The Empirical Roots of the Regulatory Reform Movement: A Critical Appraisal," (2006) 58 *Administrative Law Review* 359, 394–395.

129 IA Guidelines 2005, updated 2006, at 39, Part III s 5.1 and n. 45 and Annexes 12 and 13. As the EU moves from the hotter (less or non-)analytic side toward greater use of IA and BCA, it may need to do more to quantify impacts and compare options rigorously. One of the leaders of the Better Regulation effort recently remarked: "I will also be following with great interest the external evaluation of our Impact Assessment system which will report next year and which should provide further input for improvements. Without prejudging the results of the assessment, I personally believe that a more rigorous quantification of the costs and benefits – economic, social and environmental – will be very important. Only if we can demonstrate through hard data that the benefits of what we propose outweigh the costs will we be fully convincing." Günter Verheugen, Vice-President of the European Commission responsible for Enterprise and Industry, Better Regulation for Jobs and Growth, Former Members Dinner, European Parliament Former Members Association, Brussels, May 10, 2006, SPEECH/06/287, available at http://ec.europa.eu/commission_barroso/verheugen/speeches/speeches_en.htm.

130 IA Guidelines 2006, Part II, s 5, at 8. Similarly, "The depth and scope of the assessment respects the principle of proportionate analysis, i.e. more Impact Assessment resources will be allocated to those proposals that can be expected to have the most significant impacts." Communication of March 16, 2005, n. 4 above, at 13. See also Renda, n. 76 above, 92 (discussing the meanings of proportionality in regulatory standards and proportionate analysis in the IA process).

131 See Ezra J Mishan, *Cost-Benefit Analysis: An Informal Introduction* (London: Allen & Unwin, 1971; 4th edn, Routledge, 1994); Sunstein, n. 101 above; Jonathan B Wiener, "Risk in the Republic," (1997) 8 Duke Envtl Law & Policy F 1–21; Matthew D Adler and Eric A Posner, "Implementing Cost-Benefit Analysis when Preferences are Distorted," (2000) 29 *Journal of Legal Studies* 1105, 1146.

a lively controversy over whether and how to adjust monetized values of the value of a life to account for the expected years of life lost when risks occur at different ages, or to account for different levels of income and associated demand for risk protection. Using a single value of a statistical life (VSL) for all premature deaths seems insensitive to the timing of the death occurring early or late in life, as well as insensitive to other attributes of the risk that people find more or less undesirable.[132] But devising schedules of different VSL or value of a statistical life-year (VSLY) for different risks, populations, and ages is criticized as unfair and even as inconsistent with willingness to pay.[133] Here, I simply point out that the US and Europe are already using monetized VSL figures in regulatory IAs, but not the same figures: the US uses a range of figures clustered around $3 to $6 million per VSL saved,[134] whereas Europe is using numbers closer to $1.5 million.[135] This implies that the US puts greater value

132 See Cass R Sunstein, "Valuing Life: A Plea for Disaggregation," (2004) 54 Duke LJ 385; George Tolley, Donald Kenkel, and Robert Fabian (eds), *Valuing Health for Policy: An Economic Approach* (Chicago: University of Chicago Press, 1994).

133 Using the same VSL for all deaths appears to treat all victims alike, but it also values younger victims" remaining years of life at less per year than older victims" remaining years of life. On the other hand, using a simple VSLY (i.e. the VSL divided by years of average life expectancy at birth), which values each year the same regardless of age (and hence values younger victims more than older victims), is inconsistent with WTP if people put different values on different times of life, and in particular if they value the last few years of life (scarce time) more highly than earlier years. See W Kip Viscusi, "Regulation of Health, Safety and Environmental Risks," NBER Working Paper 11934 (January 2006), at 46–49, available at http://www.nber.org/papers/wll934 Laura J Lowenstein and Richard L Revesz, "Anti-Regulation under the Guise of Rational Regulation: The Bush Administration's Approaches to Valuing Human Lives in Environmental Cost-Benefit Analyses," (2004) 34 *Environmental Law Reporter* 109–154. The Lowenstein and Revesz article criticizes OIRA for undervaluing older people, but in fact it was EPA during the Clinton administration that began doing so (based on studies in the UK and Canada) and it was OIRA in 2003 that instructed EPA and other agencies not to use a crude "senior discount" nor a simple VSLY approach, see John D Graham, "Memorandum on Benefit-Cost Analysis and Lifesaving Rules," May 30, 2003, available at http://www.whitehouse.gov/omb/inforeg/pmc_benefit_cost_memo.pdf (noting that saving ten years of life is more valuable than saving one year of life, but not ten times more valuable). Studies to date suggest that total VSL decreases in older age, but less than proportionately, so that VSLY is increasing in older age, although with little overall impact on benefits valuation, see Viscusi, n. 59 above, at 14–17, 30–31.

134 See Sunstein, n. 132 above, table 1, at 396–398 ($1.5 to $6.5 million); Lisa Robinson, background paper for National Academy of Sciences/Institute of Medicine, Current Federal Agency Practices for Valuing the Impact of Regulations on Health and Safety (2004) ($1 m-$8 m).

135 Presentation by Matti Vainio, DG Environment, European Commission, "Impact Assessment of Thematic Strategy on Air Pollution," at the US–EU High Level Regulatory Cooperation Forum (January 25, 2006), powerpoint slide 27. In November 2000 the European Commission had issued "Recommended Interim Values for the Value of Preventing a Fatality in DG Environment Cost Benefit Analysis," at http://europa.eu.int/comm/environment/enveco/others/recommended_interim_values.pdf (from a workshop at http://ec.europa.eu/environment/enveco/others/value_of_life.htm), recommending that the VSL be 1 to 1.5 million euros, with a range from 0.65 to 2.5 million euros.

than does Europe on preventing health risks – an observation contrary to the conventional wisdom of greater European concern about such risks. Whether that difference is due to the income elasticity of demand for risk prevention, or to other factors,[136] it deserves greater attention – as does the fact that the US now uses discount rates of 7 and 3 percent (or even lower for long-term intergenerational effects), while the EU Guidelines require a discount rate of 4 percent.[137] These and other differences could serve as the point of departure for a wider comparative review of US and EU approaches to monetizing in BCA and to Cool versus Warm Analysis in general.

Using BCA to say "Yes" as well as "No"

The second institutional innovation Europe should pursue is to use RIA and BCA evenhandedly, not only to say "No" to the Bad (that is, reject or "return" regulation proposed by agencies), but also to say "Yes" to the Good (that is, "prompt" new regulation). This is especially apt in the EU, where the European Commission initiates legislation, so it could use BCA to identify the best new policies to pursue – even more directly than can the White House in the US system, because the US Presidency is so often reacting to Congressional legislation and to agencies' implementing regulations. But it is also highly important in the US, where RIA and BCA have traditionally been positioned as a one-way "No" check by the Presidency on the tide of lawmaking by the Congress and concomitant regulating by the agencies. It is this institutional posture, more than any analytic bias, that puts BCA in the position cited by critics[138] of being used more often to restrain regulation than to promote it. That posture erodes the credibility of BCA; a more evenhanded posture is needed that uses BCA to maximize net benefits by *both* adding and subtracting regulations as warranted. There are good reasons to think that, even as some proposed regulations would yield benefits that do not justify their costs and should be revised or rejected, there are other regulations that agencies are not proposing that would increase net benefits – such as health and environmental regulations that would yield broadly diffuse benefits but concentrated costs.[139] To fill this institutional gap, in the last five years, OMB/OIRA has adopted the path

---

136 On variation in the VSL across countries, see Sunstein, n. 132 above, at 415; W Kip Viscusi and Joe Aldy, "The Value of a Statistical Life: A Critical Review of Market Estimates throughout the World," (2003) 27 *Journal of Risk and Uncertainty* 5.

137 IA Guidelines 2006, Annex 12 (adding in footnote 45 that "This rate broadly corresponds to the average real yield on longer-term government debt in the EU over a period since the early 1980s").

138 E.g. Driesen, n. 97 above; Bagley and Revesz, n. 108 above.

139 This is indeed a standard prediction of public choice theory. See William N Eskridge, Jr, "Politics without Romance: Implications of Public Choice Theory for Statutory Interpretation" (1988) 74 *Virginia Law Review* 275.

breaking innovation of "prompt letters" to urge agencies to consider adopting new regulations that look attractive on BCA criteria. Such evenhanded application of BCA would increase net benefits, while incidentally shoring up the credibility of BCA. The US should develop a more routine approach to identifying promising subjects for prompt letters, such as by issuing an annual request for proposed prompt letters (as a counterpart to OIRA's annual request for burden-reducing proposals), by assigning one or more OIRA staff to identify and develop prompt letters, and by including prompt letters more explicitly in the next revision of the Executive Order.[140] Europe, too, should also develop this kind of an evenhanded approach to IA and BCA.

Wider application

Third, IA and BCA should be applied more widely, not just to health and environmental rules but also to other important policies, such as trade measures, forest management, projects such as dams and highways, and homeland security and counter terrorism. As discussed in detail above, BCA was initially applied to many of these topics, but no longer is, or is not adequately conducted. Broadening its application would, in many of these domains, position BCA institutionally on the side of health and environmental protection – and as a more powerful tool than environmental groups have often had in these arenas to date. Combined with the continued application of BCA to regulations, this broadened role for BCA would help achieve the more neutral posture to which it aspires, while also bringing more sensible policy results in each domain.[141]

BCA should be used not only to limit costs, but also to increase net benefits. That is the explicit instruction of EO 12866. Thus, if BCA indicates that a regulation should be made more stringent than proposed, that finding should be on the same footing as a BCA in another case indicating that less stringent regulation would be preferable. BCA should correct both over- and under-regulation. And BCA should be applied to deregulation as well as to new regulation.[142] There is no reason to assume in the abstract that every deregulatory move will reduce costs more than benefits; that question should be subject to BCA.

Applying BCA to legislation would be more straightforward in the EU (where the European Commission initiates legislation and is also committed to IA), than in the US (where Congress initiates legislation but is not committed to IA – unless the Congress itself would take seriously the proposals to establish a BCA process and review office, such as in the General Accountability Office or the Congressional Budget Office, and listen to the analyses produced by that office).

---

140 See Bagley and Revesz, n. 108 above.
141 See Robert W Hahn and Cass R Sunstein, "A New Executive Order for Improving Federal Regulation? Deeper and Wider Cost-Benefit Analysis," (2002) 150 *University of Pennsylvania Law Review* 1489, 1499 (advocating broader use of BCA to render it a more neutral tool).
142 See OMB Circular A-4, n. 55 above, at 1 (covering both regulation and deregulation).

Optimal analysis

Fourth, the meta-BCA idea should be incorporated in an institutional mechanism. Where BCA remains highly contested, its application should be based on its own pros and cons (judged by the implementing agency, subject to executive branch review), rather than mandated or prohibited by law. In US law, EO 12866 and Circular A-4 already give some discretion to agencies to tailor the type of BCA or C-EA to the regulatory matter in question. Going further, Congress could enact a "superauthorization" to authorize (but not mandate) agencies to use BCA or C-EA or other analytic techniques where optimal, notwithstanding prohibitions (or requirements) in existing individual laws.[143] In EU law, the European Commission should develop a regular system to animate its "proportionate analysis" criterion through routine, considered selection of the optimal type and degree of analysis for each major policy initiative.

Multiple risks

As it constructs its program of Impact Assessment, the EU can tackle a difficult but inescapable problem that risk regulators have not yet fully addressed: the phenomenon of multiple risks. Government agencies and scientists typically assess the risk of one chemical or technology at a time.[144] For the most part, agencies regulate one risk at a time.[145] Many individual risks have thereby been reduced. But increasing recognition of the interconnectedness among multiple risks poses new demands, including the need to forecast the joint effects of simultaneous exposure to multiple risks, and to analyze the full portfolio effects, including ancillary benefits (AB) and countervailing risks (CR), of any effort to reduce a target risk.

One reason for the single-risk approach is that the cost of information (COI) increases as the problem becomes more complex. Another is institutional fragmentation – dividing up problems into smaller pieces to be addressed by different government bodies – which is the logical result of special interest politics, legislators' credit-claiming, and specialization in governance. Such specialization can be desirable, and some degree of specialization is inevitable because a monolithic government entity could not handle all issues at once (and would raise other concerns about concentration of power). But fragmentation can also yield problems when issues are interconnected. Fragmentation into

---

143 See Jonathan B Wiener, Testimony on Regulatory Reform Legislation before the Committee on Governmental Affairs, US Senate, 1995.

144 International Life Sciences Institute (ILSI), *A Framework for Cumulative Risk Assessment*, ILSI Risk Science Institute Workshop Report 5 (1999), available at http://rsi.ilsi.org/file/ rsiframrpt.pdf (visited September 10, 2003) ("Traditionally, these risk assessments have been conducted on individual chemicals medium by medium; however, humans are exposed to multiple chemicals by multiple routes concurrently in daily life.")

145 See J Clarence Davies and Jan Mazurek, *Pollution Control in the United States: Evaluating the System* (Washington, DC: RFF Press, 1999).

specialized agencies with narrow missions exacerbates the inattention to risk-risk tradeoffs, by causing spillover effects into the domains of other agencies (for example the EPA asbestos ban yielding weaker brake linings and hence increased highway accidents, or EPA limits on air toxics emissions yielding increased exposures to workers inside factories). Even within an agency's own domain, these tradeoffs can occur (for example NHTSA requiring higher fuel efficiency levels without assessing vehicle safety, or requiring airbags without assessing injuries to children; or the Iraq war plans addressing cost – albeit underestimated – but omitting the countervailing risks of collateral damage, blowback, theft, degraded combat readiness, and distraction from other threats). Actions by one government entity can impose spillover effects on others – "regulatory externalities." Some version of coordination or integration is therefore needed.

The real world is one of interconnection and complexity, in which people and ecosystems are exposed to multiple risks at the same time. Naturalist John Muir famously remarked in 1869 that "when we try to pick out anything by itself, we find it hitched to everything else in the universe."[146] The modern science of ecotoxicology is moving to formalize that insight in models of simultaneous "multiple stressors."[147] Modern legal scholars see the same thing: "It only takes a moment's reflection to see that multiple-risk situations are quite common."[148] "Most of today's environmental law violates basic principles of ecology. Nature teaches the connectedness of all activities, but most current-generation law regulates separate pollutants with little consideration of ecosystems as a whole."[149]

The multirisk world poses challenges for risk assessment. First, risk assessors should develop the means to forecast the joint effects of simultaneous exposure to multiple risks. The joint effect may be synergistic (supralinear), linear (additive), or offsetting (subtractive), but the key point is that it is the joint effect rather than the sum of the individual effects that must be forecast. Second, increasing interconnections may accelerate the transmission of risks (such as disease or terrorism) across countries and continents, through increasingly dense networks among ecological, trade, travel, and telecommunications systems (including the internet). Risk assessment needs to account for these propagation vectors. Third, rather than simply forecasting single variables (such as exposure to a chemical),

146 John Muir, *My First Summer in the Sierra* (San Francisco: Sierra Club Books, 1988), 110 (journal entry for July 27, 1869).

147 See Nico M Van Straalen, "Ecotoxicology Becomes Stress Ecology" (September 1, 2003) *Envtl Sci & Tech* 325A; J A Foran and S A Ferenc (eds), *Multiple Stressors in Ecological Risk and Impact Assessment* (Pensacola, Fla: Society of Environmental Toxicology and Chemistry (SETAC) Press, 1999); S A Ferenc and J A Foran (eds), *Multiple Stressors in Ecological Risk and Impact Assessment: Approach to Risk Estimation* (Pensacola, Fla: SETAC Press, 2000).

148 Mark Grady, Book Review, "Discontinuities and Information Burdens," reviewing William Landes and Richard Posner, *The Economic Structure of Tort Law* (1987), 56 *George Washington Law Review* 658,664 (1988).

149 E Donald Elliot, "Toward Ecological Law and Policy," in Marion R Chertow and Daniel C Esty (eds), *Thinking Ecologically* (New Haven: Yale University Press, 1997).

risk assessors need to develop multiple scenarios incorporating the mix of multiple variables affecting risk, weighted by probability judgments and sensitivity analyses.[150] US OMB Circular A-4 (September 2003) now requires a formal probabilistic portfolio of scenarios for policies with impacts exceeding $1 billion.

The multirisk world also challenges risk management. In theory, BCA embraces all effects. But in practice, BCA is often limited to looking only at the reduction in the target risk (TR) versus the increase in industry compliance cost. The problem is that risk-risk tradeoffs – the phenomenon that efforts to reduce a target risk may induce new countervailing risks[151] – are thereby ignored. The focus on TR omits countervailing and ancillary effects. And the focus on industry compliance cost favors options in which the cost of shifting from a restricted product or activity to a new substitute is low; but these substitutes can pose their own countervailing risks.

The solution is a full portfolio analysis (to "treat the whole patient" rather than focusing on one risk or symptom at a time) that applies BCA more broadly, to maximize overall risk reduction (including countervailing risks (CR) and ancillary benefits (AB), as well as target risk (TR) reductions) less overall social costs (c, including administrative costs, compliance costs, and foregone innovation).[152] Thus risk-risk tradeoff analysis needs to be made an explicit part of BCA (or conducted on its own where BCA is prohibited or otherwise not used). Even opponents of BCA agree that these risk-risk tradeoffs deserve analysis.[153]

---

150 Kahn and Wiener, n. 24 above; de Jouvenel, n. 24 above; Stephen Schneider, "Can We Estimate the likelihood of Climatic Changes at 2100? An Editorial Comment," (2002) 52 *Climatic Change* 441–451 (criticizing single-scenario forecasts and calling for probability weighted portfolios of scenarios).

151 See Graham and Wiener, n. 117 above.

152 A short version is: $\max(\Delta TR - \Delta CR + \Delta AB - C)$. See Jonathan B Wiener, "Managing the Iatrogenic Risks of Risk Management," (1998) 9 *Risk: Health Safety Environment* 39–82. Equal attention to ancillary benefits (as well as countervailing risks) is urged by Samuel J Rascoff and Richard L Revesz, "The Biases of Risk Tradeoff Analysis: Towards Parity in Regulatory Policy" (2002) 69 *University of Chicago Law Review* 1763. I agree, as we stated expressly in Graham and Wiener above n. 117, at 2, 37, 232. Indeed several of the examples of ABs offered by Rascoff and Revesz are the same examples we cited in ibid. No normative bias was intended; the goal should be an evaluation of the full portfolio of consequences.

153 Thomas O McGarity, "A Cost-Benefit State" (1998) 50 *Administrative Law Review* 7, 40–42 ("There is a grain of truth in the proposition that single-minded regulation of some health and safety risks can increase others. For example, when the Consumer Product Safety Commission promulgated a flammability standard for children's sleepwear, some manufacturers responded by treating the sleepwear with the chemical TRIS, which was later found to be carcinogenic. Health and safety agencies should take care not to create more risks than they eliminate. To the extent feasible, agencies should address ancillary risks that flow in a direct causal sequence from the conduct required or induced by their regulations. [Internal footnote: All of the risk-risk tradeoffs described in the case studies of the recent book, *Risk Versus Risk: Tradeoffs in Protecting Health and the Environment*, are of this variety]. Agencies should also coordinate regulatory initiatives with other agencies to ensure that one agency's regulation does not unduly increase risks within another agency's domain.")

EO 12866 expressly requires consideration of adverse health and environmental impacts in section 6. OMB/OIRA's Circular A-4 (2003) contains narrative instructions to perform risk-risk tradeoff analysis, although the table it attaches as a scorecard to guide agency calculations does not contain a line on which risk-risk impacts (countervailing or ancillary effects) are to be entered.[154]

The EU IA Guidelines simply say: "Identify (direct and indirect) environmental, economic and social impacts and how they occur."[155] They should pay closer attention to countervailing risks and ancillary benefits, because these factors are so often neglected in the IA process.

The phenomenon of multiple risks underscores the need for Integrated Impacts Assessment – not different IA requirements segmented into particular topics. In the US the RIA is an integrated IA, but there are also specialized IAs on environment, federalism, takings, small business, children, and others. OMB Circular A-4 encourages agencies to combine these into one document. In the EU there is one Integrated IA on economic, social, and environmental impacts (but there is also talk of creating a special IA on competitiveness). The Commission's Communication of March 16, 2005 (at 13) remarks:

> Impact Assessment system was introduced to integrate and replace all previous single-sector assessments, as un-integrated analyses had been found to have little effect on the quality of policy-making. It requires the Commission to systematically assess, on an equal basis, the likely economic (including competitiveness), environmental and social implications of its proposals and to highlight the potential trade-offs. This new impact assessment system aims at helping the Commission to improve the quality and transparency of its proposals and to identify balanced solutions consistent with Community policy objectives.

Beyond risk-risk analysis in policy development, there should be networks of notification across agencies of cross-domain side effects. In the US, EPA now notifies OSHA when air toxics regulations may induce employers to stop exterior emissions by sealing the factory, thereby trapping toxics inside the

---

154 Other approaches do not achieve this full portfolio analysis. For example, "incomerisk" ("health-health") analysis translates costs into risk units by estimating the amount of household income reduction (due to regulatory cost) associated with a death (due to reduced household expenditures on health). This in effect "riskizes" costs, instead of the standard practice of "monetizing" health risks, to achieve a common numeraire; but it does not address the risk-risk phenomena of CR or AB, which are additional effects apart from regulatory costs. "Precaution" typically looks only at ΔTR and ignores CR and C (although the European Commission's Communication calls for attention to C). A focus on Administrative Costs" ("red tape") is only a subset of C, and reducing Administrative Costs could increase social costs, for example if a good BCA would necessitate some administrative costs, or if requiring industry to do more paperwork for information disclosure would save lives.

155 IA Guidelines 2006, at 26.

workplace. But this was agreed only after OSHA complained, and there is still no government-wide process for such notifications across all agencies. The EU has a process of "Interservice Consultation,"[156] but it is not yet clear whether it will address the problem of cross-domain regulatory externality, or act as a more general invitation to comment on others' proposals.

At the legislative level, a key move is toward methods of Integrated Pollution Control.[157] In the 1990s, the United Kingdom made significant efforts to adopt IPC, in its 1990 and 1995 Environmental Protection Acts and its creation of an integrated pollution control agency.[158] The EU and other countries have considered borrowing the IPC.[159] In the US, this may require statutory changes to enable, for example, EPA's program offices for air, water, and waste to develop joint multimedia regulations, or several agencies to collaborate. Ultimately, the numerous narrowly targeted statutes could be combined into a Comprehensive Environment (or Risk) Act that integrates regulatory standards and instruments while ensuring attention to multiple risks.

The EU concept of "Interservice Steering Groups" is also promising.[160] Similarly, the US White House often fosters interagency collaboration. Interagency teams assembled to deal with shared or spillover problems connect the matrix by linking horizontally across the set of vertically isolated government silos.

More aggressively, one could pursue structural integration. This could include merger of related agencies, to internalize cross-domain regulatory externalities. For example, in the United States, EPA (Environmental Protection Agency) and OSHA (Occupational Safety and Health Administration) might be merged, or

---

156 IA Guidelines, updated March 15, 2006, Part II, s 7, at 9–12.

157 Lakshman Guruswamy, "The Case for Integrated Pollution Control" (Autumn 1991) 54 *Law and Contemporary Problems* 41; Nigel Haigh and Irene Erwin (eds), *Integrated Pollution Control* (Washington, DC: The Conservation Foundation and the Institute for European Environmental Policy, 1990).

158 Richard Macrory, "Integrated Prevention and Pollution Control: The UK Experience" in C Backes and G Betlem (eds), *Integrated Pollution Prevention and Control* (The Hague: Kluwer International, 1991) 53–64; Albert Weale, "Environmental Regulation and Administrative Reform in Britain" in Giandomenico Majone (ed), *Regulating Europe* (London: Routledge, 1996) 106; Michael Purdue, "Integrated Pollution Control in the Environmental Protection Act 1990: A Coming of Age of Environmental Law?" (1991) 54 *Modern Law Review* 534; Neil Carter and Philip Lowe, "The Establishment of a Cross-Sector Environment Agency" in T Gray (ed), *UK Environmental Policy in the 1990s* (New York: St Martin's Press, 1995) 38.

159 See Chris Backes and Gerrit Betlem (eds), *Integrated Pollution Prevention and Control: The EC Directive from a Comparative Legal and Economic Perspective* (The Hague: Kluwer Law International, 1999); Johannes Zöttl, "Towards Integrated Protection of the Environment in Germany?" (2000) *12 J Envtl L 281.*

160 IA Guidelines, updated March 15, 2006, Part II, s 6, at 9 ("An Inter-Service Steering Group is compulsory for all items of a cross-cutting nature. The Roadmap asks DGs to provide valid justification in those instances when no Inter-Service Steering Group is envisaged. These groups are there to provide specialised inputs and to bring a wider perspective to the process. Involving other DGs from the early stages will also make it easier to reach agreement during the Inter-Service Consultation").

those two might be combined into a new Risk Department along with others such as the CPSC (Consumer Product Safety Commission), NHTSA (National Highway Traffic Safety Administration), the aviation safety branch of FAA (Federal Aviation Authority) (now partly of TSA, the Transportation Security Administration), and the food safety branch of the FDA. Land and resource management agencies such as the Forest Service, National Park Service, BLM (Bureau of Land Management), FWS (Fish and Wildlife Service), and NMFS (National Marine Fisheries Service) could also be merged into an integrated resource conservation agency. In the EU, one can imagine combining DG (Directorates General) such as DG Environment and DG SANCO (Health and Consumer Affairs). But all these mergers would only be worthwhile if they improved decision-making on complex multirisk problems. They would yield little if the statutory authority to regulate were not also revised, or if the cultures of the pre-existing units remained so balkanized that they continued to regulate without regard for their effects on each other. Merged agencies may continue to operate with fragmented internal structures (as EPA's different program offices are fragmented despite the integrationist agenda for founding EPA). The recent merger of several US agencies into the new Department of Homeland Security offers an opportunity to study and learn from a mega-merger of risk regulatory agencies. In addition to the concern that mergers may mean greater centralization of power, there is also the concern that more centralized management could be more rigid even as a multirisk world demands more agile and creative policymaking. All things considered, merger of agencies seems not as urgent as inculcating a multirisk approach in each agency.

Finally, the White House and the European Commission could each create a Primary Risk Manager to help coordinate risk regulation across the government.[161] Like a primary care physician who monitors the whole patient but refers more serious ailments to specialists, the primary risk manager would dispatch specific problems to expert agencies while supervising and monitoring the whole. The primary risk manager could help coordinate responses to multiple simultaneous risks, and ensure attention to ancillary effects that cross agency jurisdictions. It could also ensure within–agency consideration of ancillary effects.

One point here is that Better Regulation of multiple interconnected risks can imply the need for more, not less regulation – for more comprehensive regulation to avoid perverse shifts (induced regulatory externalities). That is, when narrow regulation creates countervailing risks, rather than regulate the target risk less, the optimal strategy may be to adopt more embracing regulation that internalizes both the market externality (target risk) and the regulatory externality (countervailing risk). Such comprehensive approaches can also be less costly than the sum of separate regulations for each risk. For example, if

---

161 Graham and Wiener, n. 117 above ch 11.

regulating CO_2 alone induces perverse shifts to emissions of methane (CH_4) that increase net global warming, the optimal solution might be to regulate both in a comprehensive multigas approach – both more protective and less costly.[162]

Administrative simplification

The leading phalanx of Better Regulation in European member states is currently the campaign to reduce administrative costs and adopt simplification measures. For example, the Netherlands developed the standard cost model to measure administrative costs, the UK is cutting red tape, the Merkel government in Germany is scaling back bureaucracy, and France hosted a June 2006 conference on administrative simplification. The EU has programs on administrative cost reduction and simplification. The OECD has developed a red tape scoreboard and is conducting a pilot exercise in the road freight transport sector.

Administrative costs are the costs of furnishing information and of processing government functions. Reducing administrative costs can be pursued both *ex ante* (in review of proposed new regulations and information requirements) and *ex post* (to reduce the costs of existing programs). "Simplification" entails combining, codifying, or repealing old laws, in order to make them easier to understand, to reduce the complexity of bureaucratic steps the public must navigate, and to remove obsolete provisions.

Administrative cost reduction and simplification can be highly desirable, especially in legal systems encumbered with outdated and uncodified rules and a labyrinth of bureaucracy. But administrative cost reduction and simplification pursued narrowly could be counterproductive. They need to be evaluated in terms of their full social costs and benefits.

Administrative costs

Reducing administrative costs can be one important way to remove barriers to business activities, facilitate new business startups, and diminish the hassles and intrusions faced by individuals. In Europe, the standard cost model (SCM) is being applied to measure and reduce paperwork burdens and time consumption due to information demands imposed on businesses and individuals by regulation. The Netherlands pioneered the SCM in 2002, and there is now an SCM Network involving at least nine EU member states.[163] Further, European

---

162 See Jonathan B Wiener, "Protecting the Global Environment" in ibid, ch. 10; Richard B Stewart and Jonathan B Wiener, *Reconstructing Climate Policy* (Washington, DC: AEI Press, 2003).

163 See the SCM Network website at http://www.administrative-burdens.com/. A brief discussion of progress to date is in European Commission, Communication from the Commission on an EU common methodology for assessing administrative costs imposed by legislation, SEC(2005)1329, COM(2005) 518 final (Brussels, October 21, 2005), at 4.

governments are setting political targets, such as a 20 or 25 percent reduction in administrative costs from a base level estimated by the SCM inventory.[164] European member states face both national (member state) and EU administrative requirements, but reducing the latter may increase the former.[165] The European Commission has developed a common methodology for measuring administrative burden[166] and is undertaking a pilot project to measure administrative costs in industry sectors (initially construction, with others to be added next year) across Europe. In May 2006, European Commission Vice President Günter Verheugen announced the EU's own 25 percent target to reduce administrative costs, to be achieved in partnership with the member states' own cost reduction programs.[167]

---

164 See examples at the SCM Network website, n. 162 above. For example, on April 27, 2006, Austria set a target of reducing administrative costs by 25 percent by 2010 using the SCM, see http://www.administrative-burdens.com/default.asp?page=1&article=69.

165 The Commission pointed out: "Administrative obligations should therefore not be presented as mere "red tape," a term normally reserved for needlessly time-consuming, excessively complicated or useless procedures. Nor should EU administrative obligations be presented as a mere cost factor, as it often replaces 25 different national legislations and thus decreases operating costs at EU level." European Commission, Communication from the Commission on an EU common methodology for assessing administrative costs imposed by legislation, SEC(2005)1329, COM(2005) 518 final (Brussels, October 21, 2005), at 2 (footnote omitted).

166 See IA Guidelines 2006, Annex 10 (on administrative cost measurement); European Commission, Communication from the Commission on an EU common methodology for assessing administrative costs imposed by legislation, SEC(2005)1329, COM(2005) 518 final (Brussels, October 21, 2005).

167 He said: "I believe that we should give particular attention to the administrative costs of regulation since these costs can be cut without affecting the objectives of the legislation itself. They are the proverbial "low hanging fruit" of our Better Regulation agenda. And they are the major irritants European citizens and businesses are confronted with in their daily lives. Crucially, work done by several Member States, notably the Netherlands, suggests that both these costs and the potential for reducing them are very significant. If these estimates are correct, Europe is spending more than 2.5 percent of its GDP – or some 275 billion euros every year – on reporting requirements and other administrative obligations linked to our regulatory system. Moreover, these costs fall disproportionally on small and medium sized enterprises – the job engine of the European economy. This is patently absurd at a time that we are putting competitiveness at the heart of our policy agenda. I am, therefore, of the opinion that we should look at cutting these costs by 25 percent and I will take a proposal to the Commission suggesting how this objective can be achieved. To lay the foundations for this proposal, I have instructed my services to launch the necessary studies, which will provide a baseline against which we can measure administrative costs, as soon as possible.... There will...have to be a shared responsibility for reaching the 25 percent objective. I am optimistic that we can achieve this partnership since 17 Member States have already announced administrative cost reduction measures in their Lisbon National Reform Programmes. Through the newly created High Level Group on Better Regulation we are working closely with experts from all the Member States to prepare this ambitious project." Günter Verheugen, Vice President of the European Commission responsible for Enterprise and Industry, Better Regulation for Jobs and Growth, Former Members Dinner, European Parliament Former Members Association, Brussels, 10 May 2006, SPEECH/06/287, available at http://ec.europa.eu/ commission_barroso/verheugen/speeches/speeches_en.htm.

In the US, the Paperwork Reduction Acts of 1980 and 1995, and OMB Circular A-130,[168] established the objective and methods of cutting administrative costs. OMB measures the time spent by businesses and individuals in filling out each form, works to reduce that time, and requires new surveys and other information-gathering projects to receive OIRA approval. But OIRA has gone beyond that task – as directed by EOs 12291 and 12866 – to assess the full social costs and benefits of policies.

Better Regulation should address administrative costs, but should not focus solely or predominantly on administrative costs. "Cutting red tape" is popular, but does not assess the full costs or benefits of a policy. The political targets of 20 or 25 percent reductions in administrative costs are like Procrustes' insistence that guests be cropped to fit his bed: these targets arbitrarily crop information-based programs without considering the benefits of such information collection or the other costs that might increase if information collection is curtailed. Even granting that administrative costs are too high in many countries, the 20 or 25 percent reduction targets have not been based on an analysis of the optimal reduction in such costs. In some countries or sectors the optimal reduction in administrative costs might be greater than 25 percent; in others it might be less than a 20 percent reduction, or even an increase in administrative costs if gathering new information would yield net benefits.

Focusing exclusively on cutting administrative costs could be perverse. It could forfeit the large social benefits of some information disclosure programs, such as the US Toxics Release Inventory[169] and similar European pollutant discharge registries.[170] Cutting administrative costs could be accomplished by swiftly adopting highly precautionary regulations, based on little information or analysis, that impose high social costs in foregone innovation. Administrative costs could also be cut by eschewing the information demands of BCA and proceeding to adopt regulations that impose lower administrative costs but greater social costs.[171] Vice President Verheugen's remarks (just quoted) express

---

168 44 USC s 35; OMB Circular A-130, Management of Federal Information Resources, at http://www.whitehouse.gov/omb/circulars/al30/al30trans4.html.

169 See James T Hamilton, *Regulation through Revelation: The Origin, Politics and Impacts of the Toxics Release Inventory Program* (Cambridge: Cambridge University Press, 2005).

170 See Peter H Sand, "Information Disclosure" (2003) 63 *Heidelberg Journal of International Law (Zeitschrift für ausländisches öffentliches Recht und Völkerrecht)* 487–502 (revised as Peter H Sand, "Information Disclosure and the Atlantic Divide" in Jonathan B Wiener *et al* (eds), *The Reality of Precaution: Comparing Risk Regulation in the United States and Europe* (forthcoming 2006)).

171 Consider these four hypothetical policies and their associated costs and benefits:
    Policy A: Admin cost 10, Full cost 13, Benefit 20. Net Benefit = 7.
    Policy B: Admin cost 7, Full cost 10, Benefit 19. Net Benefit = 9.
    Policy C: Admin cost 4, Full cost 7, Benefit 12. Net Benefit = 5.
    Policy D: Admin cost 2, Full cost 16, Benefit 10. Net Benefit = –6.
    To reduce administrative costs alone, one would prefer option D. To reduce full costs alone: prefer C. To maximize benefits alone: prefer A. To maximize net benefits: prefer B.

optimism that administrative costs "can be cut without affecting the objectives of the legislation itself," but in many cases administrative costs support valuable information collection efforts that are necessary for policies to yield benefits or reduce other costs. The 20 or 25 percent targets to reduce administrative costs do not appear to take these benefits and other savings into account.

To reduce administrative costs while avoiding these potentially counterproductive results, rather than simply setting targets to cut administrative costs alone, European Union institutions and member states should use IA and BCA to assess the full social costs and benefits of policy changes to reduce administrative costs. This point was recently recognized by the European Commission: On March 15, 2006 the Commission inserted a warning to this effect, as a new "Box 11" in the updated version of the IA Guidelines. Box 11 now reads:

> The fact that one option would impose lower administrative costs is *not* in itself a sufficient reason to prefer it. For example, a measure ... likely to impose relatively fewer administrative costs [by mandating specific technical standards, instead of requiring labels that disclose product data] ... could give manufacturers less flexibility and could reduce consumer choice, [so that] its overall costs may be higher than the "administrative" requirement to display data ... [172]

This Box 11 was not present in the June 2005 IA Guidelines. Its addition in the updated 2006 Guidelines indicates that the Commission is responding to the zeal for cutting red tape and tempering that zeal with attention to full costs.[173] The Commission should now go further to add explicit consideration of benefits as well as costs, and should address this issue in the member states as well.

Simplification

The EU and several member states have also embarked on ambitious programs of simplification. In October 2005 the European Commission announced "a three year programme to simplify the existing thousands of pages of EU legislation ("acquis") adopted since 1957," including a proposal "to repeal, codify, recast or modify 222 basic legislations and over 1,400 related legal acts in the next three years" and "to tackle administrative burden, especially for small business, by simplifying cumbersome statistics form-filling or by modernizing the customs

---

172 See EU IA Guidelines 2006, Part III, s 5.1, at 39, Box 11.
173 As the Commission remarked, "Regulatory costs, of which administrative obligations are just one element, must be analysed in a broad context, encompassing the economic, social and environmental costs and benefits of regulation." European Commission, Communication from the Commission on an EU common methodology for assessing administrative costs imposed by legislation, SEC(2005)1329, COM(2005) 518 final (Brussels, 21 October 2005), at 3.

code to facilitate electronic exchange of information."[174] The Communication issued to launch this policy outlined each of these strategies (repeal, codify, recast, modify), as well as efforts to make greater use of information technology, to use performance standards instead of technical design standards, and to replace some EU "directives" (which call on member states to transpose their instructions into national law – akin to "cooperative federalism" in the US) with EU "regulations" (which are effective throughout the EU without such transposition – akin to federal pre-emption in the US), in order to achieve more uniform and hence simpler rules across the European single market.[175]

The best understanding of simplification is that it attempts to modernize a body of law by editing, pruning, organizing, and streamlining the laws so that they are more clear, understandable, and effective as well as less burdensome to navigate. It may well be that legal rules in some countries in Europe (and in the US) are so labyrinthine that businesses and individuals must incur high costs just to figure out what the law means. Simplification in the EU is thus reminiscent of the codification movement in the US led by David Dudley Field in the mid-1800s, and the effort in the last several decades in some US states and the federal government to write laws in plain understandable language. This was one of the goals of the Clinton–Gore "National Performance Review" and the Presidential Memorandum of June 1, 1998. As simplification moves beyond consolidation and codification to undertake the repeal of obsolete or superfluous laws, it is also expressing the view that venerable vintage is not a sufficient reason to preserve a law – perhaps best crystallized by US Supreme Court Justice Oliver Wendell Holmes, Jr:

> It is revolting to have no better reason for a rule of law than that so it was laid down in the time of Henry IV. It is still more revolting if the grounds upon which it was laid down have vanished long since, and the rule simply persists from blind imitation of the past.[176]

But in the EU simplification effort there is also an unmistakable bent of, if not deregulation, then selective excision of obsolete laws. The French example is

---

174 See DG Enterprise and Industry, "Better Regulation–Simplification," October 25, 2005, posted at http://ec.europa.eu/enterprise/regulation/better_regulation/simplification.htm.

175 European Commission, Communication of the Commission to the European Parliament, the Council, the European Economic and Social Committee and the Committee of the Regions, "Implementing the Community Lisbon Programme: A Strategy for the Simplification of the Regulatory Environment," COM(2005) 535 final (Brussels, October 25, 2005), available at http://ec.europa.eu/enterprise/regulation/ better_regulation/simplification.htm.

176 Oliver Wendell Holmes, Jr, "The Path of the Law" (1897) 10 *Harvard Law Review*, 469. Holmes was referring to common law rules, which judges can change. Statutes enacted by the legislature may be more difficult for judges to reform and may deserve reform programs or phaseout schedules to enable periodic review and revision or repeal. See Guido Calabresi, *A Common Law for the Age of Statutes* (Cambridge, Mass: Harvard University Press, 1983).

telling: after laws enacted in 2003 and 2004 to reduce costs to businesses and individuals, France is now considering enactment in 2006 of the *loi anti-loi* – the so-called "anti-law law" or "killer law," which can be used to abrogate outdated or meaningless laws. Belgium has a "Kafka test" to identify maddening bureaucratic puzzles. These may be a good idea – casual observation and a series of World Bank studies[177] both hint at the possibility that some European law could use some tidying up, flexibility, and codification (rather than the opaque system of citation by date of enactment) – but success depends on the *criteria* for determining which laws to rescind or revise or reorganize, and who has the power to make these decisions. At a meeting on Administrative Simplification in Paris on June 9, 2006, I asked what these criteria might be, and the response was that laws that "have been in disuse for a long time" *(en désuétude)* would be deemed obsolete and slated for repeal. This standard is too vague, inviting biased selective enforcement. And it neglects the possibility that while some old laws are indeed obsolete, others may be dormant because they are widely accepted and rarely violated, but the act of repealing them signals open season to transgress the old norm in undesirable ways.

The Mandelkern Group emphasized that simplification does not mean simplistic deregulation:

> The Group's concept of simplification is not to be mistaken with deregulation. The two concepts cannot be regarded as synonyms. Deregulation simply refers to the abolition of rules in a certain sector, whereas simplification – a more advanced stage in governing regulation – is aimed at preserving the existence of rules in a certain sector, while making them more effective, less burdensome, and easier to understand and to comply with.... Therefore, by simplification we refer to the process of reform of existing regulation, which seeks to streamline administrative procedures and to reduce the burden of compliance on citizens, businesses and the public sector itself, while preserving the intended (political) goals of the regulation.[178]

But sometimes the original intended goals of the legislation also become obsolete. Changes in economics, technology, and social values may well call for repeal or replacement of old laws. The key, again, is the criteria for such choices.

---

177 World Bank, "Doing Business in 2006: Creating Jobs" (2006), "Doing Business in 2005: Removing Obstacles to Growth" (2005), and "Doing Business in 2004: Understanding Regulation" (2004), all available at http://www.doingbusiness.org/. In the 2006 report, in the summary ranking on "Ease of Doing Business," France ranked 44th and Italy 70th, while Denmark, the UK, and Ireland were eighth, ninth, and 11th. The top three spots in both 2006 and 2005 were held by New Zealand, Singapore, and the USA. These reports focus on economic (price and entry) regulation, not on risk (health, safety and environmental) regulation. There can also be debates about the methodologies used to compile the rankings.

178 Mandelkern Group Report (2001), n. 2 above, at 33.

Standing alone, the simplification initiative lacks clear criteria for identifying and modifying laws.

Instead, I suggest applying IA and BCA to decide on the rescission or revision of existing laws. IA and BCA should be used to evaluate existing regulations as well as new regulations, and to evaluate deregulation and simplification as well as new regulatory proposals. Such evenhandedness would reduce the current new/old bias in regulatory review. It would also correct the bias toward cutting regulatory costs or repealing old laws without considering benefits. Some existing laws and regulations should be phased out, and others strengthened, depending on new information and learning, but this process should be guided by sensible analysis rather than only by political impulses. More blunt approaches – such as predetermined "sunset" dates at which regulations automatically expire, or political targets to cut administrative costs by a certain percentage, or deregulation without BCA, or simplification programs to rescind laws on the ground that they have not been used recently – are crudely effective but arbitrary; they neglect the benefits of existing policies and administrative requirements (including costly policies that generate worthwhile benefits, and laws that have not been used recently because compliance is universal as long as the law is in effect). Applying BCA criteria to the review of existing policies would be better: it would put the focus on benefits as well as costs, and it would enable net benefits to be maximized by strengthening, revising, weakening, or eliminating these policies, as the merits warrant.[179]

One promising tack for simplification programs would be to rescind perverse subsidies.[180] Governments spend billions of taxpayer dollars (and euros) on subsidizing agriculture, energy, mining, water use, logging, and many other industries. Such policies often endure long after their initial usefulness has ebbed, yet continue to support activities that are both environmentally harmful and economically wasteful. They are resilient in part because they are supported by concentrated beneficiary constituencies, and impose diffuse costs on the general tax-paying public who face free-rider incentives not to complain. To surmount these rent-seeking pressures in favor of subsidies, the EU and the US could

---

179 The Commission appears to be heading in this direction: "Simplification is not merely an exercise in improving accessibility and readability. It is intended to operate within the Competitiveness policy and for this reason a reinvigorated simplification programme, to be launched in 2006/7, will reinforce the mechanisms for identifying legislation that requires simplification; namely legislation which careful assessment shows to be disproportionately burdensome for EU citizens and businesses in relation to the public interests that the legislation aims to safeguard.... It is only when the assessment of proportionality clearly confirms that public interests might be equally well served by simpler means that the repeal or modification of the legislation should be considered." DG Enterprise and Industry, "Better Regulation–Simplification," October 25, 2005, posted at http://ec.europa.eu/enterprise/regulation/better_regulation/simplification.htm.

180 See Norman Myers and Jennifer Kent, *Perverse Subsidies* (Washington, DC: Island Press, 2001); Barton Thompson, n. 93 above (suggesting rescission of perverse subsidies in order to protect biodiversity).

consider setting up non-political commissions to identify subsidies for rescission (based on BCA), with the recommendations to take effect unless the relevant legislature acts to preserve them. Transitions to systems of support payments that are not tied to output could be added to assist dependent communities to wean themselves off subsidies. This approach would be similar to the US military base closure commission. And it would use the power of simplification under Better Regulation to address a problem of enormous domestic and international concern. Such a "subsidy-closing commission" could not only save costs and the environment in the US and EU, but also benefit farmers in poor countries, and make progress in the stalemate over international trade liberalization.

Oversight

All of this analysis and reform will not make Better Regulation succeed if it does not influence policy decisions. Impact assessment can change minds, but it can also become merely cosmetic – a "relookage" as they say in France – if there is no oversight mechanism to ensure that the analysis is taken into account in decisions. Some mechanism to check, review, and shape legislation is needed in the EU institutions.

In the US, environmental impact assessment under NEPA has persistently faced the criticism that agencies do the EIA, but merely attach it to the decision they would have made anyway. This is despite the availability of judicial review of NEPA law, including the courts' power to issue injunctions halting projects. One reason is that judicial review is infrequent enough to be a weak deterrent. Another is that NEPA has been held by the US Supreme Court to be "purely procedural," a "stop and think" law, requiring agencies to assess environmental impacts but not imposing substantive criteria or constraints on the ultimate decision.[181]

By contrast, RIA is sometimes criticized as overly influential, binding agencies too much as they seek to satisfy OIRA's criteria for BCA; and yet sometimes criticized as inadequately influential, because only about half of agency RIAs monetize the benefits and costs. Still, OIRA's own data show that net benefits have increased over time in response to the RIA and BCA requirements.[182] Yet there is no judicial review of RIAs (although courts can and do take note of RIAs in their decisions under other laws, such as the "arbitrary and capricious" standard of the Administrative Procedure Act). The reason for even the partial success of the RIA process is undoubtedly the role of OIRA in reviewing the RIAs and returning

---

181 See *Strycker's Bay Neighborhood Council v Karlen*, n. 65 above. Others have, to be sure, criticized NEPA and judicial review of the EIS for delaying federal projects. See Holder, n. 68 above. One study found that NEPA impact analyses usually imposed low costs of delay and did influence agencies to consider and avoid environmental impacts. Serge Taylor, *Making Bureaucracies Think: The EIS Strategy of Administrative Reform* (Stanford, Calif: Stanford University Press, 1984).

182 See OMBOIRA Annual Report, 2005 n. 103 above.

proposed rules when the criteria are not met. OIRA is more successful at supervising RIA than the courts are at supervising EIA because judicial review is decentralized and non-expert, whereas centralized executive branch oversight is expert and potent while helping to obthroughte judicial oversight.[183]

In the EU, at least at the European Commission, the Better Regulation initiative is still in search of an oversight mechanism. The Mandelkern Group Report suggested several options, including central, lateral, interinstitutional, and external models.[184] The crucial criterion is an effective ability to influence decisions. As the Mandelkern Group wrote:

> [T]he issue of appropriate **structures** is an absolutely **crucial topic.** The success of efforts on better regulation will ultimately depend on this very issue.... Based on the experience in various administrations there are four main elements that seem to be essential for the chosen structure to be effective:
>
> – **Strong political support** Better regulation programmes need very strong political support to produce the desired outcome;
> – **Support from the centre** The best results are often achieved with the Head of Government personally and/or at least institutionally interested and involved;
> – **A horizontal approach** Very clearly, an all-government approach is necessary; sectoral approaches limited to individual Ministries or Directorates-General will not achieve optimum results and a coherent, horizontal approach is needed; and
> – **A strategic approach** Close connection to the strategic planning of the government/administration is of real benefit."[185]

---

183 Justice Breyer's suggestion in *Breaking the Vicious Circle* (1993), n. 26 above, was an elite expert group that could manage the risk regulation system to avoid the distortions of interest group politics and heuristic errors. He cited the French *Conseil d'Etat* as a potential model. Some criticized this proposal as unduly technocratic and insulated from democratic input. That same year, President Clinton issued EO 12866, maintaining OIRA authority over regulation while expanding its transparency and public accountability.

184 The Mandelkern Group Report (2001), at 50, considered several options: "There are five main best practice options for effective structures, of which the first is recommended by OECD guidelines:

– A primary unit based at or near the centre of the administration, with or without a network of satellite units across the main Ministries or Directorates-General;
– A primary unit based in a part of the administration other than the centre (e.g. Public Administration or Economic Affairs Ministry), probably with a network of satellite units;
– An inter-ministerial co-ordination committee;
– A network of units/responsibilities across the main Ministries or Directorates-General, with or without support from a primary unit; and
– A body external to the administration (a body of such type may especially be apt to be integrated into the evaluation of the consequences of already existing regulation)."

185 Mandelkern Group Report (2001), at 47–48 (emphasis in original).

This body/structure must, by virtue of its qualified staff with a range of expertise, its specific position in the administration, its recognised authority and its expertise in managing regulatory quality tools, be able to ensure adherence to the process that contributes towards improving regulatory quality. At the same time this body/structure must have an appropriate level of autonomy, as well as objectiveness with regard to the policy officials who prepare regulations ... the body/structure might also be given a gate-keeping function."[186]

Yet despite this advice from 2001, and the US model in place since at least 1981, the European Commission appears still to be searching in 2006 for the best way to handle the oversight question. Constructing an oversight mechanism is a work in progress. Vice President Verheugen recently declared:

> I will be campaigning for three major new initiatives: First, President Barroso and I will significantly strengthen central oversight in the Commission to police the quality of our Impact Assessment. While the Impact Assessments must be carried out by the services responsible for the development of the proposals, we must also ensure that they are rigorously scrutinised by an 'independent party' within the Commission but with no involvement in the preparation of the file. This is why as a first step, we are creating a standing committee of senior officials who will be tasked with ensuring that the Impact Assessments are in full conformity with the exacting requirements we have set ourselves. These officials should report directly to the President and myself. In this way we can strengthen the system of checks and balances in the Commission.[187]

Where this independent review will be located is still an open question. Within the European Commission, the office of the Secretariat General has the authority to perform this function, but does not yet have the expert staff to review IAs, and has not yet issued an *avis negatif* based on an IA. Perhaps it will soon bolster its capacity. Other options for a central oversight body include the Bureau of European Policy Advisors attached to the Presidency; a new Presidential office; or a shared group of DGs or an interinstitutional body linking several units such as DG Enterprise, DG EcoFin, DG Environment, DG SANCO, the Legal Service, and others with expert staff.

But none of these has yet been adopted at the EU level.[188] The structure of power in the Commission to some extent inhibits a strong central role, because

---

186 Mandelkern Group Report (2001), at 49.
187 Günter Verheugen, Vice-President of the European Commission responsible for Enterprise and Industry, Better Regulation for Jobs and Growth, Former Members Dinner, European Parliament Former Members Association, Brussels, May 10, 2006, SPEECH/06/287, available at http://ec.europa.eu/commission_barroso/verheugen/ speeches/speeches_en.htm.
188 Several have been tried at the member state level. See Hahn and Litan, n. 19 above. The UK has a central expert body in its Better Regulation Executive. Finland assigns the oversight role to its

the President of the Commission is not popularly elected and remains one member of the College of Commissioners, all of whom are appointed at the same time and are expected to work together. Moreover, the objective of the European Union is in substantial part to prevent conflicts among the countries of Europe, and as a result the collegial and courteous style of work within the Commission seems, at least to an outsider accustomed to the tough debates within the White House "family," to be unreceptive to the sharp and hierarchical confrontations over policies that central regulatory oversight might entail. The question is whether a Commission could decide collegially to establish an oversight office with real power, an office that would sometimes oppose the position of one or another individual Commissioner, or whether instead such a reform must await more radical governance reform such as the advent of a popularly elected European President who could install such an office.

Meanwhile, filling the open niche, DG Enterprise has developed substantial staff expertise and appears to be acting, in effect, as the "lateral" oversight arm. If so, this is progress, but it is not yet the ideal. Lateral oversight offers staff capacity, but typically lacks the power to enforce supervisory decisions on other co-equal units. And lateral oversight lacks the perspective and legitimacy of central oversight. Even if DG Enterprise does a very fine job, its lateral posture will yield the appearance (if not the reality) of factionalized or parochial review, if it appears to represent the interests of business rather than of full social impacts, in turn raising questions about its credibility and hence its sustainability.[189] The review function (including staff with expertise) should thus be relocated to the center, that is, to the Presidency of the Commission. DG Enterprise could continue its review activities in support of this central office, or the current review team at DG Enterprise could (along with others) be promoted to become the staff of the central office.[190]

This central oversight office should not be just a referee, nor simply a check on regulation percolating up from the DGs. That is too reactive a posture. The central oversight office should be closely attached to the Presidency of the

Trade Ministry, and Hungary to its Justice Ministry. Recently, France shifted its Better Regulation office from the office of *Réforme de l'Etat*, attached to the Prime Minister, to the Ministry of Finance, Economy and Industry. Although this creates a lateral review rather than a central office, its objective was to combine regulatory review with fiscal budgetary review in the Finance Ministry and thereby to add effective teeth to the review function.

189 Radaelli, n. 28 above, at 940, argues that "credibility is the Achilles heel of impact assessment. [If] RIA is tilted towards one actor's preferences to the detriment of others, there is no economic analysis that can compensate for the credibility deficit."

190 Consistent with this recommendation, as this paper was going to press in late 2006, the European Commission announced the creation of a new Impact Assessment Board (IAB), reporting directly to the president, composed of selected high-level commission officials, with the role of commenting on the quality of Impact Assessements. See communication from the commission, A Strategic Review of Better Regulation in the European Union: COM (2006)689 final, November 14, 2006, at http://ec.europa.eu/governance/impact/docs/key_docs/com_2006_0689_en.pdf. But it remains to be seen how this IAB will operate, with what staff expertise and with what authority to influence policy decisions.

Commission and should carry out the President's strategy for regulatory policy (such as Better Regulation using IA).[191] Of course the Commission President could lead this initiative along with one of the Vice Presidents (just as the US Executive Orders originally designated the Vice President to oversee OMB/OIRA, a role now transferred to the White House Chief of Staff by EO 13258). In addition to waiting for regulatory proposals to arrive from the DGs for review, the central oversight office should play an early role in shaping the regulatory priorities of the Commission, working with DGs to identify subjects warranting regulation, to improve their policy proposals, to reconcile tradeoffs, and to ensure best practices across DGs. It should issue "prompt" letters to stimulate new regulation that its expert analysis deems desirable, and "return" letters (or *avis negatifs*) to reject regulations where the analysis is inadequate.

In the EU system the Commission initiates new legislation, so IA within the Commission is important, especially at a central oversight office that can reconcile competing interests across the DGs. Otherwise the lead DG may simply carry the day, or there may be horse trading among DGs (among Commissioners) in which each gets its priority initiatives adopted but none is truly assessed for overall net benefit to the EU.

> Complicated regulation arises in large part from current practice of the Commission, by which regulation is drafted primarily by more than 20 Directorates-General, with an imperfect degree of co-ordination among them. This does not optimise collegiate action and often forsakes the benefits that could be gained by a more deliberative form of decision-making. On this crucial topic, it has been widely observed that different DGs draw up draft directives in themselves perfectly compatible with the objectives and administrative culture of a particular DG, but compatibility with general EU interests is weakly ensured.[192]

Central oversight of the IA process in the Commission would thus be important to ensure that EU-wide net benefits are considered in important regulatory policies.

Even if the Commission does establish centralized review, there may also be a need for an external check on the Commission because of the Commission's monopoly on initiating legislation. This external check could be situated in the Council, the Parliament, or an Interinstitutional body.

---

191 See Kagan, n. 18 above, ("We live today in an era of Presidential administration . . . presidential control of administration, in critical respects, expanded dramatically during the Clinton years, making the regulatory activity of the executive branch agencies more and more an extension of the President's own policy and political agenda"); James F Blumstein, "Regulatory Review by the Executive Office of the President" (2001) 51 *Duke Law Journal* 851. For doubts whether the Presidential agenda and expert BCA can fully coexist in regulatory review, see Stuart Shapiro, "Politics and Regulatory Policy Analysis," (summer 2006) *Regulation* magazine 40–45.
192 Mandelkern Group Report (2001), at 64.

The Council is currently ill-suited to this task because the Council members who meet on a particular matter, although ostensibly representing each member state's prime minister or government, in fact tend to be the ministers from the single ministry concerned with the specific issue of the legislation (for example all the Environment ministers), and therefore tend to support the legislation. "At the European level, even if the proposals have to come from the Commission, which, operating in collegiate fashion, seeks to weigh the various demands and interests, the competent Council is composed of just the sectoral ministers, who are in charge of the final decision. This asymmetry leads to a systematic tendency towards the growth of regulation."[193] The Council's role in IA could be strengthened if the member states insisted on a full consideration of impacts before deciding on instructions for their delegates to the Council, and, furthermore, if the member states conducted their own IAs. There is now talk of member state parliaments doing so in order to assess EU directives before they are adopted and must be transposed into member state law. The Council's role in EU-level Better Regulation could be best supported if the member states created a network or pool of member state experts (drawn from each member state's own central regulatory oversight office) – the Council's own "regulatory analysis review group," to borrow the title of President Carter's interagency body – available to conduct IAs for the Council and to deliberate together on regulatory proposals. The Commission's Communication of March 16, 2005, at 10, announces a "group of high-level national regulatory experts," although this group may or may not be in a position to advise the Council.

Apart from the Council, external oversight would be left to the European Courts or the European Parliament. The Courts are not equipped with the staff or expertise to perform IA, and they tend to defer to the Commission and the Council (as in the *Pfizer* case discussed above). But if the other EU institutions do not effectively oversee regulatory policy, the courts may step in. The European Parliament, meanwhile, has the motivation to check legislative initiatives coming from the Commission, but so far does not have the political clout. In the US, the adoption of the Congressional Review Act in 1996 authorized a special procedure for Congress to reject an agency regulation (a power Congress always had through legislation, so long as the President did not veto the law or Congress could override the veto), but Congress did not create an expert body to conduct IA, so exercise of the CRA remains an essentially political act. And it remains rare – of almost 42,000 rules including 610 major rules promulgated in the last ten years, the Congressional Review Act has only been used to reject one: the ergonomics rule rescinded in March 2001.[194] Adding

---

193 Mandelkern Group Report (2001), at 64.
194 Statement of Morton Rosenberg, Congressional Research Service, before the House Subcommittee on Commercial and Administrative Law, Committee on the Judiciary, Concerning Oversight of the Congressional Review Act on the Tenth Anniversary of its Enactment, March 30, 2006, http://judiciary.house.gov/media/pdfs/rosenberg033006.pdf, at 3.

an expert body equipped to perform IA in the US Congress and in the European Parliament (as a counterpart to IA by the White House and the Commission) could raise the Parliament's stature and enable it to engage actively in reasoned debate over regulatory policy (to reject, revise, or prompt policies, as the net benefits warrant). In the US, such a body could also, perhaps even more importantly, enable IA of legislative proposals in Congress, which currently are not subject to IA. But if no such expert IA body is created, then Congressional or Parliamentary review of regulatory policy could be seriously dysfunctional: driven by the vicissitudes of political winds and caprice, unrelated to societal net benefits, it could mark a return to horse trading among parties and parochialisms that would harm rather than help yield Better Regulation.

In sum, a central oversight office is needed in the EU regulatory system, but the unique features of EU governance imply that "centralized" could be within the Commission (overseeing the DGs), at the Council (with support from the member states), at the Parliament, or in a new interinstitutional body. This oversight office needs the capacity to conduct excellent analysis, embracing the broad set of topics outlined above, with skills not only in economics but in other fields as well, including the science underlying benefits estimates and risk assessments. It needs the power to influence decisions: to say no (return), yes (prompt), or revise. It needs to follow clear procedures of transparency, posting its meetings and decisions for public view, to avoid the appearance of backroom deals.[195] And it needs the expertise not only to evaluate regulatory proposals and IAs, but also to assist the DGs with their policy development and analyses:

> Education as to the usefulness of the tool in assisting the policy process is vital – policy officials need to see what is 'in it for them' in using the system. But there must also be a credible deterrent element – if the process is not completed properly (timing and quality), the progress of the policy can be delayed, halted completely or challenged subsequently.[196]

At present, the most likely candidate for such a central oversight office is within the Commission, either in the Secretariat General or in a new body attached to the Presidency (and a Vice President). The Commission's Competitiveness Council might play this role, if it were equipped with an expert staff and if it took a full-portfolio view of overall impacts rather than focusing only on competitiveness. But over time the creation of oversight mechanisms in the Council and the Parliament could supplement and check the Commission's oversight role. A new interinstitutional body remains the least well-defined option; it would be the most "central" but perhaps the least potent. Failing all these options, the courts may begin to take a tougher role in reviewing EU regulatory policies.

195 This was a key improvement made in EO 12866 in 1993, and redoubled by OIRA after 2000 when it posted all its activities on a public website at www.omb.gov.
196 Mandelkern Group Report (2001), at 24.

Ex post evaluation and adaptive management

Do policies actually work? With what results? This question is often neglected, perhaps because agencies have scarce resources which they prefer to devote to new initiatives. Most wealthy countries currently conduct some kind of *ex ante* assessment through IA, but few conduct *ex post* review. In the US, EO 12866 requires *ex ante* review of major rules but does not require *ex post* evaluation.

One reason to conduct *ex post* evaluation is to improve policies over time based on the updated information about effectiveness, benefits, costs, and unintended countervailing or ancillary effects.[197] The use of performance monitoring data to revise policies is often called "adaptive management." A second reason to conduct *ex post* evaluations is to determine how accurate the *ex ante* RIA estimates were, and to validate and improve the *ex ante* methodologies for subsequent decision-making. As noted above, initial retrospective studies by OMB and by Harrington *et al*,[198] while not representative samples, find both over- and underestimates in the *ex ante* analyses.[199]

As it implements Better Regulation, the EU and its member states should take the opportunity to build in regular *ex post* evaluations of policies and of *ex ante* IAs. In the future, *ex post* evaluation exercises should address a representative sample of past IAs rather than a convenience sample. They should quantify the degree of error rather than just whether the *ex ante* IA over- or underestimated. They should address countervailing risks and ancillary benefits (both those

---

197 Charles Herrick and Daniel Sarewitz, "Ex Post Evaluation: A More Effective Role for Scientific Assessments in Environmental Policy," (2000) 25 *Science, Technology, and Human Values* 309–331.

198 See OMB, n. 103 above; Harrington *et al*, n. 103 above. An early call for such evaluations was W Kip Viscusi, *Risk by Choice: Regulating Health and Safety in the Workplace* (Cambridge, MA: Harvard University Press 1983), 162–163 (criticizing the absence of *ex post* evaluation of cost estimates, and urging creation of a staff group to conduct these analyses).

199 *Ex post* evaluations face methodological challenges. See James K Hammitt, "Risk Assessment and Economic Evaluation," ch.112 in William N. Rom (ed), *Environmental and Occupational Medicine* (4th edn) (Philadelphia: Lippincott-Raven, 2006), 33–36 (noting that "retrospective values are also estimates because, although one can observe some of the consequences once the rule is implemented, one cannot observe what the consequences would be if the rule had not been adopted and so the counterfactual situation must be estimated. In addition, the health benefits of a regulation may remain quite uncertain in cases where the individuals suffering the health effects due to the agent that is regulated may not be identifiable.") One should not draw the conclusion from *ex post* evaluations that *ex ante* predictions can always be easily improved. *Ex post* evaluations may yield "hindsight bias"– the misimpression that outcomes were more easily predicted *ex ante* when in fact they were difficult to predict *ex ante*. Terrorist attacks and corporate fraud may look predictable in hindsight when *ex ante* clues are turned up, but those *ex ante* clues may have been buried among many other clues pointing in other directions. See Scott A. Hawkins and Reid Hastie, "Hindsight: Biased Judgments of Past Events after the Outcomes are Known," (1990) 107 *Psychol Bull* 311, 312; Mitu Gulati, Jeffrey J Rachlinski, and Donald C Langevoort, "Fraud by Hindsight," (2004) 98 *Northwestern University Law Review* 773.

forecast *ex ante* and those observed *ex post*). Eventually, *ex post* evaluations should be undertaken as a routine matter for every major rulemaking, both to improve *ex ante* methods and to revise policies through adaptive management.

Some observers urge more *ex post* evaluation and adaptive revision, and less reliance on *ex ante* evaluation through BCA.[200] But why not do both? One cannot just do *ex post* analysis alone – because one needs some way to choose which policies to adopt at first, and then review later. One still needs some sensible criteria for initial choices.[201]

The adaptive management aspect of *ex post* review corresponds to the "provisional" character of precautionary regulation, meant to be updated as science evolves. But this still leaves open the question of who will conduct the additional research and who will apply that research to *ex post* policy evaluation and revision. JB Ruhl worries that "decision makers need to be in a position to adjust decisions based on reliable monitoring feedback [and] in a manner that is transparent and accountable [and] subject to some objective boundaries," but in practice this gets bogged down by interest groups and judicial review; it "cannot flourish... in the conventional [US] administrative law context," so we need "new institutions... that allow agencies to use adaptive management while ensuring adequate agency accountability."[202] *Ex post* review using BCA could serve this role. And perhaps Europe, with a less ossified system of judicial review, could do better at this task than the US.

Such *ex post* evaluation should also apply to the choice among regulatory instruments. There is ample theory on the different costs and effectiveness of technology standards, emissions trading, taxes, information disclosure instruments, environmental contracts, and other instrument options. But there is insufficient empirical evidence on how these tools operate in practice. *Ex post* evaluation of these interventions could go a long way to improving future policy choices.[203]

---

200 Sidney A Shapiro and Robert L Glicksman, *Risk Regulation at Risk: Restoring a Pragmatic Approach* (Stanford, Calif: Stanford University Press, 2003).

201 Cf Ackerman *et al*, n. 97 above (arguing that BCA mistakenly skews decisions against environmental protection, as illustrated by the authors' *ex post* reconstructions of *ex ante* BCA rejecting selected past decisions that they contend were good). But on what criteria do they determine that the initial decisions were good? If *ex post* BCA shows that the decisions were good but *ex ante* BCA would not have done so, this is the kind *of ex post* review that can be used to improve the methods of *ex ante* BCA. A more complete sample would also include cases where BCA did favor adoption of the policy *ex ante* but would not *ex post*, and cases where BCA would have favored adoption of the policy *ex ante* but was not used and hence the policy was not adopted.

202 See J B Ruhl, "Regulation by Adaptive Management – Is it Possible?" (2005) 7 *Minnesota Journal of Law, Science and Technology 21*, 53–55.

203 One recent effort is Winston Harrington, Richard Morgenstern, and Thomas Sterner (eds), *Choosing Environmental Policy* (Washington, DC: RFF Press, 2004), collecting *ex post* studies of the impacts of technology-based and incentive-based environmental policies in the US and Europe.

The move toward regular *ex post* evaluations of regulations has been slow, but recent activity is promising. US EPA only began to conduct *ex post* evaluations in the late 1990s,[204] including a major retrospective study of the Clean Air Act required by Congress.[205] US OMB/OIRA is now beginning to conduct *ex post* evaluations of agency RIAs, as noted above.[206] The OECD held a meeting on *ex post* evaluations in 2003.[207] The European Environment Agency has attempted to conduct *ex post* analyses (of effectiveness and cost-effectiveness, though not necessarily of BCA), but has been hampered by lack of comparable information across member states.[208]

204 According to a GAO report, of the more than 100 major rules issued by EPA from 1981 to 1998, only five were subject to *ex post* evaluations, with all of those five reviews occurring after 1997. GAO, "Environmental Protection: Assessing the Impacts of EPA's Regulations through Retrospective Studies," GAO/RCED-99-250 (September 1999). GAO concluded: "While EPA devotes substantial resources to cost-benefit analyses when developing new regulations, the agency seldom looks back at the actual costs and benefits after those regulations have been implemented." Ibid at 13. GAO recommended that EPA develop a plan for systematic *ex post* evaluations, ibid at 14. See also Thomas O McGarity and Ruth Ruttenberg, "Counting the Cost of Health, Safety, and Environmental Regulation" (2002) 80 *Texas Law Review* 1997 (criticizing *ex ante* cost estimates and the lack of *ex post* evaluation).

205 US EPA, "The Benefits and Costs of the Clean Air Act, 1970–1990, Section 812 Retrospective Study" (October 1997).

206 OMB, n. 103 above. Scholars' *ex post* evaluations of BCA include Harrington *et al*, n. 102 above; James K Hammitt, "Are the Costs of Proposed Environmental Regulations Overestimated? Evidence from the CFC Phaseout" (2000) 16 *Environmental and Natural Resource Economics* 281–301; P W Kolp and W Kip Viscusi, "Uncertainty in Risk Analysis: A Retrospective Assessment of the OSHA Cotton Dust Standard" (1986) 4 *Advances in Applied Microeconomics* 105–30. For more general reviews of OIRA's influence on regulatory policy (as opposed to *ex post* validation of BCAs), see e.g. OMB/OIRA Annual Report 2005, n. 103 above (finding that OIRA *ex ante* reviews have yielded rules promising substantial net benefits); Steven Croley, "White House Review of Agency Rulemaking: An Empirical Investigation" (2003) 70 *University of Chicago Law Review* 821 (finding that OIRA has had a discernible and beneficial influence on rules, with little evidence of bias); Hahn and Muething, n. 61 above (finding fully monetized BCA in about half of US agencies' RIAs); Scott Farrow, "Improving Regulatory Performance: Does Executive Oversight Matter?" (draft July 2000, available at http://www.aei-brookings.org/admin/authorpdfs/page.php?id=123) (finding little impact on rejections of rules); Stuart Shapiro, "Unequal Partners: Cost-Benefit Analysis and Executive Review of Regulations" (2005) 35 *Environmental Law Report* 10433 (arguing that BCA has had little effect on rulemaking because OIRA has put more emphasis on coordinating Presidential priorities); Bagley and Revesz, n. 108 above (arguing that BCA has had a significant impact on rulemaking, but that OIRA should instead put more emphasis on coordinating Presidential priorities); Richard D Morgenstern (ed), *Economic Analysis at EPA: Assessing Regulatory Impact* (Washington, DC: RFF Press, 1997) (finding beneficial impact). A challenge in these studies is to identify the counterfactual baseline of what would have happened absent regulatory review. See Cary Coglianese, "Empirical Analysis and Administrative Law," (2002) *University of Illinois Law Review* 1111.

207 OECD, *Regulatory Performance: Ex Post Evaluation of Regulatory Policies* (Paris, September 22, 2003) (noting at p 5 the increasing interest in evidence-based empirical evaluation of policy impacts).

208 European Environment Agency (EEA), "Reporting on Environmental Measures: Are We Being Effective?" Environmental Issues Report no. 25 (November 2001) (calling for greater attention to data collection and comparability to enable *ex post* evaluations); EEA, "Effectiveness of

To address that need, the EU IA Guidelines now direct attention to planning for *ex post* review in the initial policy design and *ex ante* IA.[209]

The lesson for Better Regulation is to learn from medicine: Treat the whole patient, not just one ailment at a time, and measure success by "evidence-based" *ex post* review or "outcomes studies" of patients after treatment.[210] Better Regulation should develop large-scale outcomes studies to track the effects of regulatory policy choices over time, and across jurisdictions (where policies vary spatially). These *ex post* outcomes studies could be conducted by regulatory agencies and oversight offices, but could also be delegated to an independent body to ensure greater objectivity. In this effort, the US and EU could collaborate on a transatlantic policy laboratory – a joint effort in the *ex post* epidemiology of regulatory interventions and their empirical impacts.

Conclusions

In many respects, the Better Regulation initiative promises salutary reforms, such as wider use of regulatory impact assessments (IAs) to evaluate regulatory decisions *ex ante*. In other respects, including some of its rhetoric, its focus on administrative costs and simplification, and its institutional structure, the EU initiative speaks more of deregulation than of better regulation. Questions also remain whether particular regulatory programs, such as those regarding genetically modified foods and chemicals (REACH), can be reconciled with the tenets of Better Regulation.

Truly better regulation – maximizing societal well-being – would involve reducing or eliminating some regulations, but strengthening or expanding others, depending on the full social consequences of each choice. Better Regulation will often mean cutting costs. But it will also sometimes mean more regulation, or more comprehensive regulation: of issues that BCA shows warrant more regulation; of risks understated by risk assessment; of multiple simultaneous risks; of countervailing risks induced by intervention to reduce a target risk; and of risks addressed through more cost-effective instruments that reduce costs and hence make the optimal degree of regulation more protective. The "less versus more"

Packaging Waste Management Systems in Selected Countries: An EEA Pilot Study," Report 3/2005 (2005) (noting at p 8 that "The sixth environment action programme of the European Community (6EAP) highlights the need to undertake "*ex-post* evaluation of the effectiveness of existing measures in meeting their environmental objectives," but finding such analysis inhibited by non-comparable data across member states).

209 IA Guidelines 2006, at 44–46.

210 See Wiener, n. 152 above (advocating evidence-based outcomes studies for risk regulation, as in medical care). See also Cary Coglianese and Lori Snyder Bennear, "Measuring Progress: Program Evaluation of Environmental Policies" (2005) 47(2) *Environment* magazine 22–40 (lamenting lack of *ex post* evaluation and advocating establishment of systematic program evaluation to measure policies' actual impacts); Cary Coglianese and Lori Snyder Bennear, "Program Evaluation of Environmental Policies: Toward Evidence-Based Decision Making," in *Social and Behavioral Science Research Priorities For Environmental Decision Making* (Washington, DC: National Research Council, National Academies Press, 2005) 246–273.

dichotomy is fairly unhelpful in making regulatory policy choices. "Better" can be neither less nor more.

The EU is borrowing the concepts of Better Regulation from US regulatory reform and from initiatives in the EU member states, but Europe can make Better Regulation even better. Regulatory tools and institutions can be improved based on learning from past approaches, and tailored to suit European governance. The problems with impact assessment and benefit-cost analysis to date appear to be institutional: not that they are used too much, but rather too little and too narrowly or one-sidedly. IA and BCA in Europe would be more successful and credible if they were expanded to become self-reflective proportionate Warm Analysis of full portfolio impacts, to say yes to the good as well as no to the bad, to apply to a wider array of public policies (such as trade and counter terrorism) beyond the current focus on risk regulation, to embrace multiple countervailing risks and ancillary benefits, and to guide administrative simplification to consider benefits as well as costs. In addition, Europe should establish a centralized expert oversight body with the authority to use IA to influence decisions, and a system of *ex post* policy evaluations for adaptive revision and for improvement of *ex ante* assessment methods. These reforms would help Better Regulation become even better and achieve its true objective: better, not less or more.

Europe should experiment with these institutional innovations under its Better Regulation strategies, and evaluate their performance over time. Europe has an opportunity to develop new and improved approaches to regulation, not only borrowing but also adapting and creating anew. The innovations suggested here can help Europe manage its regulatory system, facilitate trade in the Single European Market, and advance European competitiveness, while ensuring that Better Regulation really means better. In turn, the US could improve its own regulatory regime by monitoring and borrowing from Europe's successes.

The exercise of legal borrowing involved in Better Regulation, and the normative evaluation of that borrowing that I have offered, show that – at least in this case – the focus is, and should be, on the particular merits of legal ideas, not on abstract ideology or supposedly fixed national legal mentalities. Blake overstated the case: "To generalize is to be an idiot. To particularize is alone the distinction of merit."[211] That itself is a hasty generalization, perhaps unintentionally proving its point, because some generalizations are useful.[212] But the point remains that particularization adds insight; the details matter, even when they are difficult to grasp. Observed La Rochefoucauld: *Pour bien savoir les choses, il en faut savoir le détail, et comme il est presque infini, nos connaissances sont toujours superficielles et imparfaites.*[213] Better Regulation itself consists in

---

211 William Blake, Annotations to Sir Joshua Reynolds' *Discourses* (1814).

212 For a provocative discussion, see Frederick Schauer and Richard Zeckhauser, "Regulation by Generalization," AEI-Brookings Joint Center, Working Paper 05–16, August 2005.

213 La Rochefoucauld, *Maximes* (Montreal: Les Editions Variétés, 1946), no 106 (p 61) (translated into English, "To know things well, one must know the details, but as these are almost infinite, our understanding is always superficial and imperfect.").

large measure of knowing the important details, without seeking perfection in every last detail, and in using those details to offer and to test different reasons for alternative regulatory choices, toward a considered judgment about the better course of action. Mr Franklin's advice to avoid "rash steps" by a prudential evaluation of the consequences now finds fruition in what Mr Blair has called "regulation after reflection."

Chapter 5

The development of environmental assessments at the level of the European Union

Ludwig Krämer

Environmental assessments and planning

Environmental assessments were, at EU level, first announced in 1977, when the European Commission, inspired by legislation in the United States and in France and by a failed attempt in Germany to introduce such assessments,[1] declared that it was to examine the possibility of proposing legislation in order systematically to examine the incidences of certain plans and projects on the environment.[2] Having discussed twenty-three internal draft texts, it made a proposal in 1980 for a directive on the environmental impact assessment of certain public and private projects.[3]

Within the EC Member States, the principle of environmental assessment was hardly contested in general: experts and public opinion agreed that there should be such an assessment, wherever possible, as it was accepted that the environment was fragile. Objections, however, came from the different national or regional, general or sectoral administrations that were afraid of losing the power which the monopoly over planning and permitting procedures gave them. Apart from this general aspect, detailed problems influenced the evolution of the discussion. For example, the Netherlands was keen to see plans and programmes that affected the

---

1 In the United States, the National Environmental Policy Act of 1969 required in Section 102(2) (c) that the federal administration 'shall...include in every recommendation for major Federal actions significantly affecting the quality of the human environment, a detailed statement on the environmental impact of the proposed action'. In France, legislation of 1 July 1976 imposed the assessment of the impact which public or private projects could have on the natural environment, before such projects were authorised. In Germany, the Federal government and the Länder did not agree to have environmental impact legislation, which led, in June 1976, to internal instructions that were limited to the federal administrations to examine, whether future public measures were compatible with the environment.

2 Commission, Second EC Environmental Action Programme, OJ 1977, C 139 1, paras 203ss. See also Commission, State of the Environment, 2nd report, Bruxelles-Luxembourg 1979, 58ss.

3 Commission, OJ 1980, C 169 14; explanatory memorandum in COM(80) 313 of 11 June 1980. The proposal was based on the present Art 94 EC and its adoption required a unanimous decision by the Council.

environment also included in the legislative proposal, but met stiff opposition from the majority of Member States which wanted the field of application of the directive as narrow as possible and limited to projects only. Denmark planned to bridge the Oeresund between Denmark and Sweden and did not wish to have any environmental interference in its decision-making process; for that reason, it insisted that projects which had been adopted by Parliamentary decisions in Denmark should not be covered by the directive. France wanted in particular nuclear installations to be excluded from the future legislation. Furthermore, it insisted that in cases where a project had effects in another Member State, the planning administration should only be allowed to make contacts with the (central) government of that other Member State, but not directly with the citizens of the other Member States – an attitude also influenced by its nuclear policy. The UK government did not consider it appropriate to legislate at European level, contrary to the opinion of the influential House of Lords.[4] Germany was afraid that its existing administrative system – which was based on strong administrative permitting procedures – could be affected by the requirement of an environmental impact assessment with public participation.

The Directive was adopted in 1985, after five years of protracted bargaining among Member States.[5] The joint venture of national administrations and the requirement of unanimous decisions led to reducing the Directive's field of application, but in particular to fixing the principle of impact assessment but then leaving a large discretion to the administrations with regard to the details of the procedure, the forms of consultation and the follow up of the impact assessment.

Directive 85/337 as a first step

Field of application

Right from the beginning of the EC discussions, it was considered that the Directive should apply to all measures and projects which had or were likely to have a significant impact on the environment. Member States' administrations, however, considered this approach to be too broad. The final text therefore established so-called positive lists: a first list (list I) grouped projects which always had to undergo an environment impact assessment before development consent was given. Projects of a second group (list II) had to undergo an environment impact assessment where the projects were 'likely to have significant effects on the environment by virtue, *inter alia*, of their nature, size or location'.[6] For projects which did not fall into either of these groups, an environmental impact assessment

---

4 See for details N Haigh, *Manual of Environmental Policy: the UK and Britain*, Loose-leaf (Leeds, Maney), ch. 11.2.

5 Directive 85/337 on the assessment of the effects of certain public and private projects on the environment, OJ 1985, L 175 40. The Directive was based on the present Arts 94 and 308 EC Treaty.

6 Ibid, Art 2(1).

was not required. The same applied to measures not considered to be 'projects', such as sheep grazing.[7]

List I was made relatively precise. Thus, a mandatory environment impact assessment (EIA) was only required for installations, for example, 'solely designed for the permanent storage or final disposal of radioactive waste' or incinerators and landfills for hazardous waste, for airports with a basic runway length of 2100 metres or for ports which permitted the passage of vessels of over 1350 tonnes. In contrast to that, List II was much less specific: it included such broad items as 'extraction of peat', 'reclamation of land from the sea', 'yacht marinas', 'hotel complexes' and 'urban-development projects'. Lobbying was successful in having golf courses altogether exempted from the lists. Attempts by the Commission to include all projects that were to be realised in designated nature protection zones[8] failed.

Alternatives

More relevant, though, were other omissions. Indeed, the Directive laid down the obligation of the operator of a project to submit some information to the planning authority, and in particular (Art 5(2)):

1 a description of the project comprising information on the site, design and size of the project;
2 a description of the measures envisaged in order to avoid, reduce and, if possible, remedy significant adverse effects;
3 the data required to identify and assess the main effects which the project was likely to have on the environment;
4 a non-technical summary of the information mentioned in the previous indents.

Thus, operators neither had to examine alternatives – alternative places, sizes etc – for the project, nor had they to assess the effects of the project on the environment. And operators were not obliged to envisage measures to avoid, reduce or remedy significant adverse effects of their projects.

Assessment document

As it was not the operator's task to make an impact assessment, this obligation fell on the administration, although this was nowhere explicitly specified in the Directive.

---

7 See Court of Justice, C-392/96 *Commission v Ireland*, [1999] ECR I-3901.
8 These are zones of EC-wide importance, which were designated by Member States under Art 4 of Directive 79/409 on the conservation of wild living birds, OJ 1979, L 103 1, and later under the provisions of Directive 92/43 on the protection of habitats and of wild fauna and flora, OJ 1992, L 207 6.

It could indirectly be derived from Art 3 which stated that the 'environmental impact assessment will identify, describe and assess' the direct and indirect effects of a project on the environment. From a legal perspective, the assessment of impacts would thus, at least in my opinion, require some form of an 'assessment document' which evaluates in detail all direct and indirect effects of the project. And it would only have been logical that the requirement of Art 9 – 'the competent authority…shall inform the public concerned of…the reasons and considerations on which the decision is based' – was complied with by a specific section in such a document. However, once more, the influence of administrations can be noticed here: the obligation of Art 9 only existed 'where the Member States' legislation so provides'. Furthermore, the detailed arrangements for such information were to be determined by the Member States (Art 9(2)). Finally, a number of administrations understood the provision of Art 3 as not to require a written assessment, although it is unclear how an impact can be described in a form other than writing.

Anyway, Directive 85/337 and in particular the environmental impact assessments were not only handled by lawyers, and the lack of precision in the text of the Directive led to the situation that a written assessment document was not always available. The Commission satisfied itself by declaring that the whole procedure under Directive 85/337 was 'the impact assessment'.

Bad assessment

The Directive was silent of how to handle cases where an environment impact assessment was made, but was of bad quality. An example – a real case – is an environment impact assessment which was made within three days and was two pages long, though it dealt with the impact of some 300 kilometres of a motorway on natural habitats, farmland and rural communities and had been produced by former government officials, which had set up a consultancy. Directive 85/337 left the handling of such cases to Member States. However, as the process of impact assessments was also new in Member States, most of them had not provided for any mechanism to deal with such cases.

The Commission, under its monitoring function of the application of environmental law, took the line that where an impact assessment was of bad quality, this normally had to be accepted. Only where the assessment was so deficient and the errors and omissions so flagrant and obvious to any reasonable person, such that the spirit of Directive 85/337 was disregarded, could a bad assessment be considered equivalent to the absence of an impact assessment. This line was respected in most cases,[9] but led to numerous protracted discussions with complainants and Member States.

---

9 There is one famous exception. At a certain moment, the Flemish Government wanted to construct a waste incinerator in the community of Drogenbosch, close to Uccle, a high-standing residential area of Bruxelles. In this case, the Commission, after strong intervention from interested persons, decided to tackle the Belgian decision under Art 226 EC Treaty, though the deficiencies of the impact assessment were only minor. The case was later solved under Belgian law.

At the end of 2006, however, the Court of Justice gave a very remarkable judgment. In Case C-239/04,[10] it was decided that an administration which had made an impact assessment, but had not examined a reasonable alternative to the project in question – a motorway – did not make an impact assessment. Though the judgment concerned an impact assessment under Art 6 of Directive 92/43 (the Habitats Directive), it may also have a considerable effect on the interpretation of Directive 85/337.

Sanctions

The Directive did not indicate what should happen when a project was realised without an impact assessment, although such an assessment was required. Rather, the answer to this question was left to the Member States. The consequence was that in some States, such as Germany in particular, the courts decided that the omission to make an environmental impact assessment was an administrative failure, but had no consequences for the project unless it could be proven that in a given case, the planning decision would have been different, had the environmental impact assessment been made. And as in Germany individual persons were not considered either to have been attributed subjective rights by the Directive,[11] the administrations could be rather generous with their discretion not to make an impact assessment, or not to make a very elaborate one. The Court of Justice has not yet had an opportunity to decide on this matter. In a preliminary ruling, it decided that in this regard, national law played an important role.[12]

Policy decisions

The biggest omission of the Directive was probably the silence on policy decisions which preceded the subsequent procedure for obtaining planning permission of a specific project. Indeed, frequently there were plans for town and country planning, for transport infrastructure, rural development or other sectors which foreshadowed the realisation of such projects; the subsequent planning procedure was only to fine-tune its details. As a general rule, one can

---

10 *Commission v Portugal*, judgment of 26 October 2006.
11 In this regard, my own interpretation of Directive 85/337 differs. Indeed, the 'concerned public' has, in my opinion, a right of giving its opinion: in other words, a right to be heard. This is a subjective right which gives persons and environmental organisations a right of standing, even in German law.
12 Case C-201/02 *Delena Wells*, ECJ judgment of 7 January 2004: 'it is for the national court to determine whether it is possible under domestic law for a consent already granted to be revoked or suspended in order to subject the project to an assessment of its environmental effects, in accordance with the requirements of Directive 85/337, or alternatively, if the individual so agrees, whether it is possible for the latter to claim compensation for the harm suffered'.

state that the bigger a specific infrastructure or other project is, the earlier there is a political and financial decision on its realisation. Also, lesser infrastructure projects are preceded by some form of planning, and only a very limited number of industrial or agricultural projects are submitted to the procedure for planning permission without any preceding policy decision to go ahead with the project.

The Commission had been aware of the necessity to also foresee environment impact assessments for plans and programmes,[13] but had temporarily abandoned these plans in view of the resistance of Member States which had to agree the proposal at unanimity.

Other deficiencies

The Directive was drafted in a very general way which gave great, often too great, discretion to the administration on its interpretation. It did not explicitly require the administration to avoid or minimise the negative effects of a project on the environment,[14] but allowed development consent to be given, even where serious negative effects were to be expected. It did not provide for the project not to be started before the impact assessment procedure was finished. For projects with a transnational effect, it provided for intergovernmental consultation rather than for citizens' participation. And it did not request the Commission to regularly report on the Directive's application.

Implementation

Though the Directive provided for a full three year period before it became effective, this time-span was not enough for numerous Member States. Obviously, the administrations which previously had had the power to decide on specific projects without the 'cumbersome' consultation of the nature protection administration, without participation of the public and without an environmental impact assessment, needed time to renounce on their prerogatives. Only five Member States transposed the Directive in time, and 10 years later, in 1998, the Commission reported that the legislation in Spain, Ireland, Greece, Italy, Belgium and Germany still did not conform with Directive 85/337.[15]

It thus fell on the Court of Justice to try to make Directive 85/337 operational. The Court mainly decided on the direct effect of certain provisions of the Directive, on reducing the administration's discretion with regard to projects of

---

13 See e.g. COM (80) 222 of 7 May 1980, 47, where the Commission elaborated on the necessity to have environmental impact assessments for town and country planning in particular.
14 This aspect was covered by an amendment of 1997 (Directive 97/11, OJ 1997, L 73 5) which now asks the administration to include in its decision on the project 'a description, where necessary, of the main measures to avoid, reduce and, if possible, offset the major adverse effects' (Art 9).
15 Commission, 'Monitoring application of Community law', 15th Report 1997 (1998) OJ 250 1, 175.

List II, and on the interpretation of specific provisions in the Directive which were generally interpreted by enlarging the field of application of the Directive. While the Court's jurisprudence had a considerable impact on the interpretation of the Directive, its effectiveness was reduced in particular by the long procedural delays,[16] the reluctance of national courts to ask the Court of Justice for a preliminary ruling,[17] and by the refusal of the administration in one Member State to consider a judgment by the Court of Justice against another Member State to be relevant for itself.[18]

Amendment

Directive 85/337 was amended in 1997[19] in order to include some omissions which had been discovered in the meantime and partly to take into consideration the Court's jurisprudence. The structure of the legislation remained the same. Only some fine-tuning was made, in particular with regard to Lists I and II.

Application in practice

The Commission reported in 1993, 1997 and 2003 on the implementation of Directive 85/337.[20] The reports mainly deal with the legal transposition of the Directive into national law, where they show some significant differences, for example as regards the requirement of an EIA for golf courses, GMO installations, shooting ranges, military practice grounds or installations for the intensive rearing of agricultural animals. The national differences on the thresholds of List II projects are sometimes quite remarkable.[21]

---

16 In environmental matters, the procedure under Art 226 EC Treaty takes on average four to five years. See L Krämer, 'Statistics on Environmental Judgments by the EC Court of Justice' (2006) *Journal of Environmental Law*, 407.

17 It is significant that the courts of the four Member States that are beneficiaries of the EC Cohesion Fund, i.e. Spain, Greece, Portugal and Ireland, had, until the end of 2006, never addressed any question for a preliminary ruling in environmental matters to the Court, based on Art 234 EC Treaty. Cashman rightly mentions that it was these four Member States which experienced, during the 1990s, 'a phase of rapid infrastructure-building'. See L Cashman, 'Environmental impact assessment' in M Onida (ed.), *Europe and the Environment* (Groningen: Europa Law Publishing, 2004), 63.

18 See as an example, A Aragão, 'The impact of EC environmental law on Portuguese law' in R Macrory (ed.), *Reflections on 30 years of EU Environmental Law: A High Level of Protection?* (Groningen: Europa Law Publishing, 2005), 503.

19 Directive 97/11 (1997) OJ L 73 5.

20 Commission, COM (93) 28 of 2 April 1993; COM (2003) 334 of 23 June 2003. The report of 1997 is available via http://europa.eu.int/comm/environment/eia-support.htm.

21 The 2003 report indicates an afforestation project requires an environmental impact assessment when it exceeds 20 hectares in Italy, 30 hectares in Denmark, 50 hectares in Germany, 100 hectares in Belgium (Wallonia), 200 hectares in Finland and 350 hectares in Portugal. For cement manufacture the threshold is 300,000 tonnes annual production capacity in Austria, 500,000 in

Information on practical application is almost entirely based on the national administrations' data and has thus to be treated with caution. In this sense, the 2003 report expressly indicated that 'from the review of information assessed here it is very difficult to draw any firm conclusions on the role Environmental Impact Assessment (EIA) plays in project decision-making'[22] and that 'the main problem lies with the application and implementation of the directive and not, for the most part, with the transposition of the legal requirements of the directive'.[23] The number of estimated environmental impact assessments per year in Member States varied from 10 to 20 in Austria, to 6000–7000 in France, with Germany indicating more than 1000, Greece 1600, Ireland 178, Portugal 92, Sweden 3000–4000 and the United Kingdom 500.[24] The different figures show that with the exception of France, Sweden and perhaps Greece, no Member State has really made the environmental impact assessment a normal procedure for infrastructure projects.

Impact assessments and nature protection

As mentioned above, the Commission was unsuccessful in inserting a provision in Directive 85/337 that any project which affected a European protected habitat[25] should have to undergo an environmental impact assessment. It also failed in its attempt to have an EIA made for all projects in Member States that were co-financed by the EC Structural funds or the Cohesion Fund. In particular, the main receiving affected Member States considered this to be discriminating.

However, the requirement of some impact assessment was inserted, in 1992, in Art 6 of Directive 92/43[26] as a reaction to a judgment of the Court of

Belgium (Flanders), 5 tonnes per day (France), 500 tonnes per day in Italy and Belgium (Wallonia), and 1000 tonnes per day in Germany. In the Netherlands, there is no mandatory threshold, while Greece, Ireland, Denmark, Belgium (Bruxelles), and Finland always require an environmental impact assessment.

22 COM (2003) 334, n. 20 above, 95.

23 Ibid, 98.

24 Ibid, 49. These figures are estimates from Member States' administrations and have to be used with caution. In particular, in federalised Member States, i.e. Austria, Belgium, Germany, Italy, Spain, reliable central data collection systems seem not to exist.

25 Such habitats are identified and protected under Art 4 of Directive 79/409 on the conservation of wild birds (1979) OJ L 103 1, and Art 6 of Directive 92/43 on the conservation of natural habitats and of wild fauna and flora (1992) OJ L 206 7.

26 Directive 92/43, ibid, Art 6(3): 'Any plan or project not directly connected with or necessary to the management of the site but likely to have a significant effect thereon, either individually or in combination with other plans or projects, shall be subject to appropriate assessment of its implications for the site in view of the site's conservation objectives. In the light of the conclusions of the assessment of the implications for the site and subject to the provisions of paragraph 4, the competent national authorities shall agree to the plan or project only after having ascertained that it will not adversely affect the integrity of the site concerned and, if appropriate, after having obtained the opinion of the general public.'

Justice,[27] by which Member States felt unduly restricted in town and country planning with regard to protected areas. The new provision in Directive 92/43 established that plans and projects which could possibly affect a protected area had to undergo an assessment. If it turned out that they had damaging effects, they were not to be realised, unless there was no alternative solution and there were reasons of overriding public interests. The Commission had to be consulted in such a case.

There are several problems linked with this provision. First, it applies to habitats which appear on an EC-list of protected habitats.[28] However, as Member States had not designated all the habitats of EC importance by the required date,[29] the field of application of Art 6 is often uncertain. Second, the form of the impact assessment is largely discretionary, as Art 6 does not directly refer to Directive 85/337 and because there are differences as to the two assessments: Directive 92/43 refers to projects and plans. Its objective is to protect the natural environment, protected habitats and protected species, whereas Directive 85/337 protects all environmental facets. Also, Directive 92/43 refers to plans and projects which may have significant effects once they are taken in combination with other plans or projects.

In practice, the 'overriding public interest' of Art 6(4) which allows for derogations has been widely interpreted by Member States. Where central governments have decided on the realisation of a specific project, normally a considerable amount of political pressure has been exercised to obtain the agreement of the European Commission, such as high political visits to officials, letters to the EC President, confidential interventions with the responsible Commissioner, and so on. This political pressure often goes so far as to incite the Commission not even daring to publish its decision to agree to the national project. Details cannot be analysed here, but it needs to be stated that, as a whole, the provisions of Arts 6(3) and 6(4) did not succeed in striking a fair balance between the requirements of Art 6(3) and national plans and projects. Not one single project is known to have been given up or significantly amended following the Commission's consultation, in order to preserve the natural habitat

---

27 Case C-57/89 *Commission v Germany* [1991] ECR I-883. The Commission had brought that case as it considered sea dyke works largely destroyed a protected habitat. The Court accepted this destruction, because it considered that the protection of human life through sea dykes was of an overriding public interest.

28 In Case C-117/03 *Draggagi*, Judgment of 13 January 2005, the Court of Justice declared the regime of Art 6 applied only once a habitat appeared on a published EC list. Pending such publication, Member States were not obliged to comply with Art 6, although they had to take appropriate protection measures.

29 It is estimated that with regard to Directive 79/409, n. 25 above, about 70 per cent of all relevant habitats have now been designated, while they should all have been designated by 1981. With regard to Directive 92/43, n. 25 above, the EC lists should have been established by 1998. By the end of 2006, the Community lists for six bio-geographical areas had been published. However, three new lists will have to be made up, for the Pannonian, Steppic and Black Sea regions. Furthermore, the existing lists will have to be completed.

from the planned economic development. And Commission guidance on the interpretation of Art 6[30] has not had a measurable effect.

Environmental impact assessments for projects authorised at EC level

There is no legislation which requires any environmental impact assessment of projects that are approved by EC institutions. The reason, repeated time and again by the European Commission, is that the formal development consent is never given by EC institutions, but instead by national administrations. In the formal sense, this is probably correct. However, in substance, numerous projects at national level would not be realised without the EC institutions co-financing the project. Under the Cohesion Fund, such financial contribution is normally 80 per cent and may reach, in specific cases, 100 per cent of the cost. Relevant cases which were decided by the European courts concerned the financing of a motorway by-pass around Lyon,[31] the co-financing of a tourist centre in a protected area in Mullaghmore in Ireland,[32] or the co-financing of electrical power plants in the Canary Islands.[33]

In the past, this situation was of considerable concern to environmental organisations which saw specific projects authorised without a preceding environmental impact assessment. When they complained to the European Commission or the Court of Justice they were told the decision of co-financing was of no 'direct and individual concern' to them, and that any court action was thus inadmissible. While there were provisions in the different EC regulations that projects had to comply with the relevant EC environmental legislation, the Commission satisfied itself with the – often rather summary – Member State's declaration of compliance with EC legislation. No solution has yet been found for this problem which could, of course, be solved by better monitoring the application of EC environmental impact legislation by Member States.

Environmental assessment of plans and programmes in Member States

After four years of discussions and after some consensus at international level having been reached,[34] the EC adopted, in 2001, Directive 2001/42 on the

---

30 Commission, 'Managing Natura 2000: The provisions of Art 6 of the Habitats Directive 92/43/EEC' (Luxembourg, 2000).

31 Case T-460/93 *Tete v European Investment Bank* [1993] ECR II-1257.

32 Case T-461/93 *An Taisce v Commission*, [1994] ECR II-733. The appeal against this judgment was rejected. See Case C-325/94P [1996] ECR I-3727.

33 Case T-585/93 *Greenpeace v Commission* [1995] ECR II-2205. The appeal against this judgment was rejected. See Case C-321/95P [1998] ECR I-1651.

34 The Convention on environmental impact assessment in a transboundary context, concluded in 1991 in Espoo (Finland), referred to projects only but invited the contracting parties to 'endeavour to apply the principles of environmental impact assessment to policies, plans and programmes' (Art 2(7)).

environment assessment of plans and programmes.[35] This Directive required an impact assessment of Member States' plans and programmes which, at a subsequent stage, could lead to projects being consented that were covered by Directive 85/337 or plans which require an assessment under Art 6 of Directive 92/43. Plans and programmes which are adopted by way of a legislative procedure are expressly included, in the same way as national programmes which are co-financed by the EC.

Where an environmental assessment is required, the responsible administrations must make an environmental report which identifies, describes, and evaluates the likely significant effects on the environment of implementing the plan[36] and reasonable alternatives to it. The public and environmental administrations have to be consulted on the draft plan and the report. It is up to Member States to designate the authorities and the public which are to be consulted. The report and the opinions expressed shall be taken into account in the preparation of the definite plan. After adoption a statement has to be made available to the persons and bodies consulted which indicates how the environmental considerations had been taken into consideration.

The environmental report must specifically refer to protected natural areas under Directive 92/43, the 'relevant environmental protection objectives established at international, Community or Member State level', the effects of the programme, measures to prevent, reduce or offset significant adverse effects, a description of the reasons which led to the selection of alternatives, and monitoring measures. Thus, the requirements under Directive 2001/42 are much more specific than those of Directive 85/337.

As the Directive only came into force in July 2004 it is too early to assess its impact. However, it has to be underlined that no judicial remedy is foreseen when the environmental report is bad, the consulted public was unduly restricted, a consultation did not take place at all or the results of a consultation are not taken into consideration in the final plan. I am of the opinion that, at least in cases where it is obvious which public is likely to be affected by the plan, that public has the possibility of judicial review should it not be consulted. In these cases, its right to be heard is infringed.

Environmental impact assessments for EC plans and programmes

The EC institutions adopt a number of plans and programmes which, were they adopted by Member States, would come under the application of Directive 2001/42.

The Convention on access to information, participation in decision-making and access to justice in environmental matters, concluded in 1998 in Aarhus (Denmark), suggested extended public participation in the decision-making concerning projects, plans and programmes and policies. To what extent this participation is obligatory for plans and policies, is disputed among experts. The EC adhered to both Conventions.

35 Directive 2001/42, OJ L 197 30.
36 Community law uses the notions of 'plan' and 'programme' without differentiation.

It is worth mentioning, initially, the sixth EC Environmental Action Programme, and in addition the thematic strategies announced under this – the strategies on climate change, on environmentally friendly technologies transport programmes, the planning of trans-European networks for transport and energy infrastructures[37] and others. Following the signing, by the EC, of the Aarhus Convention on access to information, participation in decision-making and access to justice in environmental matters and of the Kiev Protocol under the Espoo Convention on environmental impact assessment in a transboundary context which the EC signed in 2005, Regulation 1367/2006[38] was adopted which provides for public participation in EC decision-making, although such participation is not the same as an environmental impact assessment. At present, it is not yet known when the Community will adhere to the Protocol or if and when it will adopt provisions for the evaluation of environmental impact assessments for EC plans and programmes.

The internal EC administrative resistance against environmental impact assessments for plans and programmes is considerable. In particular, it is feared such assessments would lead to slowing down the envisaged measures and would unduly delay the adoption and implementation of EC plans. Though the same argument also applies to national plans and programmes, it is better heard at EC level, because there is no public opinion which would counterbalance the administration's greed for acceleration. Considerations have gone so far as to reflect whether transboundary networks could not be declared to be of 'European interest' and thereby be exempted from the requirements of environmental impact assessments under existing EC directives.

Environmental impact assessments for EC legislation

Since 2001 the European Commission has tried to improve the rules on European governance. Its White Paper on governance included, among others, a section on 'better regulation'. In this section, the Commission announced that it would, in future, make an impact assessment for its proposals on legislation and important strategic documents. Particularly important proposals would be submitted to an extended impact assessment before the proposal was submitted to the other institutions. The assessment would examine the economic, social and environmental effects of the proposal.

Subsequently, the Commission elaborated and fine-tuned its intention,[39] though without precisely specifying the rules which should apply. The absence

---

37 See Art 154 EC Treaty. Such networks are to be developed 'in the areas of transport, telecommunications and energy infrastructures'.

38 Regulation 1367/2006 on the application of the provisions of the Aarhus Convention on access to information, public participation in decision making and access to justice in environmental matters to Community institutions and bodies, OJ 2006 L 264, p 13.

39 Commission, 'Communication on Impact Assessments', COM (2002) 276 of 5 June 2002.

of clear provisions for such impact assessments had the expected consequences at the level of the other institutions on the one hand, and at the level of the Commission on the other.

The European Parliament and the Council wanted to see, in each case, the Commission's impact assessment, in order to examine and eventually correct it. More important for them, though, was that they also wanted an impact assessment for the amendments to the proposal which they would bring to the legislative proposal. The absence of a methodology raised the concern that each institution would use its own method and develop its own assessment – with its own results. That this apprehension was not entirely theoretical was demonstrated during the discussions on the REACH proposal of the Commission,[40] where the different EC institutions, Member States and also private organisations made some 50 (!) different impact assessment studies, the result of which was often influenced by the mandating body and by the contractor chosen for the assessment.

The discussion among the institutions, about when and how to make impact assessments during the legislative elaboration of a text, has not yet come to a conclusion. It is thus likely that each institution will make such an assessment according to its own rules and that also the Council Presidency and Member States will continue their present practice. In the medium term, legislative provisions appear necessary. Indeed, the different methodologies used, the influence of vested interests, the absence of precise provisions and the almost complete lack of transparency considerably undermine the credibility of the present impact assessments.

Within its own services, the Commission continued its efforts on impact assessments. It issued internal guidelines,[41] trained its officials, and reported in 2004 on the experience over the first two years of use of impact assessments.[42] And in 2005 it came out with a report on the future role of these assessments, which had the significant title 'Better Regulation for Growth and Jobs in the EU'.[43] The title only revealed what was already clear from observing the practical application of the impact assessment and, more broadly, of the whole 'better regulation' policy: the procedures were used in order to promote growth and social concerns, but to stop environmental activities. Environmental legislation was only accepted, if and where it did not impair economic (and social) interests. And the content of environmental legislation which was proposed by the Commission since 2003 – in the same way as legislation which had been requested

---

40 Commission, 'Proposal for a Regulation concerning the Registration, Evaluation, Authorisation and Restrictions of Chemicals (REACH), establishing a European Chemicals Agency and amending Directive 1999/45 and Regulation (EC) on persistent organic pollutants, COM(2003) 644 of 29 October 2003.
41 Commission, SEC (2005) 791 of 15 June 2005.
42 Commission, Next Steps in Support of Competitivity and Sustainable Development, SEC (2004) 1377 of 21 October 2004.
43 Commission, COM (2005) 97 of 16 March 2005.

by the Council and the European Parliament, but had not been submitted – more than clearly shows that this is the reality of the Commission's policy in environmental standard setting since at least 2003.[44]

The EC's efforts to reduce 'sustainable development' to economic and perhaps social considerations, but not to include environmental considerations, have a long history which cannot be discussed here in detail. The reference to sustainable growth in Art 2 of the EC Treaty[45] may be mentioned, the infamous 'Lisbon declaration' on sustainable development of 2000 which was meant to make the EU 'the most competitive and dynamic knowledge-based economy in the world, capable of sustainable economic growth with more and better jobs and greater social cohesion', without mentioning the environment. The heads of State and Governments had to correct this statement one year later and to add, at the Göteborg summit, the protection of the environment to its own Lisbon definition of sustainable development. In substance, however, the Commission's mentality did not change, as is shown by the impact assessment approach.

In 2003 the Commission made some 20 detailed impact assessments[46] for its legislative proposals and important strategic documents, in 2004 about 30 assessments, and in 2005 more than 50. Numerous impact assessments of 2004 did not mention the environment at all or referred to it in one phrase.[47] Three cases of 2005, taken at random, demonstrate the approach: the impact assessment accompanying the Commission proposal on the reform of the sugar market[48] does not contain a word on the impact of these proposals on the European, but perhaps also the global, environment. The impact assessment accompanying the Commission proposal to fix a strategy for the EC development policy

44 Evidence is provided by the thematic strategies on air pollution, marine protection, natural resources, waste recycling and air pollution presented by the Commission under the 6th environmental action programme; the omission to implement the requirements of the 6th action programme on the interrelationship between greenhouse gas emissions and transport/energy; the omission to present legislative proposals on biological waste and construction and demolition waste; the deregulating proposal for amending the waste framework directive; and the omission to fix concentration standards for heavy metals in the air etc.

45 Version 1993–1999.

46 The Commission's terminology changed. While in the beginning the notions 'preliminary impact assessment' and 'extended impact assessment' were used, the Commission now uses the terms 'roadmap' and 'impact assessment'. This latter terminology is used here.

47 No mention of the environment was made, among others, in the following assessments: 'Interoperability of Digital Interactive Television Services' (SEC(2004) 1028); 'The Setting Up of a European Refugee Fund' (SEC(2004) 161); Framework Decision on Certain Procedural Rights in Criminal Proceedings (SEC(2004) 491); Regulation on a Visa Information System (SEC(2004)1629); on Re-insurance (SEC(2004)443); a Directive on Capital Adequacy of Credit Institutions (SEC(2004) 921); 'Legal Protection of Design' (SEC(2004)1097); 'Action Plan for Electronic Public Procurement' (SEC(2004) 1629).

48 Commission, 'Proposal for a Council Regulation on the Common Organisation of the Markets in the Sugar Sector, COM (2005) 263 of 22 June 2005; 'Accompanying Impact Assessment' SEC (2005) 808 of 22 June 2005.

towards Africa[49] limits itself to a short, half page statement that the suggested strategy will help Africa to protect its environment such as water, air or nature; the environmental problems of Africa are neither identified nor described nor assessed. And the impact assessment accompanying the proposal for measures under the Common Fisheries Policy[50] again does not contain any section on environmental impacts.

In most other cases which do not stem from the Commission's environmental department and where the environment is mentioned, there is no 'identification, description and evaluation' of the direct and indirect effects[51] of the planned measures on the environment. Rather the statements are either short or general and limit themselves to the declaration that the measures are favourable to sustainable development or to the environment. Or the 'assessment' is reduced, as far as the environmental impact is concerned, to the question of how much the measure would cost. It is clear that such a question can hardly ever be answered. Where the envisaged measure is an environmental measure, this gives room for vested interests' arguments that the costs would be immense, that the competitiveness with regard to third country producers and traders would be reduced and that jobs would be lost. Environmental groups and other bodies that are interested in ecological issues normally do not have resources in order to examine in detail the environmental impact of a proposal.

The conclusion of this is that, as far as the environment is concerned, the Commission's impact assessments lack a precise methodology, an internal control (whether the Commission's internal instructions are followed[52]) and the

---

49 Commission, 'Accompanying Impact Assessment' SEC (2005) 1255 of 12 October 2005.

50 Commission, 'Proposal for a Regulation Establishing Community Financial Measures for the Implementation of the Common Fisheries Policy and in the area of the Law of the Sea', COM (2005) 117 of 6 April 2005; 'Accompanying impact assessment' SEC (2005) 426 of 6 April 2005; see SEC (2004) 448 of 28 April 2004 on the proposal for a Regulation to set up a Common Fisheries Control Agency, which contained one line on the environmental impact of the proposal.

51 Directive 2001/42, n. 36 above, indicates in annex I that 'direct and indirect effects' include: secondary, cumulative, synergistic, short, medium and long-term permanent and temporary, positive and negative effects. The Commission's impact assessment documents do not take up any similar enumeration.

52 The Commission's internal instructions suggest the following questions should be raised and discussed: (1) does the option have an effect on emissions of acidifying, eutrophying, photochemical or harmful air pollutants that might affect human health, damage crops or buildings or lead to deterioration in the environment (polluted soil or rivers etc)?; (2) does the option decrease or increase the quality or quantity of freshwater and groundwater? Does it raise or lower the quality of waters in coastal and marine areas (e.g. through discharges of sewage, nutrients, oil, heavy metals and other pollutants)? Does it affect drinking water resources?; (3) does the option affect the acidification, contamination or salinity of soil, or soil erosion rates? Does it lead to loss of available soil (e.g. through building or construction works) or increase the amount of usable soil (e.g. through land decontamination)?; (4) does the option affect the emission of ozone-depleting substances (CFCs, HCFCs, etc) and greenhouse gases (e.g. $CO^2 \leq$, methane, etc) into the atmosphere?; (5) does the option deplete renewable resources (freshwater, fish) more quickly than they can regenerate? Does it reduce or increase the use of non-renewable

political will to be serious in identifying, describing and evaluating the direct and indirect effects of the envisaged measure on the environment. In practice, they serve to block new environmental proposals or proposals which have a precise pro-environment content and mainly serve to cut back initiatives to implement a serious EC environmental policy.

The 'impact assessment' approach by the Commission cannot, therefore, be considered a serious contribution to assess the environmental effects of proposed legislation and policy orientation. This finding is not surprising. Indeed, the methodology for environmental assessments for legislation and policies is not yet established. If one were thinking for a second that the Commission would answer the questions enumerated in note 52 above with regard to its proposal for a development strategy for Africa, one becomes aware of the problem. In the same way, the identification, description and evaluation of the change of the EC sugar policy on water and soil in Spain, compared to France or Germany, would require a very intensive research which present methods cannot or, at least, do not deliver. The impact assessments for legislation and policies thus give some pseudo-results which may satisfy those economists who favour econometric methods in policy and law and who believe that all impacts can properly be assessed. This might even be true to a large extent. However, the detail of any such research, the time needed and the bureaucracy involved appear to be prohibitive. With regard to the environment, the political requirement to make

resources (groundwater, minerals etc)?; (6) does the option reduce the number of species/ varieties/races in any area (i.e. reduce biological diversity) or increase the range of species (e.g. by promoting conservation)? Does it affect protected or endangered species or their habitats or ecologically sensitive areas? Does it split the landscape into smaller areas or in other ways affect migration routes, ecological corridors, or buffer zones? Does the option affect the scenic value of protected landscape?; (7) does the option have the effect of bringing new areas of land ('greenfields') into use for the first time? Does it affect land designated as sensitive for ecological reasons? Does it lead to a change in land use (e.g) the divide between rural and urban, or change in type of agriculture?; (8) does the option affect waste production (solid, urban, agricultural, industrial, mining, radioactive or toxic waste) or how waste is treated, disposed of, or recycled?; (9) does the option affect the likelihood of prevention of fire, explosives, breakdowns, accidents and accidental emissions? Does it affect the risk of unauthorised or unintentional dissemination of environmentally alien or genetically modified organisms? Does it increase or decrease the likelihood of natural disasters?; (10) does the option increase or decrease consumption of energy and production of heat? Will it increase or decrease the demand for transport (passenger or freight), or influence its modal split? Does it increase or decrease vehicle emissions?; (11) does the option lead to changes in natural resource inputs required per output? Will it lead to production becoming more or less energy intensive? Does the option make environmentally un/friendly goods and services cheaper or more expensive through changes in taxation, certification, product, design rules, procurement rules etc? Does the option promote or restrict environmentally un/friendly goods and services through changes in the rules on capital investments, loans, insurance services etc? Will it lead to businesses becoming more or less polluting through changes in the way in which they operate?; (12) does the option have an impact on health of animals and plants? Does the option affect animal welfare (i.e. humane treatment of animals)? Does the option affect the safety of food and feed? See Commission, SEC(2005) 791, n. 41 above, 31.

impact assessments leads to slowing down, watering down or even stopping measures to preserve, protect or improve the quality of the environment. And this might be, as indicated above, the hidden agenda of impact assessments at EC level. Until now no Commission proposal for legislation in the area of transport, energy, agriculture, fisheries, internal market, industry or trans-European networks has been stopped or significantly changed because of its negative environmental impacts. However, numerous environmental measures have been stopped, often in the embryonic stage, or watered down with the argument that their economic impacts were too burdensome.

Some final remarks

It is nowadays uncontested that environment impact assessments may be a useful tool for preparing administrative decisions on projects as well as on plans and programmes. The requirement of consulting the administrations that deal with the protection of the natural environment and, even more importantly, the compulsory consultation of the concerned public, and furthermore, the requirement to explain and even to justify the chosen option, has a healthy impact on the responsible administration. The monopoly of decision-making is, as far as the EC legislation reaches, put into question, and the improved transparency in decision-making is the greatest achievement of this legislation. A very essential part of this environmental impact assessment is the examination of alternatives for projects; for plans and programmes it is less evident that alternatives may really play a reasonable role in decision-making.

There does not appear to be much evidence that environmental impact assessments have stopped environmentally harmful projects or have led to significant changes. On this, much depends on the responsible administration's determination to properly protect the environment. Environmental impact assessments allow the protection of the environment, but the provisions are so flexible that they hardly impose such a protection on the administration. This observation seems to apply to practically all Member States of EU-27.

Environmental impact assessments take time which administrations and private businesses often do not wish to take. Furthermore, the political influence at local, regional, national or international level all too frequently leads to policy decisions being taken long before the environmental impact assessment has even started. The environmental impact assessment then often degenerates to an obligatory exercise which is made, though the result is known beforehand. This is also the case where the administration opposes the environmental impact assessment as a threat to its monopoly in decision-making, a situation which is rather widespread, for example, in Germany.

The bigger a project is – a bridge over the Oeresund in Denmark-Sweden, a bridge over the Street of Messina in Italy, the tunnel between France and the United Kingdom, the construction of a nuclear power plant or of a new airport – the more the result is known beforehand and the less impact an assessment will have on the final decision to go ahead with the project. Trans-European networks for transport are a good example: the construction of roads or railways throughout the European Union is decided at a political level; any environmental impact assessment may, at best, lead to smaller local changes, but does not put into question the projects as such. Though this influence of policy decisions on administrative planning is of particular relevance in trans-national or large national projects, the issue of dimension also plays a role at the local level.

It would probably help if environmental impact assessments were made not by the project's promoter – be they public or private – but by an independent body according to well-established, standardised requirements. However, such an option stands little chance of becoming reality, as in particular administrations it would be too uncertain whether the assessment would deliver the desired results.

Humans act according to their interests; thus, it is always difficult to give voice to the environment and it is likely that the 'affected public' with regard to plans and programmes will often not voice its opinion because it does not consider its interests affected and does not really care about the general interest to protect the environment. The new legislation on environment impact assessments for plans and programmes will, in this regard, still have to prove its added value to better decision-making.

Experience to date seems to show that environmental impact assessments for legislation and political strategies do not work. The different effects of a piece of legislation appear to be too complex to be able of being caught in such an assessment, quite apart from the question, whether the 'affected public' is not, in practice, another term for lobby groups of vested interests. I certainly would still have to be convinced of any added environmental value of such assessments. At EC level, and these remarks do not aim at going further, environmental impact assessments for legislation are, until now, more a tool for promoting deregulation than a tool for improving decision-making.

Environmental impact assessments will not work where the administration is not willing to use this tool in order to minimise the negative impacts of its decision on the environment. In a given case, public concern might lead to changes also against a reluctant administration. However, such cases are exceptional. In general, the administrations' objections or reluctance to an environmental impact assessment will have the consequence that such an assessment has no or only poor effects.

Chapter 6

Substance and procedure under the strategic environmental assessment directive and the water framework directive

William Howarth[1]

The context

The progressive adoption of 'environmental assessment'[2] in United Kingdom and European Community environmental law has to be seen as a part of a wider evolutionary process that has taken place over the past two decades. This is a progression from the concrete to the speculative and from concerns about the present to concerns about the future. Past preoccupations with the need to react to specific pollution incidents causing tangible environmental and ecological damage have been supplemented by measures aimed at anticipating environmental harm and preventing it from occurring. Prevention has, in turn, been supplemented by mechanisms directed at the avoidance of possible environmental harm, where a risk of harm may not subsequently materialise. This succession of responses, from reaction to prevention, and from prevention to precaution, may well be illustrative of wider changes in thinking in a 'risk society'[3] which is evermore fearful of the

1 I am grateful to Jane Holder, University College London, and Huw Williams, Environment Agency, for helpful comments on an earlier draft of this paper. Any errors are my responsibility alone.

2 'Environmental assessment' (hereafter EA) is used here in a general sense which may be characterised as 'a method or procedure for predicting the effects on the environment of a proposal, either for an individual project or a higher-level "strategy" (a policy, plan or programme), with the aim or taking account of these effects in decision-making'. See Office of the Deputy Prime Minister, *A Practical Guide to the Strategic Environmental Assessment Directive* (Office of the Deputy Prime Minister, 2005), 42. Alternatively, EA has been generally defined in legislation as 'a systematic interdisciplinary approach which will insure the integrated use of the natural and social sciences and the environmental design arts in planning and in decision-making which may have an impact on man's environment.' See National Environmental Policy Act 1969 42 USC 4321 to 4361 (NEPA), s.102(a) (United States). This broad sense of EA should be contrasted with 'environmental impact assessment' (EIA), which is more narrowly concerned with assessment of the impacts of particular development projects, and 'strategic environmental assessment', hereafter 'SEA', which is usually concerned with assessment of the impact of plans and programmes, although it is sometimes extended to assessment of policies and other kinds of strategic action. See R Therivel and M R Partidario, *The Practice of Strategic Environmental Assessment* (London: Earthscan Publications, 1996), 4.

3 Classically, a starting point in the literature is U Beck, *Risk Society: Towards a New Modernity* (London: Sage Publications, 1992).

prospects which lie ahead. The sociological roots of the progression lie beyond the scope of this chapter, but the interrelationship between changes in thinking about the environment and changes in the approach taken by environmental law need to be acknowledged from the outset.

The adoption and development of EA, in this broad sense, also needs to be seen as a part of an evolving European Community environmental policy, increasingly emphasising prevention and precaution as key principles. Hence, the original Environmental Impact Assessment Directive (EIAD)[4] constituted a major step from reaction to anticipation. Although the original Directive was ostensibly based on 'prevention' of recognised kinds of harm to the environment, it was, in turn, followed by an amending Directive[5] which extended its rationale to encompass 'precaution'.[6] EIA, therefore, progressed from a mechanism for preventing known kinds of environmental harm to a means of requiring anticipation of possible harms.[7] The difficulty with assessment of either known or unknown kinds of harms, however, is that assessment demands some kind of criteria as to what is to count as a 'harm' or what quality of environment is to count as 'satisfactory' or 'acceptable' or, ultimately, what kind of development will qualify as 'sustainable'. The continuing peculiarity of EIA is that it requires assessment of significant environmental impacts without seeking to formulate any explicit and precise environmental objectives against which assessments of 'significance' are to be made.[8] Put bluntly, the exercise is 'aimless', at least in some key respects that will be investigated in the discussion that follows.

Similar observations may be offered on the mechanisms provided for SEA in the European Community Strategic Environmental Assessment Directive (SEAD).[9] Whilst the extension of EA methodology from individual development projects to plans and programmes is commendable in allowing a broader scope of anticipation at a higher level of decision-making, the criteria for determining 'significance' remain obscure. The failure to relate generalities,

---

4 85/337/EEC, as amended by 97/11/EC.

5 97/11/EC.

6 The original EIA Directive (85/337/EEC) stressed that the best environmental policy consists in preventing the creation of pollution or nuisances at source, rather than subsequently trying to counteract their effects (first recital). The amending Directive (97/11/EC) also emphasised the need for precaution (second recital). See A Sifakis, 'Precaution, Prevention and the Environmental Impact Assessment Directive' (1998) *European Environmental Law Review* 349, and contrast H-J Peters, 'The Significance of Environmental Precaution in the Environmental Impact Assessment Directive' (1996) *European Environmental Law Review* 210.

7 Although the scope of the amended Directive might be seen to be limited by its application to projects which are likely to have significant effects upon the environment (Art 1.1) suggesting that such effects are probable rather than possible and a preventative rather than precautionary rationale. See *R (Jones) v Mansfield District Council* [2003] EWCA Civ 1408.

8 For a range of possible factors determining 'significance', see A Gilpin, *Environmental Impact Assessment: Cutting Edge for the Twenty-First Century* (Cambridge: Cambridge University Press, 1995), 6–7.

9 2001/42/EC.

misleadingly dubbed as 'significance criteria',[10] to objective and precise standards of what is environmentally acceptable, serves to install the same quality of aimlessness in the SEA process as has been noted in respect of EIA.

After some introductory observations, the purpose of this chapter is to compare and contrast legislation concerned with SEA with another mechanism in European Community law that provides for a related kind of 'environmental assessment'. Specifically, the contrast to be considered is between the mechanisms provided for under the SEAD and the 'reviews' of the impacts of human activity on water bodies, required under the Water Framework Directive (WFD)[11] as a precursor to adoption of plans and programmes under that Directive.

The need for an assessment process as a prelude to plan making under the WFD makes the relationship with the SEAD especially apposite and the procedural similarities will become evident from an analysis of the content of the two Directives. However, as will be seen, the WFD assessment process contrasts starkly with the requirements of the SEAD. The former is based upon explicit and reasonably precise environmental objectives and standards, against which assessments are to be made, whereas the latter is not. Contrasts with the purposeful kinds of assessment that need to be made under the WFD raise the issue of whether it is timely for a more substantive kind of EA to be developed from the EIA and SEA procedures.[12] Should the next phase in the development of EA law be to address the question of prevention and precaution against what?

Horizontality, inclusivity and scope

The EIA has a central but unique position in European Community and national environmental law. By contrast to sectoral legislation, concerning the different environmental media of water, air and land, and the habitats and biodiversity which they support, EIA involves evaluation of the significant effects of a development project across a wide range of possible environmental impacts upon all sectors and their living constituents, both human and non-human. The breadth of this cross-sectoral, or horizontal, exercise may well explain some of the difficulties encountered by Member States in giving effect to Community

---

10 See p 164 below on the 'significance criteria' under the SEAD.
11 Art 5 2000/60/EC. The WFD also provides a linkage with 'appropriate assessments' required under Art 6 of the Habitats Directive (92/43/EEC). See p 170 below on this.
12 Note similarly the call for 'a closer link with concrete policy goals, emission standards and best available techniques [that] is necessary for EIA to have more influence in decision-making', J Jaap de Boer, 'Editorial: Impact of the European EIA Directive' (2005) *Impact Assessment and Project Appraisal* 86. Contrast the view that environmental standards may be used to determine what impacts should count as 'significant' in EA. See J Holder, *Environmental Assessment: The Regulation of Decision Making* (Oxford: Oxford University Press, 2004), 14 and 239.

obligations concerning EIA, particularly where national responsibilities for the environment are entrusted to different authorities. Nonetheless, the overall aim of EIA, that decision-makers should be fully informed of the environmental implications of authorising a development project, justifies the complexities involved in seeking to ascertain what those diverse impacts are likely to be and trying to avoid, or mitigate, adverse impacts to the extent that this is feasible.

Beyond the task of introducing a greater degree of transparency into the assessment of environmental impacts, EIA provided an early inroad into the democratisation of environmental decision-making. The information derived from the EIA process is not to be seen as the exclusive property of those entrusted with making development consent determinations.[13] EIA is perhaps the first recognition of a public right to be fully informed about the implications of a development project and to have access to appropriate information to enable participation in those procedures that determine the environmental quality of the areas in which ordinary citizens must live.[14] The provision of information to enable informed public participation in environmental decision-making constitutes another dimension to EIA which, at the time of its initiation at least, set it apart from other branches of Community environmental law.[15]

Alongside the new departures following from anticipation and participation, EIA distinguished itself as a distinct kind of environmental law by virtue of its almost entirely procedural character. No amount of transparency in the provision of environmental information, or degree of public involvement in the decision-making process, necessarily dictates whether a particular project should be authorised or not, or the conditions subject to which an authorisation should be granted. Authorisation determinations are made in a context that requires a balancing of environmental impacts against economic, social and political factors. Providing this balancing exercise is properly undertaken, the EIA process provides no guarantee that projects which are recognised to have a significant environmental cost will never be authorised. Again, EIA can be seen as precocious in recognising that 'sustainable development' does not preclude development, but recognises that developmental gain must be explicitly weighed against its environmental and other costs. At the project-authorisation level, the introduction of greater transparency into the balancing exercise was a radical innovation in

---

13 For general discussion of the role of citizens in environmental decision-making, see J Steele, 'Participation and Deliberation in Environmental Law: Exploring a Problem-Solving Approach' (2001) *Oxford Journal of Legal Studies* 415.

14 See e.g. *Berkeley v Secretary of State for the Environment (Berkeley No.1)* [2000] AC 603, particularly the opinion of Lord Hoffmann, and contrast earlier decisions discussed in J Alder, 'Environmental Impact Assessment – the Inadequacies of English Law' (1993) *Journal of Environmental Law* 203, and A Ward, 'The Right to an Effective Remedy in European Community Law and Environmental Protection: a Case Study of United Kingdom Judicial Decisions Concerning the Environmental Assessment Directive' (1993) *Journal of Environmental Law* 221.

15 Although subsequently see the Environmental Information Directives 90/313/EEC and 2003/4/EC.

bringing environmental decision-making into closer alignment with the broader international imperative that was later to be adopted for the environment.[16]

Although the innovative character of EIA in emphasising anticipation, participation and procedure is properly emphasised, the form of environmental assessment initially adopted at European Community level must be seen as a compromise.[17] 'Environmental impact assessment', as understood in the United States, encompassed a requirement that all agencies of Federal Government are to include, with every proposal for legislation and other major Federal actions significantly affecting the quality of the human environment, a detailed statement by the responsible officials of the environmental impact of the proposed action.[18] Clearly, the European Community version was considerably narrower in requiring environmental assessment only in respect of particular, public or private, development projects.

The qualified and tentative steps into EA taken by the Community under the original, and later amended, European Community EIA Directive, may be seen as politically expedient at the time they were adopted.[19] Nonetheless, in the light of experience of implementing the EIA process, it was inevitable that their limitations would come to be recognised. Determination of whether a particular project should be authorised is profoundly influenced by broader policies for land and other resource use and a range of other environmental concerns which, in many cases, are at least as important as the location-specific considerations upon which EIA tends to focus. When this constraint upon the EIA process is recognised, the shortcomings of project-specific environmental assessment are readily apparent.

Sooner or later, the unavoidable response lay in a broadening of the scope of EA. This response took the form of the SEAD which extended consideration from the impacts of particular projects to the assessment of environmental effects of the 'plans and programmes' under which they fell. With a view towards further promoting sustainable development, the preparation and adoption of plans and programmes are to be subject to a process of scrutiny as to the significant effects they are likely to have upon the environment. As will be seen,[20] the scope of the 'plans and programmes' subject to SEA is extensive. Again, the cross-sectoral implications, that proved problematic in implementing EIA, are likely to be of

---

16 Significantly, the EIAD was adopted before 'sustainable development' gained general endorsement in World Commission on Environment and Development, *Our Common Future* (United Nations, 1987), and the 1992 Rio Declaration of the United Nations Conference on Environment and Development.

17 See C Wood, *Environmental Impact Assessment: A Comparative Review* (London: Longman Publishing Group, 1996), 35, recounting the 'emasculation' of earlier versions of the EIAD.

18 NEPA, s.102(c).

19 See P Wathern, 'The EIA directive of the European Community' in P Wathern (ed.) *Environmental Impact Assessment: Theory and Practice* (London: Routledge, 1988), 192, for a discussion of the background to the adoption of the EIAD.

20 See p 163 below on the scope of 'plans and programmes'.

equal concern to governments and sectoral environmental authorities in Member States that must grapple with the new obligations. Nonetheless, the progression from projects to plans and programmes, as the target for EA, is a welcome one, in view of the widening of requirements for informed environmental decision-making that are involved and the potential enhancement of the assessment of sustainability of development that this may allow.

Against this introductory background, the issue must be raised whether environmental assessment has been taken as far as it can sensibly go. Is environmental assessment now so comprehensively provided for that no decision, or activity, that might significantly effect the environment may lawfully be reached, or undertaken, without a sufficient level of assessment of its environmental impacts?

In respect of international environmental impacts, the Espoo Convention[21] requires the parties, either individually or jointly, to take all appropriate and effective measures to prevent, reduce and control significant adverse transboundary environmental impacts from proposed activities and, for this purpose, to establish EIA procedures in relation to specified projects.[22] The transboundary dimension to EA is further extended by the Protocol to the Espoo convention relating to SEA,[23] which makes similar provision for SEA of plans and programmes to that provided for in the SEAD. However, a revealing contrast is to be seen in relation to the further extension of SEA to 'policies and legislation'. On this, the Protocol requires the parties to ensure that environmental concerns are considered and integrated, 'to the extent appropriate', in the preparation of policies and legislation that are likely to have significant effects upon the environment, including health.[24] The rather timid formulation of the obligation in relation to policies and legislation may reflect the difficulties and national sensitivities of applying EA in these sectors and the reason for hesitancy in extending it further in these directions.[25]

Nonetheless, a fair amount of headway has been made in relation to the application of EA methodology in relation to policy and legislative proposals. The original EIAD excluded the application of EIA to projects, the details of which are adopted by a specific act of national legislation, because it was

---

21 The UN ECE Convention on Environmental Impact Assessment in a Transboundary Context, 25 February 1991, signed by the European Community on 25 February 1991 (Com(92)93, OJ C104, 24 April 1992, as amended by Com(93)131, OJ L112, 22 April 1993).

22 Espoo Convention, Art 2, implemented in the European Community under Directive 97/11/EC.

23 UN ECE Protocol on Strategic Environmental Assessment to the Convention on Environmental Impact Assessment in a Transboundary Context (open for signature 21 May 2003).

24 Protocol to Espoo Convention on SEA in a Transboundary Context, Art 13.

25 In relation to the need for public participation concerning plans, programmes and policies relating to the environment (under Art 7 Aarhus Convention, see p 178 below on this) the European Commission took the view that the 'exhortatory reference' to public participation in relation to policies is 'soft law' which does not require Community legislation (see COM (2000)839 final, the proposal for the SEAD, para 6.1.1).

envisaged that the objectives of the Directive, including that of supplying public information, were fully achieved through the legislative process.[26] However, the assumption that scrutiny of a proposal through the legislative process is invariably sufficient to meet the needs of EIA, including the need for public participation, has been the subject of consideration by the Court of Justice, which has taken the view that national legislative procedures may be investigated to ensure full compliance.[27]

At EC level, the adoption of an 'impact assessment' methodology to improve the quality and coherence of the Community's policy development process, and to enable more coherent implementation of sustainable development, is another mechanism involving informal use of SEA at the level of policy formulation and legislative enactment. Hence, all major legislative and other policy proposals that have a potential economic, social and/or environmental impact and/or require some regulatory measures for their implementation will be subject to a preliminary, and in some cases an extended, assessment of their economic, environmental and/or social impacts before adoption.[28] Recognising the increasing degree to which policies and legislation involve issues of political judgment, the potential for further formalisation of EA requirements in these areas is likely to be increasingly problematic and to offer limited scope for further extension.

Substance

The culmination of the developments recounted suggests that EA methodology has reached the limits of its useful range measured, at least, in terms of the extent of decision-making that can profitably be made subject to EA. On the other hand, although the present breadth of EA requirements may allow little scope for further extension, the depth of the EA process is a different matter. A limitation that needs to be investigated is the exclusive reliance upon procedural constraints in EA and the lack of any specification of the substantive objectives as to what constitutes an environmentally acceptable decision.

The limitations of EA, in relation to its lack of any substantive content, are well illustrated in the context of the United States' National Environmental Policy Act 1969. The 'rise and fall' of substantive EA in this jurisdiction is pertinently recounted.[29] The early basis for inferring substantive content was that

---

26 EIAD, Art 1.5. On the national approach to scrutiny of policy and legislative proposals, see Cabinet Office website at www.cabinetoffice.gov.uk which gives details of 'regulatory impact assessment', a process intended to give effect to principles of better regulation. Among other matters, regulatory impact assessment guidance incorporates a 'costs and benefits checklist' intended to assist in the assessment of economic, social and environmental impacts of a proposal.

27 Case C – 287/98 *Luxembourg v Linster* [2000] ECR I–6917.

28 See European Commission, *Communication from the Commission on Impact Assessment*, COM (2002), 276 final, and see J Holder, *Environmental Assessment*, 164–181.

29 Ibid, Holder, *Environmental Assessment*, 250–256.

the obligation upon federal bodies to undertake EA was capable of being read alongside environmental policy objectives that are articulated in an adjacent section of the Act. This states that the Federal Government is to:

> use all practicable means and measures...in a manner calculated to foster and promote the general welfare, to create and maintain conditions under which man and nature can exist in productive harmony, and fulfil the social, economic and other requirements of present and future generations of Americans.[30]

In furtherance of this policy, Government is to:

> use all practicable means consistent with other essential considerations of national policy, to improve and coordinate Federal plans, functions, programs and resources to the end that the Nation may [amongst other things] attain the widest range of beneficial uses of the environment without degradation, risk to health or safety, or other undesirable and unintended consequences.[31]

The critical issue arising from these provisions was the extent to which the policy declaration, and the indication as to the manner of its implementation, gives rise to substantive obligations that must be met through the EA process. Put the other way around, to what extent may EA be used to reach outcomes that are contrary to the stated national policy?

The high water mark in substantive judicial interpretation of EA came in the *Calvert Cliffs* decision,[32] where the argument was accepted that the environmental policy in the National Environmental Policy Act 1969 imposed substantive duties upon federal agencies. Hence, it was the proper role of the judiciary to review the merits of administrative decisions alongside the policy declaration. However, subsequent decisions have effectively extinguished substantive review by reasserting that only procedural rights are created by EA requirements.[33] The decline of the substantive interpretation was sealed by a ruling of the Supreme Court affirming that EA has only the narrower procedural purposes of ensuring that agencies consider environmental impacts and disclose relevant information to the public: 'NEPA does not mandate particular results, but simply prescribes the necessary process. If the adverse environmental effects of the proposed action are adequately identified and evaluated, the agency is not constrained by NEPA from

---

30 NEPA, s 101(a).

31 Ibid, s 101(b).

32 *Calvert Cliffs' Coordinating Committee v Atomic Energy Commission* 449 F2d 1109 (DC Circ 1971).

33 *Stryker's Bay Neighbourhood Council Inc v Karlen* 44 US 223 (1980); *Robertson v Methow Valley Citizens Council* 490 U.S 332, 104 Led2d 351 (1989), cited by Holder, *Environmental Assessment*, 254.

deciding that other values outweigh the environmental costs.'[34] In short, the argument for substantive interpretation of EA requirements has come to nothing in the United States.

Turning from the American experience to the position in the EC, the question needs to be raised whether there are any stronger arguments for the incorporation of substantive content in EA as it is provided for in Community law. Perhaps the best starting point is the SEAD, where the recitals note that Community policy on the environment is intended to contribute to the preservation, protection and improvement of the quality of the environment, the protection of human health and the prudent and rational utilisation of natural resources.[35] Reference is also made to the Fifth Environment Action Programme of the Community, emphasising the need for action in relation to the environment and sustainable development.[36] More broadly, the Directive may be seen as a means of furthering the overall tasks of the Community of promoting 'a harmonious, balanced and sustainable development of economic activities' and 'a high level of protection and improvement of the quality of the environment'.[37] The issue is whether any of these policy objectives might be construed as requiring EA to be undertaken in a substantive manner, so as to ensure only those outcomes consistent with the identified policy objectives are acceptable. The answer is almost certainly in the negative. The affirmation that the SEAD is of a 'procedural nature',[38] seems explicitly to rule out any substantive content to EA deriving from the policy principles that might have been used for this purpose.

Even if the procedural character of the SEAD was not so unqualifiedly proclaimed, the suggestion that general policy principles such as the need for a 'high level of environmental protection' or 'sustainable development' should somehow guide the EA process is unhelpful. The use of abstractly stated policy principles as a guide to practical decision-making in EIA or SEA is a matter of no small difficulty. Deciding the extent to which a particular plan or programme is conducive to the attainment of sustainable development is either heavily subjective or as impossibly abstract as that of defining the practical meaning of 'sustainable development' itself. Defining the precise points at which environmental resources are permissibly traded off for greater social or economic benefits involves an algebra of incommensurables in which 'fine words' are of little help in getting the sums right.[39]

---

34 Per Stephens J in *Robertson v Methow Valley Citizens Council*, ibid, 350.
35 SEAD Recital 1.
36 Ibid Recital 2, referring to Fifth Environment Action Programme, *Towards Sustainability – A European Community programme of policy and action in relation to the environment and sustainable development* (1993), as supplemented by Council Decision No.2179/98/EC affirming the importance of assessing the likely environmental effects of plans and programmes (OJ L 275, 10 October 1998, 1).
37 Art 2 EC Treaty.
38 SEAD Recital 9.
39 Similar difficulties arise where decision-makers are made subject to general duties with regard to 'sustainable development'. See s 39 Planning and Compulsory Purchase Act 2004 which

On this, national experience with sustainability appraisal of development plans is illuminating.[40] Sustainability appraisal has emerged as a part of the strategic approach towards integrating sustainable development into strategic options for land use planning, initially, at a regional level.[41] 'Sustainability appraisal' is seen as 'a systematic and iterative process undertaken during the preparation of a plan or strategy, which identifies and reports on the extent to which the implementation of the plan or strategy would achieve the environmental, economic and social objectives by which sustainable development can be defined.'[42] The approach focuses upon the formulation of objectives and targets which seek to define sustainable development by headline indicators, against which an emerging strategy can be appraised.[43]

While progress towards, or regress from, sustainable development is helpfully informative in regional planning, as in other sectors, the absence of any specific quantifiable objectives in the sustainability appraisal process should be noted. Indeed, the criticism has been raised that the approach may actually serve to marginalise environmental appraisal against the more dominant role of economic criteria in the assessment of regional plans. At the very least, the environmental component needs to be bolstered if sustainability appraisal is to be worthy of

imposes a statutory duty upon persons or bodies responsible for the preparation of regional spatial strategies and local development documents to exercise their functions with the object of contributing to the achievement of sustainable development, having regard to policies on guidance on sustainable development issued by central Government.

40 Initially, sustainability appraisal was provided for in Department of Environment, Transport and the Regions, *Good Practice Guide to Sustainability Appraisal of Regional Planning Guidance* (DETR, 2000) building upon earlier guidance in Department of the Environment, *Environmental Appraisal of Development Plans: A Good Practice Guide* (DoE, 1993). Subsequently, s 5(4) Planning and Compulsory Purchase Act 2004 has provided for sustainability appraisal for the draft revision of proposals for regional spatial strategies. Guidance on the details of the process is provided for in Planning Policy Statement 11, *Regional Spatial Strategies* (Office of the Deputy Prime Minister, 2004), paras 2.36–2.39. Section 19(5) of the 2004 Act also provides for sustainability appraisal in the preparation of local development documents and guidance on this is provided in Planning Policy Statement 12, *Local Development Frameworks* (Office of the Deputy Prime Minister, 2004), para 3.17. A consultation paper, *Sustainability Appraisal of Regional Spatial Strategies and Local Development Frameworks*, was issued by the Office of the Deputy Prime Minister in September 2004.

41 See M Stallworthy, *Sustainability, Land Use and Environment: a Legal Analysis* (London: Cavendish, 2002), 156–157, 177–180.

42 Department of Environment, Transport and the Regions, *Good Practice Guide to Sustainability Appraisal of Regional Planning Guidance* (DETR, 2000), para 2.1.

43 The focus of sustainability appraisal on objectives may be seen as a point of contrast with the approach taken in the SEAD, which focuses upon impacts. See S P Smith and W R Sheate, 'Sustainability appraisal of English regional plans: incorporating the requirements of the EU Strategic Environmental Assessment Directive' (2001) *Impact Assessment and Project Appraisal* 263; and see also R Therivel and P Minas, 'Ensuring effective sustainability appraisal' (2002) *Impact Assessment and Project Appraisal* 81.

retention.[44] Even with such bolstering, it is difficult to see what response could be offered to the criticism that the kind of qualitative assessment involved is based solely upon the assessor's subjectivity:

> Attempts to quantify impacts, using scoring systems in matrices, for example, only result in subjectivity being built into the results. One assessor might rank an impact on the air quality very high and an impact on water quality less high in comparison, whereas another assessor would do the contrary, both using their own sensitivity to decide on the ranking.[45]

Despite these concerns about the national approach towards sustainability appraisal, the idea of consolidating and extending EA into a more holistic process of 'sustainable development assessment' seems to have some support at European Community level. The Commission's development of an assessment regime for its internal procedures, noted above,[46] may be seen as a testing ground for application of a more holistic kind of assessment. A suggestion is that the experience gained from applying this kind of assessment to Community actions might serve as a precursor to the introduction of broader kinds of sustainability assessment being required by the Member States.[47] If so, it will be revealing to see how this kind of assessment can be defended against criticisms of the kind that have been raised nationally against sustainability appraisal. The national concern, that sustainability assessment has the effect of marginalising environmental concerns, has tremendous scope for a parallel at Community level where the weightier concerns of the Commission, with trade and competition, have the potential to gain the upper hand.[48]

All these points of criticism may be subsumed in the broader appreciation that sustainability appraisal is just that, appraisal. An appraisal does not incorporate any substantive requirements. In the same way that EA has been characterised as 'aimless' because of its lack of precision in securing any particular quantifiable environmental objective, sustainability appraisal is equally aimless lacking a guarantee of any satisfactory environmental outcome. Clearly, it is informative to ascertain that a particular plan or programme is likely to have consequences that are environmentally catastrophic, but sustainability assessment does nothing by itself to prevent the approval of the plan or programme despite that finding.

Some care is needed in the interpretation of the above comments. Saying that EA is 'aimless' is not the same as saying that it is of no value or no benefit.

---

44 Royal Commission on Environmental Pollution, Twenty-Third Report, *Environmental Planning*, Cm.5459 (2002), para 7.47. The Government broadly accepted the need for the environmental component of sustainability appraisal to be strengthened: United Kingdom Government, *The Government's Response to the Royal Commission on Environmental Pollution's Twenty-Third Report on Environmental Planning England*, Cm 5887 (HMSO, 2003), 13.

45 C Roger-Marchart and S Tromans, 'Strategic Environmental Assessment: Early Evaluation Equals Efficiency' [1997] *Journal of Planning and Environment Law* 993, 996.

46 See p 155 above on the commission's impact assessment regime.

47 Holder, *Environmental Assessment*, 166.

48 Ibid, 295.

Indeed the opposite of this is equally arguable, to the extent that EA may have a positive effect upon the quality of environmental decision-making. It may plausibly be maintained that more widely informed environmental decisions necessarily result in environmentally better outcomes. It is not improbable that EA requirements are a force for changing institutional cultures, so that decision-making bodies better appreciate the significance and importance of environmental resources. Another persuasive line of argument is that the democratisation of environmental decision-making, through provision of public information and encouraging public involvement, is invariably a means of securing better protection of the environment. Despite the vigour with which these views have been presented by numerous and diverse commentators, it remains an open question, which seems to be empirically unprovable either way, whether EA has actually resulted in environmentally better decisions than would have been reached if it did not exist.[49]

Conversely, in relation to EIA at least, it might be contended that the procedures have merely added legitimacy to decisions that involve an inbuilt bias towards those developers who use environmental statements to direct the flow of information in a pro-development direction.[50] More sceptically still, the extreme view might be taken that the central premise upon which EIA is based, that detailed articulation of reasons for administrative decisions necessarily enhances the integrity of the decision-making process, is simply a 'dubious example of wishful thinking', put colourfully, 'nine parts myth and one part coconut oil.'[51]

The lack of, probably unobtainable, hard evidence that EA actually produces environmentally better decisions, and the absence of logically compelling reasons why it should produce such decisions, makes positioning oneself on the converts-sceptics spectrum of views on EA largely a matter of faith. Whatever the unprovable benefits or otherwise of EA, the position taken here is that its environmental quality objectives remain unclear. If there are benefits to EA, they are the incidental rather than necessary results of the legal forms in which it has been established. The only incontrovertible way of showing EA will necessarily produce environmentally better decisions is through the explicit incorporation of substantive content.

Hence, the aim of the following discussion is to investigate what potential exists for more substantive environmental objectives and standards to be incorporated into EA. The basis for this discussion is a comparison and contrast between EA methodology, particularly that provided for in the SEAD, and obligations that arise in relation to assessments, plans and programmes that are

---

49 See e.g. European Commission, *Report from the Commission on the implementation of Directive 85/337/EEC on the assessment of the effects of certain public and private projects on the environment* COM(93)28, s 4.5, and table 4.9.

50 Holder, *Environmental Assessment*, 285.

51 J L Sax, 'The (Unhappy) Truth About NEPA' (1973) 26 *Oklahoma Law Review* 239, quoted by Holder, *Environmental Assessment*, 283.

provided for under the Water Framework Directive.[52] The purpose of these comparisons and contrasts is to appreciate that EA need not be purely procedural in character and to highlight those respects in which substantivisation is possible, and arguably desirable, in relation to procedures under the EIAD and SEAD.

Assessment and planning under the Water Framework Directive

It is beyond dispute that the Water Framework Directive is one of the most ambitious pieces of environmental legislation ever adopted at EC level. The strategy of water management at river basin level, through a diverse range of mechanisms directed towards securing the good status of waters, has far-reaching implications that go beyond the simple consolidation or integration of previous water legislation. However, it is not the purpose of this chapter to provide a detailed review of the content of the WFD or the national mechanisms that will be required to secure its comprehensive and effective implementation.[53] The narrower focus is upon the role of planning under the WFD, the extent to which this involves EA methodology and the contrasts between the WFD and the SEAD in this respect. As will be seen, a major advancement of the WFD, as compared with previous water legislation, is the introduction of approaches towards achieving satisfactory water quality that involve assessing and addressing impacts upon the aquatic environment, including those arising from a range of land-based activities, and anticipating what must be done to realise specified environmental quality objectives. To emphasise the similarities and contrasts between SEA and WFD assessment and planning, some central points from the WFD must, first, be briefly recounted.

Under the WFD, the key administrative obligation upon Member States is that of ensuring a river basin management plan (RBMP) is produced for each river

52 For a general discussion see, J Carter and J Howe, 'The Water Framework Directive and the Strategic Environmental Assessment Directive: Exploring the Linkages' [2006] *Environmental Impact Assessment Review* 287.

53 For general academic literature on the Water Framework Directive see D Matthews, 'The Framework Directive on Community Water Policy: A New Approach for EC Environmental Law' (1997) *Yearbook of European Law* 191; W Howarth, 'Accommodation without Resolution? Emission controls and environmental quality objectives in the proposed EC Water Framework Directive' (1999) *Environmental Law Review* 6; D Grimeaud, 'Reforming EU water law: towards sustainability' (2001) *European Environmental Law Review* 41–51, 88–97, 125–135; A Farmer, 'The EC Water Framework Directive' (2001) *Water Law* 40; G Kallis and D Butler, 'The EU Water Framework Directive: Measures and Implications' (2001) *Water Policy* 125; and see W Howarth and D McGillivray, *Water Pollution and Water Quality Law* (hereafter *'Water Pollution'*) (Shaw and Sons, 2001) Ch. 5. From the perspective of environmental non-governmental organisations, see World Wide Fund for Nature and European Environmental Bureau, *'Tips and Tricks' for Water Framework Directive Implementation* (World Wide Fund for Nature and European Environmental Bureau, 2004) available at www.eeb.org.

basin district lying entirely within its territory.[54] The elements of a RBMP are set out in Annex VII to the Directive. These elements encompass a general description of the characteristics of the river basin district, and specified details concerning surface waters, groundwaters and significant human impacts; information concerning protected areas; monitoring arrangements and information on the status of waters; a statement of environmental objectives; and information on the economic analysis of water use. Perhaps most significantly for present purposes, a RBMP must also include a summary of the Programme of Measures (PoMs) that are to be adopted and, by means of which, the environmental objectives of the Directive are to be achieved, and various specific details concerning the PoMs.

PoMs are to be established for each river basin district and are to take into account the results of analyses of the characteristics of the river basin district, a review of the impact of human activity and an economic analysis of water use.[55] Hence, account needs to be taken of the most significant anthropogenic pressures on waters and assessments of the impacts of those pressures upon water quality.[56] PoMs also need to be established for the purpose of achieving the environmental objectives of the Directive.[57] Broadly, this means that deterioration in the status of waters should be avoided and that waters should be protected, enhanced and restored with the aim of achieving 'good status' for most waters by 2015.[58] However, various exceptions and qualifications are provided for in relation to artificial and heavily modified waters, and situations where less stringent objectives are justified for reasons of feasibility of disproportionate expense.[59]

More specifically, PoMs are stated to require 'basic' measures and, where necessary, further 'supplementary' measures. In summary, the basic measures encompass the need for mechanisms to address the following issues:

(a)   implementation of certain Community water legislation;
(b)   cost recovery for water services;
(c)   promotion of efficient and sustainable water use;
(d)   protection of water abstracted for drinking water supply;
(e)   abstraction and impoundment controls;
(f)   artificial recharge or augmentation of groundwater;
(g)   control of point source discharges;

---

54 WFD, Art 13.1. In respect of international river basin districts falling entirely within the Community, coordination is to be ensured with a view to producing a single international river basin management plan, but where this is not done, RBMPs covering national territories are to achieve the objects of the Directive. See WFD, Art 13.2.
55 WFD, Art 11.1.
56 Ibid, Art 5 and Annex II, para 1.4 and 5 (surface waters) and similarly para 2.3 (groundwaters).
57 Ibid, Art 11.1.
58 See the more detailed statement of the environmental objectives of the WFD at p 174 below.
59 Art 4 WFD.

(h)   control of diffuse sources;
(i)   significant adverse impacts, including hydromorpological conditions;
(j)   prohibition of certain direct discharges to groundwater;
(k)   elimination of pollution by priority substances; and
(l)   prevention of losses of pollutants from technical installations.[60]

The categories of supplementary measures are specified, non-exclusively, to include measures such as economic or fiscal instruments; negotiated environmental agreements; codes of good practice; restoration measures; and demand management measures.[61]

In short, implementation of the WFD requires the adoption of RBMPs encompassing PoMs, covering the specified matters, to achieve the environmental objectives of the Directive by the required deadline.

Activation of SEA in WFD planning

The first comparative issue needing to be addressed is the relationship between WFD assessment and planning, and the requirements for SEA. Specifically, this is the issue of whether WFD assessment and planning, as outlined above, is within the categories of activity that activate a requirement for SEA. While it might have been expected that this crucial issue would have been clearly and explicitly dealt with under Community law, it appears that it has not been and Member States are left to resolve some rather fundamental uncertainties. For example, draft guidance issued in the United Kingdom[62] has incorporated an 'indicative list' of plans and programmes that may be subject to SEA and are to serve for the purpose of reporting to the European Commission on the implementation of the SEAD. The indicative list makes reference to RBMPs and PoMs, but it is recognised that the list is not definitive and that case-by-case screening of particular plans or programmes, such as those under the WFD, may be required to determine their significant effects. The reasons for the uncertainties, as to whether WFD planning is subject to the SEAD, need to be examined.

Turning back to the SEA Directive, the pertinent requirements are that SEA must[63] be undertaken in respect of a plan or programme which is likely to have significant environmental effects and, among other things, is prepared for stated purposes and sets the framework for future development consent for projects listed in Annex I or II of the EIAD or is likely to have to have an effect on sites

---

60   Ibid, Art 11.3.
61   Ibid, Art 11.4 and Part B of Annex VI.
62   See, Office of the Deputy Prime Minister, *A Practical Guide on the Strategic Environmental Assessment Directive* (HMSO, 2005) Appendix 1, 45.
63   Although an element of discretion is given to Member States to broaden this requirement under the obligation to determine whether plans and programmes other than those that are explicitly identified are likely to have significant environmental effects. See SEAD, Art 3.4.

falling under the Habitats Directive.[64] Within this statement five distinct, but mostly cumulative, requirements may be isolated: first, whether a plan or programme is likely to have significant environmental effects; second, whether it is prepared for a stated purpose; third, whether 'it sets the framework for future development consent'; fourth whether that future development consent relates to a project within Annex I or II of the EIAD; and fifth, as an alternative to the fourth requirement, whether it is likely to have an effect upon certain protected habitats. In relation to RBMPs and PoMs under the WFD, the application of these five criteria for SEA needs elaboration.

Significant environmental effects

On the first issue, it might be immediately inferred that a RBMP or PoMs is clearly likely to have 'significant environmental effects', albeit beneficial effects,[65] since that is the essential purpose of such plans and programmes. Conceivably, but improbably, there might be a situation where all waters within a river basin already meet the ecological objectives of the WFD and where no actions are needed to bring about significant environmental improvement, but the remoteness of this possibility is such that it may be swiftly discounted.

The intuitively obvious inference, that WFD planning should require SEA because it involves significant environmental effects, may be confirmed by reference to the SEA 'significance criteria'. These are criteria that need to be applied to those categories of plans and programmes that may become subject to SEA through a determination of Member States that they are likely to have significant environmental effects.[66] Hence, the 'significance' of a plan or programme is to be determined by having regard to: the degree to which it sets a framework for projects and activities, either with regard to the location, nature, size and operating conditions or by allocating resources; the degree to which it influences other plans and programmes, including those in a hierarchy; its relevance for the integration of environmental considerations, particularly with a view to promoting sustainable development; the relevant environmental problems; and the relevance for the implementation of Community environmental legislation.[67] If any doubts remain about whether the implementation of RBMPs or PoMs is likely to have significant environmental effects, they are surely

---

64 SEAD, Art 2 and 3.1. In relation to the Habitats Directive (92/43/EEC), this is a reference to the need for an 'appropriate assessment' on sites under Art 6 or 7.

65 Note that there is no requirement that 'significant environmental effects' should be limited to adverse effects. Annex I SEAD requires information to be provided on...(f) the likely significant effects on...water...including secondary, cumulative, synergistic, short, medium and long-term permanent and temporary, *positive and negative* effects [emphasis added]. See *British Telecommunications plc v Gloucester City Council* [2001] EWHC Admin 1001.

66 SEAD, Art 3.4–3.5.

67 Ibid, Annex II para 1.

dispelled by considering these criteria. Against each criterion, WFD plans and programmes may be seen to have considerable significance. The purposive approach that courts are likely to take towards interpretation of the SEAD should place the issue beyond dispute.[68]

The stated purposes

On the second issue, the 'stated purposes' for which SEA is required expressly encompass plans and programmes which are prepared for 'water management' purposes. Although this phrase is not defined, it would seem wide enough to encompass a range of water quality and water quantity issues[69] and there seems little room for doubt that RBMPs and PoMs under the WFD are prepared for 'water management' purposes.[70]

Setting the framework

On the third issue, the question of what kinds of plan or programme 'set the framework' for future development consent for relevant projects is critical, but not clearly explained in the SEAD. It has been suggested that this would normally mean the plan or programme contains criteria or conditions that would guide the way a consenting authority would determine an application for development consent for a particular project falling under the plan or programme. This might involve placing limits on the type of activity or development which may be

---

68 An analogy may be drawn with EIAD, where the European Court of Justice has adopted a purposive approach to interpretation of the terminology used to identify different kinds of 'project' and restricted the discretion of Member States to exclude categories of project from the ambit of the Directive. See Case C-72/95 *Aannemersbedrijf P K Kraaijeveld BV and others v Gedeputeerde Staten van Zuid-Holland Environnement et consommateurs* [1996] ECR I–5403; Case C–435/97 *World Wildlife Fund (WWF) EA and others v Autonome Provinz Bozen EA 7 others* [1999] 1 CMLR 149.

69 It should be noted that the WFD was adopted under Art 175.1 of the EC Treaty. The significance of this is that Art 175.2 derogates from the usual co-decision procedure by reserving certain areas of legislation for the Council alone, subject to consultation requirements. Among the matters where legislation may only be adopted by a unanimous decision of the Council are measures concerning 'management of water resources'. The scope of this phrase is not defined, but it has been suggested it refers to measures mainly concerned with issues of water quantity, rather than water quality. Although the WFD does encompass some issues of water quantity, it seems to have been generally conceded that the main focus of the Directive on water quality made adoption under Art 175.1 uncontroversial. See Commission, *Framework for Community Action in the Field of Water Policy*, COM (97) 49 s.2.6; Case C–36/98; *Spain v Commission* [2001] ECR I–779, where the European Court of Justice held that the Convention for the Protection of the Danube, 30 January 2001, being mainly concerned with water quality issues, was properly adopted under EC Treaty, Art 175.1; and see Howarth and McGillivray, *Water Pollution*, s.4.10.1, for general discussion of the issues.

70 SEAD, Art 3.2.

permitted, perhaps to preserve characteristics of the area concerned.[71] Hence, the issue of whether adoption of a plan or programme requires SEA is to be determined by the degree to which it determines whether subsequent projects and other activities will be authorised. More specifically, this determination may be with regard to location, nature, size and operating conditions of activities or by allocating resources.[72]

The ambiguity of what is required for a plan or programme to 'set the framework' for consent for future projects has prompted the rather uninformative observation that whether a RBMP under the WFD sets the framework for future consents 'depends on the contents' of that plan.[73] This seems a rather evasive conclusion, since RBMPs are to contain PoMs which indicate quite specifically what kinds of control mechanisms are to be applied in relation to the environmental objectives that are being sought for particular water bodies. On the other hand, the character of what is to count as a 'measure' in a PoM is not entirely clear from the wording of the Directive.[74] It seems equally possible to construe 'measure' as a regulatory regime that needs to be adopted, such as a system of prior authorisations, or as the particular actions taken in pursuance of the regime, in the granting of individual authorisations. Notwithstanding this ambiguity, either the adoption of regulatory regimes or the application of those regimes in individual circumstances for the purpose of achieving the environmental objectives of the Directive, must surely 'guide', if not determine, the manner in which an authorisation for a particular project is formulated. This is particularly so where the project is likely to have an adverse impact upon the aquatic environment. If PoMs are not for that purpose, then it is difficult to see what purpose, if any, they are intended to serve.

Even if the ambiguities in what is involved in 'setting a framework' for future development consent are acknowledged, the additional status of RBMPs in guiding decisions about land use must also be considered. It seems to be accepted that land use plans, containing criteria determining what kinds of development may be permitted to take place in a particular area, are a 'typical' example of a plan which sets the framework for future development consent.[75] While recognising that land use plans may differ in the manner and extent to which they 'guide' consenting practice in individual cases, in principle at least, they are acknowledged to be a clear example of the kind of plan that would fall within the scope of the SEAD. The secondary issue, therefore, is whether RBMPs can be regarded as a kind of land use plan.

---

71 European Commission, *Implementation of Directive 2001/42 on the Assessment of the Effects of Certain Plans and Programmes on the Environment* (undated), hereafter *'SEAD Guidance'*, para 3.23. Although it must be noted the Guidance represents the views of the Commission and is not of a binding nature. See *SEAD Guidance*, para 1.5.

72 SEAD, Annex II para 1.

73 *SEAD Guidance*, 55.

74 See WFD, Art 11.

75 *SEAD Guidance*, para 3.26.

Land use planning differs from one Member State to another and even within Member States, but the situation in England may be taken as an illustration. In this jurisdiction, the planning system is 'plan-led'. That is, individual determinations of whether a proposed development should be authorised must follow the relevant development plan unless material considerations indicate otherwise.[76] The national system of development plans has recently been subject to major reforms,[77] including a streamlining of the hierarchy of plans provided for, but the system remains essentially plan-led one.

Under the new planning arrangements, the 'development plan' that must be followed in determining planning applications is a combination of the 'regional spatial strategy' and the 'local development framework' adopted or approved for a locality. Local development frameworks are envisaged as a 'portfolio' of documents relevant to planning matters and which, taken as a whole, comprehensively set out the policies of a local planning authority with respect to development and use of land in its area. This encompasses any document, or proposed document, containing statements or policies regarding, among other things, any environmental, social and economic objectives which are relevant to encouraging development or use of land.[78] Most significantly, the new emphasis upon 'spatial planning' seeks to integrate policies for the development and use of land with other kinds of policy and programme influencing the balance which needs to be drawn between competing land uses, with particular emphasis upon sustainable development. Hence, supplementary planning documents could include policies relating to diverse matters including regeneration, economic development, education, housing, health, waste, energy, biodiversity, recycling, protection of the environment, transport, culture and social issues.[79]

76 S 38 Planning and Compulsory Purchase Act 2004, replacing s 54A Town and Country Planning Act 1990. As national planning policies are regarded as 'material considerations' in planning determinations, it has been noted that 'the boundary between national/regional policy and development plan policy as plans or programmes which 'set the framework for future development control decisions' of EIA development and which are 'subject to preparation and/or adoption at national, regional or local level' is not therefore a clear one. Given a broad approach to interpretation, there is scope for argument that some forms of regional or national policies ought to be considered 'plans' within Art 2(a) SEAD. See D Elvin, 'Inclusivity and integration: some recent legal developments' [2004] *Journal of Planning and Environment Law (Occasional Papers No.32)* 11; D Elvin, 'The New Planning System: Inclusive, Sustainable and Spatial' [2004] *Journal of Planning and Environment Law* 26–27.

77 Under the Planning and Compulsory Purchase Act 2004. The new measures are not being fully implemented until 2007. For the policy background to the 2004 Act, which substantially amends the Town and Country Planning Act 1990, see the Department for Transport, Local Government and the Regions consultation paper, *Planning: Delivering A Fundamental Change* (HMSO, 2001); and see Office of the Deputy Prime Minister, *Sustainable Communities – Delivering through Planning* (HMSO, 2002), setting out the legislative proposals.

78 2004 Act, s 17(1)(a), and Town and Country Planning (Local Development) (England) Regulations 2004, SI 2004 No.2204, Reg. 6.

79 See generally W Upton, 'Planning Reform: the requirement to replace Supplementary Planning Guidance with Supplementary Planning Documents' [2005] *Journal of Planning and*

Despite the apparently all-encompassing range of policies that regard is to be had to in preparing local development frameworks, the inclusion or exclusion of WFD RBMPs amongst these policies remains somewhat indirect.[80] Guidance requires regional planning bodies to take into account a list of European Community, central government or central government agency national policies, guidance, research and related material when undertaking revisions of regional spatial strategies. Within this list is featured the national legislation transposing the WFD.[81] Because local planning authorities must have regard to regional spatial strategies in preparing local development documents,[82] which constitute a part of the local development scheme, they are implicitly bound to have regard to the need to implement the WFD. The indirectness of the planning law and guidance, however, contrasts markedly with the national legislation that transposes the WFD. Here it is explicitly stated that each public body, in exercising its functions so far as they affect a RBD, must have regard to the relevant RBMP.[83] The circuitous obligations arising under planning guidance are effectively displaced by a more specific duty under the WFD transposition legislation.

The inference from this is that, alongside their status for water management purposes, it is arguable at least that RBMPs also 'set the framework' for development consents because of their role in the land-use planning system. They are documents to which regard must be had by bodies making planning determinations and, in principle, this may be an overriding consideration unless material considerations indicate otherwise. In a system that is plan-led, such as in England, there is good reason to suppose that WFD plans act as a 'guide' to future development. Therefore, even if, read in isolation, WFD plans did not 'set

Environment Law 34; and see A Chaplin, 'Planning for Local Development Frameworks: a new development plan regime' [2004] *Journal of Planning and Environment Law* 260.

80 The Environment Agency has called for planning authorities and development agencies to be 'duty-bound' to take account of WFD objectives when developing regional spatial strategies and local development plans. See Environment Agency, *The Water Framework Directive: Position Statement* (Environment Agency, 2005). On the need for integration between land development plans and RBMPs, see Environment Agency, *The Relationship between the land use planning system and the Water Framework Directive* (Environment Agency, 2004), (a report prepared by Baker Associates) para 4.8.

81 The Water Environment (Water Framework Directive) (England and Wales) Regulations 2003 (hereafter 'the WFD Regs 2003'), SI 2003 No.3242; Office of the Deputy Prime Minister, *Planning Policy Statement 11: Regional Spatial Strategies* (HMSO, 2004), Annex A, 57.

82 S 19(2)(b) Planning and Compulsory Purchase Act 2004.

83 The WFD Regs 2003, Reg. 2(1), which defines 'public body' as a person holding an office under the Crown or created of continued in existence by public general Act of Parliament. Similarly, see Department for Environment Food and Rural Affairs, *Third consultation paper on the implementation of the EC Water Framework Directive (2000/60/EC)* (hereafter, *'EC WFD Consultation Paper 2000/60/EC'*) (HMSO, 2003) which states 'planning authorities are required to take account of environmental considerations and, although the WFD contains no explicit provisions in relation to land use planning, planning authorities will need to take account of the objectives which it creates', para 2.241.

the framework' for future development – which is disputed – their status in planning determinations means that they are capable of having this role within the land use planning system.

Projects under the EIAD

As regards the fourth issue, of the kinds of development project that are relevant, it is fairly clear that matters which fall within a RBMP or a PoMs under the WFD will be closely related to future development consent for projects listed within Annex I or II of the EIAD. To take one example, the need for controls over the artificial recharge or augmentation of groundwater[84] is a matter which must be provided for under the basic measures in a PoMs. Hence, when fully implemented, PoMs will determine criteria against which permission will be given for a project involving artificial recharge or augmentation of groundwater. In effect, projects of this kind will not be authorised where they are likely to prevent the environmental objectives for a particular water body being achieved.

Projects involving the artificial recharge of groundwater also fall within the scope of the EIAD.[85] It is to be expected that the form of PoMs, adopted in different RBMPs in different Member States, will differ. Despite this variation in content, however, it is difficult to resist the conclusion that WFD plans and programmes will 'set the framework' for future authorisations for relevant groundwater projects, as they will for other kinds of project or activity which fall within both a PoMs and Annex I or II of the EIAD. Again, this view is supported by the likelihood that courts will take a purposive interpretation of the SEAD in interpreting any ambiguities in terminology in the light of the broader environmental purposes of the Directive.[86]

Assessment under the Habitats Directive

The final requirement, concerning assessment under the Habitats Directive, may arise independently of whether or not the plan or programme at issue sets the framework for future development consent for projects under Annex I or II of the EIAD. SEA is required where the plan or programme, in view of its likely effects on certain conservation sites, has been determined to require an assessment under the Habitats Directive.[87] More specifically, the Habitats Directive requires

---

84 See (f) in the list at p 162 above.
85 EIAD, Annex 1(11) and Annex 2(10)(l).
86 See p 165 above on purposive interpretation.
87 Notably, also SEAD Recital 3, which refers to the obligation under the Convention on Biological Diversity requiring Parties to integrate as far as possible and as appropriate the conservation and sustainable use of biological diversity into relevant sectoral plans and programmes. See Convention on Biological Diversity, Art 14.1, and Decision VI/7 of the Conference of the Parties on guidelines for incorporating biodiversity related issues in SEA.

an 'appropriate assessment'[88] of 'any plan or project[89] not directly connected with or necessary to the management of a site but likely to have a significant effect thereon.'[90] This encompasses plans or projects which have impacts on special protection areas, under the Wild Birds Directive,[91] and proposed sites of Community importance, under the Habitats Directive.[92] The purpose of an assessment of this kind is to enable competent national authorities to ascertain the implications of the plan or project upon the site, in view of its conservation objectives, and whether the plan or project will adversely affect the integrity of the site.

In interpreting these requirements, it has been suggested that the terms 'plan or project' should be broadly construed to encompass land use plans and sectoral plans such as water management plans.[93] Conversely, the exclusion of plans or projects 'not directly concerned with or necessary to the management of the site' should not be narrowly construed to encompass only those relating to the conservation management of the site, though conservation management may fall within a 'mixed' plan which has conservation among its other objectives.[94] This raises the issue of whether a RBMP under the WFD would be excluded from requiring an assessment under the Habitats Directive, and possibly from the requirements for SEA, because, in part at least, it is 'directly' concerned with the conservation management of relevant sites.

Certainly, nature conservation is a strong theme in the WFD. Its first-stated purpose is that of establishing a framework which 'prevents further deterioration and protects and enhances the status of aquatic ecosystems and, with regard to their water needs, terrestrial ecosystems and wetlands directly depending on the aquatic ecosystems'.[95] To some extent these objectives are addressed through broadly based mechanisms which seek to protect water quality generally, but in other respects more specific provision is made in relation to conservation management. Hence, the WFD required Member States, by the end of 2004, to establish a register of areas, lying within each river basin district, which has been designated as requiring special protection under Community legislation for the conservation of habitats and species directly dependent upon water.[96] The register must include bodies of water

88 Commission guidance suggests that an 'appropriate assessment' under the Habitats Directive is narrower in scope than assessment under the EIAD, in that it is confined to the implications for the conservation objectives of the site. Nonetheless, there are similarities in the methodology involved in the two kinds of assessment. See European Commission, *Managing Natura 2000 Sites: the provisions of Art 6 of the Habitats Directive 92/43/EEC*, hereafter *'Managing Natura 2000 Sites'* (Office for Official Publications of the European Communities, 2000), para 4.5.2.

89 Notably, assessment under Art 6.3 Habitats Directive does not encompass 'programmes'.

90 Habitats Directive, Art 6.3.

91 See Wild Birds Directive 79/409/EEC, Art 4.

92 Ibid.

93 See *Managing Natura 2000 Sites*, para 4.3.2.

94 Ibid, para 4.3.3.

95 WFD, Art 1(a).

96 Ibid, Art 6; and see Art 4.1(c), on environmental objectives for protected areas.

and areas designated for the protection of habitats and species, where the maintenance or improvement of the status of water is an important factor in their protection, including relevant sites designated under the Wild Birds and Habitats Directives.[97] The measures to be included in a PoM under the WFD must encompass measures required under other Community environmental legislation including the Wild Birds and Habitats Directives.[98] Monitoring of water status is specifically required for protected areas with specifications for this being determined by the Community legislation under which the individual protected area has been established.[99] The upshot of all this is that, although a RBMP under the WFD would be categorised as a 'mixed' plan, there is a fair amount of evidence on which to base an inference that it is, at least in part, 'directly' concerned with conservation management of relevant sites under the Habitats Directive and, therefore, should not require an appropriate assessment under that Directive.

Commission guidance on appropriate assessment under the Habitats Directive suggests some degree of severance may be possible between different objectives of a 'mixed' plan and this may be required in some cases to ensure that a non-conservation component of the plan is subject to assessment. The example is given of a commercial timber harvesting plan, which forms part of a conservation management plan for a designated woodland, but also incorporates a commercial dimension which is not necessary to conservation management. Here, it is suggested that the mixed plan would need to be considered for assessment.[100] Similar considerations might arise in relation to a RBMP under the WFD. Although the issue is far from being clearly resolved, this would suggest that an assessment under the Habitats Directive would be required for those elements of a RBMP which are not directly concerned with conservation management of relevant sites. On the other hand, Commission guidance on the SEAD is ambivalent about this conclusion, in suggesting that whether a RBMP requires an assessment under the Habitats Directive 'depends on the contents' of the RBMP.[101]

It is somewhat difficult to reconcile the Commission guidance documents on assessment under the Habitats Directive and on the SEAD. A RBMP would appear to be a clear example of the sort of 'mixed' plan that the Habitats Directive guidance would require to be subject to assessment because of the potential impacts of its non-conservation management elements upon designated sites.[102] Depending on the contents of a particular RBMP, the SEAD guidance seems to envisage one or other of two possibilities: either that a RBMP might be

---

97 Ibid, Annex IV, para 1(v).
98 Ibid, Annex VI.
99 Ibid, Art 8.1 and Annex V, para 1.3.5; and see p 177 below on monitoring.
100 See *Managing Natura 2000 Sites*, para 4.3.3.
101 *SEAD Guidance*, 55.
102 This view is reinforced by broad interpretation of 'plan or project' adopted by the European Court of Justice in the *Waddenzee Shellfishery* case (Case C–127/02 *Landelijke Vereniging tot Behoud van de Waddenzee and Nederlandse Vereniging tot Bescherming van Vogels v*

excluded from Habitats Directive assessment because it is 'directly' and exclusively relevant to the conservation management of designated sites or because the implementation of a RBMP would not be likely to have significant effects upon designated sites. Both of these possibilities seem rather remote when it is appreciated that a large part of water planning under the WFD is concerned with water utility functions, particularly those arising from supplying water for human use. This coverage seems to place RBMPs squarely in the category of 'mixed' plans, with substantial components that are not concerned with conservation management but are capable of having significant effects upon designated sites. Hence, the need for an economic analysis of water use in each river basin district under the WFD,[103] the need for that analysis to be taken into account in the PoM for that district[104] and the need to implement a cost recovery principle in relation to certain water services[105] are all matters that could have significant impacts upon designated sites. Because of this, it is difficult to see how these non-conservation elements in a RBMP could evade assessment under the Habitats Directive or exclude the need for SEA of a RBMP. The SEAD allows for integrated assessments, meeting the requirements of different Community legislation at the same time, in order to avoid duplication of assessment procedures,[106] but this would not justify a RBMP failing to incorporate any kind of assessment of its overall impact upon designated conservation sites.

The inference

Summarising the five preceding subsections, there are sound reasons why adoption of RBMPs and PoMs under the WFD should require SEA in accordance with the criteria under the SEAD. In each respect, it has been seen that there are strong, if not always compelling, reasons why WFD planning should fall within the scope of the SEAD. It is regrettable that some of the uncertainties that have been ranged over have not been laid to rest by an explicit statement in the SEAD that RBMPs and PoMs are intended to be within its scope. Nonetheless, the similarity between WFD assessment and planning, and SEA, is evidenced by the finding that the former is within the requirements of the latter.

Staatssecretaris van Landbouw, Natuurbeheer en Visserij, ECJ 7 September 2004), where it was found that mechanical cockle fishing, that had been carried on for many years subject to licences granted following an annual assessment, fell within a 'plan' or 'project' under Art 6(3) Habitats Directive. Licences needed to be subject to a precautionary approach towards appropriate assessment of the significant effects upon the site's conservation objectives, so an activity may only be authorised if no reasonable scientific doubt remains as to such effects. See J Verschuuren, 'Shellfish for Fishermen or for Birds? Art 6 Habitats Directive and the Precautionary Principle' (2005) *Journal of Environmental Law* 265.

103   WFD, Art 5.1.
104   Ibid, Art 11.1.
105   Ibid, Art 9.
106   SEAD, Art 11.2; and see p 182 below on integrated assessment.

Procedural requirements for SEA and WFD planning

Having concluded that WFD assessment and planning activates the requirement for SEA, the next issue needing to be addressed is the extent to which the procedural requirements under the WFD are sufficient to meet the requirements for the process of undertaking SEA under the SEA Directive. For purposes of exposition, it is convenient to set aside the procedural requirements concerning consultation and monitoring issues for later consideration.[107]

As has been noted, the SEAD requires the EA of plans and programmes which are likely to have significant environmental effects.[108] In brief, the key procedural requirements for SEA are that it must be carried out during the preparation of a plan or programme and before its adoption or submission to legislative procedure.[109] An environmental report must identify, describe and evaluate the likely significant effects on the environment of implementing the plan or programme and the reasonable alternatives available taking into account its objectives and geographical scope.[110] Specified information must be included in the environmental report, taking account of current knowledge and methods of assessment; the contents and level of detail; the stage in the decision-making process; and the need to avoid duplication of assessment.[111]

Turning back to the WFD, the comparative issue to be addressed is the extent to which the procedural requirements of the SEAD are also met by the requirements for formulating WFD plans and programmes. The form of EA provided for in the WFD requires RBMPs and PoMs to be prepared according to a formalised procedure based upon the gathering, analysis and application of specified kinds of information. In particular, Member States must ensure that, for each river basin district, there is undertaken: an analysis of its characteristics; a review of the impact of human activity on the status of surface waters and groundwater; and an economic analysis of water use.[112] The three kinds of 'assessment' must be carried out in accordance with technical specifications set out in Annexes II and III to the Directive. Annex II sets out in some detail the principles that must be applied to the characterisation of surface waters and the classification by ecoregions; the type-specific reference conditions that are to be applied; and the identification of pressures and assessment of impacts. Annex III identifies the information that needs to be gathered, among other things, to make estimates of the volumes, prices and costs associated with the provision of water services. The overall impression is that a challengingly wide-ranging and detailed

---

107 See p 178 below on consultation and p 183 below on monitoring.
108 SEAD, Art 3.1; and see p 163 above.
109 Ibid, Art 4.1.
110 Ibid, Art 5.1.
111 Ibid, Art 5.2.
112 WFD, Art 5.

amount of environmental information will need to be gathered and analysed as a precursor to formulating the RBMPS and PoMs that the WFD requires.

Perhaps most critically, for the present discussion, a purpose of the initial 'characterisation' reports is to identify those water bodies where individual, cumulative or synergistic impacts cause them to be at risk of failing to meet the environmental objectives of the WFD by the required deadline of 2015. Concisely stated, this means that relevant waters must not fall below what is required for the following environmental objectives to be met.

1 preventing deterioration of water quality;[113]
2 protecting, enhancing and restoring waters with the aim of achieving good status (encompassing both good chemical status and good ecological status of surface waters) by 2015;[114]
3 protecting, enhancing and restoring artificial or heavily modified waters with the aim of achieving good status by 2015;[115]
4 progressively reducing pollution by priority substances and phasing out emissions, discharges and losses of priority hazardous substances;[116]
5 preventing or limiting inputs of pollutants into groundwaters;[117]
6 Reversing significant upward trends in the concentration of any pollutant in groundwater;[118] and
7 Complying with standards and objectives for protected areas by 2015 including objectives for areas for the abstraction of drinking water.[119]

The initial characterisation exercise

The reality of the initial exercise of characterising waters and assessing pressures and impacts against the stated ecological objectives has not fully met the high expectations that might have been raised by the wording of the WFD. The deadline for the first characterisation exercise was set as the end of 2004.[120] By then, Member States were to have accomplished the formidable task of assessing the risk that individual water bodies would fail to meet the environmental objectives of the Directive. However, at the time of the initial assessment, those environmental

113 WFD, Art 1.a.i and b.i.
114 Ibid, Art 4.1.a.ii and b.ii.
115 Ibid, Art 4.1.a.iii.
116 Ibid, Art 4.1.a.iv.
117 Ibid, Art 4.1.b.ii.
118 Ibid, Art 4.1.b.ii.
119 Ibid, Art 1.c and Art 7.
120 More precisely, 22 December 2004 (under WFD, Art 5.1) with national reports required to be submitted to the Commission within three months of completion. See WFD, Art 15.2.

objectives were not fully defined. Particular problems arose in relation to the quality specifications for groundwater, priority substances and ecological quality.

In respect of groundwater, uncertainties arose because the environmental objective of preventing or limiting inputs of pollutants into groundwater does not specify which pollutants are involved. This matter is intended to be clarified by a daughter directive[121] in relation to groundwater, incorporating criteria to be applied in determining whether a 'significant and sustained' upward trend in groundwater contamination exists.[122] Until these criteria have been established at Community level, Member States have to formulate their own criteria. Similar uncertainties surround the environmental quality standards for priority substances[123] which will not be finalised until agreement is reached on a daughter directive relating to these standards.[124] Likewise, there is considerable uncertainty about the boundaries between the ecological status classes for surface waters which are needed to determine whether good ecological status is met. Criteria for ecological status are not expected to be finally determined until after the end of an intercalibration exercise that is being conducted across a network of sites to ensure comparability of ecological data[125] and the establishment of a monitoring network in 2006.[126]

Alongside the formal reasons why the initial assessments were bound to be incomplete or uncertain, there are other, more practical, limitations that must be recognised. Broadly, these limitations arise because much of the data on water quality pressures and impacts has not previously been required to be gathered or analysed for the purposes of Community or national law. Even where data on the existing state of water bodies is available, the futuristic and cumulative assessment of how it is likely to change over the next decade, due to plans, projects and implementation of other Community environmental legislation is bound to generate a high level of speculation. Given the relatively short timescale involved, the likelihood of Member States having the expertise to be able to collect, collate and analyse the new kinds of information, in the comprehensive and consistent manner envisaged by the Directive, was remote.

To a degree, the imperfections of the initial assessments were widely recognised. The WFD is distinguished from previous Community environmental legislation by the initiatives that have been put in place to secure its coherent and harmonious implementation across the Member States. For this purpose,

---

121 Ibid, Art 17. See European Commission, *Proposal for a Directive of the European Parliament and of the Council on the protection of groundwater against pollution*, COM (2003) 550 final.
122 Ibid, Art 4.1.b.iii.
123 Ibid, Art 4.1.a.iv.
124 Ibid, Art 16. See Decision No.2455/2001/EC of the European Parliament and of the Council establishing the list of priority substances in the field of water policy and amending Directive 2000/60/EC. The Commission is preparing a proposal for Community-wide environmental quality standards (under WFD, Art 16.7) and emission controls (under WFD, Art 16.6).
125 Ibid, Annex V, para 1.4.
126 Ibid, Art 8.

a Common Implementation Strategy has been adopted for the Directive, involving working groups of experts and stakeholders from the Member States producing a series of guidance documents addressing practical issues in respect of implementation.[127] The Common Implementation Strategy documentation which is most relevant to the assessment of risks to the attainment of the objectives of the WFD arising from human activity is *Analysis of Pressures and Impacts*.[128] Although recognised not to be legally binding, this guidance seeks to establish a common understanding as to what must be done by Member States to assess the likelihood that waters will fail to meet the environmental objectives of the WFD.

Pertinently, this Guidance recognises the limitations of the initial analysis of pressures and impacts that have been noted above and acknowledges that it will be necessary for some compromises to be made. An example of this is to be seen in the assessment of those surface water bodies that are to be designated as 'artificial or heavily modified', so that the environmental objective of 'good ecological status' is reduced to the lesser objective of 'good ecological *potential*'.[129] In respect of such waters, it is advised that the first impacts analysis should concentrate upon the risks of such waters failing to meet the good ecological status requirement, leaving for later consideration the assessment of whether those bodies subsequently designated are at risk of failing to meet the good ecological potential requirement, although this should be done 'as soon as practical'.[130]

More generally, the *Guidance* recognises that initial analyses of pressures and impacts must be 'proportionate' to the difficulties involved in their assessment and that Member States must recognise and record their uncertainties in their reports.[131] 'Proportionality' is widely used as justification or recognition of the limitations of initial assessment exercise. Hence, the complexity of, and therefore effort expended on, assessing the effects of pressures on any particular water body, or group of water bodies, should be proportional to the difficulty of deciding whether that water body is at risk of failing to meet the environmental objectives of the Directive. The assessment effort should be proportional to the difficulty in designing effective monitoring programmes and programmes of measures. Proportionality is also applied through the adoption of screening criteria to identify pressures that are not significant and water bodies that are clearly at risk or clearly not at risk of failing to achieve their objectives. It is

127 See generally, European Commission, *Common Implementation Strategy for the Water Framework Directive (2000/60/EC), Strategic Document* (European Commission, 2001) and subsequent strategic documents of 2003 and 2004.

128 European Commission, *Common Implementation Strategy for the Water Framework Directive (2000/60/EC), Guidance Document No. 3, Analysis of Pressures and Impacts* (European Commission, 2003). Hereafter '*CIS Guidance No. 3*'.

129 WFD, Art 4.1.a.iii, emphasis added.

130 *CIS Guidance No. 3*, 5.

131 Ibid, 6.

advised that generic screening criteria should be used to identify pressures of magnitudes that may be expected to have obviously significant or obviously insignificant effects, taking account of the characteristics and susceptibility of particular water bodies to pressures. Grouping of water bodies is also seen as a means of ensuring the most cost-effective approach taken towards the analysis of pressures and impacts.[132] It must be reiterated that this 'practical' guidance has no status in law, but it gives a clear indication why the initial assessments are likely to fall below the thoroughness envisaged by the Directive.

This background of uncertainty or incompleteness has also been recognised by the UK competent authorities who have summarised the limitations of the initial characterisation exercise and reviewed the refinements that will be needed to improve the degree of certainty that can be achieved in future characterisation exercises.[133] Hence, it seems to be generally conceded that quite a lot more needs to be done before meaningful assessments can be made of the states of waters against the environmental objectives required by the Directive.

The limitations that have been noted might cause the unsatisfactory initial assessment of pressures and impacts to be 'written off' as the inevitable result of the misguidedly short time period that was allowed for the exercise to be completed. Indeed, a critical view might be that it suffered from the same fault of 'aimlessness' that has been alleged in relation to EA generally. Alternatively, the exercise might be seen more positively as a 'trial run' in an ongoing process of reassessment and refinement that will eventually become genuinely useful as a guide to the measures needed fully to meet the environmental objectives of the WFD. From this positive perspective, it might be noted that the initial assessments are of significant importance in relation to the monitoring programmes that must be put in place by the end of 2006.[134] Although the next formal assessment of pressures and impacts is not required until the end of 2013,[135] the initial assessment has served the purpose of identifying those waters needing special monitoring to inform that process, albeit imperfectly. With hindsight, requiring the initial assessment to be completed before the monitoring network is established might be seen as anomalous. Conversely, requiring monitoring of those waters that are 'at risk' would be incoherent without some means, however imperfect, of identifying which waters are at issue. Initial monitoring of water bodies at risk is likely to inherit many of the problems that have been identified in the initial assessment of pressures and impacts, but the relationship between the two activities is one of progressive mutual refinement. That is, a 'rough and ready' initial assessment will be enhanced by the information

---

132 Ibid, 8–9.
133 Welsh Assembly Government, Scottish Executive, Department of the Environment Northern Ireland and Department for Environment Food and Rural Affairs, *Water Framework Directive (WFD): Note from the UK administrations on the next steps of Characterisation* (Department for Environment Food and Rural Affairs, 2005).
134 See p 183 below on monitoring.
135 WFD, Art 5.2.

gained from monitoring, and an improved assessment will enable progressively better targeted monitoring, and so on.

As a point of contrast, environmental reports prepared under the SEAD must be of sufficient quality to meet its requirements and Member States must communicate to the Commission any measures they take concerning the quality of these reports.[136] No corresponding 'quality assurance' requirement is provided for in the WFD. Certainly, in relation to the initial characterisation exercise, it would have been difficult to have met any meaningful requirement for the quality of the first reports but, for the reasons given, this should not be taken to be indicative of the way that future assessments of water quality will be undertaken. In principle at least, there is no reason why the methodology for assessment under the WFD should not become at least as stringent as that required for SEA under the SEAD.

Consultation requirements

As has been noted,[137] a key characteristic of EA in all its different forms is inclusivity, whereby members of the public, relevant authorities, and other interested parties nationally and internationally, are given the opportunity to make representations concerning an environmental decision. Moreover, the basic tenet of EA is that an environmental decision will be informed, and thereby improved upon, by taking into account the widest possible range of intelligence and opinion. For that reason, in most instances, it is the explicit duty of the decision-making body to 'take into account'[138] representations of this kind, though not to be bound to follow any particular representation. Broadly, these principles are followed in both the SEAD and the WFD, with some notable points of contrast.

More generally, public participation in environmental decision-making is also addressed by the Aarhus Convention,[139] which requires 'appropriate practical and/or other provisions for the public to participate during the preparation of plans and programmes relating to the environment, within a transparent and fair framework, having provided the necessary information to the public'.[140] Endorsing the principle that Community law should be properly aligned with the Convention, with a view to its ratification by the Community,[141] Directive 2003/35/EC has been

---

136 SEAD, Art 12.2.
137 See p 152 above on consultation.
138 SEAD, Art 6, and EIAD, Art 8, which uses the expression 'taken into consideration'.
139 UN ECE Convention on Access to Information, Public Participation in Decision-making and Access to Justice in Environmental Matters, 25 June 1998. See also Principle 10 of the Rio Declaration (1992) on access to information on the environment and the opportunity to participate in decision-making processes.
140 Aarhus Convention, Art 7.
141 See European Commission, *Proposal for a Decision on the conclusion of the Aarhus Convention* COM (2003) 625 and, subsequently, Council Decision of 17 February 2005 on the conclusion, on behalf of the European Community, of the Convention to access to information, public participation and decision-making and access to justice in environmental matters (2005/370/EC) approving the Convention on behalf of the Community.

adopted to amend certain directives that do not contain sufficient provision on public participation to meet the requirements of the Convention.[142] Notably, while the Directive makes amendments to other environmental directives, the provisions on public participation concerning plans and programmes are specifically stated not to apply to the SEAD or the WFD.[143] The reason for this is that the public participation provisions in both the SEAD and the WFD are already thought to be in conformity with the requirements of the Convention.[144]

Consultation is provided for under the SEAD by way of a requirement that the draft plan or programme and the environmental report must be made available to authorities likely to be concerned with its effects and to the public.[145] An 'early and effective' opportunity must be given for the authorities and the public likely to be affected, including relevant non-governmental organisations, to express their opinion before adoption of the plan or programme.[146] Further provision is made for transboundary consultation where implementation of a plan or programme is likely to have significant effects upon the environment of another Member State or where another Member State so requests. Where this applies, detailed arrangements need to be agreed to allow relevant authorities and the public in the Member State that is likely to be significantly affected to express their opinions within a reasonable time.[147] Opinions expressed by consultees, including those arising from transboundary consultation, must be taken into account during the final preparation of the plan and before its adoption.[148] Consultees must be informed that the plan or programme has been adopted and a statement must be provided as to how environmental considerations have been integrated; how opinions have been taken into account; and the reason for adopting the plan in preference to reasonable alternatives.[149] The information on the decision must also include information on monitoring, which is required in relation to the significant

142 Directive 2003/35/EC providing for public participation in respect of the drawing up of certain plans and programmes relating to the environment and amending with regard to public participation and access to justice Council Directives 85/337/EEC and 96/61/EC.

143 Directive 2003/35/EC, Art 2.5.

144 In relation to the WFD, see European Commission, *Proposal for a Directive of the European Parliament and of the Council Providing for Public Participation in respect of the Drawing up of Certain plans and programmes relating to the environment and amending Directives 85/337/EEC and 96/61/EC*, COM (2000) 839 final, para 3.5.

145 'The public' is defined to mean one of more natural or legal persons and, in accordance with national legislation or practice, their associations, organisations and groups: see SEAD, Art 2.d. Notably, authorities with specific environmental responsibilities must be consulted in relation to any determination whether certain, non-listed, kinds of plan or programme are to be subject to SEA. See SEAD, Art 3.6.

146 SEAD, Art 6.

147 Ibid, Art 7.

148 Ibid, Art 8.

149 Ibid, Art 9.

environmental effects of implementation, to identify unforeseen adverse effects and to undertake appropriate remedial action.[150]

The WFD emphasises that its success relies upon 'information, consultation and involvement of the public'[151] and it makes explicit provision for 'public information and consultation' which contrasts with requirements under the SEAD and goes beyond consultation requirements found in other environmental directives. The general duty imposed upon Member states is to 'encourage the active involvement of all interested parties' in the implementation of the Directive and to ensure consultation and access to background information. In particular, this duty arises in relation to production, review and updating of RBMPs. Accordingly, the following information is to be published and made available for public comment: a timetable and work programme for the production of plans; an interim overview of the significant water management issues; and draft copies of the plan. On request, access must be given to background documents and information used for the development of the draft plan. Six months are to be allowed for comments, in writing, on any of the documents in order to allow active involvement and consultation.[152]

The obligation to encourage active involvement seems to suggest something beyond the ordinary elements of a consultation process, involving a 'potentially much deeper form of participation, although there is little compulsion here',[153] perhaps indicating a shift towards a model of 'active citizenship' in which power is shared between a wide range of stakeholders.[154] However, the obligation to 'encourage' involvement falls short of a duty to ensure that this actually occurs and the WFD gives no further indication as to what kind of 'encouragement' is needed.[155] By contrast, the Common Implementation Strategy Guidance affirms that 'participation' involves more that mere consultation, so that 'interested parties participate actively in the planning process by discussing issues and contributing to their solution'. The guidance notes that, beyond consultation, still

---

150 SEAD, Art 10.
151 WFD Recital 14.
152 Ibid, Art 14.
153 M Lee and C Abbot, 'The Usual Suspects? Public Participation Under the Aarhus Convention' (2003) *Modern Law Review* 80, 100. Similarly, respondents to national consultation on WFD 'stressed that public involvement included, but did not stop at, providing information and consulting'. See Department for Environment Food and Rural Affairs, *Third consultation paper on the implementation of the EC Water Framework Directive (2000/60/EC)* (2003) para 2.273.
154 R Macrory and S Turner, 'Participatory Rights, Transboundary Environmental Governance and EC Law' (2002) *Common Market Law Review* 489, 505.
155 In relation to proposed RBMS and PoMs, the national transposing legislation requires the Environment Agency to take such steps 'as it thinks fit', or as directed, to (i) provide opportunities for the general public and those persons likely to be interested in or affected by its proposals to participate in discussion and the exchange of information or views in relation to the preparation of those proposals; (ii) publicise its draft proposals to those persons; and (iii) consult those persons in respect of those proposals. See the WFD Regs 2003, Regs. 10(2)(b) and 12(2). It is far from clear how these measures are intended to encourage involvement.

higher levels of participation are shared decision-making and self-determination. 'Shared decision-making' implies that interested parties not only participate actively in the planning process, but also become partly responsible for the outcome. 'Self-determination' implies that at least parts of water management are handed over to the interested parties. The view taken in the guidance is that encouraging consultation should be considered the core requirement for active involvement, but although the latter two forms are not specifically required by the Directive they may often be considered as best practice.[156]

In summary, the contrasts between the SEA Directive on consultation and corresponding provisions for 'public information and consultation' under the WFD are as follows. The WFD is more stringent than the SEAD in that it encourages active involvement; encompasses consultation on documents other than draft RBMPs; and is explicit about the time period for consultation. The WFD is less stringent than the SEAD in that it makes no explicit provision for transboundary consultation, though the involvement of 'all interested parties' might be construed to encompass this. Apparently,[157] it only allows consultees to respond 'in writing', makes no explicit provision requiring the opinions of consultees to be taken into account in the adoption of the final plan, and imposes no requirement that consultees should be informed as to how their opinions have been taken into account. However, the final plan is required to provide a summary of the public information and consultation measures taken, their results and the changes to the plan made as a consequence.[158] Given the two Directives were adopted within a few months of each other, it is remarkable that their consultation requirements are not more fully harmonised. Nonetheless, in those respects in which consultation under the WFD is narrower than under SEAD, it seems unavoidable that WFD consultation would have to be overridden or extended to meet the stricter requirements of the SEAD.[159]

The environmental report

Perhaps the most outstanding procedural contrast between the SEAD and the WFD is that consultation under the WFD does not require the preparation of any separate environmental report, detailing the likely significant environmental effects of implementing a RBMP or PoMs and its reasonable alternatives, as required by SEAD.[160]

156 European Commission, Common Implementation Strategy for the Water Framework Directive (2000/60/EC), Guidance Document No. 8, *Public Participation in relation to the Water Framework Directive* (European Commission, 2003), para 2.2.
157 Although the contrasting view that oral responses are permissible is taken in guidance, see ibid.
158 WFD, Annex VII, para A9.
159 The requirements for EA under SEAD are stated to be 'without prejudice' to any requirements under the EIAD and to any other Community law requirements. See SEAD, Art 11.1. That is, requirements under the SEAD are in addition to those that apply in other Community legislation.
160 SEAD, Art 5 and Annex I.

It is difficult to gauge how far the content of an environmental report on a draft RBMP would differ from that of the draft RBMP itself. The categories of information required to be provided in an environmental report, set out in Annex I to SEAD, seem to be substantially the same matters that would also need to be encompassed within a draft or final RBMP, the essential elements of which are set out in Annex VII to the WFD. Certainly, there are differences between the wording of Annex I to SEAD and Annex VII to WFD, with the latter reflecting the more specific requirements relevant to the aquatic environment. Nevertheless, in substance, it is difficult to discern any elements of an environmental report that would not also be present in a draft RBMP. If this is the case, the only remaining point of contrast is that the process of SEA seems to be integral to WFD planning, with the consequence that production of a separate environmental report appears to be superfluous. The critical question is whether SEA necessarily requires a separate environmental report to be prepared and consulted upon, even where a draft WFD plan already contains the categories of information required to assess the likely significant environmental impacts of implementing the plan.

The SEAD makes various provisions for minimising the administrative burden of implementation through incorporating its provisions into existing procedures. In general terms, this is addressed by a statement that its requirements may be integrated into existing procedures to avoid establishing new procedures specifically to comply with the Directive. Where plans and programmes form part of a hierarchy, avoidance of duplication of assessment should take into account that assessment may take place at different levels in that hierarchy.[161] Hence it is recognised that environmental reports should take account of the fact that certain matters may be more appropriately assessed at different levels in decision-making processes to avoid duplication of assessment. Also, relevant information on environmental effects of plans and programmes obtained at other levels of decision-making or through other Community legislation may be used for providing the information that must be contained in an environmental report.[162] All this tends to suggest that the information gathering and analysis undertaken in the adoption of a RBMP or PoMs should not be duplicated in SEA or other kinds of plans and programmes that relate to the aquatic environment. It does not however directly address the question of whether it is mandatory to have distinct and separate requirements for adopting WFD plans and for SEA of the adoption process.

More illumination may be drawn from the definition of 'environmental report' provided under the SEAD. This states that the 'environmental report shall mean the part of the plan or programme documentation containing the information required' to identify, describe, and evaluate the likely significant effects of implementing the plan or programme and its reasonable alternatives.[163] As

161 SEAD, Art 4.2–4.3.
162 Ibid, Art 5.2–5.3.
163 Ibid, Art 2.3, 5, and Annex I.

mentioned in Commission guidance, this implies the environmental report should be 'a coherent text or texts', but the Directive does not specify whether the environmental report should be integrated in the plan or programme itself or provided in a separate document. If the environmental report is integrated, it should be clearly distinguishable as a separate part of the plan or programme, and be easy to find and assimilate for the public and authorities.[164] The implication is that the SEAD could be complied with by preparation of a single document, such as a RBMP or PoMs, providing all the other requirements for SEA were met.

The possibility of integrating SEA and WFD planning is envisaged by the SEAD in stating that:

> for plans and programmes for which the obligation to carry out assessments of the effects on the environment arises simultaneously from SEAD and other Community legislation, Member States may provide for co-ordinated or joint procedures fulfilling the requirements of the relevant Community legislation in order, *inter alia*, to avoid duplication of assessment.[165]

This has been interpreted as inviting Member States to provide co-ordinated or joint procedures which fulfil the requirements of all the relevant Community legislation.[166] More specifically, because the WFD and the SEAD are 'complementary and provide for a broadly similar environmental assessment', they are seen as measures where joint transposition could readily be provided. This might be done, for example, by making the competent national authority for WFD planning also responsible for ensuring the requirements of SEA are adequately covered in RBMPs. Differences in the requirements under the SEAD and WFD, for example, in relation to public participation, would have to be considered, but application of SEA could be of especial value to implementation of the WFD, for example, in relation to assessing the basis for derogation from the environmental objectives of the WFD.[167]

Monitoring requirements

Both the SEAD and the WFD recognise that the kinds of planning at issue are sequential, in requiring plans to be revised periodically, and revisions must be undertaken against a background of information about the operation of existing plans. However, there are dramatic differences in the level of detail of information that must be gathered from monitoring the effects of implementing an existing plan and how that information needs to be employed in its revision.

164 *SEAD Guidance*, para 5.4.
165 SEAD, Art.11.2.
166 *SEAD Guidance*, para 9.13.
167 Ibid, para 9.16; see also WFD, Art 4, on derogations.

In respect of the SEAD, the requirements as to monitoring are tersely stated as requiring Member States to monitor the significant environmental effects of the implementation of a plan or programme. A purpose of monitoring, among other things, is to identify, at an early stage, unforeseen adverse effects and to be able to undertake appropriate remedial action.[168] For this purpose, it is noted that existing monitoring arrangements may be used with a view to avoiding duplication of monitoring[169] and an environmental report will need to provide a description of the measures envisaged for monitoring.[170] Beyond these generalities, the SEAD gives no further indication of what needs to be monitored, how frequently, to what technical standards, or by whom. Even where monitoring does detect an unforeseen significant adverse environmental effect of implementing the plan or programme, the Directive does not prescribe any particular 'remedial action' that should be taken or the circumstances in which the existing plan or programme will need to be revised in the light of such a finding.

The lack of detail on how monitoring should be undertaken under the SEAD may reflect the lack of experience that exists in the Member States as to the monitoring of environmental effects resulting from the implementation of plans and programmes. Moreover, it has been emphasised that the scope, depth and method of monitoring that are required will be greatly dependent upon the type of plan or programme.[171] The breadth of the range of possible environmental impacts that may be at issue in relation to different kinds of plan and programme has, therefore, the consequence that monitoring possibilities are extremely 'flexible', but difficult to specify in advance.

By contrast, the WFD imposes an explicit obligation upon Member States to establish programmes for monitoring water status in order to establish a 'coherent and comprehensive' overview of that status within each river basin district. Specifically, for surface waters, the monitoring programme must cover the volume and level or rate of flow and the chemical and ecological status. For groundwater, monitoring must cover chemical and quantitative status. For protected areas,[172] the

---

168 It has also been suggested that monitoring may be of assistance in relation to the area of quality control (under SEAD, Art 12, Member States are to ensure that environmental reports are of sufficient quality to meet the requirements of the Directive) if monitoring reveals that a certain effect is systematically overlooked or underestimated in environmental assessments of a certain type of plan or programme. See *SEAD Guidance*, para 8.19.

169 SEAD, Art. 10. Hence *SEAD Guidance* suggests that data collected under the WFD may be used for monitoring purposes if it is relevant to a particular plan or programme and its environmental effects. See *SEAD Guidance*, para 8.16.

170 SEAD, Annex I (i). Art 9.1 SEAD requires relevant authorities and the public to be informed of monitoring measures in relation to individual plans and programmes. It is likely the public would also have a right to this information under the Directive on Public Access to Environmental Information 2003/04/EC.

171 See IMPEL (European Union Network for the Implementation and Enforcement of Environmental Law) Project, Implementing *Art 10 of the SEA Directive* 2001/42/EC (2003).

172 See p 170 above on protected areas.

previous monitoring must be supplemented by specifications under which individual protected areas are established. These programmes of monitoring, which may be subject to technical specifications and standardised methods of analysis,[173] are normally to be operational by the end of 2006 and are subject to more detailed specifications set out in Annex V to the WFD.[174]

Annex V to the WFD goes on to explain that, on the basis of the initial characterisation and impact assessments,[175] Member States are to establish a 'surveillance monitoring programme' and an 'operational monitoring programme' for surface waters within each river basin district, and may also need to establish programmes of 'investigative monitoring'. Surveillance monitoring is intended to provide information to supplement the initial characterisations of waters and further to assess changes in natural conditions and the impacts of human activity. Operational monitoring is intended to establish the status of waters previously identified as being at risk of failing to meet their environmental objectives and to assess changes in status resulting from a relevant PoM. Investigative monitoring may be required where the reasons for a water body failing to meet its environmental objectives are unknown or to ascertain the magnitude and impacts of accidental pollution. In each instance, fairly detailed requirements are imposed in relation to the selection of monitoring points and quality elements and the frequency of monitoring activities.[176] Beyond these matters, Annex V goes into some detail on the monitoring requirements for protected areas and groundwater. The overall impression is that monitoring requirements are set out as comprehensively and thoroughly as could be hoped, to ensure that water quality data will be collected in a consistent and comparable manner across different kinds of water body in different Member States.[177]

The contrast between the detailed and comprehensive requirements for monitoring under the WFD and the lack of specificity as to monitoring requirements under the SEAD may well reflect the respective breadth of the two Directives. The wider sectoral scope of SEAD may well have had the consequence that it would have been impractical to set out explicit and comprehensive monitoring requirements for the wide range of potential impacts involved. Nonetheless, it is likely that the wide discretion that has been given to Member States in relation to monitoring of projects within the SEAD will, sooner or later, necessitate a greater degree of harmonisation in the manner in which monitoring is undertaken within different sectors. Perhaps also, the

---

173 Under the procedure under WFD, Art 21.

174 Ibid, Art 8.

175 Required under WFD, Art 5 and Annex II. Discussed at p 174 above.

176 WFD, Annex V, para 1.3.

177 European Commission, *Common Implementation Strategy for the Water Framework Directive (2000/60/EC), Guidance Document No.7, Monitoring under the Water Framework Directive* (2004).

consequences of monitoring information revealing unforeseen environmental effects will need to be clarified.

Substantive outcomes

The most significant contrasts between the kinds of EA provided for under the SEAD and the WFD are in relation to the degree of substance provided for in regard to the outcomes of the respective assessment processes. On this, the contrast is that, while the SEAD imposes almost entirely procedural requirements relating to the way in which the assessment process must be undertaken, the WFD is far more stipulative as to the permissible outcomes of the assessment process. Put bluntly, the WFD specifies the environmental objectives that must be met in a way that the SEAD does not.

Taking the SEAD first, the preamble recognises that the 'Directive is of a procedural nature'[178] which seeks to harmonise different EA systems operating within Member States so they 'contain a set of common procedural requirements'.[179] The purpose of adopting common minimum EA procedures across the Community is to include a wider set of factors in decision-making to 'contribute to more sustainable and effective solutions'.[180] However, it is far from clear how its procedures will guarantee any particular level of environmental protection. This is because the overriding obligation, that specified kinds of environmental information should only be 'taken into account' in environmental decision-making,[181] does not determine what weight should be given to significant environmental effects in the final decision. An environmental report must provide information on the environmental protection objectives, established at international, Community or Member State level, which are relevant to the plan or programme, and the way those objectives and any environmental considerations have been taken into account during its preparation.[182] But there is no mandatory requirement that the decision reached must be in conformity with these objectives. Hence, the identification of significant adverse environmental effects[183] of implementing a plan or programme does not prevent it being authorised in accordance with the SEAD. Notwithstanding a finding that a plan or programme is relevant to the implementation of other Community environmental legislation,[184] and is likely to prevent or obstruct effective implementation of that other legislation, the SEAD provides no bar to the plan or programme being adopted. If the consequences of implementation are that other Community legislation is

178 SEAD Recital 9. See discussion of substance at p 155 above.
179 SEAD Recital 6.
180 SEAD Recital 5.
181 SEAD, Art 8. See p 178 above.
182 Ibid, Annex.
183 As determined by the 'significance criteria' under SEAD, Annex II, discussed at p 150 above.
184 As identified as a criterion of significance under SEAD, Annex II, para 1.

breached, implicitly, that matter is then left to be dealt with under the other legislation.

The lack of substance in the SEAD contrasts markedly with the emphasis upon measures needed actually to achieve environmental quality objectives in WFD planning. Assessment of human impacts upon the aquatic environment is undertaken purposively. Its purpose is to ascertain how much adverse impacts need to be reduced in order to achieve specified environmental objectives within a stated timescale. A RBMP or a PoMs would therefore be unacceptable if it were not formulated in a manner likely to achieve those environmental objectives. It would not be sufficient to embark upon a process of plan formulation that merely involved 'taking into account' the environmental objectives needing to be achieved.

Moreover, the specification of environmental objectives under the WFD goes further than setting out the generalised requirements that noted above as the 'environmental objectives' of the Directive. In various ways the environmental objectives also relate to environmental quality standards that establish precise chemical and biological quality criteria that need to be realised if the environmental objectives of the Directive are to be met.

An appreciation of the ways in which the WFD assessment and planning is driven by environmental quality standards must start from the premise of 'non-deterioration' of water quality. As an environmental quality objective of the Directive, it has been noted that this means that implementation must be by measures that prevent deterioration of the existing quality of surface and groundwaters.[185] Beyond that, the Directive states that implementation 'is to achieve a level of protection of waters at least equivalent to that provided in certain earlier acts', which are to be repealed once the relevant provisions of the WFD are fully implemented.[186] The broad implication is that where an environmental quality standard has been provided for in a previous water directive, at least equally stringent requirements are imposed by the WFD. More specifically, where pre-existing legislation requires a quality objective or standard to be met, and this cannot be achieved by existing controls upon emissions, stricter conditions must be imposed to ensure the objective or standard is met.[187] In part, this has the consequence that environmental quality standards established pursuant to the Dangerous Substances Directive must be adhered to in implementing the WFD,[188] but the same approach applies to 'other' existing legislation setting relevant objectives or quality standards.[189]

185 WFD, Arts 4.1.(a).i and 4.1.(b).i.
186 Ibid, Recital 51.
187 Ibid, Art 10.3, providing for a 'combined approach' to point and diffuse sources.
188 Directive 76/464/EEC. The five 'daughter' directives to the Dangerous Substances Directive, setting environmental quality standards for specific substances, are listed in WFD, Annex IV.
189 Although the WFD is not explicit as to what 'other' legislation is relevant here, it is possible that water quality standards provided for under the Agricultural Nitrates Directive (91/676/EEC) and the Drinking Water Quality Directive (80/778/EEC, as amended) might be examples that fall within this category.

Beyond non-deterioration below existing water quality standards, the WFD incorporates mechanisms for the adoption of further water quality standards for substances that have not been provided for under previous legislation. Hence, the 'framework' character of the Directive envisages additional measures being adopted against pollution of water by individual pollutants or groups of pollutants presenting a significant risk to or through the aquatic environment.[190] Among other actions for this purpose, the Commission is bound to submit proposals for quality standards applicable to the concentrations of priority substances in surface water, sediments and biota.[191]

Although the environmental quality standards referred to above concentrate upon precisely determined parameters for maximum levels or particular pollutants which may be present in the aquatic environment, the exercise of standard setting is not limited to chemical parameters. As has been noted,[192] the WFD also incorporates requirements for good ecological status of surface waters involving determination of biological standards which must be met by relevant waters. The substantial challenge involved in securing good ecological status is rapidly becoming as precisely quantified as that involved in securing good chemical status.[193]

In relation to both chemical and ecological status, precise quantified criteria are provided, or are soon to be provided, which will determine what is required for RBMP or PoMs to be acceptable. The overriding point to be reiterated is that WFD assessment and planning is being undertaken for the purpose of actually realising explicit and precisely stated environmental objectives and standards, not merely 'taking into account' the need for a high level of protection of the environment as is otherwise required in EA.

Conclusion

The preceding discussion has drawn attention to the many points of similarity between the processes of assessment involved in formulating RBMPs and PoMs under the WFD and the requirements for SEA under the SEAD. On points of detail, many contrasts have been noted and, in respect of specificity, the WFD is markedly more stipulative as to the assessment procedures that need to be followed. Nonetheless, the overall similarities may be seen as greater than the differences. The WFD and SEAD share admirably comparable and compatible approaches

---

190 WFD, Art 16.1, on strategies against pollution of water.
191 Ibid, Art 16.7. 'Priority' substances are identified in accordance with Art 16.2, and listed in Annex X. See WFD, Art 2.30. See Decision No.2455/2001/EC of the European Parliament and of the Council establishing the list of priority substances in the field of water policy and amending Directive 2000/60/EC, establishing WFD, Annex X.
192 See p 174 above on ecological standards under the WFD.
193 Although see W Howarth, 'The Progression Towards Ecological Standards' (2006) *Journal of Environmental Law* 18(1), 3–35, expressing some reservations as to the basis for ecological valuation in setting ecological standards under the WFD.

to SEA. This is evidenced by the strong likelihood that fulfilment of the WFD requirements will leave little more to be done to meet the requirements of the SEAD.

The fundamental contrast between the WFD and the SEAD, however, lies in the balance between procedure and substance. While assessment under the SEAD is almost entirely procedural in character, the WFD incorporates many points of substance which ensure that assessment and planning processes are directed towards ensuring that precisely stated environmental objectives and standards are actually met. The possibility that a faultless environmental scrutiny procedure could still lead to an environmentally unacceptable decision being reached is ruled out in the WFD assessment and planning processes. This is because the WFD procedures go beyond informing decision-makers of the existence of environmental factors which need to be 'taken into account'. They instruct decision-makers as to the weight to be attached to those factors. Certain outcomes of the WFD decision-making process are made unacceptable by the specification of mandatory thresholds, below which the environmental impact of a RBMP or a PoMs should not be allowed to fall.

If, as argued, substantive EA can be implemented in the water sector, there seems to be no reason of principle why it should not be achieved in other sectors, or cross-sectorally through the EIA and SEA processes. Most simply, this might be accomplished, in the short term at least, by the incorporation of existing environmental objectives and standards from Community environmental legislation as a threshold for acceptability of any project, plan or programme. This could be done by a relatively minor tweak of wording, albeit accompanied by a momentous amount of political will. While the existing wording of the SEAD merely requires account to be taken of the relevance of a plan or programme for the implementation of other Community environmental legislation,[194] this needs to be bolstered. Quite simply, the step needs to be taken from taking cognisance of existing environmental objectives and standards to requiring that they should actually be adhered to before a project, plan or programme may be authorised. Authorisation for any project, plan or programme that cannot be shown to be in conformity with all requirements of Community environmental law should be mandatorily declined. In effect, it seems indefensible that the step from procedure into substance has already been taken in WFD assessment planning, allowing the EIAD and SEAD to lag behind.

Environmental standards should be seen as a means to an end, rather than an end in themselves. In the longer term, the effectiveness of SEA must be measured by the extent to which it yields decisions in conformity with the requirements of

---

194 WFD, Annex II, para 1, and see also Annex I (e) which requires an environmental report to provide information on environmental protection objectives, established at international, Community or Member State level, which are relevant to a plan or programme. WFD, Art.8 requires these matters to be 'taken into account' before the adoption of a plan or programme.

sustainable development. However, as has been seen, the difficulty with this objective is that criteria for what is to count as 'sustainable development' are notoriously inaccessible. Possibly, in the distant future, precise quantified criteria might be devised to assess the sustainability of a proposed project, plan or programme. But for the foreseeable present at least, adherence to environmental standards in decision-making is the most feasible option for progress. The introduction of environmental standards into EIA and SEA is the next step in the progression.

Chapter 7

Access to justice and the EIA directive: the implications of the Aarhus Convention

Áine Ryall

Introduction[1]

This chapter examines the implications of the Aarhus Convention for access to justice in Environmental Impact Assessment (EIA) matters with particular emphasis on national judicial review procedures.[2] Practical difficulties in accessing review mechanisms have proven to be a persistent problem for individuals and non-governmental organisations (NGOs) in cases where it is alleged that the requirements of the EIA Directive have not been met. The main concerns here relate to restrictive standing rules, the costs associated with judicial review procedures, and the intensity of the standard of review applied by national courts when called upon to examine decisions taken by public authorities in the planning and environmental law field. The Aarhus Convention attempts to address the access to justice problem head-on and it has already had a marked impact on the development of European Community environmental law.[3]

The particular focus of this chapter is the new Art 10a recently inserted into the text of the EIA Directive pursuant to Directive 2003/35/EC.[4] Art 10a, which

---

1 This chapter draws on research undertaken for a more substantial work on environmental impact assessment law and access to justice in Ireland. See Á Ryall, *Effective Judicial Protection and the Environmental Impact Assessment Directive in Ireland* (Oxford: Hart Publishing, 2007).

2 United Nations Economic Commission for Europe, *Convention on access to information, public participation in decision-making and access to justice in environmental matters* 1998 (the Aarhus Convention). The full text is available at www.unece.org/env/pp/treatytext.htm.

3 J Jendrośka, 'Aarhus Convention and Community Law: the Interplay' [2005] *Journal for European Environmental and Planning Law* 12; J Verschuuren, 'Public Participation regarding the Elaboration and Approval of Projects in the EU after the Aarhus Convention' (2005) 4 *Yearbook of European Environmental Law* 29; Á Ryall, 'Strengthening rights of participation in environmental decision-making' (2001) 8 *Irish Planning and Environmental Law Journal* 103, and 'Implementation of the Aarhus Convention through Community Environmental Law' (2004) 6 *Environmental Law Review* 274.

4 Directive 85/337/EEC on the assessment of the effects of certain public and private projects on the environment, [1985] OJ L/175/40 as amended by Directive 97/11/EC [1997] OJ L/73/5. The directive was again amended in 2003 pursuant to Art 3 of Directive 2003/35/EC (the public participation directive) [2003] OJ L/156/17. Member States were required to implement the

aims to give effect to the access to justice pillar of the Aarhus Convention so far as EIA matters are concerned, sets down minimum standards for access to review procedures.[5] The second part of this chapter, Access to Justice: the EIA Directive, attempts to tease out the practical implications of Art 10a. With a view to illustrating the difficulties involved in giving effect to the obligations created in Art 10a, the Irish experience is then examined.

Ireland is an interesting case study for a number of reasons. First, Irish planning law was substantially revised and consolidated in the Planning and Development Act 2000.[6] Section 50 PDA sets down a special judicial review procedure governing challenges to the validity of certain planning decisions.[7] The scheme established in s.50 introduced a number of significant amendments to the previous legislative framework with the aim of restricting access to judicial review and facilitating the timely determination of any challenges. For present purposes, the new *locus standi* test introduced in s 50(4)(b) PDA is of interest and will be considered further below. Second, the Irish planning system is distinctive in that it has long provided for a third party right of appeal.[8] Both the applicant for development consent, the developer, and third party 'objectors' enjoy a right to appeal a decision taken by a local planning authority on an application for development consent under Part III PDA to *An Bord Pleanála*, the Planning Appeals Board.[9] The Board, which was established in 1976,[10] is an independent, quasi-judicial tribunal that determines appeals *de novo*, that is, there is a full rehearing on the planning merits of the original decision taken at

public participation directive by 25 June 2005. For a detailed analysis of EA as a regulatory mechanism see J Holder, *Environmental Assessment: The Regulation of Decision Making* (Oxford: OUP, 2004).

5 Note that Directive 2003/35/EC also introduced important amendments to Directive 96/61/EC (the Integrated Pollution Prevention and Control (IPPC) directive). In particular, Art 4(4) of Directive 2003/35/EC inserted a new Art 15a (headed 'Access to justice') into the text of the IPPC directive. Art 15a is cast in similar terms to Art 10a of the EIA directive.

6 Hereafter 'the PDA'. The bulk of the PDA came into force in March 2002, so it is still a relatively new statutory scheme. The supporting regulations were also revised and consolidated at this time. See Planning and Development Regulations 2001 ('The Planning Regs') (SI No 600 of 2001). The PDA was subsequently amended by a number of diverse enactments including the Local Government Act 2001; Planning and Development (Amendment) Act 2002 and the Protection of the Environment Act 2003. The text of PDA, Planning Regs 2001–2005 and other relevant documentation, including guidance notes, is available at www.environ.ie. For a detailed account of the Irish planning system see G Simons, *Planning and Development Law* (Dublin: Thomson Round Hall, 2004), and see Y Scannell, *Environmental and Land Use Law* (Dublin: Thomson Round Hall, 2006), ch.2.

7 Section 50 replaced s 82(3A) and (3B) of the Local Government (Planning and Development) Act 1963. Section 82(3A) and (3B) was introduced into the 1963 Act by s 19(3) of the Local Government (Planning and Development) Act 1992.

8 See Simons, *Planning and Development Law*, n. 6 above, ch.9.

9 PDA, s 37. See generally 'How Bord Pleanála works – and who's on it' *Irish Times Property Supplement* 26 January 2006.

10 Prior to the establishment of the Board the Minister for Local Government heard appeals.

local level.[11] The scope of the Board's jurisdiction to determine questions of law is rather unclear.[12] While the Board can correct errors made by a planning authority in the application of the relevant statutory scheme, disputes over whether or not Ireland has correctly implemented the EIA Directive fall to be determined by the High Court.[13] The Board may refer a point of law to the High Court for decision.[14] This power is rarely deployed, however, presumably because of the potential costs and delay involved. The Board is an 'emanation of the State' and is obliged as a matter of Community law 'to take all the general or particular measures necessary' to ensure that the requirements of the Directive are observed.[15] The Board rarely engages with legal arguments in practice and prefers to leave such matters to the courts. The Board is a 'court or tribunal' for the purposes of Art 234 EC, but has never referred a question of Community law to the European Court of Justice (ECJ).

Certain disputes concerning the correct application of national and Community EIA law may be resolved by way of an appeal to the Board without the necessity of recourse to the courts. For example, a planning authority may take the view that a particular project does not require assessment and may decide to grant development consent without EIA. A third party objector may pursue this point on appeal to the Board and may argue that the planning authority's decision on the EIA point was incorrect. Where the Board takes the view that the proposed development falls within the classes of project for which EIA is mandatory it must require the developer to submit an Environmental Impact Statement (EIS) and the Board must carry out an EIA.[16] A similar obligation arises where a planning authority has not carried out an EIA in respect of a sub-threshold project and the Board considers that the proposed development is likely to have significant effects on the environment.[17] An appellant may also argue that the EIS submitted by the developer is inadequate having regard to the requirements set down in the EIA Directive and/or the relevant national implementing measures and it falls to the Board to determine this issue afresh on appeal.[18] These examples demonstrate the value of the Board as an alternative to

---

11 PDA, s 37(1)(b).
12 The judgment of O'Higgins CJ in *State (Abenglen Properties Limited) v Lord Mayor, Aldermen and Burgesses of Dublin* [1984] IR 381, 393, indicates the Board has jurisdiction to address what may be loosely described as straightforward questions of law.
13 *O'Brien v South Tipperary County Council and An Bord Pleanála*, unreported, High Court, 22 October 2002, Ó Caoimh J, 27–28.
14 PDA, s 50(1).
15 Case C-72/95 *Aannemersbedrijf P.K. Kraaijeveld BV and Others v Gedeputeerde Staten van Zuid-Holland* [1996] ECR I-5403, [61]; Case C-201/02 R *(Wells) v Secretary of State for Transport, Local Government and the Regions* [2004] ECR I-723, [64]–[65]; and *Power v An Bord Pleanála*, unreported, High Court, 17 January 2006, Quirke J, 23.
16 Planning Regs 2001, Art 109(1).
17 Ibid, Art 109(2).
18 Ibid, Art 111.

judicial review for correcting clear-cut errors. During 2004, the percentage of planning decisions appealed to the Board was 5.5 per cent, declining from approximately 7 per cent in previous years.[19] Almost 95 per cent of planning cases are therefore concluded at local authority level without an appeal to the Board. Only 2.6 per cent of planning appeals involved EIA during 2004.[20] Of the planning appeals formally determined in 2004, 50 per cent were 'third party only' appeals.[21] In third party appeals against decisions to grant permission the Board confirmed just 1 per cent of the original planning decisions without varying any conditions.[22] Permission was granted with revised conditions in 60 per cent of third party appeals and refused in 39 per cent.[23] These figures indicate that third parties generally enjoy a considerable measure of success before the Board.[24]

The existence of a third party right of appeal means that fewer EIA controversies come before the Irish courts than is the case for example in the United Kingdom. Consequently, the Irish courts are presented with fewer opportunities to rule on EIA matters and to develop and clarify the law on important practical issues; for example, the thorny problems surrounding 'horizontal direct effect' of the EIA Directive in the case of private projects.[25] It is not surprising, therefore, to find that the Irish EIA jurisprudence is underdeveloped when compared with the significant body of case law that has now emerged in England and Wales.[26] Furthermore, the Irish Superior Courts have never referred an environmental question to the ECJ pursuant to Art 234 EC. As a result, the Irish courts, and the relevant competent authorities, have never had the benefit of a ruling from Luxembourg on the compatibility or otherwise of Irish planning law, and national judicial review practice and procedure, with the EIA Directive and the ECJ's extensive case law on effective judicial protection.

---

19 *An Bord Pleanála, Annual Report 2004*, 5. The text is available at www.pleanala.ie.

20 *An Bord Pleanála*, 'Planning Appeals Involving Environmental Impact Statements' (1996–2004). Data is available at www.pleanala.ie.

21 Ibid, 35. A further 3.7 per cent of appeals were combined first and third party appeals.

22 Ibid.

23 Ibid.

24 Data published by the Board does not indicate the proportion of third party appeals that involved EIA. Limited data on EIA in the specific context of local authority projects is noted in *An Bord Pleanála, Annual Report 2004*, 20–21.

25 See *Wells*, n. 15 above. For commentary see R Harwood, 'EIA, Development Consent and Duties on the Member State' (2004) 16 *Journal of Environmental Law* 261.

26 For an overview of the Irish case law, see Scannell n. 6 above, ch.5; and see Ryall, n. 1 above, ch.5. Good overviews of the current state of the case law in England and Wales include V Moore, *A Practical Approach to Planning Law* (9th edn) (Oxford: OUP, 2005), ch.13; S Bell and D McGillivray, *Environmental Law* (6th edn) (Oxford: OUP, 2006), ch.14, especially 516–549; P Stookes, *A Practical Approach to Environmental Law* (Oxford: OUP, 2005), ch.24; and see M Stallworthy, 'Once More Unto the Breach: English Law Rationales and Environmental Assessment' [2004] *Journal of Planning Law* 1472.

A third reason why Ireland provides an interesting case study on the theme of access to justice in the context of the EIA Directive is that the EC Commission continues to receive the highest number of environmental complaints *per capita* from Ireland. This situation is not particularly surprising given the strong tradition of public participation in planning matters since the foundation of the modern Irish planning system in 1963. It also serves to demonstrate the continuing frustration amongst Irish environmental NGOs over poor application of European environmental rules at local level. Dissatisfaction with responses received from the competent authorities, together with the costs, delay and unpredictability associated with judicial review proceedings are the main spurs for complaints. The volume of Irish complaints must also be set in the context of heavy demands placed on the Irish planning system during a prolonged period of intense economic development and the official drive to deliver badly needed strategic infrastructure. The current high volume of planning applications and subsequent appeals has put a serious strain on the limited resources of the Irish competent authorities, that is local planning authorities and the Board on appeal. The fact that the Board finds it difficult to recruit and retain professional planners and experienced inspectors is a cause of particular concern.[27] Reservations about the quality of decision-making within competent authorities confirm the importance of an effective system of judicial review to ensure that these authorities apply the requirements set down in the EIA Directive correctly and consistently.

Access to Justice: the EIA Directive

Recent (and long overdue) advances in access to justice are a direct result of the rights and obligations created in the Aarhus Convention. The Convention is a groundbreaking instrument designed to strengthen information and participation rights in environmental matters.[28] It is built around the three 'pillars' of public participation. Three inter-connected procedural rights: the right to information; the right to participate in decision-making; and the right of access to justice are identified as playing a crucial role in supporting the right of every person to live in an environment adequate to health and well-being. One of the most striking features of the Convention is the access to justice pillar.[29] Art 9 sets down a set

---

27 *An Bord Pleanála, Annual Report 2004*, 4–5; and see 'Bord Pleanála to get more planning staff' *Irish Times* 25 November 2005.

28 For a good overview see J Jendroska and S Stec, 'The Aarhus Convention: Towards a New Era in Environmental Democracy' (2001) *Environmental Liability* 140; and see J Wates, 'The Aarhus Convention: A Driving Force for Environmental Democracy' (2005) *Journal for European Environmental and Planning Law* 2.

29 On the access to justice pillar, see S Stec and S Casey-Lefkowitz, *The Aarhus Convention: An Implementation Guide* (New York and Geneva: UNECE, 2000), 123–136; and see S Stec (ed.), *Handbook on Access to Justice under the Aarhus Convention* (2003). Both texts are available at http://www.unece.org/env/pp/.

of core requirements governing access to review procedures with the overall aim of ensuring that the information and participation rights established in the Convention are effective and enforceable in practice. This sharp focus on access to justice is most welcome in the EIA context where problems with implementation and enforcement at national level are well documented.[30] The Aarhus Convention entered into force on 30 October 2001. At the time of writing (January 2006), there were 36 Parties to the Convention including the Community itself and twenty of the Member States. Though Ireland signed the Convention in June 1998, it is not, as yet, a Party to the Convention. Work towards ratification is ongoing within the Irish Department of the Environment, Heritage and Local Government but there is no firm indication as to when Ireland intends to ratify.

The Convention has already had a marked influence on the development of Community EIA law. The Public Participation Directive[31] introduced a number of important amendments to the EIA Directive that were due to be implemented in the Member States by 25 June 2005. For present purposes, the most significant amendment is the new Art 10a inserted into the text of the EIA Directive. Art 10a purports to give effect to the access to justice pillar of the Convention in so far as EIA matters are concerned. It provides as follows:[32]

[1] Member States shall ensure that, in accordance with the relevant national legal system, members of the public concerned:[33]

(a) having a sufficient interest, or alternatively,
(b) maintaining the impairment of a right, where administrative procedural law of a Member State requires this as a precondition,

have access to a review procedure before a court of law or another independent and impartial body established by law to challenge the substantive or procedural legality of decisions, acts or omissions subject to the public participation provisions of this Directive.

[2] Member States shall determine at what stage the decisions, acts or omissions may be challenged.

---

30 *Report from the Commission to the European Parliament and the Council on the Application and Effectiveness of the EIA Directive (Directive 85/337/EEC as amended by Directive 97/11/EC): How successful are the Member States in implementing the EIA Directive?* 23 June 2003. The Report highlighted the inadequacy of national judicial review procedures in the case of alleged breach of the EIA directive. See para 4.8.2. Text available at www.europa.eu.int/comm/environment/eia/report_en.pdf.

31 Directive 2003/35/EC, n. 4 above.

32 Paragraph numbers have been inserted into the text of Art 10a for ease of reference.

33 The concept of 'the public concerned' is defined in Art 1(2) of the EIA directive as meaning: 'the public affected or likely to be affected by, or having an interest in, the environmental decision-making procedures referred to in Art 2(2) [of the EIA directive]; for the purposes of this definition, non-governmental organisations promoting environmental protection and meeting any requirements under national law shall be deemed to have an interest'.

[3] What constitutes a sufficient interest and impairment of a right shall be determined by the Member States, consistently with the objective of giving the public concerned wide access to justice. To this end, the interest of any [NGO], meeting the requirements referred to in Art 1(2) shall be deemed sufficient for the purpose of subparagraph (a) of this Article. Such organisations shall also be deemed to have rights capable of being impaired for the purpose of subparagraph (b) of this Article.

[4] The provisions of this Article shall not exclude the possibility of a preliminary review procedure before an administrative authority and shall not affect the requirement of exhaustion of administrative review procedures prior to recourse to judicial review procedures, where such a requirement exists under national law.

[5] Any such procedure shall be fair, equitable, timely and not prohibitively expensive.

[6] In order to further the effectiveness of the provisions of this article, Member States shall ensure that practical information is made available to the public on access to administrative and judicial review procedures.

The core obligation set down in Art 10a requires Member States to provide access to a review procedure where qualified members of 'the public concerned' can challenge 'the substantive or procedural legality' of decisions subject to the participation requirements established in the EIA Directive. This obligation is qualified by an express reference to 'the relevant national legal system' in the opening paragraph of Art 10a, indicating that Member State discretion continues to play an important role in shaping the overall character of the review procedure. Member States remain free to determine the stage at which decisions may be challenged and any national requirement to exhaust available administrative remedies before proceeding to judicial review is not affected.[34] Member States are also obliged to provide the public with practical information on access to administrative and judicial review procedures.[35]

A number of aspects of Art 10a merit special attention. First, as regards the structure of the review procedure, Art 10a[1] provides for review before a court of law or, in the alternative, review before 'another independent and impartial body established by law'. The obligation created here must be read in light of the overarching principle of effective judicial protection developed by the ECJ.[36] This principle aims to give effect to the Rule of Law through access to judicial control. It is grounded in the constitutional traditions of the Member States and

---

34 See Art 10a[2] and [4].
35 Art 10a[6].
36 See generally M Dougan, *National Remedies Before the Court of Justice: Issues of Harmonisation and Differentiation* (Oxford: Hart Publishing, 2004), especially ch.1; and see S Prechal, *Directives in EC Law* (2nd edn) (Oxford: OUP, 2005), 134–145.

in Art 6 and Art 13 of the European Convention on Human Rights (ECHR).[37] Essentially, the principle of effective judicial protection requires that 'an individual who considers himself wronged by a measure which deprives him of a right or advantage under Community law must have access to a remedy against that measure and be able to obtain complete judicial protection'.[38] It follows that where a Member State purports to comply with the requirements of Art 10a[1] by putting in place a system of review before a body that is not a court, the principle of effective judicial protection demands that access to judicial control must also be available. A right of appeal to an administrative tribunal is not sufficient to satisfy this fundamental principle of Community law.[39] The principle of effective judicial protection therefore provides an important supplement to the minimum requirements set down in Art 10a[1].

Second, Art 10a[1] does not establish a rigid standing requirement. Rather it provides considerable flexibility for Member States. Two alternative tests for standing are presented and Member States are free to choose the test that best fits their national legal system. Member States may require 'the public concerned' to demonstrate 'a sufficient interest' in the contested decision. In the alternative, 'the public concerned' may be required to demonstrate 'the impairment of a right' where this is a condition of national administrative law. The two alternative tests presented here are designed to accommodate the diverse approaches to standing found throughout the Member States. According to Art 10a[3], Member States must determine standing requirements in a manner that is consistent with the objective of giving the public concerned 'wide' access to justice. This proviso creates a potentially interesting constraint on Member State discretion when elaborating national standing rules. While it is difficult to identify what exactly is envisaged by the concept of 'wide' access to justice in this context, the proviso essentially stipulates a liberal attitude to standing. It is difficult to square this mandate with the far more deferential approach to national standing requirements articulated in Art 10a[1]. This inbuilt contradiction will lead to difficulties of interpretation in cases where a challenge is mounted to a restrictive national standing rule on the basis of alleged non-compliance with Art 10a[1] and [3].

Special rules apply in the specific case of environmental NGOs. The definition of 'the public concerned' found in Art 1(2) of the EIA Directive provides that NGOs that promote environmental protection and meet any requirements specified under national law are deemed to have an interest in the decision-making procedure.

---

37 See Case 222/84 *Johnston v Chief Constable of the RUC* [1986] ECR 1651 [18]; Case C-50/00 P *Unión de Pequeños Agricultores v Council* [2002] ECR I-6677 [38]–[39]; Joined Cases T-236/04 and T-241/04 *European Environmental Bureau (EEB) and Stichting Natuur en Milieu v Commission* [2005], [65].

38 Ibid, *Unión de Pequeños Agricultores* [39].

39 Case C-424/99 *Commission v Austria* [2001] ECR I-9285 [45].

Art 10a[3] then goes on to provide that NGOs that meet any requirements set under national law automatically enjoy standing to invoke the review procedure. This approach holds the potential to expand access to review procedures for qualified NGOs in a rather dramatic way. At the same time, the fact that Member States remain free to prescribe the criteria that must be met before NGOs will qualify for the benefit of the relaxed standing requirement creates an important limitation that could be exploited by Member States.

Third, the review procedure prescribed in Art 10a[1] must meet the minimum standards articulated in Art 10a[5]. The procedure must be 'fair, equitable, timely and not prohibitively expensive'. The express reference to the cost factor here is noteworthy in light of ongoing concerns about the deterrent effect of costs at national level.[40] It is difficult to elaborate on the precise meaning of the 'not prohibitively expensive' requirement. The use of phrase 'prohibitively' indicates that a relatively high threshold of expense is envisaged here. It is useful to recall the principle of effectiveness developed by the ECJ which dictates that national procedural rules must not make it 'impossible in practice' or 'excessively difficult' to enforce Community law rights.[41] Experience has shown that these twin requirements set a malleable standard against which national rules are to be measured and leave national courts with plenty of room for manoeuvre. So, for example, a national court may well take the view that a contested procedural rule is indeed compatible with the principle of effectiveness without making a reference pursuant to Art 234 EC. A questionable national rule may therefore escape scrutiny by the ECJ. In Member States where the substantive or procedural legality of a decision may only be challenged before a court, the financial resources of the parties seeking to mount judicial review proceedings and the availability of civil legal aid and advice will be critical. In the case of individuals and NGOs with limited funds, national procedural rules and judicial practice (governing such matters as security for costs, undertakings as to damages and liability for costs) may operate to obstruct effective access to justice. Art 3(8) of the Aarhus Convention acknowledges that national courts may award 'reasonable' costs. There is no explanation of what is meant by 'reasonable' costs, however, and Art 10a is silent on the question of costs as such, apart from the 'not prohibitively expensive' formula. Art 9(5) of the Convention requires Parties 'to consider' establishing 'appropriate assistance mechanisms to remove or reduce financial or other barriers to access to justice'. It is disappointing to note that this positive initiative, it is not cast in terms of an obligation, is not reflected in any shape or form in Art 10a.

While Art 10a is a welcome addition to the EIA Directive, which was previously silent on remedies, the brief overview set out above demonstrates the

---

40 In the Irish context, see Friends of the Irish Environment, *The Transposition into Irish Law of Directive 2003/35/EC* (7 July 2005). Text available at www.friendsoftheirishenvironment.net.

41 See, e.g. *Wells*, n. 15 above, [67].

continuing role for Member State discretion in the design and organisation of review procedures at national level. As is the case with many environmental directives, the scope of Member State discretion on various points, such as standing, costs and the standard of review, is not exactly clear from the text of Art 10a. Furthermore, the principle of effective judicial protection provides an important supplement to the basic requirements articulated in Art 10a. It follows that the text of Art 10a does not provide a self-contained source of the rules governing remedies in EIA cases. It is necessary to look beyond the text of Art 10a for a complete picture of the relevant Community law principles. The extensive body of case law from the ECJ on the principle of effective judicial protection assists, to some degree, in clarifying aspects of the obligations created in Art 10a. For example, it is clear from the Court's remedies case law that Member States may determine national standing requirements subject always to the principle of effectiveness, that is, national standing rules must not render it 'virtually impossible' or 'excessively difficult' to exercise rights conferred by Community law.[42] Art 10a[1] and [3] elaborates on this general principle in the specific context of review proceedings involving the EIA Directive. Notwithstanding the ubiquitous references to the situation prevailing within the relevant national legal system, Art 10a[1] and [3] supports the idea of 'wide' access to justice and provides a firmer basis on which to question restrictive national standing rules – particularly in the case of environmental NGOs. As regards liability for costs, the ECJ has ruled that where a directive is silent on costs, then this matter falls to be determined by the Member States subject to the principle of effectiveness.[43] As noted earlier, Art 10a[5] requires that review procedures must not be 'prohibitively expensive'. The extent to which this new obligation goes beyond the ECJ's general mandate that national rules must not make it 'virtually impossible' or 'excessively difficult' to enforce Community law rights remains to be seen.

The ECJ's *Upjohn* ruling is instructive on the standard of review to be applied by national courts where a challenge is mounted to the decision taken by a competent authority.[44] On this occasion, relevant national legislation, that is, the Medicines Act 1968, provided that any person concerned by a decision of the national authority could make an application to the High Court in England and Wales contesting its validity. The national court's inquiry was confined to examining whether the decision taken by the authority could reasonably have been reached on the basis of the material before it. The ECJ ruled that limited judicial review, as opposed to full-blown review of the merits of the decision, is acceptable where competent authorities are required to act in circumstances

---

42 Joined Cases C-87/90, C-88/90 and C-89/90 *Verholen* [1991] ECR I-3757; and see Case C-13/01 *Safalero* [2003] ECR I-8679 [50].

43 Case C-63/01 *Evans* [2003] ECR I-14447 [74]–[75].

44 Case C-120/97 *Upjohn Ltd. v The Licensing Authority* [1999] ECR I-223.

involving 'complex assessments'.[45] Though the *Upjohn* judgment shows considerable deference to national procedural autonomy, the Court concluded by stressing the fundamental importance of the principle of effectiveness in the following terms: '... any national procedure for judicial review of decisions of national authorities revoking marketing authorisations must enable the court or tribunal seised of an application for annulment of such a decision effectively to apply the relevant principles and rules of Community law when reviewing its legality'.[46]

While *Upjohn* did not involve the EIA Directive, it seems clear that planning and environmental decision-making falls squarely within the category of 'complex' decisions contemplated by the ECJ in that case. If this view is correct, then Member States are not required to put in place a system of judicial review that empowers the national courts to reconsider the merits of planning and environmental decisions taken by the relevant, and usually expert) competent authorities. Beyond this general principle, the standard of review to be applied by national courts is not at all clear from the *Upjohn* judgment.[47] The ECJ requires at the very minimum that the national system of judicial review must provide 'effective' protection for Community law rights. It is difficult to identify the content and meaning of this vague minimum requirement of 'effective' protection. How closely is a national court required to scrutinise the contested decision in order to ensure the effectiveness of Community law? As noted earlier, Art 10a of the EIA Directive contemplates a system of review where the 'substantive or procedural legality' of the contested decision is open to challenge. While this formula is more specific than the general principle articulated in *Upjohn*, the actual content of this important obligation remains uncertain. The reference to 'legality' indicates that Art 10a does not require merits review as such. This begs the question: what, if anything, does Art 10a add to the principle established by the ECJ in *Upjohn*? This question is considered further below in the Irish case study.

The ECJ's remedies case law attempts to draw a careful balance between national procedural autonomy on the one hand, and the effectiveness of Community law on the other. The text of Art 10a in turn, aims to achieve a similar balance. The sharp variation in the administrative law systems operating across the Member States demands a reasonably flexible approach to local remedies. The challenge lies in providing an appropriate degree of flexibility for Member States while ensuring that discretion is not deployed to undermine the core objective of delivering effective judicial protection for Community law

---

45 *Upjohn* was recently affirmed in Joined Cases C-211/03, C-299/03 and C-316/03 to C-318/03 *Warenvertrieb* [2005] ECR I-5141 [75]–[79]; see also the Opinion of Poiares Maduro AG in Case C-136/03 *Dörr* [2005] ECR I-4759 [48]–[50].

46 *Upjohn* [36]; and see *Warenvertrieb* [77].

47 See *R (Noble) v Thanet DC* [2005] EWCA Civ 782, [2006] 1 P. & C.R. 13 [58]–[60] per Auld LJ.

environmental rights. The ECJ has adopted a consistently prescriptive approach towards the role of national courts in overseeing the effective implementation and application of the EIA Directive at local level. The Court can therefore be expected to draw on the text of the Aarhus Convention, and its strong recitals, to support an equally vigorous approach to Art 10a.

The following section examines the likely impact of the obligations set down in Art 10a for the Irish system.

Case study: EIA and remedies in Ireland

Overview

Depending on the factual and legal context, an appeal to *An Bord Pleanála* may provide an alternative non-judicial remedy in cases where it is alleged that EIA requirements were not applied correctly at local authority level. The availability of this potential avenue of redress raises an interesting question: does a right to appeal to the Board, where this option is available, satisfy the Art 10a[1] obligation to provide for a review procedure? Recall that Art 10a[1] gives the Member States a choice between providing for review before a court or offering review before an independent body established by law. The Board is an independent body established by statute.[48] Appeals to the Board are certainly faster and cheaper than judicial review. The sticking point here however is the requirement that 'the substantive or procedural legality' of the contested decision must be open to challenge through the domestic review procedure. The Board has limited jurisdiction to determine questions of law. It follows that, notwithstanding the existence of a third party right of appeal, there are cases where judicial review is the most appropriate remedy.[49] For example, it is clear from the decision in *O'Brien* that disputes over whether or not Ireland has correctly implemented the EIA Directive fall to be determined by the High Court.[50] Consequently, a right to appeal to the Board is not in itself sufficient to meet the Art 10a[1] obligation. In the Irish context, judicial review before the High Court is the main remedy by which to challenge the substantive or procedural legality of contested planning decisions.[51] If Ireland is to fulfil the obligation created in Art 10a, then judicial review in cases involving challenges to decisions subject to EIA must meet the minimum standards set down in that Art. Judicial review practice and procedure must also satisfy the principle of effective judicial protection.

---

48 PDA, Part VI.
49 Simons, n. 6 above at paras 11.92–11.102.
50 See *O'Brien*, n. 13.
51 Note that in the context of challenges to IPPC licences or waste licences granted by the Environmental Protection Agency (EPA), there is no equivalent of *An Bord Pleanála*, i.e. there is no appeal system for either first or third parties Such decisions can only be challenged before the High Court.

Turning then to judicial review in the Irish context. Judicial review is a discretionary remedy involving a two-stage process. First, the potential challenger must apply to the High Court for leave or permission to bring judicial review proceedings. If leave is granted, the case may then proceed to a substantive hearing. Special rules apply to judicial review in the planning context. Section 50 PDA prescribes 'a mandatory statutory scheme'[52] that must be followed where an applicant seeks to challenge prescribed planning decisions, including the decision of a planning authority on an application for permission under Part III PDA or a decision of the Board on appeal.[53] Any such challenge must be made by way of judicial review pursuant to Order 84 of the Rules of the Superior Courts.[54] The application for leave must be made within the prescribed time period[55] and must be made by way of motion on notice to specified parties, thereby adding significantly to the overall costs involved.[56] The three statutory conditions that an applicant is required to satisfy before leave to apply for judicial review may be granted are of interest for present purposes.

First, the applicant must demonstrate that there are 'substantial grounds' for contending that the contested decision is invalid or ought to be quashed.[57] It is now well established that if a ground is to be 'substantial' it must be 'reasonable', 'arguable' or 'weighty' and must not be 'trivial or tenuous'.[58] The equivalent standard in ordinary judicial review proceedings is less demanding and requires the applicant to establish 'an arguable case'.[59] Second, the High Court must be satisfied that the applicant has 'a substantial interest' in the matter which is the subject of the application for judicial review. Prior to s.50 PDA, the *locus standi* requirement was one of 'sufficient interest'.[60] Third, an applicant must establish that he

---

52 *Brick v Burke and An Bord Pleanála* [2001] 2 ILRM 427, 434 per Denham J. The special judicial review procedure set out in s 50 PDA is examined in detail by Simons, n. 6 above, ch.11. Scannell, n. 6 above paras 2.429–2.444, provides a very useful overview of the core elements of the procedure.

53 The prescribed decisions are listed in s 50(2) PDA as amended by s 12 Planning and Development (Amendment) Act 2002.

54 Hereafter 'RSC'. See S I. No. 15 of 1986.

55 PDA, s 50(4)(a)(i) prescribes that an application for leave to bring judicial review proceedings involving a decision of a planning authority on an application for permission, or of the Board on any appeal, must be made within the period of eight weeks commencing on the date of the decision. An application may be made to the High Court for an extension. However, pursuant to s 50(4)(a)(ii) the court 'shall not' extend time 'unless it considers that there is good and sufficient reason for doing so'. Extensions of time are rarely granted in practice. See *Kelly v Leitrim County Council* [2005] IEHC 11.

56 PDA, s 50(4)(a).

57 Ibid, s 50(4)(b).

58 *McNamara v An Bord Pleanála* [1995] 2 ILRM 125, 130 per Carroll J. Carroll J's interpretation of 'substantial grounds' was cited with approval by the Supreme Court in *Re Art 26 and ss 5 and 10 of the Illegal Immigrants (Trafficking) Bill 1999* [2000] 2 IR 360.

59 *G. v DPP* [1994] 1 IR 374 at 378 per Finlay CJ.

60 RSC, Order 84, rule 20(4).

participated in the statutory planning process or must demonstrate that there were 'good and sufficient reasons' for non-participation.[61] The rationale behind this third requirement is to encourage members of the public to get involved in the planning process at the earliest possible opportunity in the hope of avoiding subsequent judicial challenges.[62]

Section 50(4)(f) provides a very limited possibility of appeal to the Supreme Court from refusal of an application for leave and from the determination in the substantive hearing.[63] Essentially, the High Court must certify that its decision involves a point of law of exceptional public importance and that it is desirable in the public interest that an appeal is taken to the Supreme Court.[64] It is extremely difficult to meet this high threshold in practice. Section 50(5) PDA requires the courts to determine challenges to certain categories of planning decisions 'as expeditiously as possible consistent with the administration of justice.'[65] A recent survey by *An Bord Pleanála* indicated that the average time taken to determine cases that were judicially reviewed was 92 weeks.[66] It is difficult to see how this state of affairs could be compatible with the express requirement in Art 10a[5] that the review procedure must be 'timely'.

Following the template for national review procedures set down in Art 10a, three aspects of Irish judicial review law and practice are selected for attention in this short case study: *locus standi*; liability for costs; and the standard of review applied by the courts in EIA cases.

Locus standi

Prior to s.50 PDA, an applicant was required to demonstrate 'a sufficient interest' in the subject matter of the application for judicial review.[67] A close analysis of the pre-PDA case law confirms that the Irish courts generally adopted a liberal approach to standing in planning cases.[68] *Lancefort* is the leading modern

---

61 PDA, s 50(4)(c)(i) and (ii). No statutory guidance is provided as to what would amount to 'good and sufficient reasons' in this context.

62 The origin of this statutory requirement can be traced back to the 1998 *Lancefort* judgment where the Supreme Court stressed that the EIA argument put forward in that case should have been raised at the appeal stage before *An Bord Pleanála*. See *Lancefort Ltd. v An Bord Pleanála* [1999] 2 IR 270, 315 per Keane J. See generally Simons, n. 6 above, paras 11.88–11.91.

63 See *Irish Asphalt v An Bord Pleanála* [1996] 2 IR 179; and see *Irish Hardware v South Dublin County Council* [2001] 2 ILRM 291.

64 PDA, s 50(4)(f)(i) and (ii). See generally Simons, n. 6 above, paras 11.186–11.207.

65 Ibid, s 50(5)(a)–(c). Section 50(5)(c) envisages that rules of court may make provision for the expeditious hearing of the categories of cases covered by section 50(5). No such rules had been made at the time of writing.

66 An Bord Pleanála, *Annual Report 2004*, 6.

67 RSC, Order 84, rule 20(4).

68 See, e.g. *Electricity Supply Board v Gormley* [1985] IR 129, 156–157 per Finlay CJ; *Fallon v An Bord Pleanála* [1992] 2 IR 380; *Chambers v An Bord Pleanála* [1992] 1 IR 134; and see *Village Residents Association v An Bord Pleanála* [2000] 1 IR 65, 71–72 per Geoghegan J.

decision. On this occasion, a majority of the Supreme Court highlighted the unambiguous legislative strategy to eliminate unnecessary delays in the planning process.[69] *Lancefort* established that the merits of the case presented by the applicant are relevant in determining standing. Furthermore, an applicant may be denied standing to pursue a particular argument where he failed to raise that argument in the course of an appeal before the Board.[70] Keane J, as he then was, cited *Kraaijeveld* and noted *obiter* that there may be circumstances in which national standing rules may have 'to yield to the paramount obligation on national courts to uphold the law of the European Union'.[71] Though the decision in *Lancefort* pre-dated s.50 PDA, the majority opinion delivered by Keane J continues to influence the courts' approach to standing under the new statutory scheme.

The main question for present purposes is the meaning of a 'substantial interest' in the context of s.50(4)(b) PDA.[72] A measure of guidance is provided in s 50(4)(d) which expressly states that a 'substantial interest' is not confined to 'an interest in land or other financial interest'. This proviso indicates that 'substantial interest' is a broad and flexible concept. In *O'Shea*, however, Ó Caoimh J ruled that the applicant, a local resident, must provide specific details of the manner (if any) in which he will be affected by the proposed development in order to demonstrate a 'substantial interest'.[73] This approach stands in marked contrast to pre-PDA decisions such as *Chambers*[74] and *Gormley*,[75] where the courts had no difficulty in accepting that local residents had standing, without undertaking any real inquiry as to the impact of the proposed development on their particular situation.[76] More significantly, Ó Caoimh J expressed the view that 'an interest in seeing that the law is observed' does not amount to a 'substantial interest' within the meaning of s 50(4)(b).

Subsequently, in *Harrington*, Macken J stressed the clear legislative intention to further tighten the criteria governing challenges to planning decisions pursuant to s.50 PDA.[77] This state of affairs prompted Macken J to adopt 'an equally rigorous approach' to the substantial interest requirement, including the proviso in s.50(4)(d). Macken J was careful to explain however that the standing

---

69 *Lancefort Ltd*, n. 62 above, at 309–310 per Keane J.
70 Ibid, 315.
71 Ibid, 312–313. See also *Martin v An Bord Pleanála (No. 2)*, unreported, High Court, Smyth J, 30 November 2004, cited in Scannell, n. 6 above, para 5.03. Note that in both *Lancefort* (n. 62 above) and *Martin No. 2* the pre-PDA 'sufficient interest' test applied.
72 For an early analysis of the concept see Simons, n. 6 above, paras 11.69–11.87.
73 *O'Shea v Kerry County Council* [2003] 4 IR 143, 160–161.
74 *Chambers v An Bord Pleanála* [1992] 1 IR 134.
75 *ESB v Gormley* [1985] IR 129.
76 See *R (Edwards) v Environment Agency* [2004] EWHC 736 (Admin) [15]–[16].
77 *Harrington v An Bord Pleanála* [2005] IEHC 344.

requirement must not be deployed 'in such a restrictive manner that no serious legal issue legitimately raised by an applicant could be ventilated or which would have as its effect the inability of the courts to check a clear and serious abuse of process by the relevant authorities'.[78] *Harrington* confirmed that where an applicant could have pursued a point on appeal before the Board yet failed, without adequate explanation, to do so, then he does not have standing to invoke that point in subsequent judicial review proceedings.[79] Notwithstanding the absence of a 'substantial interest', where the applicant can demonstrate 'substantial grounds' for contending that the contested decision is invalid, then the court is not precluded from scrutinising 'a serious failure properly to apply the law'. The courts' strict approach to the 'substantial interest' requirement is grounded on the fact that the planning system provides for a full right of appeal to the Board. Nevertheless, the courts remain alert to the need to ensure that unlawful decision-making by public authorities does not escape judicial scrutiny due to the absence of a suitably qualified challenger. This latter point is of particular relevance in cases involving constitutional rights or where it is alleged that the State or its emanations has acted in breach of Community law.[80]

In principle, a company may have *locus standi* to challenge a planning decision notwithstanding the fact that it cannot demonstrate a property interest or other economic interest that may be affected by the contested decision.[81] The question arises as to the likely impact of the 'substantial interest' requirement on the standing of limited companies and environmental NGOs. Ó Caoimh J's narrow approach to standing in *O'Shea* suggests that it will be difficult for an environmental NGO to establish that it will be 'directly affected' by a proposed development. Though *Harrington* is further authority for a strict approach to the 'substantial interest' requirement, Macken J's ruling leaves open the possibility of access to judicial review by satisfying the 'substantial grounds' requirement, even where the applicant has failed to satisfy the 'substantial interest' test. The Supreme Court has not as yet, had an opportunity to consider and clarify the 'substantial interest' requirement. It remains to be seen whether the courts will accept that a public interest in planning or environmental matters qualifies as a 'substantial interest'. This point is especially relevant to the standing of environmental NGOs.[82]

---

78 See *Lancefort*, n. 62 above, 312–314 per Keane J.

79 See *Ryanair Ltd. v An Bord Pleanála* [2004] 2 IR 334; *Casey v An Bord Pleanála* [2004] 2 ILRM 296.

80 *Crotty v An Taoiseach* [1987] I.R. 713; *Lancefort*, n. 62 above, 308–314; and see *Martin (No. 2)*, n. 71 above.

81 *Lancefort*, n. 62 above, 317–318. See Simons, n. 6 above, paras 11.81–11.87.

82 *Construction Industry Federation v Dublin City Council* [2005] IESC 16, is interesting as it suggests a particularly narrow approach to the standing of a representative body by the Supreme Court. Note this was not a planning law case and the 'sufficient interest' test applied.

Liability for costs[83]

Costs lie in the discretion of the court and the general rule is that costs usually follow the event.[84] There is no doubt that the risk of liability for costs has had, and continues to have, a serious chilling effect on anyone of modest means who is considering a challenge to a decision taken by a public authority.[85] The Irish courts have demonstrated that they are not averse to awarding substantial costs against an unsuccessful applicant for judicial review in the planning and environmental law field. Rulings on costs in a series of high-profile, but ultimately unsuccessful, challenges based *inter alia* on alleged non-compliance with the EIA Directive provide graphic examples of the financial risks inherent in mounting a challenge to decisions of *An Bord Pleanála* and the Environmental Protection Agency (EPA).[86] Rules governing security for costs[87] and undertakings as to damages[88] create additional financial restraints on access to judicial review. The situation is further compounded by an underdeveloped system of civil legal aid and advice where the primary focus is on family law matters.[89] The Minister for Justice, Equality and Law Reform is currently examining proposals for reform inspired by public concern over high legal costs

---

83 See generally K Costello, 'Costs Principles and Environmental Judicial Review' (2000) XXXV *Irish Jurist* 121.

84 RSC, Order 99. But see *McEvoy v Meath County Council* [2003] 1 IR 208; and see *Dunne v Minister for the Environment, Heritage and Local Government* [2005] IEHC 79, where the High Court awarded costs in favour of the unsuccessful challengers in both cases on the ground that the cases involved public law issues of general importance.

85 See, e.g. Friends of the Irish Environment, *Transposition into Irish Law of Directive 2003/35/EC* (7 July 2005). Text available at: www.friendsoftheirishenvironment.org. See also *R (Burkett) v London Borough of Hammersmith and Fulham* [2004] EWCA Civ 1342, [2005] JPL 525, per Brooke LJ, in an important Addendum to his judgment.

86 By way of example, substantial costs were awarded against the unsuccessful applicants for judicial review in the following EIA cases: *McNamara v An Bord Pleanála* [1998] 3 IR 453; *McBride v Galway* [1998] 1 IR 485; *Lancefort*, n. 62 above; *O'Connell v Environmental Protection Agency* [2003] 1 IR 530; and see *Martin v An Bord Pleanála* [2002] 2 IR 655 (this case is under appeal to the Supreme Court). Costs in judicial review proceedings are very high in practice. To take a recent example, in *O'Connell*, the taxed costs awarded against the unsuccessful applicant against the first notice party alone amounted to €250,000. See also 'Anti-incinerator campaigner faces €200,000 legal bill' *Irish Times* 8 December 2004 (ruling on costs following the unsuccessful challenge before the High Court in *Martin*).

87 RSC, Order 29 and Companies Act 1963, s 390. See *Village Residents Association v An Bord Pleanála* [2000] 4 IR 321; and see *Usk District Residents Association Ltd v Environmental Protection Agency and Greenstar Recycling Holdings Ltd.* [2006] IESC 1.

88 RSC, Order 84, rule 20(6). See e.g. *Broadnet Ireland v ODTR* [2000] 3 IR 281; *O'Connell v EPA*, [2001] 4 IR 494; *Martin*, n. 86 above; *O'Brien*, n. 13 above; and *Dunne and Lucas v Dún Laoghaire-Rathdown County Council* [2003] 1 IR 567.

89 Free Legal Advice Centres (FLAC), *Access to Justice: a Right or a Privilege? – A Blueprint for Civil Legal Aid in Ireland* (July 2005). Text available at www.flac.ie. See also M Cousins, *Public Interest Law and Litigation in Ireland* (Dublin: FLAC, September 2005), 22–31.

and the unpredictability and general lack of transparency surrounding costs.[90] Apart from this long overdue official interest in improving access to legal services, recent case law has produced some interesting developments on liability for costs in so-called public interest challenges.

A 'pre-emptive costs order', or a 'protective costs order' (PCO), is one mechanism that holds the potential to address the chilling effect of costs in the planning and environmental law context. Essentially, it involves the court dealing with costs 'at an interlocutory stage in a manner which ensures that a particular party will not be faced with an order for costs against him at the conclusion of the proceedings'.[91] The advantage of such an order is that it eliminates the uncertainty regarding potential future liability for costs which may otherwise deter a potential challenger. In *Village Residents Association* it was accepted that the Irish courts had jurisdiction to make such an order, although the order was refused in that case.[92] Laffoy J adopted the principles set down by Dyson J in *R v Lord Chancellor, ex p Child Poverty Action Group*[93] *(CPAG)* where the court had distinguished between 'ordinary private law litigation' on the one hand, and 'public interest challenges' on the other. A public law challenge raises issues of 'general importance' where the applicant has no private interest in the outcome of the case.[94] Dyson J stressed that the courts' discretion to make a pre-emptive costs order, even in the case of a public interest challenge, should only be exercised in 'the most exceptional circumstances', and he proceeded to elaborate a set of criteria to be applied by the courts in considering whether or not to grant such an order.[95] Laffoy J observed it was difficult in the abstract to identify the type or types of cases in which 'the interests of justice' would require the court to deal with the costs issue by way of a pre-emptive costs order and that it would be unwise to attempt to do so.[96] The approach followed by Dyson J in *CPAG* appeared 'to meet the fundamental rubric that the interests of justice should require that the order be made'.[97] Laffoy J noted the potential role of pre-emptive costs orders in cases involving 'a true public interest issue of general importance' and cited 'a heritage protection issue' or 'an environmental issue' as examples.[98] It is difficult to predict the circumstances in which an applicant will be successful in obtaining a pre-emptive costs order in Ireland in the absence of

---

90 See *Report of the Legal Costs Working Group* (December 2005), which recommended the establishment of a new regulatory body to provide guidelines on costs Text available at: www.justice.ie.
91 *Village Residents Association*, n. 87 above, 330 per Laffoy J.
92 This jurisdiction was grounded *inter alia* on the Courts (Supplemental Provisions) Act 1961, s 14, and RSC, Order 99, rule 5.
93 [1999] 1 WLR 347.
94 Ibid, 353.
95 Ibid, 358.
96 *Village Residents Association*, n. 87 above, 330.
97 Ibid.
98 Ibid.

further case law. The recent decision of the Court of Appeal of England and Wales in *R (Corner House) v Secretary of State for Trade and Industry*, where the principles governing the grant of such orders were restated by Lord Phillips MR,[99] has not been considered by the Irish courts to date.[100]

Standard of review[101]

Judicial review is primarily concerned with the legality of the contested decision. It does not involve an appeal on the merits. The substantive merits may only be called into question indirectly by arguing that the decision taken by the public authority is unreasonable or irrational. The test of unreasonableness or irrationality in judicial review is set at a very high level and the Irish courts generally take a deferential approach to decisions taken by expert public authorities. This deference is particularly marked in the planning and environmental law field.[102] In *State (Keegan) v Stardust Compensation Tribunal*, Henchy J in the Supreme Court took the view that 'the test of unreasonableness or irrationality in judicial review lies in considering whether the impugned decision plainly and unambiguously flies in the face of fundamental reason and common sense'.[103] The leading modern decision is *O'Keeffe v An Bord Pleanála*.[104] In the words of Finlay CJ:

> ...the circumstances under which the court can intervene on the basis of irrationality with the decision maker involved in an administrative function are limited and rare...

---

99 See *R (Corner House) v Secretary of State for Trade and Industry* [2005] EWCA Civ 192.

100 See *Goodson v HM Coroner for Bedfordshire and Luton* [2005] EWCA Civ 1172 [27]–[28]; and see C George, 'Fragments from a Changing Legal Landscape – Planning Law Update' [2005] *Journal of Planning and Environment Law* 91 (Occasional Papers No. 33), paras 75–81. The judgment of Laffoy J in *Village Residents Association*, n 87 above, was considered in the *Corner House* judgment [53]–[54] (ibid). Reference was also made to the conclusions of the Irish Law Reform Commission on the issue of pre-emptive costs orders at [54] of the judgment. See also Law Reform Commission, *Report on Judicial Review Procedure* (LRC 71–2004), paras 3.33–3.38. Text available at www.lawreform.ie. The Commission recommended that the jurisdiction to make a pre-emptive costs order should be exercised only in exceptional circumstances Where there is a doubt as to the appropriateness of making such an order, it is open to the court to give an indication at an initial stage of the proceedings as to the likely outcome in relation to costs According to the Commission's report this compromise would operate 'to marry flexibility on the part of the court at a later stage in proceedings with a degree of security for the applicant'.

101 See generally G Hogan and D G Morgan, *Administrative Law in Ireland* (3rd edn) (Dublin: Round Hall Sweet & Maxwell, 1998), 641–649; A M Collins and J O'Reilly, *Civil Proceedings and the State* (2nd edn) (Dublin: Thomson Round Hall, 2004), paras 4.15–4.21; and see Simons, n. 6 above, paras 12.61–12.98. For an overview of the position in England and Wales see H W R Wade and C F Forsyth, *Administrative Law* (9th edn) (Oxford: OUP, 2004), 351–372.

102 Scannell, n. 6 above, paras 2.323 and 2.327.

103 [1986] IR 642, 658.

104 *O'Keeffe v An Bord Pleanála* [1993] 1 IR 39.

The court cannot interfere with the decision of an administrative decision-making authority merely on the grounds that (a) it is satisfied that on the facts as found it would have raised different inferences and conclusions, or (b) it is satisfied that the case against the decision made by the authority was much stronger than the case for it.

These considerations ... are of particular importance in relation to questions of the decisions of planning authorities.

Under the provisions of the Planning Acts the legislature has unequivocally and firmly placed questions of planning, questions of the balance between development and the environment and the proper convenience and amenities of an area within the jurisdiction of the planning authorities and the Board which are expected to have special skill, competence and experience in planning questions. The court is not vested with that jurisdiction, nor is it expected to, nor can it, exercise discretion with regard to planning matters.[105]

It is now well established that in order to convince the court that the decision maker acted unreasonably or irrationally 'it is necessary that the applicant should establish to the satisfaction of the court that the decision-making authority had before it no relevant material which would support its decision'.[106] The onus of establishing this material lies on the applicant.[107] Scannell has observed that 'the O'Keeffe standard is practically impossible to satisfy in Ireland so that it is almost true to say that in practice the courts will not invalidate an environmental decision because it is unreasonable'.[108]

The scope of application of the O'Keeffe principles is of interest for present purposes. Simons has argued that the weak form of judicial review mandated by O'Keeffe, by which the courts generally defer to the expert view of planning authorities or the Board, only applies to decisions on purely planning matters, usually questions of fact and degree. Decisions such as whether or not to grant planning permission fall squarely within the discretion of the competent authorities and the planning code provides for a full right of appeal to *An Bord Pleanála*. On the other hand, decisions involving questions of law should be subject to full review and there is no place for judicial deference in such cases.[109] Simons maintains that 'the standard of review set by O'Keeffe is so high that it

---

105 Ibid, 71–72. This statement was cited with approval by the Supreme Court in *Grianán an Aileach Centre v Donegal County Council (No. 2)* [2004] 2 IR 639, 639–640 per Keane CJ. See also *White v Dublin City Council, Ireland and the Attorney General* [2004] 1 IR 545, 559–560 per Fennelly J.

106 *O'Keeffe*, n. 104 above, 72. See also *Devlin v Minister for Arts, Culture and the Gaeltacht* [1999] 1 IR 47, 58; *Ryanair Ltd. v Flynn* [2000] 3 IR 240, 264–267 and the decisions cited therein; *Aer Rianta Cpt v Commissioner for Aviation Regulation*, unreported, High Court, 16 January 2003, O'Sullivan J, 47–49; and see *Kinsella v Dundalk Town Council* [2004] IEHC 373.

107 *O'Keeffe*, n. 104 above, 72. See also *P. & F. Sharpe Ltd. v Dublin City and County Manager* [1989] IR 701, 718–719.

108 Scannell, n. 6 above, para 2.429.

109 Simons, n. 6 above, paras 12.69–12.97.

effectively stymies any challenge to the decision and there is a danger that if the O'Keeffe principles are applied indiscriminately to all decisions of a planning authority, this would actually undermine the rule of law'.[110] This view has a firm basis in the case law. Finlay CJ's landmark opinion in O'Keeffe linked the weak or deferential mode of review to 'planning questions'.[111] Decisions concerning the application of the EIA Directive often involve complex, mixed questions of law and fact. In line with the principle of effective judicial protection, and following the ECJ rulings in cases such as Kraaijeveld, Bozen, and Wells, decisions taken under the Directive should be subject to robust review by the national courts.[112] While the national court is not required to engage in a detailed examination of the merits of the contested decision,[113] it is obliged to examine whether or not the substantive requirements of the Directive have been met. The case law to date indicates that the Irish courts are most reluctant to intervene where an applicant questions a competent authority's decision not to require an EIA in a particular case or where a challenge is mounted to the adequacy of the EIS submitted by the developer.[114] In the specific context of challenges to decisions of competent national authorities in the public procurement field, there are already indications that the weak mode of review established in O'Keeffe not easily reconciled with the principle of effective judicial protection.[115] It is also doubtful whether the O'Keeffe principles are compatible with Art 6 (right to a fair trial)[116] and Art 13 (right to an effective remedy)[117] of

---

110 G Simons, 'The Unreasonable Planning Authority: A Review of the Application of *O'Keeffe v An Bord Pleanála* (Part I)' (2000) 4 *Irish Planning and Environmental Law Journal* 164, 165. Part II of the article can be found at (2001) 5 *Irish Planning and Environmental Law Journal* 26.

111 See *O'Connor v Dublin Corporation*, unreported, High Court, 3 October 2000, 28, where O'Neill J ruled that the *O'Keeffe* test did not apply where it was alleged the local authority had misinterpreted conditions that had been attached to a planning permission. The appropriate test to be applied is whether the conclusion reached by the local authority 'was correct in law'.

112 *Kraaijeveld*, n. 15 above; Case C-435/97 *World Wildlife Fund (WWF) and Others v Autonome Provinz Bozen and Others* [1999] ECR I-5613; and see *Wells*, n. 15 above.

113 See *Upjohn*, n. 44 above.

114 See e.g. *Kenny v An Bord Pleanála (No. 1)* [2001] 1 IR 567; *Waddington v An Bord Pleanála*, unreported, High Court, 21 December 2000; and see *O'Connell v EPA*, unreported, High Court, 25 April 2002, Butler J.

115 *SIAC v Mayo County Council* [2002] 3 IR 148, 175–176; the opinion of Jacobs AG in Case C-19/00 *SIAC* [2001] ECR I-7725 [53]–[54]; and see *Nash v Minister for Justice, Equality and Law Reform* [2004] 3 IR 296, 307–310 per Kearns J in the High Court.

116 *Airey v Ireland* (1979) 2 EHRR 305; and see *Ortenberg v Austria* (1994) 19 EHRR 524.

117 *Hatton and Others v United Kingdom* (2003) 37 EHRR 28 (Grand Chamber). See J Hyam, 'Hatton v United Kingdom in the Grand Chamber: One Step Forward, Two Steps Back?' [2003] *Judicial Review* 631. Art 13 is not a 'Convention right' for the purposes of the Human Rights Act 1998. However, Art 13 is a 'Convention provision' within the meaning of Section 1(1) of the (Irish) European Convention on Human Rights Act 2003.

the ECHR.[118] These important points have not, as yet, been addressed in the Irish EIA case law.[119]

Appraisal

Even though Art 10a of the EIA Directive was due to be implemented in the Member States by 25 June 2005, no steps have been taken to give effect to the new European access to justice requirements in Irish EIA law.[120] This situation demonstrates the sharp tension between persistent demands for economic development on the one hand and calls for increased environmental protection, and close scrutiny of environmental decision-making, on the other. It also serves to highlight the problems of interpretation that can and do arise in practice where obligations created in environmental directives are drafted in general terms and leave the practical details of implementation to the discretion of the Member States. As noted earlier, Art 10a[1] and [3] of the EIA directive provides considerable flexibility for Member States in determining local standing rules. It is therefore difficult to predict the impact of Art 10a in the Irish context. Art 10a[1] sets a 'sufficient interest' as the basic standing requirement.[121] In Ireland, post s.50 PDA, an applicant seeking to challenge a prescribed planning decision must demonstrate a 'substantial interest'. In the recent *Harrington* ruling, Macken J confirmed that the new standing requirement is more onerous than the

118 See Á Ryall, 'Implications of the European Convention on Human rights Act 2003 for local authority decision-making', paper presented at Local Authority Solicitors Association seminar, Cork, 14 May 2004 (transcript on file with author). For a recent overview of the impact of the 2003 Act on Irish law to date see M Farrell, 'The ECHR – Practitioners' Perspectives' paper presented at University College Cork seminar, 3 February 2006 (transcript on file with author).

119 Arguments based on Arts 6, 8 and 13 ECHR are among the grounds on which the applicants were granted leave in *O'Leary & Others v An Bord Pleanála, Ireland and the Attorney General* 191/JR/2004. See 'High Court allows legal challenge to incinerator' *Irish Times* 25 January 2005. The substantive hearing has yet to come before the High Court. This case concerns a challenge to the decision of the Board granting planning permission to Indaver Ireland Ltd. for a development consisting of a waste management facility at Ringaskiddy, Co. Cork (Board Ref. No. 04.131196). The EPA's decision to grant a waste licence for this proposed facility is also the subject of a separate challenge in the High Court.

120 A detailed consultation paper on the implementation of Directive 2003/35/EC published by the Office of the Deputy Prime Minister (UK) states 'it is considered that the current judicial review procedures are sufficient to satisfy the main Art 10a requirement for the public to have access to a review procedure to challenge the legality of decisions...subject to the public participation provisions of the directive'. This appears to be a rather optimistic assessment to say the least. See *The draft Town and Country Planning (Environmental Impact Assessment) (England) (Amendment) Regulations 2005: Consultation Paper*, March 2005, para 3.19. Text available at: http://www.communities.gov.uk/pub/795/ThedraftTownandCountryPlanning EnvironmentalImpactAssessmentEnglandPDF901Kb_id1147795.pdf.

121 It is not a requirement of Irish administrative law that an applicant for judicial review must demonstrate the impairment of a right (see Art 10a[1](b)).

previous test of a 'sufficient interest'.[122] The question then arises as to whether the new Irish standing test is compatible with Art 10a[1]. The real impact of the new test in practice depends on the manner in which the courts interpret a 'substantial interest' and the relationship between the standing test and the obligation to demonstrate 'substantial grounds' in s.50 PDA. There is clear Supreme Court authority for 'a reasonably generous approach' to standing where constitutional rights are at stake.[123] In line with the principle of supremacy, and the principle of effective judicial protection, a similarly generous approach is mandated in cases involving Community law rights. Keane J acknowledged this European obligation, albeit *obiter*, in *Lancefort*. A generous approach to standing is particularly important in cases involving an allegation of serious or substantial error or an abuse of discretionary power where no other suitably qualified challenger is likely to come forward. The special recognition afforded to environmental NGOs in Art 10a, and the express obligation to set national standing requirements so as to facilitate 'wide' access to justice, may operate to temper the strict approach that the Irish High Court has taken to the 'substantial interest' requirement to date.

On the question of costs, the express requirement in Art 10a[5] that the review procedure 'not be prohibitively expensive' could be deployed to bolster arguments in favour of a pre-emptive costs order in an appropriate case. The Irish courts have adopted a very restrictive approach to the concept of a public interest challenge in the planning context to date. The courts are slow to accept that a challenge to a decision based on alleged non-compliance with the EIA Directive is primarily concerned with vindicating the rule of law or protecting the public interest, particularly where the applicant is a private individual with a property interest in the outcome of the proceedings. Art 10a[5] may encourage the courts to take a more flexible approach to the concept of public interest challenges when called upon to make a pre-emptive costs order. Taken in conjunction with Art 6 ECHR, in particular the principle of 'equality of arms', Art 10a[5] provides an interesting basis on which to develop arguments in favour of civil legal aid and financial assistance for technical expertise that may be necessary in order to mount an effective challenge.

The implications, if any, of Art 10a for the *O'Keeffe* principles is unclear. The main focus of Art 10a[1] appears to be on review of legality so it is unlikely that this provision could be used to support full review on the merits particularly in cases where the applicant has already had the benefit of a full appeal before the Board. It could however be argued that the obligation to provide for review of the 'substantive or procedural legality' of the contested decision requires more robust judicial scrutiny than the approach adopted to date under *O'Keeffe*. This is an area that is likely to see interesting developments in the future.

---

122 *Harrington*, n. 77 above.
123 See e.g. *Crotty*, n. 80 above, cited with approval in *Lancefort*, n. 62 above, 309 per Keane J.

Irish judicial review practice and procedure in the planning and environmental law field has proven to be particularly resistant to European influences. There is a certain irony in the fact that the Irish system moved to tighten access to judicial review, through the strict requirements set down in s.50 PDA, at a time when the clear trend at international and European level is towards strengthening and improving public participation and access to justice in environmental matters. More far-reaching revisions of the Irish system are forthcoming at the time of writing.[124] It is anticipated that a special division of *An Bord Pleanála* will be established to deal with 'critical infrastructure', including, for example: waste facilities such as landfill and incinerators; motorways; rail and metro lines and gas and oil pipelines, and that such projects will be referred directly to the Board, thus eliminating the local authority decision-making stage. This move reflects the fact that in practice most if not all large-scale projects are the subject of an appeal to the Board. It remains to be seen what provision will be made for public participation in the new modified planning process that is envisaged by the Government for critical infrastructure projects. Further restrictions on access to the courts in planning matters are also anticipated at the time of writing.[125]

Conclusion

The new Community law obligations governing access to justice in EIA matters represent a significant challenge for Member States. In the absence of accessible and effective remedies, the role of information and participation rights as legal tools aimed at supporting the transition towards sustainable development will be weakened, if not undermined, to the detriment of the environment and future generations.

On close scrutiny it becomes clear that Art 10a leaves considerable discretion to Member States as regards the details of implementation. It is therefore very difficult to identify the real implications of the obligations set down in Art 10a for national review procedures. Given the diverse administrative law systems operating across the twenty-five Member States, a degree of deference to national legal systems and local administrative culture is essential. At the same time, the flexibility that pervades the scheme set down in Art 10a reduces the scope for harmonisation of national review procedures and remedies in the EIA field. There is a further practical difficulty with the rather vague and general nature of the obligations created in Art 10a: any dispute over the scope of Member State discretion can only be resolved definitively by recourse to a court. In other words, national courts and ultimately the ECJ will be called upon to interpret Art 10a. Even assuming that national courts are willing to make

---

124 'New system to deliver infrastructure decisions more quickly', Department of the Environment, Heritage and Local Government Press Release 1 June 2005. Text available at www.environ.ie.
125 'Roche outlines planning reform proposals' *Irish Times* 2 June 2005.

references under Art 234 EC in appropriate cases, the delays involved in having matters determined by the ECJ are well known. The consequences of Art 10a for the national legal systems will therefore remain uncertain until such time as the ECJ clarifies the scope of the various obligations created in Art 10a. In recent years, the Commission has placed considerable emphasis on the value of guidance documents to assist national authorities with effective local implementation of obligations created in environmental directives. It is surprising to find that the Commission has not published any specific guidance on Directive 2003/35/EC, the Public Participation Directive, to date. While extensive documentation including implementation guides and notes on the Aarhus Convention has been published by the United Nations Economic Commission for Europe, this guidance is again rather general.[126] The national legal context is critical when attempting to tease out the practical implications of the Aarhus Convention and Art 10a for local procedures and remedies.[127] To this end, far more attention needs to be devoted to developing jurisdiction specific training programmes for the judiciary, competent authorities, NGOs and lawyers. Practical workshops and case studies provide a valuable mechanism by which the more difficult points of local implementation may be dissected and examined in the relevant national context.

Returning to Ireland, no steps have been taken to date to implement Art 10a, or indeed any elements of Directive 2003/35/EC, at national level. The question therefore arises as to whether Art 10a may be invoked before *An Bord Pleanála* or in judicial review proceedings in the absence of national implementing measures. A detailed analysis of this important practical question lies beyond the scope of this short case study.[128] The starting point is *Kraaijeveld*, where the ECJ ruled that competent authorities and the national courts are obliged, as a matter of Community law 'to take all the general or particular measures necessary' to ensure that the requirements of the EIA Directive are observed.[129] Beyond this general obligation, the doctrine of consistent interpretation is likely to prove very useful in terms of giving effect to Art 10a within the national legal order.[130]

---

126 Documentation available at www.unece.org/env/pp.
127 The ECJ has long acknowledged the importance of assessing contested national procedural rules in their local context. See Joined Cases C-430/93 and C-431/93 *Van Schijndel and Van Veen v Stichting Pensioenfonds voor Fysiotherapeuten* [1995] ECR I-4705. For commentary see S Prechal, 'Community Law in National Courts: The Lessons from *Van Schijndel*' (1998) 35 *Common Market Law Review* 681.
128 See Ryall, n. 1 above. Ireland also failed to implement Directive 2003/4/EC on access to information on the environment by the 14 February 2005 deadline and no steps have been taken to implement this directive to date. See Á Ryall, 'Access to Information on the Environment: the challenge of implementing Directive 2003/4/EC' (2005) 12 *Irish Planning and Environmental Law Journal* 162–167.
129 *Kraaijeveld*, n. 15 above; *Wells*, n. 15 above; and see *Power*, n. 15 above.
130 See generally S Drake, 'Twenty years after Von Colson: the impact of "indirect effect" on the protection of the individual's Community rights' (2005) 30 *European Law Review* 329.

A robust approach to the effectiveness of Community law and the onerous duties falling on the national courts in this context is clear from *Pfeiffer*.[131] On this occasion, the ECJ ruled that the principle of consistent interpretation required the national court 'to do whatever lies within its jurisdiction, having regard to the whole body of rules of national law to ensure that [the directive in question] is fully effective'.[132] Following *Pfeiffer*, the national courts are under a firm Community law obligation to interpret the relevant body of local rules on access to justice in light of the wording and purpose of Art 10a of the EIA Directive.

In sum, the access to justice provisions of the Aarhus Convention, and Art 10a of the EIA Directive, set down a formidable challenge for national courts to ensure that the right to effective judicial protection is delivered in practice at local level. It remains to be seen whether the national courts are prepared to rise to this challenge and take the lead in adapting national principles to Aarhus requirements with a view to safeguarding the procedural rights set down in the EIA Directive.

Postscript

Irish planning law has undergone dramatic changes since this chapter was completed in January 2006. The Planning and Development (Strategic Infrastructure) Act 2006 introduced a new consent procedure for specified projects of strategic importance to the State with effect from 31 January 2007.[133] The basic scheme established in the 2006 Act is that applications for planning permission for 'strategic' projects must now be made directly to *An Bord Pleanála*.[134] The essential aim here is to streamline the planning process even further and to provide for the expeditious determination of such applications. New planning regulations (in force since 31 January 2007) amend the previous planning regulations[135] and purport to implement the enhanced public participation requirements set down in the EIA directive (as amended by Directive 2003/35/EC).[136]

The rules governing judicial review in planning cases have also been reworked. Section 13 of the 2006 Act substituted two new sections, s 50 and s 50A, for the previous PDA s 50. The overall structure of the restrictive judicial review scheme has been retained, but there are a number of significant changes

---

131 Joined Cases C-397/01 to C-403/01 *Pfeiffer* [2004] ECR I-8835 [111].

132 Ibid, [118]–[119].

133 Planning and Development (Strategic Infrastructure) Act 2006 Pt. 2; Planning and Development (Strategic Infrastructure) Act 2006 (Commencement) (No 3) Order 2006 (SI No 684 of 2006); and Planning and Development Regs 2006 (SI No 685 of 2006) Pt 18.

134 For an excellent overview of the main features of the 2006 Act see J Macken, 'Planning and Development (Strategic Infrastructure) Act 2006' (2006) 13 *Irish Planning and Environmental Law Journal* 139.

135 Planning and Development Regs 2001 to 2006.

136 Planning and Development Regs 2006 (SI No 685 of 2006).

including, in particular, special *locus standi* rules for certain ENGOs. The new Irish rules provide that ENGOs that meet specified criteria are automatically deemed to have standing in EIA cases.[137] This innovation is designed to give effect to the specific obligation in Art 10a of the EIA directive concerning standing requirements and ENGOs.

The *locus standi* test articulated in PDA s 50(4)(b) (prior to the changes introduced through the 2006 Act), has been the subject of further judicial analysis. It will be recalled from the main text above that the High Court has generally taken a restrictive approach to the 'substantial interest' requirement. The contemporary case law confirms this trend.[138] In *Harding v Cork County Council (No. 2)*, Clarke J reviewed the case law to date and articulated the following criteria by which the importance of the interest asserted by the applicant might be measured: the scale of the project and the extent to which it might give rise to a significant alteration in the amenity of the area concerned; the extent of the connection of the applicant to the effects of the project; and such other factors as may arise on the facts of an individual case.[139] Clarke J determined that the applicant had not established a 'substantial interest' in this case.[140] However, the judge subsequently granted a certificate for leave to appeal to the Supreme Court on the basis that his decision on the *locus standi* point involved a point of law of exceptional public importance within the meaning of PDA s 50(4)(f).[141] This is a most welcome development as the law on this important practical point lies in a state of uncertainty, notwithstanding a series of High Court decisions.

The Irish High Court has recently been called upon to consider the impact of Art 10a on domestic rules governing judicial review proceedings. In *Friends of the Curragh Environment*, Kelly J approved the principles established by the Court of Appeal in Corner House,[142] but dismissed the application for a PCO.[143] Kelly J noted that the *Corner House* principles did not differ in any substantive sense from the principles articulated by Laffoy J in *Village Residents Association*.[144] Essentially, a court will only make a PCO 'in most exceptional

---

137 PDA s 50A(3)(b).
138 *O'Brien v Dún Laoghaire Rathdown County Council* [2006] IEHC 177 (1 June 2006), *O'Neill J*; *Harding v Cork County Council (No. 2)* [2006] IEHC 295 (12 October 2006), Clarke J. and *Friends of the Curragh Environment Limited (No. 2) v An Bord Pleanála* [2006] IEHC 390 (8 December 2006), Finlay Geoghegan J.
139 *Harding (No. 2)*, n. 138 above, [3.11].
140 For a detailed account see, (2006) 13 *Irish Planning and Environmental Law Journal* 171.
141 *Harding v Cork County Council (No. 3)*, unreported, High Court, 30 November, 2006. See further, (2006) 13 *Irish Planning and Environmental Law Journal* 174.
142 *Corner House*, n. 99 above.
143 *Friends of the Curragh Environment Limited v An Bord Pleanála* [2006] IEHC 243 (14 July 2006) Kelly J.
144 *Village Residents Association*, n. 87 above.

circumstances and where the interests of justice require such a course to be taken'; and the issue(s) raised must be of general public importance.[145] The applicant company argued that it was entitled to a PCO not only by reference to the relevant common law principles, but also on the basis of obligations created for Member States in Art 10a of the EIA directive. It will be recalled that Art 10a[5] provides *inter alia* that the review procedure must be 'fair, equitable, timely and not prohibitively expensive'. It was common case between the parties that Ireland had failed to implement Art 10a.[146] In the absence of national implementing measures, the applicant maintained that Art 10a had direct effect and that the means of rendering it fully effective in the instant case was to make a PCO. Kelly J refused to accept that Art 10a had 'the clarity, precision and unconditionality so as to make it directly applicable.'[147] It will be recalled that Art 10a requires Member States to provide a review procedure before a court of law or another 'independent or impartial body established by law.' Kelly J suggested that an appeal to *An Bord Pleanála* fulfilled the Art 10a obligation and that is was not clear whether a further layer of challenge by way of judicial review was covered by Art 10a.[148] He also held that the meaning of the words 'not prohibitively expensive' was also unclear as it could be taken to refer to either court fees or to legal costs.[149] This disappointing ruling provides a sharp illustration of the many difficulties posed by the general manner in which Art 10a is drafted – particularly in terms of the flexibility that it offers to Member States when determining the structure and mechanics of national review procedures.[150]

As at April 2007, Ireland stands alone as the only Member State that has failed to ratify the Aarhus Convention. The Irish Minister for Environment, Heritage and Local Government made regulations purporting to implement Directive 2003/4/EC on public access to environmental information on 28 March 2007 – over two years after the formal deadline for transposition had passed. The long-awaited European Communities (Access to Information on the Environment) Regulations 2007 were made pursuant to European Communities Act 1972 s 3 and will come into operation on 1 May 2007.[151]

---

145 *Friends of the Curragh Environment*, n. 11 above at 17–18.
146 Ibid, 35.
147 Ibid, 36.
148 Ibid, 37–38.
149 Ibid, 38–39.
150 For a detailed analysis of the implications of Art 10a for Irish judicial review proceedings see, Ryall, n. 1 above, chs 5 and 6.
151 SI No 133 of 2007. Text of the regs and Guidance Notes available at: www.environ.ie. See further, Á Ryall, 'Access to Information on the Environment Regulations 2007' (2007) 14 *Irish Planning and Environmental Law Journal* (forthcoming).

Chapter 8

Bringing environmental assessment into the digital age

Daniel A Farber[1]

Introduction

Environmental assessments[2] are one of the key mechanisms for developing information about current environmental conditions and future prospects. The paradox is that society spends huge sums of money to develop these assessments of proposed projects, then buries them in inaccessible archives.

Society's investment in environmental assessment should not be underestimated. In 1995, for example, a single federal agency, the federal Department of Energy (DOE), spent $20–30 million on "routine" assessments, plus $90 million on more elaborate assessments for special projects – a total of around $120 million for that one agency alone.[3] The amount of information produced is substantial. A 1996 study by the US Environmental Protection Agency found the text of the average environmental impact statement was 204 pages (or 472 pages including tables, appendices, and correspondence).[4] Given the reported number of impact statements annually,[5] this adds up to about 50,000 pages per year for the major federal assessments, plus an unknown quantity of information for more routine,

---

1 I would like to thank Jessica Yarnall for her research assistance, and Holly Doremus, Dianne Farber, Jane Holder, Brad Karkkainen, Myron Orfield, Cymie Payne, Paul Schwartz, and Matt Zinn, for their exceptionally helpful comments.
2 I will use "environmental assessments" as a general term to cover all forms of project assessments, which go by various different names depending on the scale of the assessment and whether the assessment is state or federal. The federal government uses the term "Environmental Assessment" to refer to a particular form of streamlined assessment, in contrast to environmental impact statements, which are much more elaborate. When the term is being used in this specific sense, it will be capitalized or replaced with the initials EA. It should be noted that some progress in making EAs accessible on-line took place while this article was in press. These developments are discussed in footnotes.
3 National Academy of Public Administration, *Managing NEPA at the Department of Energy* July 20, 1998, available at www.eh.doe.gov/nepa/process/napa_rep/napa_rep.html.
4 B C Karkkainen, "Toward a Smarter NEPA: Monitoring and Managing Government's Environmental Performance" (2002) 102 *Columbia Law Review* 903, 918. n. 64.
5 See B C Karkkainen, "Whither NEPA" (2004) 12 *New York University Environmental Law Journal* 333, 347–349 (reporting 250 EISs per year).

small-scale assessments. The trouble is that this information can be extremely hard to locate after it is produced. Thus, an extraordinary amount of money and information are being dropped into a black hole, never to be seen again.

Imagine, for example, that you are a researcher who is interested in the environmental impacts of projects affecting a particular species of animal or watershed. No central registry exists with this information. The only way of locating the relevant environmental assessments would be to identify each potential government agency, federal, state, and local, that might be involved in such projects, and then to make a document request from each individual agency. Some of the documents would be available only in hard copy once they were found, although more recent documents might be available on compact disk. Moreover, many agencies might be unable to locate the documents themselves because there is no systematic tracking of the most common forms of environmental assessments. This problem might not be particularly serious if our environmental data were otherwise fairly complete. But the opposite is true. Unfortunately, our information about the environment is plagued by gaps. This makes it all the more serious that much of the information we do actually have, in the form of environmental assessments, is for most practical purposes incapable of being retrieved.

The general inadequacy of our environmental data is common knowledge among environmental scholars. For instance, pollution monitoring has been strikingly inadequate.[6] To quote an influential scholar: "virtually every prominent expert panel convened to consider the effects of industrial activities on health and the environment expresses alarm at the dearth of research and basic information."[7] As of 1996, for example 80 percent of waterways had not been monitored for water quality.[8]

Similar problems exist with natural resource-related data. As the US Council on Environmental Quality (CEQ) reports: "For example, even today, many agencies with large land holdings do not know the extent or location of archeological sites, wetlands, or other important environmental features."[9] Of course, much of this information may already be contained in environmental assessments – but who would know, since the assessments are as a practical matter inaccessible.

In short, society urgently needs better information about the present condition of the environment. Otherwise, we will never be capable of discovering problems or monitoring the effectiveness of our current efforts, which are prerequisites of learning to do better. It is no secret, after all, that "environmental decision-making

---

6 For a survey of environmental monitoring and calls for improvement, see Council on Environmental Quality, *Environmental Quality: Twenty-Second Annual Report* (1992), 43–56. For continuing complaints about monitoring capacities, see National Research Council, *Air Quality Management in the United States* (2004), 284 .

7 W E Wagner, *Commons Ignorance: The Failure of Environmental Law to Produce Needed Information on Health and the Environment* (2004) 53 *Duke Law Journal* 1619, 1625.

8 Ibid, 1628.

9 Council on Environmental Quality, *The National Environmental Policy Act: A Study of Its Effectiveness After Twenty-Five Years*, January 1997, 27 ("*Effectiveness study*").

critically depends on data and analysis."[10] Indeed, it seems rather painfully obvious that society cannot expect to improve environmental quality if we do not even know the current state of the environment. Developing new information should be a priority, but it is equally important to ensure the accessibility of existing information. Our failure to make effective use of existing information is all the more unfortunate because modern technology creates abundant opportunities to promote access.

It would be premature to offer a blueprint for remedying this situation. But we are already in a good position to diagnose the shortcomings of the current system and to consider possible solutions. We will begin with an overview of US environmental assessment to provide background for considering access issues. We will then consider in somewhat painful detail the shortcomings of the current system, and then, somewhat more happily, the potential of technology to redress these shortcomings. Finally, we will consider some initial steps that might be taken along this path.

As a long-term goal, we can imagine a kind of virtual global ecosystem, where all available environmental information would be linked to a detailed geographic information system (GIS). Environmental assessments would be a significant part of the effort to put all of the relevant data at our fingertips. But we could make tremendous progress through far less ambitious actions. Simply ensuring that all environmental assessments were available online would be a big step forward. A further step would be to combine them in an easily searchable archive. Future steps could include linkages to other environmental information, especially monitoring of developments at project sites. The problem is not at all one of finding the path forward. The problem is simply one of beginning the necessary steps.

Although Congress has not addressed this problem specifically, the general issue of effective public access to government documents has received some attention. The Bush Administration has launched an effort to make rule making proceedings accessible on line.[11] In addition, s 207 of the E-Government Act:[12]

> ...aims to improve the way Federal government information is organized, preserved, and made accessible to the public. To accomplish these goals, the Act requires the Office of Management and Budget (OMB), an agency within the White House, to establish an interagency committee to recommend to OMB policies for agency public websites and indexing and categorizing government information.[13]

10 D C Esty, "Environmental Protection in the Information Age" (2004) 79 *New York University Law Review* 115, 118.
11 See C Coglianese, "E-Rulemaking: Information Technology and the Regulatory Process" (2004) 56 *Administrative Law Review* 353, 365.
12 E-Government Act of 2002 (P.L.107–347).
13 Office of Management and Budget, *FY 2004 Report to Congress on Implementation of The E-Government Act of 2002*, http://www.whitehouse.gov/omb/inforeg/2004_egov_report.pdf (1 March 2005).

So far, environmental assessments have been a major gap in these efforts. Whatever the cause, it is time to remedy this blind-spot.[14]

Addressing this problem would offer many benefits in terms of improving the general availability of environmental information. Specifically, another benefit – that of increased accountability – is equally crucial. An effective online database could go some way toward responding to the frequent criticism of assessments as rationalizations for foregone conclusions, less than thorough analyses, and failures at proposing feasible mitigation measures. Easy, centralized access to existing assessments would allow third parties to police public agencies' production of new assessments, eliminating the use of assessments as glorified public relations pieces and interfering with the cozy relationship of agencies and project proponents. The system would serve, for example, as a library of potentially feasible mitigation measures, and an agency's failure to use such mitigation would be immediately obvious. Similarly, it would be easy to find the agency's promises of mitigation and compare them with the agency's later performance. This may be an uncomfortable development for some agencies, but one that would improve the democratic legitimacy of the regulatory process.

Bringing the assessment process into the digital age seems like the proverbial "no brainer." One might wonder, accordingly, why it has not already happened. One reason may be a fear by agencies and development interests of greater transparency and public accountability. Another reason may be that no one really knows what fuller environmental information would teach; risk averse organizations on both sides of disputes may prefer not to take the gamble that they would like the outcome. And finally, environmental disputes in the United States in recent years have often involved bitter disputes about potential

---

14 There has been some progress in considering the use of the Internet in connection with EISs. The Environmental Assessment Division at Argonne National Laboratory has a project "to advance informed environmental decision-making." The focus has been on using the web to expedite participation in the public comment process: "Applications developed by EAD have shown the huge potential of the Internet to support the EIS process. Internet-based document repositories provide near-zero cost distribution of EISs and related documents while web-based commenting and EIS web sites extend the geographic reach of public information/involvement programs." See http://www.ead.anl.gov/inetapp/dsp_inetarea.cfm?areaid=13. In addition, commercial services now provide some access. A company called CSA provides abstracts of EISs. For a listing of their products, see http://md3.case.com/e_products/databses-collections.php. In addition, CEQAdocs.com provides access to many California documents. (Although one of its services is called CEQAmap, it does not in fact include a mapping function.) The company describes CEQAmap as follows:

> CEQAmap is California's only searchable digital database of environmental impact reports, summaries of mitigations, community plans and development documents. The database is FREE to all users who include: scientists, engineers, attorneys, agency staff, faculty and students, journalists and the general public.

These encouraging developments took place while this article was in press.

regulatory roll-backs, leaving little energy for new initiatives. But whatever the reason, the situation has certainly gone on too long already.

An overview of US environmental assessments

To understand the access issues, we need to begin with an overview of the environmental assessment system. The US has a multi-tiered system of environmental assessment for projects.[15] At the federal level, projects receive various forms of assessment depending on the likelihood of successfully mitigating any adverse environmental impacts. Many state governments also have their own impact assessments. In some respects, the system of environmental assessment in the US seems to function in ways that deviate from the original expectations of its founders, with important implications in terms of the types of information available and their relative utility.

The federal scheme

Environmental assessments of all kinds – federal, state, and even international – have their origin in a 1970 federal statute. S 101 of the National Environmental Policy Act (NEPA)[16] proclaims the policy of the federal government to administer federal programs in an environmentally sound fashion. In practice, the most significant provision of NEPA is undoubtedly s 102(2)(c). This section is designed to force agencies to take environmental factors into consideration when making significant decisions. The crucial language of this subsection reads as follows:

> The Congress authorizes and directs that, to the fullest extent possible: ... (2) all agencies of the federal government shall
> (c) include in every recommendation or report on proposals for legislation and other major federal actions significantly affecting the quality of the human environment, a detailed statement by the responsible official on
>
> (i) the environmental impact of the proposed action,
> (ii) any adverse environmental effects which cannot be avoided should the proposal be implemented,
> (iii) alternatives to the proposed action ... [17]

Section 102(2)(c) goes on to require the federal agency to consult other agencies with jurisdiction over or special expertise concerning the environmental problem

---

15 It would clearly be useful to extend this discussion into the international sphere, but for purposes of this preliminary inquiry the focus will be on the US. Adding a comparative dimension would be the next step in researching the issue.

16 42 U.S.C. s 4331.

17 Ibid, 42 U.S.C. s 4332(2)(c).

involved. Copies of the environmental impact statement (EIS) are to be circulated among relevant government agencies and to the public, although in practice access by the general public may be more of an aspiration than a reality. Under s 102, the EIS is also supposed to "accompany the proposal through the existing agency review processes." Other provisions of NEPA establish the CEQ, which has been designated as the lead agency in implementing the EIS requirement.[18]

In essence, the statute requires a federal agency to prepare a detailed explanation of the environmental consequences of its actions, and to make that report available to higher-level agency officials, other agencies, and the public. Three requirements must be met before an EIS is necessary. The proposed action must (1) be federal, (2) qualify as "major," and (3) have a significant environmental impact. Only the issue of significant impact has turned out to be difficult to resolve. To determine whether the impact of a project will be "significant," the CEQ regulations instruct agencies to consider factors such as impact on public health, unique features of the geographic area, the precedential effect of the action, and whether the action is highly controversial. Even after considering these factors, a determination must be made about their magnitude. This is a judgment call about which very little can be said, except to observe that courts seem to have some tendency to resolve close cases in favor of requiring an impact statement.[19] In any event, the significance of the impact is generally the critical factor in determining the need for the EIS. Note that there is a certain circularity here: in order to determine whether it is necessary to study and report on the environmental impacts of a project, the agency must first determine the possible scope of those impacts. There is thus a certain amount of overlap between the initial decision-making process about whether to prepare an EIS and the actual preparation of the EIS.

The language of NEPA suggests that a detailed assessment is required in the presence of "significant" impacts, but no assessment at all is needed otherwise. There is no mention of the need for any formal assessment except when significant impacts are predicted. Thus, there seems to be a binary choice between a "detailed statement" and no statement at all. The system has evolved differently. In practice, the question is usually not whether to perform an environmental assessment, but how detailed the assessment needs to be. Essentially, if significant impacts exist and cannot be mitigated successfully, the project receives a full-scale assessment. A less intense assessment is used if

---

18 NEPA ss 202–209 42 U.S.C. ss 4342–4347.

19 For extensive background materials on these issues, see R W Findley, D A Farber, and J Freeman, *Cases and Materials on Environmental Law* 6th edn. (West Group, 2003), 149–172. The difficulty of the "significance" determination seems to be universal. See J Holder, *Environmental Assessment: The Regulation of Decision Making* (Oxford: Oxford University Press, 2004), 37, calling this factor "a highly subjective and difficult evaluation."

the agency believes the impacts are not significant or can be eliminated through mitigation.

The environmental assessment process

The CEQ regulations now contain detailed procedural requirements for the entire EIS process. This process is shown in detail in Figure 8.1. The process

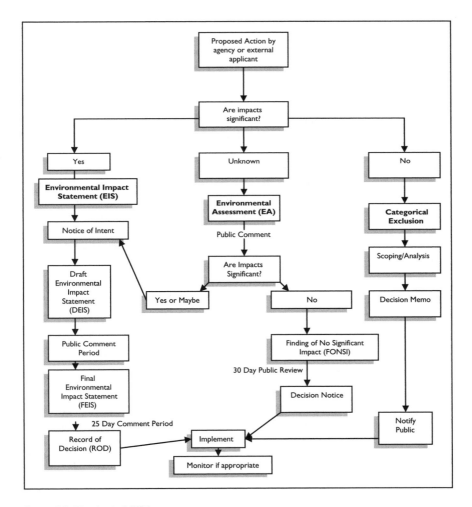

Figure 8.1 The basic NEPA process.

Sources: EPA (Federal Register) http://www.epa.gov/reg3esd1/nepa/NEPAFlowChart.pdf and Wild Law NEPA flow chart http://www.wildlaw.org/Eco-Laws/nepaflow.htm.

begins with an "Environmental Assessment" (EA), which is a brief analysis of the need for an EIS.[20] The EA must also consider alternatives to the proposed action, as required by s.102(2)(E) of NEPA. If the agency decides not to prepare an EIS, it must make a "finding of no significant impact" (FONSI) available to the public. Some agencies provide for public comment before the FONSI determination is made, but others do not.[21]

If the agency does decide to prepare an EIS, the first step in the EIS process is "scoping". Scoping is intended to obtain early participation by other agencies and the public in planning the EIS, to determine the scope of the EIS, and to determine the significant issues to be discussed in the EIS. The actual preparation of the EIS itself involves a draft EIS, a comment period, and a final EIS. Agencies with jurisdiction or special expertise relating to the project are required to comment. Major inter-agency disagreements are to be referred to CEQ for its recommendation. When an agency reaches a final decision on the project, it must prepare a "record of decision" summarizing its actions and explaining why it rejected environmentally preferable alternatives and mitigation measures.[22]

Mitigation measures have become an increasingly important part of the assessment process. When a formal EIS is required, it must include a discussion of the alternatives to the proposed action, including mitigation measures. The leading case on the issue of what alternatives must be included in the EIS is *NRDC v Morton*.[23] The impact statement must discuss all reasonable alternatives within the jurisdiction of any part of the federal government, even if a particular alternative is outside the authority of the specific agency in charge of the project. The court also held that the EIS must discuss the environmental effects of all the reasonable alternatives. The test for deciding these issues is whether a reasonable person would think that an alternative was sufficiently significant to warrant extended discussion.[24]

---

20 As noted earlier, when this specific form of environmental assessment is involved, the term will be capitalized or the abbreviation EA will be used, as opposed to the use of the term as a generic description of project assessment.

21 CEQ, *Effectiveness Study*, n. 9 above, 19.

22 The CEQ has attempted to clarify both the timing and scope issues. The current regulation, 40 C.F.R. s 1508.23, defines the term "proposal" as follows: " 'Proposal' exists at that stage in the development of an action when an agency subject to the Act has a goal and is actively preparing to make a decision on one or more alternative means of accomplishing that goal and the effects can be meaningfully evaluated." Other CEQ regulations make it clear that the EIS should be prepared early enough so that it can serve practically as an important contribution to the decision-making process, not simply to rationalize or justify decisions already made: 40 C.F.R. s 1502.5. The CEQ regulations also require the EIS to consider (a) connected actions which are closely related, (b) actions which may have a cumulative effect with the proposed action under consideration, and (c) similar actions that should be considered together in view of other reasonably foreseeable or proposed agency action: 40 C.F.R. s 1508.25.

23 *NRDC v Morton* 458 F.2d 827 (D.C. Cir. 1972).

24 Ibid. This test was endorsed by the Supreme Court in *Vermont Yankee Nuclear Power Corp. v NRDC* 435 U.S. 519 (1978).

If the EIS is to be more than a checklist of alternative actions, the consequences of each alternative must be discussed in detail. One frequently litigated issue is whether the discussion of the environmental impacts of the alternatives was adequate. In deciding which impacts must be discussed, the test once again is the "rule of reason." Speculative impacts need not be discussed. Much the same is true for the EA in situations where the agency does not find a need for a full-scale EIS.

Agencies have also relied increasingly on promises of mitigation to avoid the need to prepare an EIS. "Mitigated FONSIs" are increasingly common, meaning approval for projects which would otherwise have significant environmental impacts except for the use of mitigation measures.[25] This development can be seen as an effort to evade the statutory requirements, but it can also be seen in a positive light.

The use of the mitigated FONSI is the best evidence we have that NEPA is actually altering agency decision-making and improving environmental performance. Agencies are redefining projects to include mitigation measures that reduce adverse environmental impacts below the "significant" threshold. Moreover, through use of the mitigated FONSI, they are presumably achieving these environmentally beneficial results at a lower cost and in less time than would be required if they went through the full-blown EIS process. That is a positive outcome, not a negative one. It is evidence that NEPA works.[26] The following table may be helpful for the reader who is confused by the jargon:

Table 8.1 US environmental assessment terminology

Abbreviation	Term	Meaning
CEQ	Council on Environmental Quality	Executive office with loose oversight over impact statements
NEPA	National Environmental Policy Act	Statute creating modern environmental assessments
EIS	Environmental Impact Statement	Full-scale evaluation of impacts
EA	Environmental Assessment	Streamlined evaluation
FONSI	Finding of No Significant Impact	Formal finding that no EIS is required
Mitigated FONSI	Mitigated Finding of No Significant Impact	Finding that no EIS is required by significant impacts that would otherwise exist are eliminated through mitigation measures
DEIS	Draft EIS	The initial version of the EIS for public comment
CEQA	California Environmental Quality Act	The state law that mandates environmental assessments

25 Ibid, 348.
26 Ibid, 348–349.

Compared to other environmental statutes, NEPA is strikingly simple and seemingly mild. It provides neither for elaborate penalties or enforcement mechanisms, nor for complex regulatory standards. Nevertheless, it became an important tool of environmentalists soon after it was passed. The statute is also thought to have had an important effect on decision-making by agencies, though rigorous empirical evidence on this question does not exist.[27]

Implementation of NEPA has shifted over time. There has been a long-term decline in the number of EISs, with a corresponding expansion of EAs. This is a ground for concern because EAs are, as we will see, even less accessible to the public. In recent years, the number of full-scale EISs has declined, so that we are seeing only about 250 projects with EISs annually compared to about fifty thousand environmental assessments leading to FONSIs.[28] The bulk of federal EISs (70 percent) have come from four agencies: the Department of Transportation, the Department of Agriculture, the Department of the Interior, and the Army Corps of Engineers.[29] The average cost of an EIS at DOE was $6 million, whereas EAs cost around $100,000.[30]

In terms of information production, this means that a full-scale evaluation of environmental impacts is performed for approximately 250 projects a year. But in two hundred times as many cases, only an EA is performed. In an unknown percentage of those EAs, the justification for finding no significant impact is based on projections about the effectiveness of mitigation measures. As we will see later, however, there is at best haphazard monitoring of the success of mitigation measures, and even if there were compulsory monitoring, the difficulty of obtaining the EAs themselves would prevent any systematic comparison of predictions with outcomes.

In short, the following information is contained in environmental assessments, at varying levels of scope and detail: descriptions of current environmental conditions at project sites; projected impacts of the proposed project and of reasonable alternatives; and predictions about the effectiveness of various mitigation measures. Although NEPA could be interpreted to impose substantive policies on agencies, the US Supreme Court has interpreted the statute merely as imposing a disclosure requirement.[31] This development makes the accessibility of environmental assessments all the more important. If NEPA were considered to be primarily a form of policy guidance to agencies, the availability of

---

27 See Findlay *et al*, n. 19 above, at 212–213.
28 Karkkainen, "Whither NEPA," n. 5 above, 347–349.
29 National Academy of Public Administration, *Managing NEPA at the Department of Energy* July 6,1998, available via www.eh.doe.gov/nepa/process/napa_rep/napa_rep.html.
30 Ibid, 26–27.
31 *Robertson v Methow Valley Citizens Council*, 490 U.S. 332 (1989): "Although these procedures are almost certain to affect the agency's substantive decision, it is now well settled that NEPA itself does not mandate particular results, but simply prescribes the necessary process"; and see *Strycker's Bay Neighborhood Council Inc. v Karlen*, 444 U.S. 223 (1980), the agency "considered the environmental consequences of its decision ... NEPA requires no more."

information to the public might be considered a secondary consideration. But since NEPA does not function as a binding substantive directive to agencies, but merely as an information forcing mechanism, availability to the public is a central issue.[32] What is the point of a disclosure statute that does not in fact make information available in usable form to the public?

State environmental assessments

As Karkkainen explains: "Whatever its faults, real or imagined, NEPA is without question the most widely emulated of the major US environmental laws. It has inspired dozens of 'little NEPAs' at the state and local levels, numerous progeny around the globe, and countless imitators in other fields".[33] For purposes of manageability, we will focus on the system used in the most populous state, California. The California system is explicated in Figure 8.2.

California requires an impact statement "whenever it can be fairly argued on the basis of substantial evidence that the project may have significant environmental impact."[34] Thus, an impact report is required if there is substantial evidence of significant impact, even if there is also substantial evidence for the opposite conclusion.[35] This is more expansive than the federal standard, which allows the agency to determine that impacts are insignificant despite conflicting evidence so long as the agency's determination is reasonable. The output of impact statements is actually higher in California than at the federal level for the entire nation. In 2004, over 600 draft environmental impact reports were filed in California.[36]

Moreover, a California statute directs agencies not to approve projects "if there are feasible alternatives or feasible mitigation measures available which would substantially lessen the significant environmental effects of such projects."[37] Thus, unlike NEPA, the California statute has some substantive "bite" – it actually provides a constraint on agency decisions, not merely a mechanism for developing information.

---

32 EISs are generally available by making a specific request under the Freedom of Information Act unless one of FOIA's specific exemptions applies. One exemption that may have increasing relevant to EISs was recently enacted to limit public disclosure of "critical infrastructure." See C Coglianese, R Zeckhauser, and E Parson, *Seeking Truth for Power: Informational Strategy and Regulatory Policymaking*, 89 *Minnesota Law Review*. 277, 338 (2004), discussing the critical infrastructure exemption.

33 Karkkainen, n. 4 above, 905.

34 *No Oil Inc. v City of Los Angeles* 520 P.2d 77 (Cal. 1975).

35 *Heninger v Board of Supervisers of Santa Clara County* 224 Cal. Rptr. 409 (Cal. App. 1986). For further discussion, see Daniel B Mandelker, *NEPA Law and Litigation: The National Environmental Policy* Act s.12.06[2] (1984 with updates).

36 State Clearing House Newsletter, 1–15 April 2005, 2, available at http://opr.ca.gov/clearinghouse/PDFs/April_1-15-2005.pdf. Further statistics from this report are found in Appendix A.

37 Cal. Pub. Res. Code s 21081.

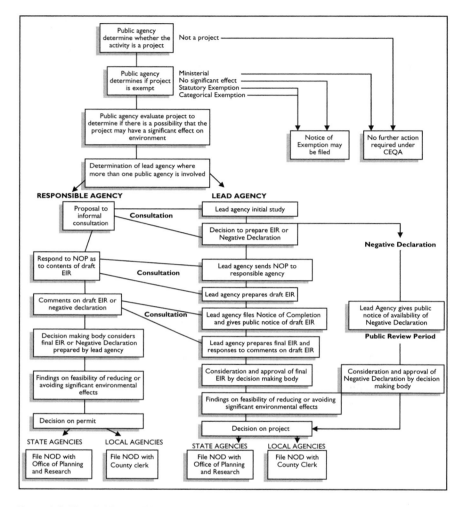

Figure 8.2 The California EA system.

Source: California Resources Agency's General Council. http://ceres.ca.gov/topic/env_law/ceqa/flowchart/index.html.

Another significant difference between the federal and California systems relates to coverage. The federal system is limited to projects with some significant degree of involvement by the federal government. The state system is much broader and includes thousands of routine land use determinations throughout the state. Notably, under California law, local governments such as municipalities are covered by the EIS requirement, which means that most building and land use decisions are subject to environmental review.[38] A third significant difference relates to monitoring. Unlike the federal government, California makes at least some effort at monitoring the success of mitigation; the federal system takes it on faith.

California requires monitoring and reporting when mitigation measures are implemented.[39] This requirement has been at least moderately effective. A 1999 survey[40] found that three-quarters of planning departments routinely require monitoring with environmental impact reports, and half have performances standards or thresholds of significance. By 1999, about a third of agencies had taken enforcement actions for failure to comply with mitigation requirements, and an equal number have procedures for modifying mitigation measures if they turn out to be infeasible. Some agencies maintain lists of standard mitigation measures, but it is recommended that agencies establish feedback procedures to track the relative success of mitigation measures and modify future use.[41]

Given the increased centrality of mitigation at both the state and federal levels, the California monitoring requirement could provide a key information source about the success of mitigation measures. Of course, for that to happen, both the mitigation measures and the monitoring data would have to be accessible by the public. In this respect, as in others, it turns out that the current data system is sadly defective.

Informational inadequacies of the current system

Both federal and state governments have developed elaborate methods of environmental assessment. The cost of the process runs into hundreds of millions of dollars annually. The output is many thousands of pages of documents, containing all manner of information and forecasting of impacts. Surely, one might suppose, this would be a treasure trove of environmental information for policymakers, researchers, and the public. Alas, this supposition would be sadly mistaken.

As observed in the Introduction, the immense efforts that go into producing assessments are largely wasted from the point of view of informing the public or future researchers. The problem is that the information is difficult if not impossible to access. As we will see, assessments are often impossible to locate at all, and only sporadically available in digital form. Ideally, environmental assessments should be readily accessed through a searchable data base, with links to other geographic and environmental information. This ideal is far removed from reality.

---

38 See D Sive, "'Little NEPAs' and Their Environmental Impact Assessment Procedures," ALI-ABA, 16–20 June 2000, 7.

39 Karkkainen, "Smarter NEPA," n. 4 above, 952.

40 See Association of Environmental Professionals, Mitigation Practices Task Force, *Environmental Mitigation Monitoring and Reporting Under the California Environmental Quality Act (CEQA)* December 15, 2000, 8.

41 Ibid, 31.

These flaws are significant for several reasons. First, public accountability is undermined when environmental assessments are not easily obtained, and when their predictions about project impacts cannot be compared with the actual impacts after the project is implemented. (To take a current example, it would be very useful to see the environmental assessments for the New Orleans levee system, which failed so badly during Hurricane Katrina.) Experience with the Toxic Release Inventory shows that public disclosures, especially when they can be easily obtainable on the Internet, can have a strong disciplining effect on private firms.[42] A similar increase in accountability might be seen if environmental assessments were easily accessible. Second, the government itself can neither readily assess the reliability of its predictions regarding impacts, nor can the researchers. Without this kind of feedback, improving the accuracy of our predictions, or even assigning meaningful ranges of uncertainty, is not feasible. Third, information developed for individual environmental assessments is lost. This may require a duplication of efforts in future assessments, or it may result in gaps in our knowledge of ecosystems and specific sites.

In assessing the current system, we can ask four key questions. First, can an environmental assessment be accessed readily, or is it necessary to engage a lengthy document request in order to obtain it? Second, can relevant environmental assessments be identified easily by someone with an interest in a particular region, ecosystem, or environmental asset, such as a type of wildlife? Third, is information about specific sites integrated so as to build a picture of the region in which they are located? Finally, are there links to later information concerning the site, such as monitoring of mitigation measures or other available data such as satellite photos? The current system flunks in all four of these dimensions.

Access issues

In today's digital world, one would expect that environmental assessments would be readily accessible. After all, it is practically a cliché that "wireless communications and the Internet portend the 'end of distance' and the 'collapse of time'. . . . Links to virtually anyone on the planet, or to data sets anywhere in the world, are now available at any time at very low cost."[43] This is undoubtedly true for many forms of information – but not for environmental assessments.[44]

---

42 For a thorough study of TRI, see J T Hamilton, *Regulation Through Revelation: The Origins, Politics, and Impacts of the Toxics Release Inventory Programme* (Cambridge: Cambridge University Press, 2005). As the first sentence of the book observes: "[t]he operation of the Toxics Release Inventory shows how freely information can circulate in the Internet age." ibid, ix.

43 Esty, *Environmental Protection*, n. 10 above, 169.

44 For a detailed discussion of the access issues, see M Gerard and M Herz, "Harnessing Information Technology to Improve the Environmental Impact Review Process" (2003) 12 *New York University Environment Law Journal* 18. Gerard and Herz provide some arguments for why electronic posting of EISs should be considered mandatory under current law. Unfortunately, agencies seem not to have taken these arguments to heart.

Not only is the information in the assessments hard to access, but there is not even a system for tracking what assessments have been performed. Federal environmental assessments and FONSIs are not subject to any formal reporting requirement, and even the agencies themselves make little effort to track them.

> Perhaps the most important reason that Environmental Assessments and FONSIs have been so little explored in the legal and policy literature is that they are maddeningly difficult to ferret out.... [A]n EA (whether it results in a FONSI or a mitigated FONSI) need not be reported to CEQ, EPA, or any other central compiler, nor is Federal Register notice required. In most agencies, even the NEPA compliance officers at agency headquarters do not track or compile EAs and FONSIs, devolving such duties to regional or subregional offices where record keeping may be lax or inconsistent across regions. Thus, in many cases it is difficult, if not impossible, for interested persons even to learn that an EA has been produced, much less to gain access to its contents.[45]

In contrast to EAs and FONSIs, EISs are subject to Federal Register notice requirements and available to the public on request. Yet access to the EIS itself remains difficult.

Electronic access remains more a hope than a reality. In 1995, CEQ activated NEPANet, which it heralded as a "one-stop shop" for NEPA information.[46] But this site does not provide actual access to environmental assessments. The DOE does maintain a site containing some EIS and EA documents, and it is increasingly common for draft EISs to be available online, although not the final product.[47] However, the data base has very limited search capacity.[48] DOE also maintains a page with links to other digital NEPA documents.[49] Many of the links, however, are non-functional. It is unclear whether the site is still under construction or whether it is falling apart.

At least it is possible to find a listing of EISs online. An EPA site provides chronological listings of all draft and final impact statements.[50] This compares favorably to the treatment of EAs. But if users actually want to see the assessments the site offers very little help. Users of the site are advised:

> EPA does not have copies of Environmental Impact Statements (EISs) available for public distribution. Instead, we recommend that you request a copy directly from the agency that prepared the EIS. A good place to start is to telephone the agency "contact person" listed in EPA's weekly Notice of

45 Karkkainen, "Smarter NEPA," n. 4 above, 946.
46 CEQ, *Effectiveness Study*, n. 9 above, 49.
47 http://www.eh.doe.gov/nepa/eis/eis_toc.html.
48 http://www.eh.doe.gov/nepa/eis/eis.htm, allowing searches by title, project number, and state.
49 http://ceq.eh.doe.gov/nepa/documents.htm.
50 http://cfpub.epa.gov/compliance/nepa/current/.

Availability of EISs. In addition, several agencies are publishing entire copies of EISs on the internet (check each agency's website to determine online availability).[51]

Users are also referred to a Northwestern University site, which provides a link to the library's on-line book catalogue and instructions on how to obtain copies through interlibrary loan.[52] The Northwestern site also links to a proprietary database of digests of environmental assessments which is available to Northwestern users.[53]

In addition, approximately a third of current EISs, and some California environmental assessments, are available at the Humboldt State University library.[54] Humboldt State also has an index and detailed abstract, but these are unfortunately available only to university users. It is also possible to search for EISs through the "First.Gov.gov" site by including the phrase "environmental impact statement" with a "subject keyword" in order to find a notice of availability or in some cases online text. EISs as well as a host of other environmental documents relating to Southern Oregon have been digitized,[55] and there may be some other similar collections for specific regions. So bits and pieces of the complete EIS data are available here and there online.

It is tempting to describe access to federal environmental documents as antediluvian. But this would be misleading: Noah's ability to find two members of all extant species strongly suggests that he had access to a much better environmental data base than the federal government currently maintains.

The California system has somewhat similar problems.[56] All draft documents must be submitted to the State Clearinghouse to allow comment by state agencies.[57] As discussed in Appendix B, the Clearinghouse now invites agencies to submit material on CD but requires printed versions of some documents. The Los Angeles public library also maintains a collection of environmental review documents: "There are now nearly 500 EIR listings, ranging from an airport dunes study to the Venice canals rehabilitation, a Warner Ridge business plan and a Wilshire Center and Koreatown redevelopment project."[58] Particularly for projects in Southern California, the library seems to provide a fairly full collection of documents, at least for individuals who are able to physically access the materials.

---

51 http://www.epa.gov/compliance/nepa/obtaineis/index.html.
52 http://www.library.northwestern.edu/transportation/searcheis.html.
53 http://er.library.northwestern.edu/details.php?rid=213948&pn=1, linking to Cambridge Science Abstracts.
54 http://library.humboldt.edu/infoservices/FEIRsandEISs.htm#fedreports.
55 http://soda.sou.edu/bioregion.html.
56 This also seems to be true in the state of New York. See Gerard and Herz, "Harnessing Information Technology," n. 44 above.
57 See wwww.opr.ca.gov/clearinghouse.
58 http://www.lapl.org/resources/guides/environmental.html. While this article was in press, some documents became available through on-line services. See note 14 supra.

The international situation may not be much better. For instance, the Canadian Environmental Assessment Agency maintains a website with summaries and contact information for all environmental assessments.[59] Submitting the final documents to the national clearinghouse is optional.

In short, the general situation is that if you know about a specific project and the agency with jurisdiction, you may be able to locate the environmental assessment, particularly if it is a major project. You may have to pay for copying, travel to a repository, or request a copy through an interlibrary loan system, assuming you have access to a participating library. Thus, getting a look at an environmental assessment can be an arduous process even if you know exactly what you are looking for. But if you do not know in advance the identity of a specific assessment, the difficulties are even greater. Identifying relevant documents is a chancy endeavor. In particular, as we will see, the ability to conduct electronic searches is quite limited.

Searchability

According to a 2003 study:

> Many agencies with NEPA-process tracking systems are planning enhancements, such as searchable libraries of NEPA analytical documents and links to geospatial data and other reference document and studies. Electronically posting and receiving comments and supplementing traditional NEPA document publication and distribution with CD-ROM and Website publication are also being adopted by agencies.[60]

At the federal level, however, the idea of a searchable library of all federal assessments seemingly remains little more than a glimmer in the eye of planners.

California has done somewhat better. The online CEQA database lists all documents that are submitted to the clearinghouse and includes basic information about the planned project.[61] The database has the project title, the name of the lead agencies, and the main environmental issues discussed in the review, but not the full impact statement. Searches can be conducted based on geography, time period, or keywords in the project description:

> [The database] can be a useful source of information for planners, consultants, and project applicants who are preparing new environmental documents [having] search capabilities to find past environmental documents based on any of the variable listed above. The purpose of the database is to

---

59 Karkkainen, "Smarter NEPA," n. 4 above, 950.

60 The NEPA Task Force, *Report to the Council on Environmental Quality: Modernizing NEPA Implementation*, s 1.2, September 2003.

61 http://www.ceqanet.ca.gov/QueryForm.asp.

streamline the environmental document preparation process by following reuse of relevant information from prior documents for similar projects.[62]

Note, however, that the environmental documents themselves are not available on this database. As early as 1996, a biologist wrote:

The Clearinghouse is the one repository to which all EIRs are sent. Regrettably, the Clearinghouse has never functioned as either a repository or a library. One cannot go to the State Clearinghouse and look at an EIR filed in Placer County in 1989. Nor can one search the text of EIRs to determine where pine marten surveys have been performed in California. The data in such EIRs is essentially lost to the professional and citizen community. In practice, each EIR relies in large part on a review – generally through the cultural memory of individuals involved with the project – of relevant EIRs performed during the last several years. In the absence of cultural memory, the EIR starts from scratch to gather and analyze field data, or with a search for titles at the Clearinghouse...Because of the lack of an adequate data tracking system, the substantial professional effort that goes into an EIR is practically lost moments after the document is finalized. [63]

He continued by explaining just why this is so deplorable:

One example of this regrettable loss is in the area of wildlife and natural resources research. In my own field of expertise it is evident that the days when universities and academic institutions performed most of the field surveys and species distribution studies are gone....

In these austere days, university and academic institutions can afford to fund precious little of this kind of basic research. Even the National Biological Survey, chartered with the objective of performing a nationwide census and description of wildlife populations is virtually bankrupt by lack of congressional support. Project developers, both private and public, however, continue to bear the onus of performing baseline biologic research. Every hydroelectric power plant, every lumber plant, every housing subdivision, and every ski area expansion requires that baseline biological surveys be performed and documented in the EIR. The unfortunate aspect is: these

---

62 *California State Clearinghouse Handbook*, January 2005, 16.
63 E J Koford, *Environmental Impact Reports on the Internet* (emphasis in original). He added: "The fundamental vision of CEQA, that this information would be available in a database to avoid delay and substantial duplication of effort has never been realized. Furthermore, the only remaining reliable source of information regarding the extent of our natural resources is being recorded in a book that is not accessible, retrievable or indexed. Remember, the function of the EIR is to document the analysis until the decision is produced. EIRs rarely are preserved more than five years after the project is approved."

documents, termed grey literature are virtually never reported in the professional literature. Since only peer-reviewed professional journals are entered into the substantial academic databases, THERE IS NO RECORD OR INDEX TO THE EIRS THAT CONTAIN THIS INFORMATION.

This situation has not gone completely unnoticed. Presently, California does have plans underway to improve access to documents through LUPIN, the Land Use Planning Information Network, a California Resources Agency program. The goal is "to establish a system for storing, making available, and providing public electronic accessibility through the CERES web information reported in environmental assessment documents that come through the State Clearinghouse, federal agencies, and related entities."[64] However, the user who attempts to make use of LUPIN for this purpose is bound for disappointment. Although one link reads "Search for EIR's deposited with Los Angeles Public Central and Branch Libraries,"[65] the only result is to pull up a "page unavailable" message.[66] Another proposal, which is reprinted in Appendix C, calls for making documents available online, with a GIS site showing the locations of the projects.

Recall that many environmental assessments rely on projections about mitigation efforts in order to avoid full-scale investigation of impacts. Yet there is no way even to identify projects in which specific forms of mitigation have been used, let alone to follow up by trying to monitor the success of mitigation. Similarly, there is no way to identify assessments dealing with particular species of plants or animals, specific soil or vegetation types, or even assessments of the same region at different times or by different agencies.[67]

Integration

Imagine a map of a city, watershed, or forest. The map would be dotted with sites that had been subjected to environmental assessments: some small dots for minor projects, large dots for bigger ones, and large circles for programmatic assessments. Yet each dot would exist in its own sealed universe, with no integration of information between the various environmental assessments:

In a metropolitan area or major natural resource area, there may have been hundreds of Federal and state impact studies conducted since 1970. These

---

64 http://www.lapl.org/resources/guides/environmental.html.
65 http://ceres.ca.gov/planning/ead/.
66 http://dbase1.lapl.org/pages/envimp.htm.
67 A similar problem exists for agencies engaged in rulemaking: "Many agencies keep compliance or incident data, but the staff who write rules often have to go out to regional offices to get this information. Data mining technologies, which range from simple web search engines to more sophisticated multi-database search and integration systems could enable rule writers to learn from the various data sources available throughout their agencies." See Coglianese, *E-Rulemaking*, n. 11 above, 369.

stand-alone reports consist of a diverse range of secondary data and new information created for the particular study. When the review is completed, the report is archived. This approach is not designed to promote community learning over time, wherein each statement contributes new transactional updates to a shared knowledge base. This one-stop approach of the impact statement is highly wasteful of scarce environmental informational expenditures, and the lack of a managed information framework condones the mediocre predictive quality that typifies many analyses.[68]

The absence of an integrated database may be related to a perceived lack of consistency and learning for EISs. A recent study concludes that

[t]here appears to be very little learning from previous years of DEIS preparation in [ratings for] informational quality of environmental impact of the preferred alternative... Documents are not of higher quality now than in the past. In fact, there were more top ratings of DEIS in the 1970s than today, even with standardizing for the large volume of documents in the 1970s vs. later years.[69]

Integrating information between documents is made difficult by the idiosyncratic nature of EISs. EISs differ both within and between agencies, often making it impossible "to make meaningful comparisons, or to aggregate or synthesize information across multiple EISs, over time, or among agencies with disparate NEPA practices."[70] In addition, because agencies buy software and hardware independently of each other, interoperability can be a serious problem.[71]

Follow-up

The one-shot nature of environmental assessment has been a frequent source of criticism. As a result, the assessment process ignores "unanticipated changes in environmental conditions, inaccurate predictions, or subsequent information that might affect the original environmental protections."[72] Follow-up is particularly important in connection with adaptive management:

Adaptive management emphasizes formal experimentation with replicates, controls, and extensive monitoring.... Adaptive management is a knowledge

---

68 J Felleman, *Deep Information: The Role of Information Policy in Environmental Sustainability* (Greenwich, Connecticut: Ablex Publishing Corporation, 1997), 175.

69 K Tzoumis and L Finegold, *Looking at the Quality of Draft Environmental Impact Statements Over Time in the United States: Have Ratings Improved?* (2000) 20 *Environmental Impact Assessment Review* 557, 576.

70 Karkkainen, "Smarter NEPA," n. 4 above, 923.

71 The NEPA Task Force, *Modernizing NEPA Implementation*, n. 60 above, s 1.8.3.

72 Ibid, 44.

driven system, and environmental impact statements can be a central supplier of the relevant data.... Because environmental impact statements continually revisit the environmental health of particular regions, environmental assessments build up the knowledge base as they accumulate over time.[73]

The NEPA does not require agencies to perform later checks on their predictions, and agencies do not generally do so.[74] What evidence does exist is not reassuring. Studies of the predictive accuracy of EISs find that the predictions are often too vague to be tested at all. Among those that can be verified, the results are no more reassuring, with fewer than one out of three being substantially accurate.[75] This is not a peculiarly American problem – studies from the United Kingdom and Canada produce similar results.[76] In contrast, however, the Netherlands does require systematic monitoring of project impacts, although compliance may be spotty.[77] Case studies indicate that "better prediction products arise more from the feedback between predictions and experience than from the introduction of more sophisticated predictive methodologies."[78] Without the check provided by such feedback, overly optimistic predictions can result from the "economic and political pressures placed on the technical consultants and the government managers, which lead them to use inadequate models and to misuse their predictive results."[79] As one study puts it:

In the absence of any inducements linked to actual performance, a decisionmaker is likely to be averse to the substantial risk that an audit will prove embarrassing by documenting a project's shortcomings. Thus, with few positive incentives to self-evaluation and substantial risks, agency managers seem to live by the maxim that ignorance is bliss.[80]

The same study found only a third of predictions in EISs were "particularly accurate", most of the remainder being "either accurate solely by virtue of the vagueness of the forecast or somewhat inaccurate in various complicated ways."[81]

---

73 J F C DiMento and H Ingram, "Science and Environmental Decision Making: The Potential Role of Environmental Impact Assessment in the Pursuit of Appropriate Information" (2005) 45 *Natural Resources Journal* 283, 299.

74 Karkkainen, "Smarter NEPA," n. 4 above, 927.

75 Ibid, 928.

76 Ibid, 928–929.

77 Ibid, 951.

78 D Sarewitz, R A Pielke Jr, and R Byerly Jr (2000) *Prediction: Science, Decision Making, and the Future of Nature* (Washington, DC: Island Press) 369.

79 R E Moran, *"Is This Number to Your Liking? Water Quality Predictions in Mining Impact Studies"* in Sarewitz *et al*, ibid, 187.

80 P J Culhane, H Paul Friesema, and J A Beecher, *Forecasts and Environmental Decisionmaking: The Content and Predictive Accuracy of Environmental Impact Statements* (Boulder: Westview Press, 1987), 146.

81 Ibid, 253.

It should be noted that the unreliability of the predictions makes the use of mitigated FONSIs a bit suspect, since we cannot have any real confidence that the mitigation measures will actually reduce the impacts below the "significance" level.

Another reason for follow-up is that mitigation plans are not always implemented.[82] Most agencies seem to have no formal procedures for ensuring that mitigation measures are actually put in place, although the US Army has recently taken the lead by imposing such a requirement.[83]

One solution to this problem is to impose formal monitoring requirements on agencies.[84] While this possible solution has appeal, it may be too expensive to institute across-the-board; after all, "[m]onitoring is not free."[85] An emerging model of assessment is tied with adaptive management, which involves a cycle of planning, implementation, and reappraisal.[86] Of course, this process can only be effective if the proposals, predictions, and appraisals are all available for study.

Even where formal monitoring processes are not in place it might be possible to perform some checks on the success of mitigation. For example, a later assessment for the same site or a nearby one might contain evidence about conditions at the site that could be used to gauge the success of mitigation. Or other public information might be linked to the original assessment, in order to make judgments about the success of mitigation. But since it is often impossible to locate even the original assessment itself to determine what mitigation was planned, actually determining the success of mitigation remains a pipe-dream.

The following table summarizes the status quo as of early 2006:

Table 8.2 Current availability of environmental assessments

Type of assessment	Tracking system	Archive	Online availability	Searchability of database
Federal EAs and FONSIs	None	None	None	None
Federal EISs	EPA maintains chronological listing	North western University Library	Some on DOE or other agency websites	Nw. Univ. collection indexed through library catalogue
California	State Clearinghouse	L.A. Public Library (partial)	None	Document summaries searchable by keyword

82 R G Dreher, *NEPA Under Siege: The Political Assault on the National Environmental Policy Act*, (Washington, DC: Georgetown University, 2005), 21.
83 Ibid, 22.
84 Karkkainen, "Smarter NEPA," n. 4 above, 938.
85 Ibid, 940.
86 See D P Lawrence, *Environmental Impact Assessment: Practical Solutions to Recurrent Problems* (Chichester: Wiley, 2003), 464–487.

The potential of digital environmental assessments

At the risk of mixing metaphors, environmental assessments might be considered a train wreck on the information superhighway. We have vast quantities of information that are for all practical purposes lost soon after they are created. But wait, you say, this is the twenty-first century. Surely this problem can be cured. The answer is that, yes, of course, the technology exists. We could make environmental assessments a critical part of our environmental information infrastructure. Simply putting the information into digital form and placing it online would be a major breakthrough. And we could well do more, using geographic information systems that would allow users to access a host of other relevant data. As CEQ has observed:

> [T]echnological innovations are improving the ability of analysts to obtain and manipulate data. The most promising technologies are modern computers, internet communications, and geographic information systems (GIS). GIS provides the analyst with management of large data sets, data overlay, and analysis of development and natural resource patterns, trends analysis, mathematical impact modeling with locational data, habitat analysis, aesthetic analysis, and improved public consultation. Using GIS has the potential to facilitate the efficient completion of projects while building confidence in the NEPA process.[87]

This technology creates exciting prospects for transforming access to environmental assessments.

Access and searchability

The potential benefits of making environmental assessments available online are obvious. First, it would make it possible for the public to readily obtain copies of information about projects affecting them. In theory, this information can be obtained already, if only by making a formal request under the Freedom of Information Act. But there is a vast difference between making information available to the strongly motivated, legally informed observer and making it available to the average member of the public. It is somewhat pathetic that routine information about high school sporting events is easily available while barriers must be leaped to find out about local environmental issues.[88]

Second, online information would become immediately searchable. Even without being organized into a formal data base, search engines such as Google would make it possible to access information through the Internet. This would

---

87 CEQ, *Effectiveness Study*, n. 9 above, 28.
88 Gerrard and Herz, "Harnessing Information Technology," n. 44 above, make a compelling case for electronic posting as a means of public access.

likely be a somewhat inefficient process. The researcher seeking assessments concerning a particular species or project type might have to work through considerable extraneous information. Searches would be expedited by creating a database with its own search engine, designed to efficiently retrieve information from environmental assessments.

Third, follow-up on mitigation would be much easier if the environmental assessments themselves were readily available. This would make it possible to quickly determine what mitigation measures had been promised and what the predicted results were supposed to be. This is the necessary precondition for any effort at follow up: you cannot follow up on predictions whose existence is unknown to you, or monitor mitigation promises that have vanished into the archives.

Fourth, the environmental assessment process, like the common law, consists of a series of individual decisions that may cumulatively establish the contours of accepted practice.[89] Just as the publication of opinions accelerated the development of the common law, so making environmental assessments available on line will help build a body of known "precedents" for reviewing environmental impacts. Similarly, making assessments readily accessible and searchable would prompt the emergence of "best practices" standards based on the diverse approaches taken by different agencies.[90]

There should be nothing controversial about the recommendation that we establish online archives for environmental assessments.[91] Surely the idea of putting public documents on the Internet should not be a controversial one.[92] It is somewhat astounding that environmental assessments are not already available online. After all, virtually everything else conceivable is already only a few

---

89 See E Bregman and A Jacobson, "Environmental Performance Review: Self-Regulation in Environmental Law" in G Teubner, L Farmer, and D Murphy (eds), *Environmental Law and Ecological Responsibility* (Chichester: Wiley, 1994), 230–232.

90 The emergence of best practice guidance in partially decentralized systems is explored in J Scott and J Holder, "Law and New Environmental Governance in the European Union," UCL Workshop, *Law and New Approaches to Governance*, May 2006, available via http://www.ucl. ac.uk/laws/clge/docs/Scott%20and%20Holder.pdf.

91 DiMento and Ingram, "Science and Environmental Decision making", n. 73 above, 300, recommend the creation of regional clearinghouses/repositories for environmental information and data, so that assessments can be grounded "in a well-structured regional database of environmental quality information." The Internet would provide the most accessible form of such a clearinghouse. As DiMento and Ingram put it, the "benefits of Internet access are well known: the power of retrieval, the access to immense amounts of information, the ability to categorize and to benefit from the categorization of others . . . ." ibid, 303. As they also point out, data quality assurance is important. One advantage of using environmental assessments is that they have already gone through a vetting process.

92 The most obvious solution would be for the government to maintain the website. It might also be possible, however, for NGOs to undertake this role. For example, a conservation group now maintains extensive online information about endangered species and their habitats. See http://www.natureserve.org.

keystrokes away, from maps of distant cities and recipes for exotic dishes to every imaginable variety of pornography. Why not environmental assessments?

Integration with GIS

Creating a database of the kinds of documents we are already producing would be a great step. But we could actually do much more than that. Geographic information systems (GIS) make it possible to produce environmental assessments in a much more useful form and to link them with other relevant information, in a way that could transform the usefulness of environmental assessments.[93]

The GIS is an increasingly well-known concept. One of the most popular and accessible forms of GIS has been provided by Google:

> The idea is simple. It's a globe that sits inside your PC. You point and zoom to anyplace on the planet that you want to explore. Satellite images and local facts zoom into view. Tap into Google search to show local points of interest and facts. Zoom to a specific address to check out an apartment or hotel. View driving directions and even fly along your route.[94]

Viewers can also superimpose other layers, such as road maps, shopping locations, parks, and other facilities. Microsoft has a similar, although as yet less elaborate, site.[95] All of this is fun and moderately useful, but it only scratches the surface of GIS.[96]

A couple of examples may help illustrate the environmental applications of GIS. In the UK, the Nuclear Industry Radioactive Waste Executive[97] has used GIS to help identify suitable radioactive waste disposal sites. The first step was

---

93 As DiMento and Ingram, "Science and Environmental Decision Making," n. 73 above, 303, explain, "GIS can visually represent environmental impact and baseline information in ways that are understandable to the participating public and to decision makers ... GIS can plot where controversial projects and facilities are sited and where others are being considered."

94 http://earth.google.com/earth.html.

95 See http://local.live.com.

96 Note the following from a press interview with the originator of Google Earth: " 'A lot of good things come out of making information available', he said, and proceeded to list a few: 'disaster relief, land conservation and forest management for fighting wildfires.' " See K Hafner and S Rai, *Government's Tremble at Google's Bird's-Eye View*, New York Times, December 20 2005. As the title of the article indicates, a number of governments are concerned by the availability of information through Google Earth. The best response seems to have come from an analyst who said: "When you have multiple eyes in the sky, what you're doing is creating a transparent globe where anyone can get basic information about anyone else ... Times are changing, and the best thing to do is adapt to the advances in technology." ibid. For further discussion of the application of GIS to environmental issues, see R Goldstein, "Putting Environmental Law on the Map: A Spatial Approach to Environmental Law Using GIS" in J Holder and C Harrison (eds), *Law and Geography* (Oxford: Oxford University Press, 2003).

97 Hereafter "NIREX."

to establish digitalized "data layers" based on maps showing geology, transport networks, conservation areas, and population statistics. These layers were refined, for example, by identifying which geological conditions were suitable for waste disposal sites. Finally, GIS software was used to combine the layers, producing a map that showed all of the relevant factors. One advantage of this technique, as opposed to the use of paper maps and documents, is that the map can be modified in order to identify the effects of changes in siting criteria or to include updated information.[98]

Another example comes from the Czech Republic. GIS was used to integrate information about the Zdarke Vrchy region as a basis for planning. The GIS integrated data from maps, aerial and satellite images, field studies, pollution monitoring, and socioeconomic data. To help identify conservation sites, scientists were asked to identify the soil types, topography, land uses, and drainage systems that were relevant for water retention and flow control. An iterative process then took place, where the scientists used the GIS to study existing water retention zones, the results were used to develop a model, and the model was used to identify additional sites suitable for water flow control.[99]

The GIS is still under development. Two of the biggest challenges are to move from two to three-dimensional mapping and to include a temporal dimension so that changes over time can be easily tracked. Moreover, better modeling of the ways that different features interact is needed.[100] Even today, however, GIS is beginning to find important uses in environmental assessment. For example, in one use of GIS for environmental assessment, the area was broken into cells of areas with similar vegetation, climate, and soils. Then a model was used to predict, on a cell-by-cell basis, the growth and ageing of a forest, including the size and distribution of each forest type. Those calculations in turn were used together with a habitat suitability model to predict impacts on wildlife.[101]

In another instance, the Bureau of Reclamation made good use of GIS in performing an assessment of the operations of the Glen Canyon Dam. Public interest was very high, with more than thirty thousand people commenting on the draft EIS.[102] As CEQ has explained:

> GIS provides the analyst with management of large data sets, data overlay and analysis of development and natural resource patterns, trends analysis,

---

98 I Heywood, S Cornelium, and S Carver, *An Introduction to Geographic Information Systems* (London: Longman, 1998), 5–6.

99 Ibid, 7.

100 Ibid, 246–247, 250.

101 W Eady, "The Use of GIS in Environmental Assessment" (1995) 13 *Impact Assessment* 199, 202. For a brief discussion of possible uses of GIS under NEPA, including linkages with remotely sensed data, see K Markowitz, *Using 21st Century Technologies to Implement NEPA* (SGO026 ALI-ABA 155) (Dec. 2001).

102 CEQ, *Effectiveness Study*, n. 9 above, 26.

mathematical impact modeling with locational data, habitat analysis, aesthetic analysis, and improved public consultation. Using GIS has the potential to facilitate the efficient completion of projects while building confidence in the NEPA process.[103]

Besides the Glen Canyon project, GIS has also been used for the Pacific Northwest Forest Plan and for the Upper Columbia River Basin Study.[104]

The GIS has received enthusiastic reviews because of its ability to catalyze public input:

> According to the Western Governors' Association, GIS is a vital component of successful NEPA processes that address land management decisions because the decisions are spatial and stakeholders relate to location; therefore, location is often the focus of stakeholder comments and concerns. The U.S. Air Force commented that a Website developed by Eglin Air Force Base to accomplish interdisciplinary reviews of environmental impact analyses uses GIS to illustrate proposals. Their GIS also provides simultaneous access to operational and environmental information, thereby increasing awareness of environmental issues.[105]

The GIS technology is not a panacea. There are some subtle pitfalls. Source maps often do not contain adequate quality information, and errors may be compounded when translating existing maps into digital format.[106] In addition: [G]eospatial data holdings are widely dispersed. Compiling available data across jurisdictional boundaries is often difficult due to differences in data element definitions, sampling methodologies, spatial and temporal resolution, technology, and standards. Lack of adequate metadata and documentation also inhibits the use of non-Federal information.[107] In an effort to combat this problem, the Office of Management and Budget established the National Spatial Data Infrastructure and the Federal Geographic Data Committee as the coordinating body for geospatial data.[108]

California has been a leader in the use of GIS. One project involved the creation of a GIS layer, containing almost 1500 natural resource projects.[109] Another mapped natural resource values and conservation opportunities for 6500 square

103 Ibid, 28.
104 Ibid.
105 The NEPA Task Force, *Modernizing NEPA Implementation*, n. 60 above, s 1.4.1.
106 Felleman, *Deep Information*, n. 67 above, 69.
107 The NEPA Task Force, *Modernizing NEPA Implementation*, n. 60 above, s 1.3.2.
108 Ibid, s 1.3.3.
109 C D Shook, *Applied Geographic Information Systems in Cooperative Natural Resources Projects: A California Example* (February 1, 1999), http://repositories.cdlib.org;/jmie/ice/icepubs/Shook1999a.

miles in the Sacramento area.[110] Much of this work is now publicly available. For instance, one site provides complete information relating to range, habitat, spawning, management plans, and land uses for key species of fish.[111] California is actively engaged in upgrading its GIS resources. The California Geographic Information Association is a non-profit, state-wide organization formed in 1994, devoted to improved sharing and use of geographic information.[112]

The GIS offers the prospect of making environmental assessments much more user friendly. It can also be used as a basis for linking assessments with other maps and data sources. We are just at the beginning of this important development in environmental assessment.

Not every environmental assessment may be a good fit with GIS because of the multiple scales on which "proposals for major federal actions" operate. Some are site-specific projects, and these seem the easiest to integrate into GIS as "dots on a map." But some EISs operate on much larger spatial scales or deal with issues that lack specific geographic locations, such as projected new technologies. These EISs do not fit easily into the "dots on a map" paradigm. There also been a movement toward the use of "strategic" assessments at the broadest policy level, based on the argument that project-based EISs tends to overlook or underestimate cumulative and synergistic effects among multiple actions. Thus, there may be some limitations on our ability to capture all relevant environmental information in GIS-mappable form. GIS is well-suited, however, for information about the urban and natural landscapes of the world. It may provide an alternative way of capturing cumulative and synergistic effects of multiple projects while maintaining the advantages of site-specific decision-making.

Some of the potential of GIS can be seen in the Everglades restoration process,[113] which seems on the way to achieving a GIS-based information management for EA/EIS purposes. The South Florida Water Management District[114] and the Army Corps of Engineers are the lead agencies in the main part of the restoration effort, the Comprehensive Everglades Restoration Plan; they share data on a GIS-based system that is also used by independent scientists, the federal EPA and its state equivalent, and many other participants in the project.[115]

---

110   M C McCoy, J F Quinn, and N B Kalman, *Identifying Environmental and Agricultural Values and Opportunities for Regional Planning: A GIS Approach* (October 1,2002), http://repositories. cdlib.org/jmie/ice/icepubs/McCoy2002a.

111   http://www.calfish.org/DesktopDefault.aspx?tabId=64#any_URL.

112   See http://www.cgia.org/.

113   http://www.evergladesplan.org/facts_info/science_maps.cfm.

114   http://www.sfwmd.gov/site/index.php?id=40.

115   For example, a project map allows viewers to locate projects, retrieve project information, print custom-made maps, and link to descriptive project web pages. In addition, the interface provides a legend listing map features, buttons for map navigation and querying, and a locator tool that selects and zooms to specific projects. http://www.evergladesplan.org/pm/projects/cerp_gis.cfm.

Beyond using GIS to present EIS information, GIS is used to actually conduct the environmental impact analyses.[116]

Dynamic updating

The technology for obtaining environmental data is rapidly improving. Some of the emerging possibilities include the use of mobile platforms for measuring air pollution, the use of personal exposure monitors, and the use of microsensors to monitor hazardous air pollution.[117] Integrating all of this data will not be easy.

Different software systems may generate significantly different maps from the same database.[118] There are additional problems with archival data.[119] Because of some of these problems, the federal government has attempted to standardize content and establish a national clearinghouse for spatial information.[120] If the information generated by impact statements is to have broader use, it too must be subject to standardization:

> Although the impact statement approach is a well-articulated administrative process, it never evolved into an integrated deep information system. There are no standards for the data, maps, or models used in impact statements. Since this information is communicated in hard-copy format, there is no potential for integrating information from multiple statements.[121]

If we combine GIS, dynamic updating, online availability, and search engines, we begin to see the outlines of a global environmental information system. Such a system could link with environmental assessments for specific sites, as well as follow-up information about current environmental conditions and the success of mitigation measures. Researchers, policymakers, and members of the public could readily access this information. Perhaps most importantly, gaps in current information would be immediately apparent in the form of blank areas on the map. This would be a graphic reminder of the need to improve our information systems.

---

116 See e.g. http://www.esri.com/news/arcuser/0701/topogrid.html. As this site explains: The application of GIS technologies in this particular project provided a quick and direct means for water managers to interpret the spatial significance of hydrologic model simulations on water resources. This provided valuable feedback that helped them validate that iterative changes in model simulations were producing the desired effects and evaluate the trade-offs associated with each modification. Adaptation of the model data in GIS further allowed manipulations and overlays of other spatial data to more fully evaluate the hydrologic context and potential impacts on adjoining areas. Future analysis and assessment using GIS will include evaluations of topography and land recontouring to reclaim wetlands.

117 National Research Council, *Air Quality Management*, n. 6 above, 315.

118 Felleman, *Deep Information*, n. 68 above, 66.

119 Ibid, 92.

120 Ibid, 86.

121 Ibid, 175.

Possible pilot projects

The potential for online GIS-based environmental assessment is almost breathtaking. But imagining the possibilities is a long way from actually realizing them. In order to establish the benefits of improvement and to work out many of the technical details, we may need to begin with smaller-scale projects.

One possibility would be to focus on a particular geographic area, such as California or even a sub-region such as Los Angeles.[122] This would make the quantity of data more manageable, and might also make it easier to deal with technical issues such as getting agencies to standardize their data formats. Focusing on a particular watershed might also be useful, given the interaction among effects of particular projects on the watershed as a whole. Alternatively, one might focus on Southern Louisiana. Given the major efforts that will be required to rebuild the city of New Orleans, reconstruct the flood control system, and restore vital wetlands, an integrated digital system of environmental assessments could be of great assistance.

A focus on California would also have another advantage. Recall that California, unlike the federal government, requires monitoring for at least certain kinds of mitigation measures. It would be extremely useful to develop a database containing project assessments along with monitoring data, searchable by type of mitigation, local geographic conditions, and form of environmental impact. Considering how heavily we rely on mitigation efforts as part of project planning, and how heavily mitigation figures in environmental assessments, it is scandalous that we have made no effort to study systematically the effectiveness of mitigation. California could provide a database that would allow researchers to conduct such studies with relative ease.

Another option would be to begin with a specific federal or type of project such as onshore oil facilities. For example, one might begin with DOE, since that agency seems to have made more progress towards organizing and digitizing its assessments. A particularly intriguing possibility might be to start with the area overseen by CalFed.[123] CalFed is a unique cooperative venture of federal and state agencies which has been attempting to address environmental issues in the San Francisco Bay and Sacramento River basin. One advantage would be that the opportunity for federal and state agencies to work together in order to achieve interoperability.

Such a pilot project would not only demonstrate the utility of the concept. It would also provide the opportunity to work out the details and technical issues. This experience could be used as the basis for drafting model

---

122 The California Center for Environmental Law and Policy at Berkeley is currently undertaking a preliminary effort to construct a prototype of such a pilot project, with assistance from the university's GIS Center.

123 CalFed is discussed extensively in J Freeman and D Farber, "Modular Environmental Regulation" (2005) 54 *Duke Law Journal* 795.

regulations for use by federal agencies and state governments in constructing similar databases.

An additional question is whether to make the project retroactive. Should we go back, digitalize and link existing environmental assessments? Or should we work prospectively, by imposing digitalization, format, and archiving requirements on agencies? In the abstract, the retroactive option is more attractive since it captures more data and a longer timeline. But it would also be much more expensive because of the need to locate and digitalize the documents and because the documents themselves would be less standardized.

It is always easy to imagine useful projects. Actually implementing those projects will undoubtedly take a great deal of hard work and technical ingenuity. By beginning with some smaller scale pilot projects, we may be able to learn how to solve the technical problems before scaling up to state-wide or nation-wide coverage.

At either the pilot stage or full-scale implementation, making information available online is only half the battle. Information overload is a very real problem, especially given the massive extent of many impact statements. The key lies in the creation of efficient, user-friendly search engines and GIS links so that people can readily find the information that is most relevant for them. Otherwise, more availability could simply result in more information overload.

Conclusion: towards global environmental assessment

Environmental assessment can become much more powerful if it draws on extant geographic, hydrological, biological, and environmental data, including information from previous assessments that is now lost in agency files. GIS provides a convenient platform for integrating all this. It also provides a convenient way to plot post-decision monitoring data against pre-decision predictions, allowing for error correction, adaptive mitigation, and improvements in our predictive models over time. All of this data is far more powerful and useful as a tool for informed decision-making if it can be combined, distributed, and updated on a regular basis – none of which is contemplated in our current environmental assessment system.

The previous section suggests some modest pilot projects that could lead us toward greatly improved access to environmental assessments. But over the longer term, we can envision a much grander transformation of our access to environmental information.

Google's Earth project promises to create a "globe inside your PC." Current technology allows us to envision something beyond that: a "global ecosystem inside your PC." Imagine, if you will, what it would be like to have instant access to everything we know about the global environment. We can already begin to see the outlines of such an information system, which would provide "one-stop shopping" for all environmental information. Current and historic information about pollution levels, water flows, animal and plant populations, soil, and ecosystem types, would be available through a single interface. The website would incorporate information from environmental assessments of particular sites, and would link to full project assessments for individuals with an interest in particular projects. The site could easily be expanded to include documents compiled under the Endangered Species Act, including biological surveys and habitat conservation plans.

In this perhaps utopian conception, the entire body of environmental information would be readily searchable. The researcher who wanted to know about the use of a particular form of mitigation in particular circumstances would only need to key in a search request to have the data instantly at hand. The public interest group that wanted to know about all government projects of a certain description would have similarly ready access. Historical trends could be easily seen by dynamic maps, flowing between time periods to display changes graphically. Other tools would make it possible to easily graph such information.

Even if this database contained only the kind of information we have currently available, it would transform the business of environmental assessments. But we are actually on the verge of having much broader information instantly available through remote sensing, the use of "smart dust" for environmental monitoring, and other new technologies. So it would be much easier to track conditions at a site or to get a handle on the effectiveness of mitigation measures. Someday, we may have a continuous, real-time view of the global ecosystem – even in the literal sense of being able to zoom in to see small patches of the Amazon or the Himalayas and track their changes over time. Until the virtual global ecosystem has been achieved, we will be more or less groping in the dark as we seek to protect the environment.

It was a major step for environmental awareness when people were able for the first time to see the Earth from space.[124] It would be another major step if they could see the world's environment, zooming in to inspect local environmental conditions and back out again to see global trends. Humans are visual animals, and we can only fully appreciate that which we can see.

The creation of a virtual global ecosystem is years away from achievement, if it happens at all. Sadly, current environmental assessment is largely a creature of the nineteenth century. Hard copies of documents languish in obscure file cabinets, just

---

124 "[T]he ultimate human psychological effect of the first photographs of Earth from the lunar orbiters and the first manned flight to the surface of the Moon in 1969 was far different. The Earth on which life depended seemed more, not less, fragile after these events. By expanding our horizons, we appeared smaller, more vulnerable, and less secure than ever before. It was, of course, hardly news that humankind resided on a planet traveling through space, but those first photographs from space drove home that reality in a way that was both exhilarating and unsettling. The Earth thereafter was frequently characterized as a 'spaceship' and as a 'lifeboat'." See R J Lazarus, *The Making of Environmental Law* (Chicago: University of Chicago Press, 2004), 57.

as they might have done in the days of Dickens' "circumlocution bureau." The government spends millions of dollars to develop information that is supposedly for the benefit of the public, but members of the public have no realistic way of accessing the information. Even the government itself has no way to track environmental assessments or to monitor the accuracy of their predictions.

It would be a substantial achievement simply to make environmental assessments available online. Beyond that, we can begin to combine them with GIS, and we can work on making databases efficiently searchable. We can also try to link assessments with monitoring and other later site information, so that we can begin to evaluate our predictions and mitigation measures. Unlike the "global ecosystem in your PC," none of this is particularly visionary or utopian. The technology is within reach; what is required is the effort and resources to apply that technology.

We should not underestimate the barriers to even modest improvements in our environmental information infrastructure. Yet, the potential for improvement is so great that these difficulties are well worth overcoming. Some realistic first steps can be made in the near future, and their success may pave the road for further progress. If we cannot be sure of solving the world's environmental problems, surely a precondition to solving them is at least to see them. And if we cannot fully control or predict the environmental impacts of projects, at the very least we should be able to examine these environmental assessments at will. Only then will environmental assessment begin to fulfill its true promise.

Appendix A[125]

MEMORANDUM
Governor's Office of Planning and Research
State Clearinghouse

Date: December 5, 2003

To: All CEQA Lead Agencies

From: Terry Roberts, Director, State Clearinghouse

Re: Submission of Electronic CEQA Documents to State Clearinghouse

In order to take advantage of the cost and time savings associated with electronic documents, the State Clearinghouse will accept electronic documents under

---

125 Drawn from State Clearinghouse Report, n. 36 above, 1.

the following conditions:

1. Electronic documents shall be on CD, and the file format shall be either Adobe PDF or Microsoft Word.
2. For EIRs, each CD must be accompanied by a printed copy of the Executive Summary. This allows the State Clearinghouse and the reviewing agencies to efficiently route the document to the proper persons.
3. Negative Declarations and Mitigated Negative Declarations will not be accepted on CD. However, any separately bound technical appendices to the document may be submitted on CD.
4. For certain projects, particularly large infrastructure projects such as airport expansions, the State Clearinghouse may request a certain number of hard copies. In addition, the lead agency shall honor a special request from a responsible or trustee agency which requires a hardcopy for purposes of review and comment.
5. This policy does not invalidate CEQA Guideline s 15205, which requires a public agency submitting printed documents to the State Clearinghouse to send, in addition, an electronic copy of the document, if available.

If you have any questions regarding the submission and circulation of environmental documents,please contact the State Clearinghouse at (916) 445–0613 or state.clearinghouse@opr.ca.gov.

Appendix B

Environmental document filings with the state clearinghouse 1999 through 2004

Year	NOP	ND/ MND	EIR	NOD	NOE	EIS	EA	Other	Total document
1999	602	2007	481	1808	2699	22	41	177	7,837
2000	613	2243	475	2580	3840	16	78	386	10,231
2001	703	2612	524	2851	6083	13	75	422	13,283
2002	642	2676	544	3102	5737	14	66	409	13,190
2003	757	2972	577	3243	6078	8	57	360	14,052
2004	766	2903	625	3304	5898	11	55	339	13,901

Key:

NOP	Notice of Preparation
EIR	Draft Environmental Impact Report
ND/MND	Negative Declaration/Mitigated Negative Declaration
NOD	Notice of Determination
NOE	Notice of Exemption
EA	Environmental Assessment (federal)
EIS	Draft Environmental Impact Statement (federal)
OTHER	Other types of documents, including Final EIRs, Early Consultation notice, plans, etc.

Appendix C

RES15 Use technology to streamline the state-level environmental review process

Summary[126]

The California Environmental Quality Act (CEQA) requires the state to review studies that assess the potential environmental impacts of proposed projects. The state is also responsible for posting notices prepared pursuant to CEQA. The state's review and notice posting process is a cumbersome, manual, paper process. This process should be automated to reduce paperwork and streamline the environmental review process.

California environmental quality act

The law that governs environmental review in the state is known as CEQA.[127] CEQA's purpose is to inform decision makers and the public of potential significant environmental impacts of proposed projects. CEQA applies to significant public projects and private development projects that require discretionary governmental approvals.[128]

The public agency legally responsible for complying with CEQA is called the "lead agency." During project development, a lead agency is responsible for the preparation of environmental documents (studies that assess the project's impacts on the community) and making these documents available for public review and comment prior to project approval.[129] For example, an environmental document would assess the noise, traffic, air quality, and aesthetic impacts of a project on the surrounding community, including the impact on biological resources, wetlands, the coastal zone and cultural and historical resources. During the public review period, a public agency or member of the public can submit comments on the environmental document.

In addition to environmental documents, lead agencies also file notices as part of the CEQA review process. Notices inform the public of the action taken on a project. Filing of the notices starts statutorily-defined legal challenge periods.[130]

---

126 This material can be found at http://cpr.ca.gov/report/cprrpt/issrec/res/res15.htm.
127 Pub. Res. C. S 21000.
128 R E Bass, A I Herson, K M Bogdan, *CEQA Deskbook, A Step-by-Step Guide on How to Comply With the California Environmental Quality Act*, 2nd edn. (Point Arena: Solano Press Books, 1999), 1–2.
129 Ibid, 13–14.
130 Pub. Res. C. S 21083(c); and Title 14 California Code of Regulations, Chapter 13, S 15024. The public comment period for environmental documents and notices varies from 30–45 days. Generally, the notices that are filed to inform the public of proposed projects have a 30–35 days public comment period.

CEQA specifies that some projects must go through a state-level environmental review process. For the state-level review process, lead agencies submit environmental documents to the State Clearinghouse for distribution to state agencies, which then have the opportunity to comment on the environmental documents and work with lead agencies to mitigate project impacts.

The State Clearinghouse

The State Clearinghouse is a unit of the Governor's Office of Planning and Research. The State Clearinghouse is responsible for posting notices and coordinating the state-level review of environmental documents. The State Clearinghouse processes thousands of documents each year, ranging from simple one-page notices to multi-volume environmental documents. The number of documents submitted to the State Clearinghouse has increased steadily from 8000 notices and environmental documents in 1999 to over 14,000 in 2003, an increase of 75 percent. In 2003, 9300 notices and 4700 environmental documents were filed with the State Clearinghouse.[131]

State law requires the State Clearinghouse to physically post the notices in its office during the legal challenge period. It also requires the State Clearinghouse to make these notices available to the public through the Internet.[132] The notices inform the public when a proposed project has been exempted from environmental review or when the environmental review process for a project has been completed and been approved by a lead agency.

The State Clearinghouse database

The State Clearinghouse maintains an electronic database of summary information for each notice and environmental document that is submitted to the Clearinghouse pursuant to CEQA. The database does not contain the actual documents. In 2003, State Clearinghouse staff manually entered summary information from paper documents into the database for over 14,000 notices and environmental documents.[133] The State Clearinghouse has three full-time clerical staff and two part-time temporary staff manually inputting information into the database.[134] The environmental documents and notices are entered manually because an electronic filing system has not been implemented.

131 Governor's Office of Planning and Research, State Clearinghouse, Environmental Document Filings with the State Clearinghouse, Calendar years 1999–2003 (Sacramento, California, 2004).
132 Pub. Res. C. Ss 21091 and 21159.9.
133 Governor's Office of Planning and Research, State Clearinghouse, Environmental Document Filings with the State Clearinghouse.
134 Governor's Office of Planning and Research, State Clearinghouse, State Clearinghouse Roles and Responsibilities, (Sacramento, California, March 8, 2004); and interview with Scott Morgan, senior planner, State Clearinghouse, May 14, 2004.

The State Clearinghouse has attempted to automate data entry through an Internet-based online submission process that could reduce its staff costs and provide faster, more efficient service to public agencies and provide more timely information on proposed projects to the public.[135] Development of an online submission process, called CEQAnet II or "application," was completed in 2002 by the Information Center for the Environment at the University of California, Davis (UC Davis).[136] CEQAnet II would allow lead agencyies to file the notice online, provide instant acknowledgement of filing, and immediately post the notice on the website. This would eliminate manual entry of the document summaries by State Clearinghouse staff and make the information available to the public immediately.

An additional function of the application includes GIS mapping capability. The GIS mapping will display the geographic location of all projects in the database as they are entered. The benefit of mapping is state agencies can quickly identify proposed projects that could impact state facilities or environmentally sensitive areas.

[I]f the application was implemented the State Clearinghouse notice processing timeline would be reduced from three months to one month, inclusive of the statutorily required legal challenge period. Although the manual entry process has a backlog of up to two months, the State Clearinghouse meets its statutory

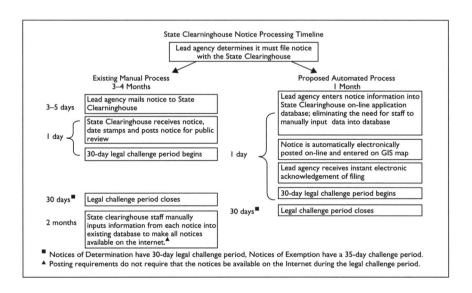

135 Memorandum from Terry Roberts, Director of the State Clearinghouse to Becky Curler, Manager, Governor's Office Information Technology Unit (February 3, 2004).
136 Ibid.

posting requirements. With the current process, manual entry into the database occurs after the legally challenge period has closed. In contrast, CEQAnet II would post notices on the Internet during the legal challenge period.

Despite its benefits the application has not been implemented due to concerns raised b the Department of Finance, Teale Data Center, and the information technology staff of the Governor's office. The concerns include identifying the appropriate host for the database, security, resources and adequate staffing. The main concern from the Department of Finance was that a state database should be hosted by the state data center, Teale Data Center. Firewall issues prevented UC Davis from hosting the application. In addition, the Governor's Office Information Technology Unit does not believe it could adequately support the application because of staffing and resource limitations.[137] According to Department of Finance staff, the Feasibility Study Report was approved in June 2000. The next step is for the Office of Planning and Research to complete a Special Project Report and submit it to the Department of Finance, which can then complete its review and incorporate costs in the regular budget cycle.[138]

Long-term solution

Implementation of the application is a short-term solution to streamlining the state-level environmental review process. A long-term solution is to implement California Technology Enabled Services (Smart Services). Smart Services, including web portals, would create a framework for the automation of state business processes. The state-level environmental document review and notice filing processes are well-suited to the web portal concept. A web portal would incorporate the application and expand it to include the filing of large environmental documents online. A web portal creates a workspace on a server that can collect electronic files from lead agencies and make them available to state agencies for review and comment. It allows for quick access to all documents, document sharing, interactive comments among reviewers, email notifications and reminders, and a centralized document library that can be searched. This system would help state agencies gain review time and be able to identify important projects more readily.

The State Clearinghouse application and state agency electronic document management systems should be incorporated in the state web portal to full automate the state-level environmental review process. Centralized document management systems through the state web portal should be available to provide online review of CEQA documents within one to two years.

137 Email from Becky Curler, Manager, Governor's Office Information Technology Unit, to Terry Roberts, Director of the State Clearinghouse (February 4, 2004).
138 Interview with Jim Esarte, Department of Finance, Sacramento, California (March 25, 2004).

Electronic document management system

The State Clearinghouse coordinates the state-level intergovernmental review process for environmental documents. The State Clearinghouse sets the comment period for each environmental document and identifies the appropriate reviewing agencies which are selected for their expertise in a particular subject matter or geographical area or their responsibility for particular types of projects.[139]

Once a state agency receives a document from the State Clearinghouse it must coordinate its internal review and compile comments to be sent to the State Clearinghouse prior to the close of the comment period. This is currently a cumbersome process requiring circulation of the large environment documents through various functional units, and gathering, compiling, and submitting comments to the State Clearinghouse. California Department of Transportation District 3 has implemented electronic document management software to automate the internal review process. The software enables quick, simultaneous distribution of scanned documents to individuals in multiple locations. This gives document reviewers more time by eliminating mailing and other document distribution process delays. The software generates and distributes automatic and electronic due-date reminders. Reviewer comments are compiled and automatically forwarded to the document manager, who can then forward them to the State Clearinghouse prior to the close of the comment period. The document history, reviewer comments, action dates and other items are maintained in the database, thus eliminating costly storage of paper documents.

Caltrans District 3 did an extensive post-implementation review of the benefits and costs of the electronic document management system.[140] The cost savings amounted to less staff time spent copying, mailing and physically routing of documents among various staff locations. Caltrans District 3 reviews about 2200 environmental documents per year and estimated that the electronic document management system produces an annual cost savings of about $78,000.

Recommendations

1. The State Clearinghouse and Teale Data Center should implement the CEQAnet II application at the State Clearinghouse.
2. The State Clearinghouse and Teale Data Center should create a web portal that incorporates CEQAnet II and an electronic document management system to streamline the state-level environmental review process.

139 Governor's Office of Planning and Research, State Clearinghouse Handbook (Sacramento, California, January 2004), 5–8.
140 Department of Transportation, District 3, Planning and Local Assistance Sacramento Office, Lotus/IBMDomino.Doc Pilot Program Report/Statewide Deployment Recommendation, internal draft final report (March 21, 2004).

Fiscal impact

Assuming implementation in January 2005, the CEQAnet II application would cost $48,000 in Fiscal year (F) 2005–2006, but would result in savings each year thereafter. After the first year, the application would cost about $56,000 for annual licensing, maintenance, and Teale Data Center costs, but this would be offset by larger savings in personnel costs.[141] B F 2006–2007, the decreased data entry work load should reduce one full-time clerical position costing $57,000. B F 2007–2008, two clerical positions should be eliminated for an annual savings of $114,000. Based on past document growth through the State Clearinghouse, a total of three positions should be saved by FY 2008–2009, for an annual savings of $171,000. Since the number of environmental documents and notices is expected to continue to increase the State Clearinghouse would need to employ additional data entry staff if CEQAnet II is not implemented.

The cost of a centralized document management system through a centralized web portal solution cannot be estimated at this time.

General fund (dollars in thousands)

Fiscal year	Savings ($)	Costs ($)	Net savings ($)	Change in PYs
2004–2005	0	0	0	0
2005–2006	0	48	(48)	0
2006–2007	57	56	1	(1)
2007–2008	114	56	58	(2)
2008–2009	171	56	115	(3)

Note
The dollars and PYs for each year in the above chart reflect the total change for that year from FY 2003–2004 expenditures, revenues and PYs.

141 Interview with Terry Roberts, Director, State Clearinghouse, Sacramento, California (April 14, 2004).

Chapter 9

The prospects for ecological impact assessment[1]

Jane Holder

Introduction

The initial impetus to develop environmental assessment came from a perceived need to integrate ecological principles and knowledge in political decision-making. However, the law relating to environmental assessment currently fails to reflect the richness and diversity of ecological systems, which have been described so graphically by Ruhl as 'a mess...highly complicated, organised disorder'.[2] For example, current environmental assessment law (contained primarily in the EU's EIA Directive[3] or derived from this) contains relatively weak provisions on predicting cumulative and indirect effects, which are hallmarks of the complex and connected nature of relationships between species and habitats and the resilience or otherwise of these. Factors which further work against an ecological approach to environmental assessment include the frequent need to reach a decision on a particular application for development consent. This tends to prevent the use of generous timescales to establish baseline conditions and curtails post-assessment monitoring. Restrictive regulatory timescales also tend to make the ecological success of compensatory mitigation, such as the creation of a wetland area, difficult to evaluate over a long period of time. This means environmental assessment is unlikely to capture fully the creation, or loss, of ecosystems. The drawing of boundaries to establish the physical limits of the area to be subject to environmental assessment more often than not reflects the boundaries of the development site according to its ownership, rather than the contours of ecological features which are likely to extend beyond the limits of the development site and its immediate environs. Finally, environmental assessment methodologies tend to be reductionist in nature, so that species and habitats are looked at in isolation rather than as connected parts of a larger whole.

---

1 This title is taken from Jo Treweek's *Ecological Impact Assessment* (Oxford: Blackwell, 1999).

2 J B Ruhl, 'Thinking of Environmental Law as a Complex Adaptive System: How to Clean up the Environment by Making a Mess of Environmental Law' (1997) 34 *Houston Law Rev*, 101.

3 Directive 85/337/EEC on the assessment of the effects of certain public and private projects on the environment, OJ 1985 L 175, p. 40, as amended by Directive 97/11/EC, OJ 1997 L 73, p 5.

Overall, I aim to provide a critique of law's part in these limitations. I offer a 'back to the future' analysis of environmental assessment by returning to its roots in ecological science and suggesting that in future it should be more firmly embedded in an on-going 'ecosystems' approach to environmental management, embodying 'ecological governance through law'.[4] This Chapter is also a reaction to the steady broadening of environmental assessment to encompass sustainability criteria of social and economic impacts, of the sort now commonplace in the European Union as 'sustainability analysis', and located in a broader movement of 'better regulation' initiatives as described, respectively, by Ludwig Krämer and Jonathan Wiener in this book. Both of these developments are a product of the 'mainstreaming' of environmental assessment in policy-making, in an effort to incorporate environmental concerns and considerations into everyday, and wide-ranging, decision-making. The process of broadening the remit of environmental assessment appears to have permeated beyond policy-making at the EU level, so that for example environmental statements for project-based assessments habitually include references to the local economy, and the (invariably positive) contribution of the project to this. In other words, the 'environment' is capable of being lost in environmental assessment. I argue that whilst there is a place for economic and social considerations to be taken into account in the broader (political) decision-making processes, there is also a real risk that environmental assessment might be used to prejudge, or package, such choices by the inclusion of economic factors in environmental statements. I therefore consider the prospects for the development of a form of environmental assessment which is capable of studying the linkages and relationships between habitats and species and assessing impacts upon these. This suggests the need for an expansion of the scales of time and space within which environmental assessment usually operates and ideally replacing the emphasis upon an individual process, site, or project, with a more complex picture of natural dependency, variation, and resilience in the broader ecosystem.

In considering the prospects for the development of such 'ecological impact assessment', I draw upon Ruhl's argument for the interdependence and complexity of ecological systems to inform the content and structure of environmental law, based on a theory of complex adaptive systems. In summary, Ruhl outlines the desirability of a compatible coevolution of ecological science and environmental law, so that ultimately law reflects the complex ('messy') characteristics of the ecosystems which it is used to protect.[5] According to Brooks, Jones and Virginia, however, an *episodic* coevolution of ecology and environmental law has been taking place in the United States since the 1970s (they characterise this in terms of a relationship – the 'lover's quarrel' between law and ecology, the 'shy embrace',

---

4 R Brooks, R Jones, and R Virginia, *Law and Ecology: The Rise of the Ecosystem Regime* (Aldershot: Ashgate, 2002), p 2.
5 Ruhl, 'Thinking of Environmental Law as a Complex Adaptive System', pp 105–106.

courtship, and finally 'marriage' in the form of 'ecological planning for environmental law'). They describe that ecology has already shaped important areas of environmental law including coastal management, endangered species protection, forest management and a variety of global pollution problems.[6]

With this evolution in mind, I focus on environmental assessment law in the United Kingdom. I begin by tracing the apparently close relationship between law, environmental assessment and ecology, and the recent turn towards sustainable development which has altered both the structure and content of environmental assessment, and is primarily responsible for the expansion of environmental assessment beyond environmental boundaries, and its subsequent entry into the mainstream of law and policy-making processes. In this context I follow Brooks, Jones and Virginia's understanding of ecology as 'the scientific study of the systematic interdependencies of the biotic and abiotic environment',[7] or in laymen's terms the study of the relationship between organisms and their environment (thus distinguishing ecology from 'environment' which is traditionally regarded as relating to the quality of environmental media – air, water, and land). I also adopt their definition of law sensitive to ecosystems (what they refer to as 'ecosystemic laws') as 'laws which seek to regulate human activities with explicit awareness of the structure, function and integrity of the ecosystems and the biodiversity within those systems affected by those activities'.[8]

Relating environmental assessment, ecology and sustainable development

Although undoubtedly drawing upon several disciplines, the driving force of environmental assessment, and indeed of environmental law, has been ascribed to ecological science.[9] The best example of this, the United States' National Environmental Policy Act (NEPA) 1969, which required federal agencies to conduct environmental assessment of their policies and activities, has been described as 'the most enduring legal application of ecology...the first piece of federal legislation to raise ecology to a star status'[10] because it rests on the premise that ecological information could guide administrative action, triggering the 'coevolution of ecology and environmental law'.[11]

6　Brooks, Jones, and Virginia, *Law and Ecology*, p 3.

7　Brooks, Jones, and Virginia, *Law and Ecology*, then make finer distinctions between various branches, and levels of ecology in Ch.1.

8　Brooks, Jones, and Virginia, *Law and Ecology*, pp 2–3.

9　F P Bosselman and D Tarlock, 'The Influence of Ecological Science on American Law: An Introduction' (1994) 69 *Chicago-Kent L Rev*, 847, at 861.

10　Bosselman and Tarlock, 'The Influence of Ecological Science on American Law', at 864. See also L K Caldwell, *Science and the National Environmental Policy Act: Redirecting Policy Through Procedural Reform* (Alabama: Alabama University Press, 1982).

11　Brooks, Jones, and Virginia, *Law and Ecology*, p 3.

Early environmental assessment was therefore held up as an example of 'ecological science in action', synthesised with law by NEPA. The conception of ecology at the time of this enactment was one based upon the dominant paradigm of homeostasis or equilibrium between organisms and the environment – a 'balance of nature' – which could be maintained only by resistance to change.[12] Although not prescribing a particular environmental standard, environmental assessment was a culturally significant evocation of the importance of such ecological concerns in decision-making, so that the fairly strict environmental assessment requirements contained in NEPA (alongside the development of nature reserves, biodiversity preservation strategies, and the setting of emission standards) suggests the absorption of some of this thinking into environmental law.

Such sentiments were further enhanced by judgments such as *Calvert Cliffs*[13] in which it was held that NEPA's requirement of federal agencies to produce an environmental statement also required them to consider environmental issues just as they consider other matters. This has been interpreted as 'a legally mandated linkage between ecology as reflected in the environmental impact statement and government action'.[14] In short, 'ecology and law could meet in the Environmental Impact Statement'.[15]

In practice, though, the influence of ecological science in environmental assessment, and particularly in the scope and structure of environmental statements submitted by developers, was limited. As Brooks, Jones and Virginia recall, the impact assessment provisions of NEPA failed initially to install a systems, or integrated, approach to preparing a statement on the likely effects of a plan or policy on the environment. Instead it provided for a more traditional planning approach, leading them to conclude that 'NEPA's "embrace" of ecology through environmental impact assessment was 'lukewarm'.[16] The limited nature of environmental assessment (as conceived of by NEPA and also as supplemented by various regulations designed to guide agencies in preparing statements) is attributed to this factor:

> Unfortunately, these regulations, like NEPA itself, do not embody a full grasp of ecological thought. Instead, intent upon reducing paper and delay, these regulations dictated the choice of a lead agency to prepare the statement, limited the range of actions and effects through up front "scoping", "tiering" of the reports from general to specific, and breaking down of the report into actions, alternatives and impacts with little attention to the ecosystem. Instead of a comprehensive planning document or

12 Bosselman and Tarlock, 'The Influence of Ecological Science on American Law', at 866.
13 *Calvert Cliffs Coordination Committee, Inc. v US Atomic Energy Commission* 449 F2d 1109 (1971), at 1112.
14 Brooks, Jones, and Virginia, *Law and Ecology*, p 159.
15 Brooks, Jones, and Virginia, *Law and Ecology*, p 159.
16 Brooks, Jones, and Virginia, *Law and Ecology*, p 160.

a complete examination of the ecosystem affected by the proposed action, the statements were reduced to a "variety of checklists, matrices of activities, and environmental components and other devices for identifying, organizing and displaying the numerous effects of a complex project". With the focus placed upon the workability and usefulness of the environmental impact statement, the actual science in the statement suffered. A 1976 review of impact statement found them to be scientifically inadequate. This inadequacy was due in part to the lack of money and trained staff for preparation of such statements, but the report went on to indicate lack of ecological conceptualization of the statement itself.[17]

Recent developments in environmental assessment law in the United States appear to have enhanced the ecological content of environmental statements, for example by introducing specific ecological concepts, such as the importance of biological diversity and cumulative impacts to ecosystems into NEPA's functions.[18] Such reforms apart, the current minimalist approach to ecology in environmental assessment practice, as opposed to its genesis, has led to arguments for the use of specialist sub-assessments such as on biodiversity,[19] within a broad environmental assessment framework.

The roots of environmental assessment might have been in ecological science, but the procedure carries the distinct mark of modernism – prediction, assessing the likely occurrence of events, or significant effects, that have not yet occurred, indeed that might never occur. This exercise in prediction can be traced to the development in the eighteenth century of methods of collection, measurement and analysis in the fields of time measurement, astrological observation, anatomy, navigation, chemical substance analysis and mathematics. Environmental assessment has, appropriately, followed a technicist path, with the emphasis on controlling pollution control through informing decisions about siting industrial development, though with a residual concern for habitat and landscape.

The more recent close association of environmental assessment with the ideas of ecological modernisation and sustainable development may to some extent be explained by the continuing influence of ecological science, and the changing paradigms within the discipline.[20] Most importantly, the ecological paradigm of

---

17 Brooks, Jones, and Virginia, *Law and Ecology*, p 161. Note that in the UK only around a third of all local planning authorities have a trained ecologist on their staff.

18 Ibid, pp 165–182.

19 See generally Treweek, *Ecological Impact Assessment*. On biodiversity impact assessments, see specifically M Montini, 'Habitats Impact Assessment: An Effective Instrument for Biodiversity Conservation?' (2001) 9 *Env Liab* 182, in which he proposes a hierarchy of assessment, with the findings of biodiversity habitat assessments (required by Art 6 of Directive 92/43/EEC on the conservation of natural habitats and of wild fauna and flora, OJ 1992, L 206, p 7 – the Habitats Directive) taking precedence over more general environmental assessments.

20 Bosselman and Tarlock, 'The Influence of Ecological Science on American Law'.

equilibrium – the idea of a balance of nature which emphasises stability and was influential in the development of laws such as environmental assessment in the United States – underwent a revolution, with the result that ecological science now stresses the dynamic and unstable nature of ecological systems and no longer upholds as ideal the withdrawal of humankind from nature. This 'New Ecology' recognises instead the inevitability of interactions between humans and the natural environment,[21] and the inevitability of the accompanying developmental strains. The management of ecosystems therefore became a priority rather than their preservation, or restoration.

As a consequence, a broadening of analysis of environmental connections to take into account human-environmental relationships, including analysis of human behaviour, attitudes, and values, may be seen in the development of environmental science. This change in emphasis is reflected in the expanding scope of environmental assessment, which serves also to give expression to the multiple concerns and objectives of sustainable development. The reformed perspective of ecology informed the evolution of the political concept of sustainable development by providing a scientific basis for it, and the associated drive for the integration of environmental factors in all decision-making. Bosselman and Tarlock sum this up: 'Environmentalism's initial objective was to make environmental quality a relative quality to be considered. This battle has now largely been won and the movement's focus has shifted to the assured comprehensive and long-term integration, if not dominance, of this perspective in all resource decision-making.'[22] A triumvirate of law, ecology, and politics therefore acted to reconceive environmental assessment as a legal expression of sustainable development, particularly giving practical effect to the more integrative aspects of this concept, so that environmental concerns are taken into account in decision-making, but do not (by design) necessarily predominate.

This profound shift in environmental discourse and environmental law, by which sustainable development became an organising theme and objective of international environmental law (and environmental law more generally), has been reflected in the functions ascribed to environmental assessment. As mentioned above, environmental impact assessment was originally considered to assist mainly with pollution control. It has since been acknowledged to have a far broader role in implementing the principle of sustainable development by influencing decision-makers to take account of the quality of development and its effects upon the conservation of natural resources, as well as still influencing locational issues. This parallel shift in the perceived function of environmental impact assessment reflects the rejection of purely technocratic practices in

---

21 This paradigm shift is attributed to several ecologists: B T MacKibben, *The End of Nature* (New York: Random House, 1989); D B Botkin, *Discordant Harmonies: A New Ecology for the Twenty-First Century* (Oxford: Oxford University Press, 1990).

22 Bosselman and Tarlock, 'The Influence of Ecological Science on American Law', at 872.

favour of a more general reformist environmental strategy (although more extreme interpretations of sustainable development have advanced economic methodologies which are similarly technicist).[23] Encouraging popular participation in environmental decision-making formed an important part of this strategy. In this vein, the World Commission on Environment and Development (WCED) specifically identified environmental assessment of projects and policies as offering a means to achieve sustainable industrial development, alongside the use of economic instruments,[24] a role similarly identified for environmental assessment in the Rio Declaration (1992)[25] and Agenda 21[26] which followed the WCED's report. The potential contribution of environmental assessment to sustainable development has since been described by, amongst others, Jacobs who welcomed environmental assessment as 'a reasonably considered and open approach to mediating conflict within the sustainability framework by allowing those most likely to be affected by a project's environmental effects to communicate their views to decision-makers'.[27]

Environmental assessment is clearly thought capable of being further developed to include the assessment of environmental impacts on communities,[28] human health,[29] and habitats.[30] Moving further beyond environmental protection, the prediction of impacts prior to decision-making may be used to reflect a range of concerns for example human rights,[31] the burden of regulation on administration,[32] even the effect of crime on 'victims',[33] and the likelihood of criminals to reoffend. This expansion has produced an all-embracing sustainability assessment, a development which reflects the wholesale adoption of the sustainable development agenda in environmental law. Relating the evolution of environmental assessment to the ascendancy of the concept of sustainable development in law and policy offers an explanation for this. For example in the context of the European Union, the sustainable development

23 For an excellent review of this shift, see M A Hajer, *The Politics of Environmental Discourse: Ecological Modernisation and the Policy Process* (Oxford: Oxford University Press, 1997) Ch. 3.
24 World Commission on Environment and Development, *Our Common Future* (Oxford: Oxford University Press, 1987) pp 221–224.
25 UNCED (1992) 31 ILM 874, especially Principle 15.
26 UNCED, 1992.
27 M Jacobs, *The Green Economy* (London: Pluto Press, 1993) pp 220–221.
28 On the evaluation of social impacts of development, see N. Lichfield, *Community Impact Evaluation* (London: University College London, 1995).
29 See, e.g. the Royal Commission on Environmental Pollution's recommendation that human health issues be incorporated explicitly in the environmental impact assessment process, Twenty-third Report, *Environmental Planning*, Cm 5459 (HMSO, 2002), paras 7.36–7.38.
30 For example, M Montini, 'Habitats Impact Assessment: An Effective Instrument for Biodiversity Conservation?' (2001) 9 *Env. Liab.* 182.
31 As discussed by S.I.Skegly, *The Human Rights Obligations of the World Bank and Monetary Fund* (London: Cavendish, 2001).
32 B Morgan, 'The Economisation of Politics' (2003) 12 *Social and Legal Studies* 489.
33 Victim impact statements are in certain cases read out in court before sentencing.

principle has undergone a process of 'mainstreaming' which describes its adoption as a guiding principle, informing the formation and fulfilment of all policies pursued by the Union,[34] not just those with an environmental purview. Since sustainable development is predicated upon the integration of environmental considerations in decision-making in exactly the manner achieved by environmental instruments, this suggests some inevitability about the remit of environmental assessment being extended (as impact assessment or sustainability analysis) and it similarly being placed at the centre of policy-making.

Some writers have taken an evangelical view of this expansion of environmental assessment to take fuller account of social and economic (as well as environmental) factors in decision-making.[35] For example Barry Sadler considers it to be the inevitable culmination of the development of environmental assessment – from a 'first-generation' process typically concerned with mitigating the impacts of major developments rather than maintaining the capacity and integrity of natural systems',[36] through strategic environmental assessment ('a second generation process that addresses both the sources and symptoms (or effects) of environmental damage'[37]) and finally reaching a third generation form of Environmental Sustainability Assessment (ESA) involving a 'full cost analysis' of social, economic, and environmental impacts.

The enthusiasm for environmental assessment as a means to secure a weak form of sustainable development (even without its full-blown evolution into 'environmental sustainability assessment') demonstrates a key characteristic of the procedure – an ability to absorb other concerns, be they environmental, economic, or social – and thus encourage recognition of diverse concerns, and the connections between them.[38] From a more critical standpoint, environmental assessment facilitates the balancing of competing interests, or rather contributes to an impression of balance, or mediation (rather than absolute environmental

---

34 Art 2 EC Treaty, as amended states: 'The Community shall have as its task, by establishing a common market and an economic and monetary union and by implementing common policies or activities...to promote throughout the Community a harmonious and balanced sustainable development of economic activities...a high level of protection and improvement of the quality of the environment'. Art 2 Treaty on European Union similarly states that the Union shall 'promote economic and social progress to achieve balanced and sustainable development'.

35 B Sadler, 'Environmental Sustainability and Assurance', in J Petts (ed), *Handbook of Environmental Impact Assessment: Vol. 1 Process, Methods and Potential* (Oxford: Blackwell, 1999).

36 Sadler, *Environmental Sustainability and Assurance*, p 27.

37 Ibid.

38 For example the Royal Commission on Environmental Pollution discusses the prospects for sustainability appraisal which would extend appraisal to include social and economic criteria as being of equal concern to environmental criteria, See Twenty-third Report, *Environmental Planning*, paras 7.43–7.45. See, also, Department of the Environment, Transport and the Regions, *Proposals for a Good Practice Guide on Sustainability Appraisal of Regional Planning Guidance* (London: DETR, 2000).

protection) which similarly underlies the concept of sustainable development. Of course, this also facilitates the identification of trade-offs that may be made. A key point, however, is that having secured the integration of environmental concerns in land-use systems, and policy-making, the further inclusion within the scope of environmental assessment of other indicators or indices, may well lead to the marginalisation of environmental impacts as against a broader spectrum of concern.[39]

In conceptual terms, therefore, this development of environmental assessment is broadly in accordance with aspects of the efficiency-oriented ecological modernisation agenda,[40] of which sustainable development is an important part. This is particularly the case with moves to integrate environmental concerns into broader social and political issues and, correspondingly, to facilitate the identification of trade-offs.

The relegation of ecology in environmental assessment

I argued above that the close identification of environmental assessment with ecological science has been hampered by the limitations of the procedure in practice, whether because of the nature of the training received by those compiling environmental statements, the use of reductionist methodology (discussed further below), or the need to comply with strict timescales for determining applications for development consent. Most importantly, the underlying problem is that the legal requirements for environmental assessment, set out in the environment impact assessment (EIA) Directive and the Habitats Directive, currently fail to reflect basic ecological premises such as interdependence between organisms and their environments and the cumulative effects of impacts. The nearest that the EIA Directive gets in this regard is the requirement that the environmental impact assessment shall identify, describe and assess the direct and indirect effects of a project on human beings, fauna and flora, soil, water, climate and landscape, material assets and the cultural heritage and the interaction between these.[41] The EIA Directive remains silent about timescales, other than that the assessment must be completed and taken into account prior to a decision being taken about whether or not to grant development consent. Both instruments fail to mention post-assessment monitoring even though this has been on the legislative agenda for quite some time. There is also no mention of appropriate methodologies, for example the need to adopt the boundaries of the study according to some conception of an 'ecological unit'. In addition, the broadening remit of environmental assessment

---

39 See, e.g. case study on the European Commission's development of a form of sustainability assessment to review policy choices, in J Holder, *Environmental Assessment: The Regulation of Decision Making* (Oxford: Oxford University Press, 2004), Ch. 5.

40 Hajer, *Ecological Modernisation*.

41 Art 3.

has led to an ascendancy of socio-economic concerns in environmental assessment procedures. Examples of the resulting failure to adopt an ecological approach in environmental assessment procedures can be grouped as follows: (i) failure to take account of cumulative impacts; (ii) failure to draw boundaries according to ecological units; and (iii) deconstructivst and reductionist methodology.

(i)   Failure to take account of cumulative impacts

The potential indirect, cumulative, and interrelated impacts[42] of a proposed development have a direct bearing upon judgements of the likely significance of its impacts upon the environment. This is because, when viewed narrowly in terms of its component parts, separated by space ('sliced up' projects[43]) and/or time (in the case of 'staged' projects), a project may fall below a threshold for significance, but when these parts are viewed together they may have considerable, or significant, effects. Environmental assessment procedures potentially provide an opportunity to consider a development as a whole – in terms of the wider impacts of an entire project (including all its component parts), and in combination with related projects, so that the effects of incremental damage from ribbon development, in-filling, and associated projects such as road building, and damage from synergistic effects (the reaction of one impact with another) are not neglected.[44] For example, an environmental assessment of a proposed extension to a power station may include analysis of emissions from cooling towers carrying saline material, in addition to the estuarine water already used (an example of indirect and cumulative impacts), as well as emissions of sulphur dioxide and nitrogen dioxide measured in the light of similar emissions from existing power stations in the vicinity of the proposed development (cumulative impact), and the increased generation of ozone through chemical reactions (the interaction of impacts).[45]

---

42 This is a category of impacts beyond those directly related to the project, as defined by the European Commission, *Guidance on Indirect, Cumulative and Impact Interactions* (Brussels: CEC, 2001). This defines these impacts as follows, at (iii): 'indirect impacts: Impacts on the environment, which are not a direct result of the project, often produced away from or as a result of a complex pathway. Sometimes referred to as second or third level impacts, or secondary impacts; cumulative impacts: impacts that result from incremental changes caused by other past, present or reasonably foreseeable actions together with the project; impact interactions: the reactions between impacts whether between the impacts of just one project or between the impacts of other projects in the areas'. There are clearly overlaps between these categories and different interpretations of them.

43 On 'salami slicing' of projects – see J Scott, *EC Environmental Law* (London: Longmans, 1997), pp 119–120.

44 On the opportunities in environmental assessment to take account of cumulative effects, see N C Sontag and R R Everitt *et al*, *Cumulative Effective Assessment: A Context for Further Development and Research* (Quebec: Canadian Environmental Assessment Research Centre, 1987).

45 This example is the Killingholme CCGT Power Station Extension, cited in European Commission, *Guidance on Indirect, Cumulative and Impact Interactions, Op. cit.* pp 39 et seq.

The common factor of each of these impact types is that they require consideration of the effects of a project *beyond* a particular site, or a particular process. The recognition that such impacts may be significant when viewed in association is in line with ecological thinking in which delayed or indirect impacts, as well as linked impacts which occur beyond an immediate project site, are recognised as sources of stress which can permanently reduce the ability of an ecosystem to absorb impacts, or recover from them,[46] or reduce environmental quality. In conceptual terms an appreciation of cumulative impacts is also to accept the vital interrelationships of what may otherwise be considered component parts of the environment. Environmental assessment should therefore entail gauging the relationship of projects with one another, and their collective impact.

The potential for a development to be broken up into separate components with the effect that a sense of the cumulative impacts of the development as a whole is lost was not recognised in the original EC EIA Directive. Amendments to this Directive in 1997[47] required that the cumulative effects with other projects be considered when screening a project for the application of environmental assessment rules,[48] and that the developer must supply information on any indirect, secondary, and cumulative effects. In contrast, the EC Directive on strategic environmental assessment (the SEA Directive)[49] is inherently more concerned with cumulative effects because it is designed to more accurately appreciate the impact of plans and programmes, which in turn are made up of individual projects. Specifically, this Directive requires that an environmental report must be prepared in which the relationship of the plan and programme with others must be described.

A clear lead on the need to consider the cumulative effects of projects, when reaching a decision about the likely significance of a project, was given by the Court of Justice in *Commission v Ireland*.[50] This case concerned the application of thresholds which the European Commission regarded as contrary to the EIA Directive because incremental, and cumulative, effects were not taken into account. The Court cited in particular the cumulative effect of land reclamation projects: 'limestone pavement, which is characteristic of the area, has been destroyed, as have vegetation and archaeological remains, giving way to pasture. Considered together, these interventions were likely to have significant effects'.[51] Since the national provisions on environmental assessment did not

---

46 Treweek, *Ecological Impact Assessment*, p 154.

47 By Directive 97/11/EC OJ 1997 L 73, p 5.

48 See Annex III, point 1 of the EIA Directive as amended by Directive 97/11/EC: 'e characteristics of projects must be considered having regard, in particular, to…the cumulation with other projects'.

49 EC Directive 2001/42/EC (SEA Directive) on the assessment of the effects of certain plans and programmes on the environment, OJ 2000 L 197, p 30.

50 Case C–392/96 [1996] ECR I–5901.

51 At para 80.

refer to the cumulative effect of such projects, which, individually, fell below the various thresholds set, Ireland had exceeded the limits of its discretion provided in the Directive. The Court held that Member States must ensure that the objective of the Directive was not circumvented by the splitting of projects into their component parts: 'Not taking account of the cumulative effect of projects means in practice that all projects of a certain type may escape the obligation to carry out an assessment when, taken together, they are likely to have significant effects on the environment within the meaning of Art 2(1) of the Directive'.[52] The judgment is recognition that loss or damage to a part of the environment does not take place only in respect of a defined area, but that harmful effects may be combined with others and thereby exacerbated. In giving this judgment, the Court of Justice should be credited with emphasising the sensitivity of land accommodating development when deciding whether a project, or several projects when viewed together, is likely to have significant effects on an environment. The Court appears to be seeking to align the rules of environmental assessment more closely to ecological conditions and impacts upon these 'on the ground'.

This, and other cases,[53] highlight that environmental assessment forms part of national development consent systems which are rooted in the concept of the project. This state of affairs is particularly pronounced in the United Kingdom because the prevalence of interests of private property in the planning system is manifested in an emphasis upon a particular site for the purposes of development consent.[54] Although conceiving of 'projects' broadly,[55] the EIA Directive similarly draws upon the project as the central unit of environmental assessment, because of the way in which it ties environmental assessment to an application for development consent. This can lead to the (ecological) 'tyranny of small decisions'.[56] EC Directive 2001/42/EC on the environmental assessment of plans and programmes will possibly prove more capable of addressing a broader range of impacts, in temporal as well as spatial terms, so that future phases of work may be taken into account when judging the significance of

---

52 At para 76.
53 See *Lewin v Rowley v Secretary of State for Transport* (1990) 2 *Journal of Environmental Law*, 216; *R v North West Leicestershire District Council ex parte Moses* [2000] Env L Rev 443 (CA), *R v Secretary of State for Transport ex parte Surrey County Council* (1993) High Court, 24 November 1993, unreported.
54 The main consequence of this characteristic of the planning system is the reluctance to consider alternatives, in terms of sites, projects, and technology. See *R (Jones) v North Warwickshire Borough Council* [2001] EWCA Civ 315. Planning policy may, however, increase the degree of scrutiny of alternatives required (see, e.g. *Jodie Phillips v First Secretary of State* [2003] EWHC 2415, and it is notable that Planning Policy Statement 1: Delivering Sustainable Development (ODPM, 2005) refers to the pursuit of 'alternative options'.
55 I.e. Art 1(1) and Annex II, point 13.
56 Treweek, *Ecological Impact Assessment* p 151.

a plan or programme overall, though at present its practical effect remains to be seen.

(ii) Failure to draw boundaries according to ecological units

The partial drawing of boundaries is highlighted by a case brought by the World Wildlife Fund (WWF) and the Royal Society for the Protection of Birds (RSPB) in which they challenged several decisions, or omissions, relating to the grant of planning permission for a ski centre, including a funicular railway as well as offices, catering and exhibition facilities and workshops on Cairn Gorm, one of the highest summits in Scotland.[57] In particular the RSPB and WWF challenged the exclusion of certain areas, such as the summit area of Cairn Gorm (vital for skiing), from the boundaries of a Special Area of Conservation (SAC) as designated by the EU Habitats Directive, claiming that the grant of planning permission was unlawful because approval of the project was made possible by drawing inappropriate boundaries for the European conservation site. As the Save the Cairngorms Campaign argued, 'the funicular site is virtually surrounded by land proposed for designation, and yet in ecological terms is very similar to the surrounding, soon to be protected, land'.[58] In the Court of Session, Lord Nimmo Smith rejected the petitioners' arguments about the exclusion of land used for skiing (including the funicular development) from the areas notified to the European Commission as a Special Protection Areas[59] and candidate Special Areas of Conservation[60] on the basis of his interpretation of the Birds and Habitats Directives, specifically that these Directives require that a discretion be exercised in the determination of boundaries, as in other respects.[61] This meant that so long as the *criteria* applied are ornithological or ecological, in line with European Court of Justice authority on this matter, then there is a discretion to be exercised in identifying the boundaries of the site, as an integral part of the process of identifying the site itself.

(iii) Deconstructivist and reductionist methodology

I have found that in most statements individual species are dealt with in isolation, with little appreciation of their place in an integrated ecosystem.[62]

---

57 *WWF – UK and RSPB v Secretary of State for Scotland* [1999] Env LR 632.
58 Save the Cairngorm Campaign, 'Cairn Gorm: Potential for Conflict With Europe' (1997).
59 As designated under Directive 79/409/EEC on the conservation of wild birds, OJ 1979 L 103, p 1.
60 'Candidate' status means that the land is considered worthy of submission to the European Commission, but has not yet been selected by the Commission as part of the 'Natura 2000' network of European protected sites, and hence not designated as a Special Area of Conservation (SAC) by the Member State under the terms of the Habitats Directive.
61 [1999] Env LR 632, at 672.
62 See case studies in Holder, *Environmental Assessment*, especially Ch. 3.

This is the case even where there are clear patterns of dependence, for example as between birds and fish. Potential impacts are frequently treated in a fragmented manner, so that their significance on the integrity of an ecosystem as a whole is lost. The prevailing approach is distinctly environmental, with a focus upon the impacts of development upon environmental media and the quality of human life – pollution of various sorts, nuisance, and visual disturbances – rather than an ecological systems approach which would necessarily entail an examination of broad, cumulative effects, the interrelation of species and habitats, and the effects of development on this. The prevailing tendency for an atomistic treatment of issues in some environmental assessment procedures, such that nature is presented as a collection of units, amounts to a rejection of the tenets of ecology,[63] and recalls the early treatment of the environment as no more than the sum of its constituent media. This suggests that currently the integrationist quality of environmental assessment exists primarily in terms of the regulation of cross-media pollution and to a lesser extent in policy appraisal, rather than in a more complex and holistic sense of appreciating the interconnectedness of nature.

Many of these concerns were raised by the Royal Society for the Protection of Birds in the course of their campaign against the building of a windfarm on the Isle of Lewis in the Hebrides. The proposal by Amec and British Energy (Lewis Wind Power Ltd) involves the construction of 181 wind turbines on the Island, potentially creating 'the world's largest onshore wind farm',[64] with likely impacts both in terms of the possible disturbance and killing of birds and other wildlife[65] and the draining of peatland in order to provide foundations for the turbines. The turbines are planned to spread across two Special Protection Areas (the Lewis Peatlands Special Protection Area (SPA) and the Ness and Barvas SPA) and the Lewis Peatlands Ramsar site (protected under the Ramsar Convention on Wetlands of International Importance), so designated because of the importance of these habitat areas for a range of birds dependent upon diverse environmental conditions – golden eagles, merlins, black-throated divers, red-throated divers, dunlins and greenshanks.[66] The effects of the development on the hydrology of the area, as well as further indirect effects from road and pylon building, may also extend to a special area of conservation (Lewis Peatlands SAC), located within the main SPA site. The building of such a large windfarm on boggy peatland will be a great engineering feat, requiring extensive drainage operations and the building of large concrete foundations. But it also presents the likelihood of serious and enduring adverse effects on the nature conservation interests of

---

63 This point is made more generally by D. Delaney in *Law's Nature* (Cambridge: Cambridge University Press, 2003) Ch. 9 in which he discusses wilderness and law, and by D. Wilkinson, 'Using Environmental Ethics to Create Ecological Law', in J Holder and D McGillivray (eds), *Locality and Identity: Environmental Issues in Law and Society* (Aldershot: Dartmouth, 1999).

64 See RSPB briefing note 'RSPB lodges official objection to world's largest onshore wind farm'.

65 Mark Townsend, 'Wind farms threaten the red kite', *The Observer* 25 January 2005.

66 See RSPB briefing note 'RSPB lodges official objection to world's largest onshore wind farm.

the Island, some of which are detailed in the developer's environmental statement which accompanied the application for development consent for the wind farm and associated infrastructure[67] and submitted to the Scottish Executive in November 2004. Interestingly, the non-technical summary from this statement adopted the language of environmental impact assessment ('significance', 'impact', 'fragility') in describing the *socio-economic* impacts of the project but with a positive spin: 'The construction and operation phases of the Lewis Wind Farm are predicted to have a significant impact on the fragile economy of the Western Isles, particularly in terms of job creation. There are also predicted benefits to the wider Scottish economy.' The statement also emphasised the provision of financial compensation for the local community.[68]

On the assessment of the development for nature conservation, the developer's environmental statement predicted that the construction and operation of the wind farm will result in the loss, disturbance and change to 1947 acres of land, of which 1426 acres fall within the Lewis Peatlands SPA. Since this was calculated as amounting to less than 1 per cent of the total area of the SPA on the Island, it was not considered significant in relation to 'the function of the SPA'. The statement further reported that no impacts are predicted for the Lewis Peatlands (then) candidate Special Area of Conservation (cSAC) or Loch Scarrasdale Site of Special Scientific Interest (SSSI) (the principal national nature conservation designation), although it was stated that the roads and access tracks crossing the blanket bog and other habitats could cause a potential impact since these may restrict the movement of species from one area to another, potentially making them less viable. As a consequence, the statement tells us that the layout has been designed around sensitive habitats, avoiding them wherever possible and that schemes would be put in place to restore areas of plantation forests back to native blanket bog and restore areas of peatlands to alleviate the remaining impacts.

RSPB Scotland commissioned independent research to evaluate the extent to which this statement fully assessed the likely impacts of the development.[69] The resulting report by Richard Lindsay concludes that the developer's environmental statement considerably undercalculates the scope of impact, including the number of bird deaths which are likely to ensue, and includes a number of inaccuracies, including incorrectly defining the legal status of land designated for nature conservation purposes.

Most importantly, Lindsay asserts a fundamental problem with the developer's 'deconstructivist' approach to assessing environmental effects, by which

67 Made under s.36 Electricity Act 1989.
68 Lewis Wind Power Ltd, *Environmental Statement*, Non-technical summary, October 2004, Summary of Findings, pp 8–9.
69 Royal Society for the Protection of Birds, *Lewis Wind Farm Proposals: Observations on the Official Environmental Impact Statement* (2005), compiled by Richard Lindsay (The Lindsay Report), p 54.

a system is broken down into its constituent parts and assumptions are made about the way in which these various parts will react to the construction of the wind farm. Instead, looking at the way the entire system works, Lindsay reports that the large-scale drainage and construction work on the hydrological condition of the peatlands bog will seriously compromise the *wider* ecological state of the area, including the SAC. For example, the Lewis Wind Farm Environmental Statement acknowledges the existence of a blanket mire ecosystem in the peat bog in terms of its structure and classification, but shows little understanding of its broader *functional* significance. In particular the position of linked mire units means that drainage of one area of the bog will have equally significant effects on other areas, even those located well away from the original drained area (because peat is made up of 98 per cent water and 2 per cent vegetation, any drainage will lead to great instability of a broader area). Lindsay summarises this factor as follows:

> Under natural conditions, the hydrological and physical linkages between the various mesotopes [the raised areas of peatland] provide the necessary degree of collective stability for the blanket mire complex, but where hydrological disruption occurs to one or more parts of the complex, this stability can be lost. The resulting instability may lead to a breakdown of surface hydrology, expressed as peat loss through various intensities of erosion, or it may give rise to large-scale catastrophic peat movements, commonly known as bog slide. That such disruption is not merely possible but widespread can be seen from the almost ubiquitous presence of surface erosion throughout the blanket mire landscapes of Britain and Ireland and the regularity of catastrophic events.[70]

This raises an important issue about the correct 'unit' for the purpose of carrying out the environmental assessment and as a matter of decision-making, namely whether this should conform to objective legal boundaries (of the specific development site boundaries), or rather be guided by the ecological conditions on the site – in this case, peatland systems reacting as whole hydrological entities, and hence excavations for even an individual turbine having the potential to result in widespread impact in the form of draining the peatland, which is highly important.

Lindsay critiques the deconstructivist approach adopted in the developer's statement as follows:

> [B]y breaking the system down into its component parts, [the Consultant responsible for this Statement] assumes that predictions can be made about the way in which these various components will react in response to the

---

70 Lindsay Report, p 66.

construction of the wind farm. This approach might work, but it depends on three things:

- firstly, it is important that the correct information is gathered. Dismantling a stationary car to determine its functional abilities is not an approach likely to succeed if the investigator catalogues the engine as 'large, inert lump of metal';
- secondly, while an understanding of component behaviour is important, it is equally important to see the system as an entire functioning entity, an entity that generally represents more than the sum of its component parts. Thus an understanding of the way in which all the parts function in two separate cars is unlikely to help predict the outcome of a race between the two vehicles;
- finally, it is vital that this functioning entity is analysed within the context of real-life conditions rather than any idealised yet inherently imperfect models of real life conditions. Thus even with road-test reports for both cars from the manufacturer and all the auto magazines it would still be virtually impossible to predict that, two weeks later, one of the cars will be found lying destroyed in a ditch because of black ice on a sharp bend. Such predictions are impossible without an analysis of the likely journeys to be undertaken, combined with weather predictions that are more accurate than is currently possible, plus a means of predicting the driver's level of attention at any particular moment, and many other imponderables. This degree of real-life uncertainty is precisely why the UK Government has embraced the *precautionary principle* in relation to development impacts; it is important that those carrying out EIA work also embrace this principle.

After reading the EIS in detail, however, the reader is left with no real sense that peatlands function as integrated entities at all, nor that any significant uncertainties exist.[71]

As a consequence of the findings of the Lindsay Report, RSPB Scotland lodged an objection letter with the Scottish Executive early in 2005, on the ground, *inter alia*, that 'many of the impacts in the ES [are] underestimated, in particular those relating to habitat' and that the Lindsay report indicates that the level of habitat impacts may be thirty times greater than those predicted by the developer. As well as highlighting the divisiveness of many wind farm projects, this case underlines the great difficulty of drawing physical boundaries for the purpose of carrying out environmental impact assessment and that the methodology and data used in the course of environmental assessment procedures can be contested and subject to varying interpretations.

71 Lindsay Report, pp 3–4.

The categories of failures to adopt an ecological approach in environmental assessment, listed above, suggest some serious limitations in the procedure. At their root is a failure to conceptualise the environment as a whole and for this to be reflected in law. Attempts have, however, been made to more closely align ecological understanding and law. Ruhl, for example, seeks to do this by arguing that law should be made to reflect the complexity of ecological systems and that it is only by doing so that such systems can be adequately protected.[72] Having identified ecosystems as possessing many of the behavioural properties of complex adaptive systems that, ultimately, lead to their sustainability, he applies complexity theory to show up the problems of modern environmental law:

> Complex adaptive systems, because of their highly collectivized, nonlinear, dynamic behaviour, defy prediction through classical reductionist method, or any other known method for that matter. Yet we have not designed our environmental law system with this underlying property in mind. Rather, it is mired in a reductionist, linear, predictivist mentality ignorant of underlying complex system behaviours. We find ourselves as a result constantly befuddled when the intended benefits of environmental regulation fail to materialize or, worse, when consequences contrary to the intended effects materialize. To be sure, the coercive, regulatory, command-and-control state has produced some admirable results in terms of environmental protection, but the underlying reductionist premises of that approach have exhausted their usefulness and will never allow us to challenge to tackle the significant environmental challenges ahead.[73]

Ruhl proposes moving beyond the 'reinvention' rhetoric of environmental law to a radical transformation: '[T]he adaptive, dynamical, sometimes chaotic forces found in complex adaptive systems must be present if the legal system is to respond effectively and creatively to the very same qualities present in the environment and society'.[74] A central point in Ruhl's thesis is the need to promote the flow of relevant information through the environmental law system (akin to energy flows through an ecosystem) which forms one of the defining characteristics of a complex adaptive system.[75] Environmental assessment clearly has an important part to play here. Indeed, the impetus for the development of procedural forms of regulation such as environmental assessment came from the perceived inadequacies of command and control (reductionist) regulation. However, as Daniel Farber argues in his chapter in this volume, information does not necessarily flow easily and freely from environmental assessment processes.

---

72 Ruhl, 'Thinking of Environmental Law as a Complex Adaptive System'.
73 At 107.
74 At 108.
75 Ruhl describes 'flows' of some medium (of energy, money, information etc) as the force of change in complex adaptive systems – as what makes them dynamical, at 114.

Dryzek similarly proposes a closer fit between the nature of ecosystems – and environmental problems – and the regulatory response. He equally identifies the core features of ecosystems (instability, dynamism, interpenetration) as unresponsive to traditional rules of law, force, or the deployment of markets,[76] and for this reason advances an idea of ecological rationality as a rationality of living systems (an order of relationships among living systems and their environments) which emphasises particularly the interrelationship and mutual dependency of a system's individual components. The inherently interdisciplinary quality of environmental assessment means that it was considered to provide a fitting level of flexibility, coordination, and appreciation of ecological interrelationships to deal with the nature of ecological systems and disturbances to these. However, the development of environmental assessment departs in practice from Dryzek's idea of ecological rationality because it ultimately fails to uphold this as a more fundamental kind of reason, when compared to other forms, for example economic and political rationality. He states: '[T]he preservation and promotion of the integrity of the ecological and material underpinning of society – ecological rationality – should take priority over competing forms of reason in collective choices with an impact upon that integrity.'[77] This is because long-term conflict between ecological, and other forms of rationality, will result in the elimination of the other forms.[78] Doubts also remain about the effectiveness of environmental assessment when working within the constraints of more prevalent and traditional regulatory structures such as development consent regimes. This is highlighted by the restrictive opportunities for social learning (through feedback loops) as a result of environmental assessment taking place within development consent regimes organised around the making of a final decision, and the scarcity of legally sanctioned post-assessment monitoring.

From these perspectives the prospect of a form of ecological impact assessment appears remote, although for Brooks, Jones and Virginia, law and ecology have been engaged in a process of 'coevolution' since at least the 1970s, producing some fruitful results, including in relation to environmental assessment. They tend to see this coevolution as one aspect of a broader, historical, process of integration, and conclude that environmental laws are likely to become more integrated in response to a better understanding of ecological systems.

> The rise of ecosystemic regimes is part of a more comprehensive historical process of growing regional, national and global interdependence, which has found expression in economic markets, global communication, international movement of peoples and new global and international institutions of governance. A heightened awareness of the interdependence of nature is part of this historical process.[79]

76 J Dryzek, *Rational Ecology: Environment and Political Ecology* (New York: Basil Blackwell, 1987).

77 Ibid, pp 59–60.

78 As discussed by R V Bartlett, 'Ecological Reason in Administration: Environmental Impact Assessment and Administrative Theory', in R Paehlke and D Torgerson, *Managing Leviathon – Environmental Politics and the Administrative State* (London: Belhaven, 1990).

79 Brooks, Jones, and Virginia, *Law and Ecology*, p 37.

Enhancing ecological thinking in environmental assessment

I have discussed above how enhancing ecological priorities depends upon focussing on linkages and relationships between habitats and species (including the human species), and how the realisation of this has informed critiques of environmental law and encouraged proposals to bring law and ecology into line. Relating such proposals to environmental assessment in practice suggests that artificial (or unecological) constraints such as deadlines for the determination of development consent, or the drawing of boundaries according to ownership of land, should be overcome or applied more flexibly. For example, in terms of temporal restrictions, the commonplace one-off survey to establish an environmental baseline provides only a snapshot of current conditions, and fails to take account of natural spatial and temporal variation (for example, some varieties of plants such as orchids do not appear annually). Since many natural systems have moving baselines, if only short runs of data are available it may be difficult to distinguish underlying trends from superimposed impacts, particularly when compared to apparently more straightforward estimates such as noise levels. Longer 'lead times' should therefore be allowed for when trying to characterise natural systems.[80] Ideally there should be repeated surveys to establish patterns and limits of seasonal variation in population numbers, and this study should accord with the habitat, and even migratory range, of species.[81] One example of constructing baselines for impact assessment which take into account natural variation is the United States' habitat evaluation procedure developed by the Fish and Wildlife Service. This acts as a continuous field survey, with the boundaries of study influenced by knowledge gathered on the site specific behaviour of species, once the process of assessment has begun.[82] However, whilst representing a considerable advance on the atomistic 'collect and count' approach to assessing the impact of a proposal on individual species, which currently dominates environmental impact assessment practice, such expansive studies fit uneasily in the contexts within which environmental assessment currently takes place in the United Kingdom, particularly those relating to development consent, and which inevitably determine the timeframe of such inquiries.

Turning to compensation and mitigation of adverse environmental impacts, Treweek notes that currently in the United Kingdom there is so little follow up of mitigation projects that it is difficult to judge the extent to which compensatory mitigation has replaced lost ecosystem function.[83] Expanding timescales in environmental assessment may help determine the effectiveness of proposals for the mitigation of impacts outlined in environmental statements. More specifically,

80 Treweek, *Ecological Impact Assessment*, p 131.
81 Treweek, *Ecological Impact Assessment*, pp 49–50.
82 Treweek, *Ecological Impact Assessment*, pp 164–165.
83 Treweek, *Ecological Impact Assessment*, p 226.

information about vegetation changes, the likelihood of colonisation by particular species, and the necessary size of recipient sites may reduce the occurrence of insensitive translocation of species, particularly given that studies of compensatory mitigation, such as the creation of new habitat, suggest that this is rarely successful in ecological terms.[84] At the very least, a more ecologically aware approach to mitigation might guard against accepting as mitigation 'benefits' unrelated to the existing ecological condition of a site in either scale or kind. For example, along these lines, in *Smith*[85] Sedley L J quite rightly criticised as a Trojan horse a planning inspector's approval of a unilateral undertaking which included payments made by a developer for traffic safety measures in the nearby town, landscaping, and the formation of a local liaison committee as 'providing significant environmental and community benefits which would mitigate the impact of the development'.

The practice of extending timeframes for environmental assessment, such as by carrying out post-assessment monitoring, might help to carve out a place for environmental assessment in on-going 'ecosystem governance' or management. Karkkainen gives as an example of the apparently successful integration of environmental assessment procedures into such systems an attempt to restore the ecological health of the Everglades and associated ecosystems following large-scale water diversions to provide public drinking water and support urban and agricultural developments.[86] The centrepiece of the restoration effort, a large-scale project to restructure the hydrological system, was subject to environmental assessment rules. However, the NEPA-mandated Final Environmental Impact Statement associated with this project did not appear as a separate document, but was instead integrated into the planning document itself, 'reflecting a merger of environmental impact analysis into the agency's decision-making process'.[87] Karkkainen describes that rather than attempting to evaluate the many highly uncertain ecological effects of the project, the Statement acknowledges these uncertainties, establishes the need for a framework for future monitoring, and outlines a range of measures that will be integral to ongoing management efforts over the life of the project. He summarises: 'In the process, the EIS is reconceptualized as a more modest but nonetheless useful analytical exercise; it is one in a series of points at which to take stock of the expected

---

84 For example, C A Simenstad and R M Thom, 'Functional Equivalency Trajectories of the Restored Gog-Le-Hi-Te Estuarine Wetland' (1996) 6 *Ecological Applications*, 38, cited in Treweek, *Ecological Impact Assessment*, pp 226–227. See also P Edgar and R Griffiths, *An Evaluation of the Effectiveness of Great Crested Newt* (Tritus Cristatus) *Mitigation Projects in England 1990–2001*, English Nature Research Report No. 275 (English Nature, 2004).

85 *Smith v Secretary of State for the Environment, Transport and Others* [2003] EWCA Civ 262, para 62.

86 B Karkkainen, 'Towards a Smarter NEPA: Monitoring and Managing Government's Environmental Performance' (2002) 102 *Columbia Law Review* 903.

87 Ibid, at 967.

environmental consequences, rather than the sole source of '"fully informed" decision-making.'[88] Whilst this is familiar ground to lawyers in the United States, such an example might encourage embedding environmental assessment within existing environmental management and audit systems in the European Union.

In terms of a more ecologically sensitive approach to cumulative impacts, translated into law and policy, and against which existing environmental assessment rules may be compared, is the Florida courts' ruling on permits for land development in wetlands.[89] This explicitly links the impact of a permit with the achievement of environmental quality standards. (In the United Kingdom, some developers currently strive to demonstrate the compliance of a proposed project with particular quality standards and conservation objectives, but this is not yet a requirement of environmental assessment law, or policy.) The Florida ruling also highlights the 'equitable independence of several projects – past, present, and future',[90] and their effects on coastal water quality *in toto*, both of which are arguably more easily achieved in the case of permits for discharges (from developments which already exist) than development consents for projects which have yet to be formally proposed.

> In order to show entitlement to a dredge and fill permit, an applicant must show that he has provided reasonable assurance that water quality standards will not be violated and that the project is not contrary to the public interest, and both of these tests must take into consideration the cumulative impacts of similar projects which are existing, under consideration, or reasonably expected in the future.

> ... The applicant's burden of proof includes the burden of giving reasonable assurance that cumulative impacts do not cause a project to be contrary to the public interest or to violate quality standards.

> ... The purpose of cumulative impact analysis is to distribute equitably that amount of dredging and filling activity which may be done without resulting in violations of water quality standards and without being contrary to the public interest. In order to determine whether the allocation to a particular applicant is equitable, the determination of the cumulative is based in part on the assumption that reasonably expected similar future applications will also be granted.

> ... Specifically in the context of permitting access roads and bridges, it has been the policy of the Department to consider what will be at the end of the bridge or road.

---

88 B Karkkainen, 'Towards a Smarter NEPA: Monitoring and Managing Government's Environmental Performance' (2002) 102 *Columbia Law Review* 967.

89 *Peebles v State of Florida, Department of Environmental Regulation*, 12 FALR 1961 (1990), cited in Brooks, Jones, and Virginia, *Law and Ecology*, p 171.

90 Brooks, Jones, and Virginia, *Law and Ecology*, p 172.

Notwithstanding the vast differences between pollution permits (for substances which in ecological terms are capable of obvious synergistic effects), and land-use development, such a comparative example highlights the relatively low standard required under existing environmental assessment rules in the United Kingdom of developers to explain the likely effects of their proposal, in combination with others. Although official guidance recognises that '[Q]uantified thresholds cannot easily deal with this kind of "incremental" development', and advocates consideration of cumulative effects in cases of multiple applications and changes or extensions to existing or approved development,[91] a minimalist approach is still taken on this matter. For example, in line with the 1999 Regulations,[92] the principal regulations implementing the EIA Directive in England and Wales, government guidance is that only the 'main' or 'significant' environmental effects to which a development is likely to give rise need be considered in the environmental statement,[93] less so indirect, or secondary effects. This considerably lightens the onus on the developer to consider what lies 'at the end of the bridge or road' and so forth. A broader, more integrated, approach is taken by the European Commission which advocates the following:

> Indirect and cumulative impacts and impact interactions may well extend beyond the geographical site boundaries of the project. Determining the geographical boundaries will therefore be a key factor in ensuring the impacts associated with a project are assessed comprehensively wherever possible... Additional data may need to be gathered to cover wider spatial boundaries, taking into account the potential for impacts to affect areas further away from the site than if just direct impacts were considered. Consideration should be given to the distance that an impact can travel and any interaction networks.[94]

At the core of many of these issues is the determination of the space to which the environmental assessment study applies. There is a good argument for adopting the concept of an ecological unit, taking the natural ecological characteristics of an area as a starting point, instead of demarcating the boundaries of a study according to the characteristics of the development or its ownership. Although this concept is familiar in US public trust law,[95] it is by no means easy to apply because of the difficulties involved in determining

---

91 Department of the Environment, Transport and the Regions, Circular 02/99, Environmental Impact *Assessment*, para 46.
92 Town and Country Planning (Environmental Impact Assessment) (England and Wales) Regulations 1999 (SI 1999, No. 293).
93 Circular 02/99, para 82.
94 European Commission, *Guidelines for the Assessment of Indirect and Cumulative Impacts as well as Impact Interactions* (Luxembourg, 1999), para 4.2.1.
95 For example *National Audubon v City of Los Angeles* 658 P.2d 709 (1983).

the boundaries of ecosystems (an ecosystem can 'range from a dung pile, to a watershed, to an ocean, and, finally, to the entire globe').[96] Brooks, Jones and Virginia point out that this has forced ecologists to sometimes define ecosystems operationally, based upon the particular process that they are interested in studying.[97] In the context of environmental assessment, determining the boundaries of a study according to an ecological unit, or several of these, is quite simply likely to lead to the prediction of a greater level of disturbance to an ecosystem than would be the case with artificially constructed boundaries.

Conclusions

A main argument when advocating ecological impact assessment is that its effectiveness depends on the extent to which legislative frameworks are supportive. The main instruments on environmental assessment currently fail to reflect a strongly ecological approach to matters such as cumulative effects, mitigation, and alternatives, beyond a fairly basic requirement to take account of impacts in an integrated manner. Referring to the position in the United States, Brooks, Jones and Virginia consider that the growing trend of ecologists to look at the interaction of different levels of biological organisation (individuals, populations, ecosystems) will lead to environmental laws becoming further integrated and more responsive to natural, rather than administrative, boundaries.[98] This is not yet the case in the United Kingdom, although there are signs that an ecosystems, or natural resource, approach to environmental assessment is now being implemented at the local level.[99] But perhaps the clearest sign of the future prospects for ecological impact assessment is the recent publication of a comprehensive set of guidelines[100] by the Institute of Ecology and Environmental Management. This seeks to fill in the ecological gaps in environmental assessment law and policy, for example by developing in practical terms concepts such as the ecological 'zone of influence' of a project, and setting out the extensive body of contextual information needed to determine the proper spatial and temporal scope of an ecological impact assessment. Importantly this type of assessment is seen as one part of the overall environmental assessment process, not as a substitute for it.

In summary, the development of environmental assessment in the United States prompted the adoption of environmental assessment regimes by the EU

---

96 Brooks, Jones and Virginia, *Law and Ecology*, p 264.

97 *Law and Ecology*, p 264.

98 Brooks, Jones and Virginia, *Law and Ecology*, p 7.

99 For example local authorities requiring 'natural resource impact assessments' of certain developments, as discussed by P Waddy, 'Sustainable Design and Planning – The New Policy Imperative' [2006] *Journal of Planning and Environmental Law*, 4.

100 Institute of Ecology and Environmental Management, *Guidelines for Ecological Impact Assessment in the United Kingdom* (IEEM, 2006).

and Member States.[101] But in the United States this development has taken two different directions: first, regulatory impact assessment, as part of 'better regulation' initiatives and including within its scope social and cost considerations; and second, environmental impact assessment, initially developed to bring ecological science within the scope of political, and strategic decision-making, and now forming part of ecological management systems. In Europe, the development of environmental assessment has been more linear, with a slow expansion of the subject matter of environmental assessment from exclusively project-based assessment to a position in which more strategic (plans and programmes) forms of assessment now provide a framework for the 'sub-' assessment of projects, and a 'super' expanded form (impact or sustainability analysis) gives equal standing to social, economic and environmental factors, leaving little practical or conceptual space for an ecological approach beyond a limited environmental remit. It is perhaps for this reason that the ecological roots of environmental assessment have been better preserved in the United States, at least in terms of one branch of its development. Certainly, dealing with cumulative impacts, and setting up post-assessment systems seems more advanced and better entrenched in the United States (although not necessarily in NEPA),[102] in part due to the extent to which adaptive management theories have influenced law and practice.[103] At a very basic level, moving European environmental assessment in an ecological direction will require a fundamental shift away from sustainable development as the organising idea of environmental law, in favour of a greater concern with biodiversity and the interdependence and integrity of ecological systems.

101 See Jones *et al*, 'Environmental Assessment: Dominant or Dormant?', in this volume.

102 For example, see Daniel Farber, 'Bringing Environmental Assessment into the Digital Age', note 73, in this volume.

103 See, e.g. C Sabel *et al*, 'Beyond Backyard Environmentalism', in J Cohen and J Rogers (eds) *Beyond Backyard Environmentalism* (Boston: Beacon Publishing, 2000). See also Brad Karkkainen, 'NEPA and the Curious Evolution of Environmental Impact Assessment in the United States', note 99, in this volume.

Index

Case law is referred to in italics. References such as "178–9" indicate continuous discussion of a topic, whilst "66 … 69" indicates scattered references to a topic throughout a range of pages. Wherever possible in the case of topics with many references, these have either been divided into sub-topics or the most significant discussion of the topic is indicated by page numbers in bold. Page references such as "142n" indicate that the topic is referred to in footnotes only.